The USSR and the UN's

Economic and Social Activities

The USSR and
the UN's Economic
and Social Activities

HAROLD KARAN JACOBSON

UNIVERSITY OF NOTRE DAME PRESS 1963

Copyright © 1963 by

University of Notre Dame Press

Notre Dame, Indiana

JX
1977.2
.R8
.J2

Library of Congress Catalog Card Number: 63-19327
Manufactured in the United States

TO
JEAN

FOREWORD

THIS STUDY IS AN ANALYSIS OF THE SOVIET UNION'S POLICIES WITH RE-
spect to the economic and social activities of the United Nations, the reactions of other states to these policies, and the impact of the resulting interaction on the UN's institutions and functions. Activities in the field of human rights are not included, since they are significantly different from the UN's other economic and social functions. Although the specialized agencies are considered, the central focus is the United Nations. Events in the agencies are included only when they continued tasks begun in the UN, or when these events constituted essential elements of programs conducted primarily within the UN. This relatively narrow scope was chosen for obvious reasons of time—to have broadened it would have permanently buried the study under the annual outpouring of documentation from the UN and the specialized agencies—and, more importantly, so that certain practical and theoretical questions could be examined in depth.

A topic of this nature can be approached either from the point of view of the country involved or from that of the international organization. Because of my interests and capabilities, I have chosen the latter approach. Admittedly, both perspectives can and must be used a good bit of the time, but now and again a choice must be made between the two, and on these occasions, rightly or wrongly, I have chosen the concerns of international organization as the basis for my analysis.

There is also another problem in a topic of this nature. To scrutinize closely the policies of one state in a multilateral organization carries the risk of distortions in analysis and interpretation because of the lack of comparative data. This risk is especially great when the subject country's policies contradict and attack those of the author's state. I recognize this risk and have tried to guard against it and can only apologize for whatever shortcomings exist in the study in this respect.

Many—if not most—of the judgments advanced in the study are speculative. The inherent problems which are involved in the analysis of contemporary events and in attempts to establish relationships between vaguely defined and numerous variables are compounded in this case by the secretiveness of the Soviet regime and the paucity of scholarly and journalistic writing in the USSR about the United Nations. Until the middle nineteen fifties, there was hardly any Soviet literature in this field, and what has appeared since then still is not extensive.[1] Moreover, very little of it treats the UN's economic and social activities. The study is therefore based primarily on the documentary record, personal observations of meetings, and interviews with participants and observers. Grants from the Horace H. Rackham School of Graduate Studies at The University of Michigan and from the Social Science Research Council enabled me to attend the twenty-seventh and twenty-eighth sessions of the Economic and Social Council in Mexico City and Geneva in 1959. As the World Affairs Center Fellow for 1959-1960, I was able to observe the fourteenth session of the General Assembly in the fall of 1959 and the twenty-ninth session of the Economic and Social Council the following spring, and to examine the subject from the vantage point of UN headquarters. Work on another project, sponsored by grants from The Rockefeller Foundation and The Center for Research on Conflict Resolution, brought me back to Geneva and also to ECAFE headquarters in Bangkok, Thailand in the summer of 1962, and enabled me to gather more data for the study. I have interviewed members of all the states which were represented on the Economic and Social Council in 1959 and also delegates from several other states which have played prominent roles in the UN's economic and social activities. In addition, I have interviewed members of all of the relevant sections of the UN Secretariat and a number of journalists and observers representing Non-Governmental Organizations who have had long experience viewing UN affairs. The data gained through observation and interviews is interwoven throughout the text. For

---

[1] See: Alvin Z. Rubinstein, "Selected Bibliography of Soviet Works on the United Nations, 1946-1959," *The American Political Science Review*, LIV, no. 4 (December 1960), 985-991; and, "The Soviet Image of the United Nations," *Proceedings of the American Philosophical Society*, CVII, no. 4 (April 1963), 132-137.

FOREWORD

obvious reasons it is impossible to provide citations for this material.

My list of acknowledgments is long. I have benefited from the kindness and wisdom of a number of people. Walter R. Sharp originally roused my interest in this subject and has since provided advice and counsel. Gerhart Niemeyer guided my work at a crucial stage and has constantly encouraged me. Inis L. Claude, Jr. has provided boundless stimulation and assistance. In addition, at one point or another, the manuscript has profited from the insights of: Robert E. Asher, Vernon V. Aspaturian, Frederick C. Barghoorn, Antonin Basch, Lincoln P. Bloomfield, Alexander Dallin, Seymour M. Finger, William T. R. Fox, Leland M. Goodrich, Charles Hogan, Stephen D. Kertesz, George Lichtblau, Bernard S. Morris, Raymond B. Powell, Alvin Z. Rubinstein, Rudolph K. Skeete, and Arnold Wolfers. I am deeply grateful to all of these individuals. I am also indebted to those whom I interviewed, who no doubt would prefer to remain unnamed. What merits the book has are obviously attributable to others; its faults are mine.

I am grateful for the grants mentioned above which enabled me to view my subject at close hand. A Horace H. Rackham Faculty Fellowship enabled me to spend an important summer on the project and the expenses in connection with the preparation of the manuscript were borne by the Begole-Brownell Fund. I am also thankful for this assistance.

A place to work is an essential ingredient in any scholarly endeavor, and I have been fortunate to have had access to the magnificent collection in the field of international organization of the Library of The University of Michigan Law School. The Director, Hobart Coffey, and his staff have greatly facilitated my tasks.

Sections of the book appeared previously in different forms in articles. I appreciate the permission granted by *International Organization*, *Osteuropa Recht*, and *The Western Political Quarterly* to use this material again. I also appreciate the permission of *International Conciliation* to include the lengthy quotations in the first chapter from Leo Pasvolsky's pamphlet.

Finally, I want to thank my wife Jean, who has borne my preoccupation with patience and goodwill. She deserves more than the dedication of this book.

H. K. J.

July 15, 1963
Department of Political Science
The University of Michigan

CONTENTS

	Foreword	ix
	Charts	xv
	Abbreviations	xvii
1	Prologue	3
2	Constitutional Issues	16

    The Economic and Social Council, p. 16; Non-Governmental Organizations, p. 22; ECOSOC's Functional Commissions, p. 31; Relations with Specialized Agencies, p. 37; Procedural and Representational Questions, p. 44; Implementation, p. 48; The Secretariat, p. 51; Conclusions, p. 53

3	Refugees and Displaced Persons	56

    Drafting the IRO Constitution, p. 58; The Soviet Attack on IRO, p. 75; The United Nations High Commissioner for Refugees, p. 76; Other UN Activities, p. 79; Conclusions, p. 81

4	Relief and Reconstruction	84

    Economic Assistance, p. 86; The UN's Role—ECE and ECAFE, p. 95; The World Food Shortage, p. 107; Conclusions, p. 113

5	Social Welfare	117

    Advisory Social Welfare Services, p. 117; The United Nations Children's Fund, p. 121; Social Defense, p. 128; The International Control of Narcotic Drugs, p. 133; Advancing Social Welfare, p. 142; Conclusions, p. 150

6 Economic Welfare   153

Trade Union Rights, p. 155; Protection of Migrant Labor, p. 160; Equal Pay for Equal Work, p. 161; Forced Labor, p. 163; Slavery, p. 167; Unemployment, p. 170; Armaments, Disarmament and the Standard of Living, p. 178; Conclusions, p. 181

7 International Trade   183

Creating a Structural Framework, p. 185; The Cold War Period, p. 188; The Era of Soviet Initiatives, p. 196; Conclusions, p. 214

8 Economic Development   218

General Discussions, p. 219; Technical Assistance, p. 227; Financing Economic Development, p. 252; Soviet Bloc Initiatives, p. 259; Conclusions, p. 262

9 The USSR and the UN's "Non-Political" Activities: Interpretations and Implications   265

The Changes in Soviet Policy, p. 265; The Impact of the USSR's Participation on the UN's Institutions and Activities, p. 277; Implications for Functionalism, p. 284

Selected Bibliography   288

Index   299

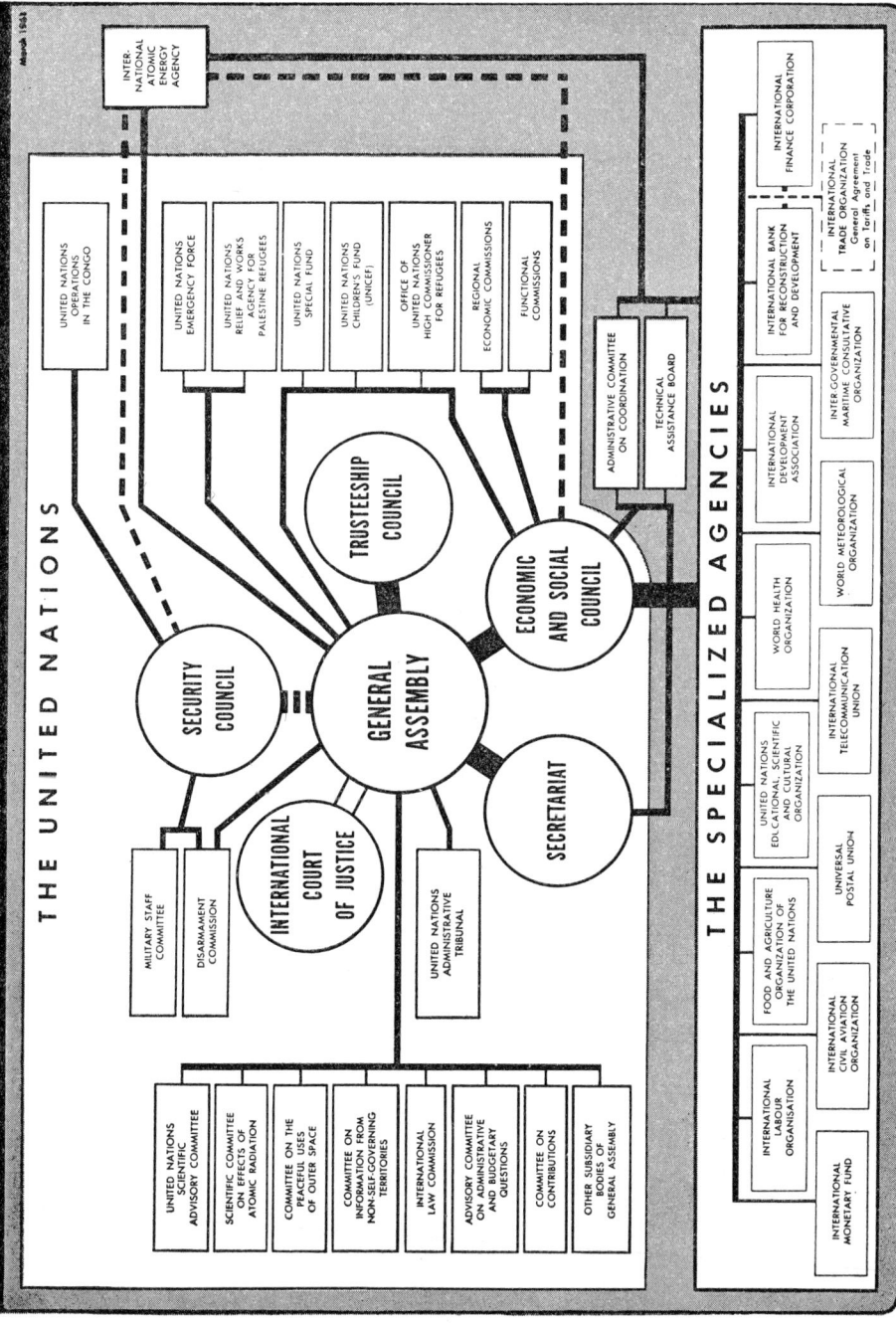

Reproduced through the courtesy of the United Nations

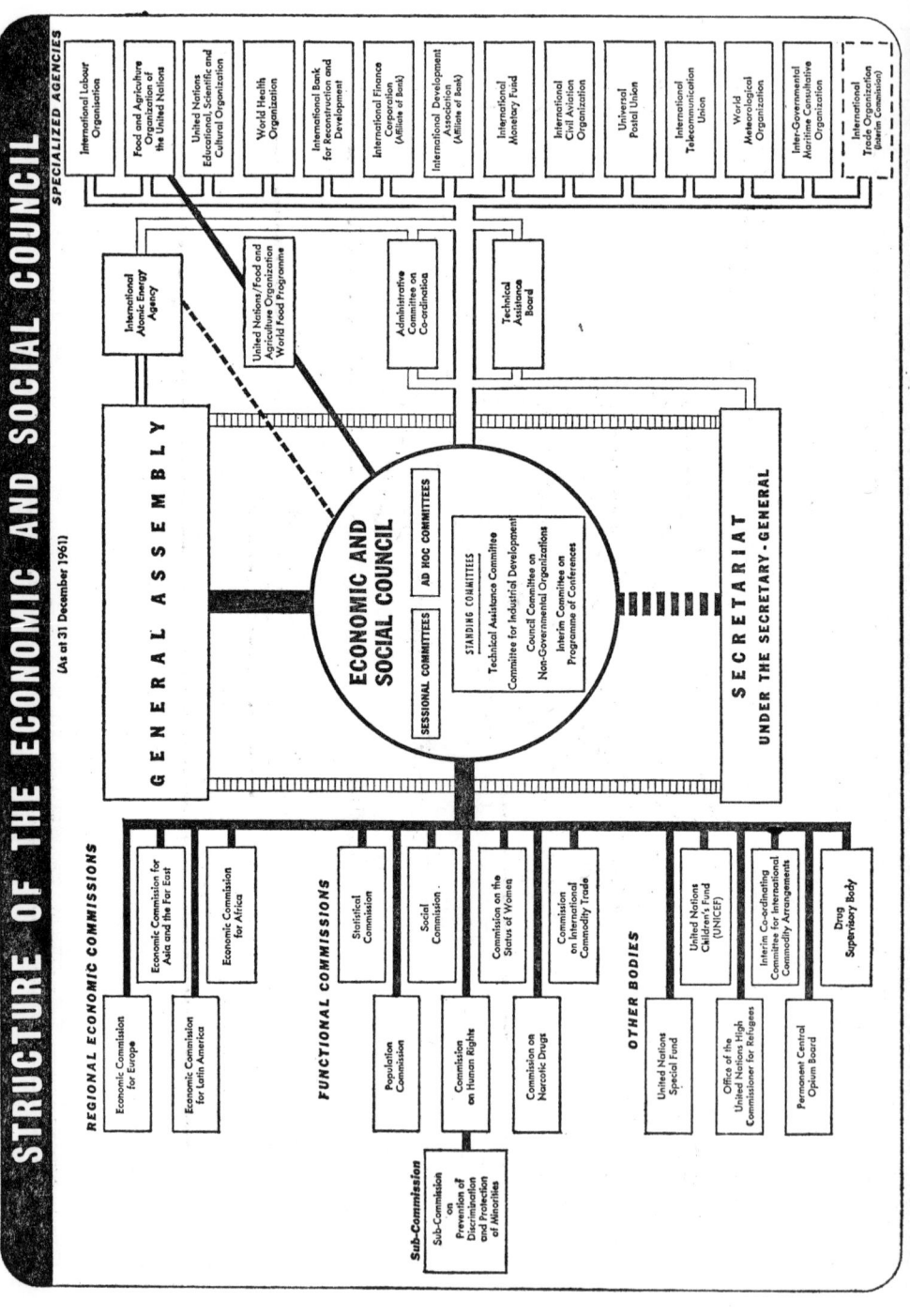

ABBREVIATIONS

ACC—Administrative Committee on Coordination
AFL—American Federation of Labor
BTAO—Bureau of Technical Assistance Operations
CIO—Congress of Industrial Organizations
CMEA—Council for Mutual Economic Assistance
COCOM—Coordinating Committee of the Consultative Group
EAEC—European Atomic Energy Community (Euratom)
ECA—Economic Commission for Africa
ECAFE—Economic Commission for Asia and the Far East
ECE—Economic Commission for Europe
ECITO—European Central Inland Transport Organization
ECLA—European Commission for Latin America
ECO—European Coal Organization
ECOSOC—Economic and Social Council
ECSC—European Coal and Steel Community
EEC—European Economic Community (Common Market)
EECE—Emergency Economic Committee for Europe
EFTA—European Free Trade Association
EPTA—Expanded Program of Technical Assistance
ERP—European Recovery Program (Marshall Plan)
FAO—Food and Agriculture Organization
GATT—General Agreement on Tariffs and Trade
IAEA—International Atomic Energy Agency
IBRD—International Bank for Reconstruction and Development (World Bank)
ICA—International Cooperative Alliance
ICAO—International Civil Aviation Organization
ICCICA—Interim-Coordinating Committee for International Commodity Agreements
ICFTU—International Confederation of Free Trade Unions
ICJ—International Court of Justice
IDA—International Development Association
IEFC—International Emergency Food Council
IFC—International Finance Corporation

IFCTU—International Federation of Christian Trade Unions
IFTU—International Federation of Trade Unions
IGCR—Inter-Governmental Committee on Refugees
ILO—International Labor Organization
IMCO—Inter-Governmental Maritime Consultative Organization
IMF—International Monetary Fund
INCB—International Narcotics Control Board (proposed)
IRO—International Refugee Organization
ITO—International Trade Organization (proposed)
ITU—International Telecommunications Union
NATO—North Atlantic Treaty Organization
NGO—Non-Governmental Organization
OEEC—Organization for European Economic Cooperation
OECD—Organization for Economic Cooperation and Development
OPEX—UN Program for Provision of Operational, Executive, and Administrative Personnel
OTC—Organization for Trade Cooperation (proposed)
PCOB—Permanent Central Opium Board
SUNFED—Special United Nations Fund for Economic Development (proposed)
TAB—Technical Assistance Board
TAC—Technical Assistance Committee
UNAC—United Nations Appeal for Children
UNESCO—United Nations Educational, Scientific and Cultural Organization
UNHCR—United Nations High Commissioner for Refugees
UNICEF—United Nations Children's Fund (formerly United Nations International Children's Emergency Fund)
UNKRA—United Nations Korean Reconstruction Agency
UNREF—United Nations Refugee Fund
UNRRA—United Nations Relief and Rehabilitation Administration
UNRWA—United Nations Relief and Works Agency for Palestine Refugees
UPU—Universal Postal Union
WFTU—World Federation of Trade Unions
WHO—World Health Organization
WMO—World Meteorological Organization

The USSR and the UN's Economic and Social Activities

1: PROLOGUE

ON SEPTEMBER 8, 1944, DURING THE DUMBARTON OAKS CONVERSATIONS, President Franklin D. Roosevelt, Under Secretary of State Edward R. Stettinius, Jr., and Ambassador Andrei A. Gromyko met to discuss the progress of the conference. During their discussion of the remaining points of difference between the United States and the Soviet Union, Ambassador Gromyko stated that although he could not yield on the question of voting in the Security Council or on the Soviet demand for separate votes for each of the USSR's sixteen autonomous republics, he could approve the American proposal to have an Economic and Social Council (ECOSOC) in the new international organization.[1] This was a major victory for United States policy, for from the earliest stages, planners in the Department of State had included economic and social functions within the mandate of their projected post-war international organization and had given them a prominent role. It is true that some Americans, including even President Roosevelt for a while, had not favored this approach, but Secretary of State Cordell Hull had supported it from the outset, and by the time of Dumbarton Oaks, it was the official United States position.[2]

Until the September 8 meeting, the USSR had strongly opposed the American position. A Soviet draft proposal, circulated shortly before the Dumbarton Oaks conversations, was significantly en-

[1] Edward R. Stettinius, Jr. (Walter Johnson, Ed.), *Roosevelt and the Russians: The Yalta Conference* (Garden City: Doubleday, 1949), p. 20.

[2] See: Louis K. Hyde, Jr., *The United States and the United Nations: Promoting the Public Welfare* (New York: Manhattan Publishing Company, 1960), pp. 31-32.

titled "Memorandum on the International Security Organization."[3] Neither this plan, the first official written statement of the Soviet position, nor those of a less official nature which had appeared earlier in the Soviet press, provided for the inclusion of economic and social functions. In the early sessions of the Dumbarton Oaks conversations, Ambassador Gromyko argued that the new organization should only be concerned with security problems.[4] In his view one reason for the ineffectiveness of the League of Nations had been a confusion of purpose. He maintained that the League had been overburdened with "secondary" matters and asserted that some 77 per cent of the items which had been discussed were not directly related to peace and security. He stated that his government was not opposed to international cooperation concerning economic and social matters, but it felt that such cooperation should occur in separate agencies, which might be linked in some fashion with the basic security organization. The extent to which the USSR would have participated in these separate agencies was not made clear.

Those within the American government who had opposed the views of the planners in the Department of State had also argued for this type of institutional arrangement, and a case could be made for it. By the fall of 1944, however, the United States, although in favor of the creation of separate specialized agencies for economic and social cooperation, was committed to a broad mandate for the new basic security organization, encompassing *inter alia* economic and social functions. The American plan provided for the creation within the organization of machinery to coordinate the work of the separate agencies and to carry out selected economic and social tasks. The emphasis in the United States plans on economic and social activities stemmed from a feeling that such work was not only valuable in itself as a means of raising living standards throughout the world, but that it would also significantly contribute to the maintenance of peace and security. The latter belief was partly based on the theories held by Secretary of State Hull and others concerning the relationship between economic factors and war. They felt that economic disputes bred political conflicts and that an economically healthy society was a prerequisite for a peaceful society.

[3] Ruth B. Russell, assisted by Jeannette E. Muther, *A History of the United Nations Charter: The Role of the United States, 1940-1945* (Washington, D. C.: The Brookings Institution, 1958), p. 393.

[4] *Ibid.*, p. 422.

In addition, the United States position was derived from the American interpretation of the experience of the League of Nations.

The economic and social work of the League had proved both useful and successful. During the organization's last years, a movement had begun to expand and develop these so-called "non-political" activities.[5] This movement was related to a school of thought about international organization, the functionalist theory, in that it drew on and, as practical movements do, gave support to the ideas advanced by writers of this persuasion.

Perhaps David Mitrany's pamphlet, *A Working Peace System: An Argument for the Functional Development of International Organization,* first published in 1943, contains the best, although also the most extreme statement, of the functionalist theory.[6] The principal tenets of the theory, however, had been advanced earlier. Briefly stated, the functionalist theory holds that, since technological developments have increasingly brought states closer together and made them more interdependent, there is an obvious and growing need for international collaboration concerning economic and social matters. The necessity of developing arrangements to facilitate communications and transportation and the clear requirement for international action to combat disease are cited as examples. Functionalist theory also sees widespread pressures among the peoples of the world for social reforms and for increased material benefits which, the theory holds, cannot be satisfied by individual states acting alone. According to the theory, the need for collaboration will override political differences and international cooperation in the economic and social fields will occur despite political differences. For example, in his pamphlet Professor Mitrany argued that: "Pivotal countries like the United States and the U.S.S.R. could become vital links in a functional network when they could not all be made parts of any formal political scheme."[7] Functionalist theory envisages the creation of a network of international agencies with specific functional

[5] See: F. P. Walters, *A History of the League of Nations* (New York: Oxford University Press, 1952), II, 749-762.

[6] The pamphlet was published by the Oxford University Press for the Royal Institute of International Affairs. See also Mitrany's article: "The Functional Approach to World Organization," *International Affairs,* XXIV, no. 3 (July 1948), 350-363. A more moderate and perhaps more realistic exposition of the theory can be found in: Philip C. Jessup and others, *International Organization* (New York: Carnegie Endowment for International Peace, 1955).

[7] *A Working Peace System,* p. 53.

tasks. The theory further holds that cooperation in these fields will contribute to the growth of a sense of community among states and in this way will tend to break down political differences. Some see functional collaboration as the most realistic way of working toward world government. In 1940, retrospectively viewing the League of Nations "nonpolitical" work, Arthur Sweetser, an American and a member of the League Secretariat, wrote that it marked "a phase in the slow transition of mankind from international anarchy to the world community." [8]

Those who supported the movement to expand the League's economic and social activities did so at least partly because of what can be termed functionalist reasons. They hoped that emphasizing this side of the League would be a way of bringing the fascist states back into membership and of bringing nonmembers—particularly the United States—into a closer relationship with the organization. They saw it as a means of saving and revitalizing the League. The movement to expand the League's economic and social functions reached a culmination in August 1939 with the submission to the League Council of a brief document[9] which was prepared by an *ad hoc* committee chaired by an Australian, Stanley M. Bruce. The Bruce Report, as it came to be known, presented the need for increased international cooperation in economic and social affairs and, in guarded language, pointed out some of the benefits which the authors hoped would result from giving this segment of the League's work greater emphasis. The Report recommended that the economic and social activities already carried on by the League should be expanded and that a special organ, the Central Committee for Economic and Social Questions, should be created to supervise this work.

It would not be accurate to say that the American insistence on the inclusion of economic and social activities within the United Nations was based on functionalist assumptions. However, the planners in the Department of State drew heavily from the Bruce Report—in terms of institutions, the Economic and Social Council was the Central Committee for Economic and Social Questions writ

---

[8] "The Non-Political Achievements of the League," *Foreign Affairs*, XIX, no. 1 (October 1940), 179-192, esp. p. 192.

[9] League of Nations Document A.23.1939, *The Development of International Cooperation in Economic and Social Affairs: Report of the Special Committee* (Geneva, 1939).

large—and they clearly believed that there was an intimate relationship between international cooperation in the economic and social fields and the maintenance of peace and security. Leo Pasvolsky, who headed the planning staff put it this way:

> . . . it is necessary that the nations of the world recognize that disputes, controversies, and frictions among them are less likely to occur if they work together in creating conditions conducive to stability and well-being within nations and, therefore, essential to the maintenance of stable and peaceful relations among nations. They must join together in creating arrangements for facilitating the solution of international economic, social, humanitarian and related problems and for cooperative action in promoting the type of international relations which are necessary for material and cultural progress.[10]

He held that, although the international cooperation concerning economic and social matters which had occurred during the League years had been "useful," it had not been "sufficiently effective," it had lacked "coordination and stimulation"; thus the American proposal. Functionalists would have argued the case somewhat differently and might not have advocated the exact institutional arrangements embodied in the American plan, but they clearly would have endorsed its objectives and they did see the need for machinery to coordinate the functional agencies which they advocated. Although the American plan was not squarely based on the functionalist theory, there was a definite intellectual connection.

On the same occasion, Dr. Pasvolsky also indicated another line of thought which had contributed to the American position.

> It would obviously be an exaggeration to say that the second world war was caused solely by the condition of international economic strife which prevailed in the twenties and even more virulently in the thirties. There were, of course, many other decisive elements in mankind's fatal drift toward the catastrophe of another war. But it is not too much to say that so long as international economic relations remained in the state in which they were in the recent decades, both peace and prosperity were forlorn hopes, and the fatal drift toward disaster could not be arrested.[11]

His statement underscored the extent to which theories of economic causation had had an impact on noncommunist thought. Many were

[10] "Dumbarton Oaks Proposals for Economic and Social Cooperation," *International Conciliation*, no. 409, section 2 (March 1945), pp. 203-210, p. 204.
[11] *Ibid.*, p. 203.

8   The USSR and the UN's Economic and Social Activities

firmly convinced that economic factors had much to do with international conflicts, even though the exact connection was seldom—if ever—explicitly stated. Certainly this explanation would not have been as fashionable as it was had it not been for Marx and his later-day interpreters. Therefore there was a certain irony in the Soviet Union's opposition to the United Nations having economic and social functions.

The USSR's position, however, was in accord with the stand that it had taken with regard to the League of Nations. Although the Soviet Union had participated in the League's economic and social activities even before becoming a member of the organization,[12] and had continued to do so thereafter, it had never participated in all of the activities and it had always held that they should not be put on the same level as the basic function of maintaining peace and security.[13] The USSR had opposed the movement to give increased emphasis to this aspect of the League.[14] The Soviet Union had joined the League of Nations primarily in the hope of gaining security against Nazi Germany, and once a member, it had sought to use the organization for this purpose. The USSR had argued for a hard policy against Germany and other fascist states. The course recommended by the Bruce Report was rather different.

Its experience with the League no doubt affected the USSR's attitude in the negotiations which led up to the adoption of the United Nations Charter. The USSR appears to have envisaged a role for the United Nations similar to that which it had hoped the League would play. The Soviet people were told through their press "that the creation of an international security organization would, above all, prevent the recurrence of a German attack." [15] This conception was not without reason. Inis L. Claude, Jr., among others, has suggested that the inclusion of the veto in the UN's collective security provisions indicated that the latter "were designed with a view to

---

[12] See: Kathryn Wasserman Davis, *The Soviets at Geneva* (Geneva: Librairie Kundig, 1934), and Charles Prince, "The U.S.S.R. and International Organization," *The American Journal of International Law*, XXXVI, no. 3 (July 1942), 425-445.

[13] See: F. P. Walters, *History of the League*, II, 757.

[14] See: J. Frankel, "The Soviet Union and the United Nations," *The Yearbook of World Affairs*, 1954 (New York: Frederick A. Praeger, 1954), pp. 69-94, pp. 75-76.

[15] Irene Blumenthal, *The Soviet Union and the United Nations* (New York, 1960), mimeographed, IV-5.

dealing with future threats to the peace by the same Axis powers which had launched World War II."[16] Soviet leaders may have regarded the American proposal to include economic and social functions in the United Nations as another diversionary Bruce Report. In any event, Ambassador Gromyko's speeches at Dumbarton Oaks made it clear that the USSR wanted the new organization to be principally and directly concerned with security issues.

Then too, for a variety of reasons the Soviet Union had had little intrinsic interest in the League's economic and social activities, except in a few cases where international collaboration was an obvious technical necessity, and it was probably equally uninterested in the economic and social functions proposed for the United Nations, since they were essentially a continuation and an expansion of the League's tasks. Communist ideology was a basic reason for the USSR's lack of interest. Although the American planners firmly believed that wars could be the product of economic and social conditions, unlike the communists, they believed that it was possible to ameliorate these conditions by techniques other than revolution. Their plans for the United Nations envisaged economic and social tasks that were essentially "reformist" solutions, and this had been the character of the League's work. To a convinced communist such activities could at best be only palliatives, and if their effect were to dull class consciousness, they might even be harmful. According to communist ideology, contradictions and tensions between the bourgeoisie and the proletariat, between the imperialist states and the colonies, and between the imperialist states themselves, which result in exploitation and oppression and possibly in violent conflict, are inherent features of capitalism. The only—and in communist dialectics, the inevitable—solution is to move to a higher form of social organization, to socialism and eventually to communism.

It is hardly necessary to state that communists would have little in common with functionalists. Each group offers quite different prescriptions for the achievement of world harmony and peace. Although both emphasize economic factors, functionalists hold that economic cooperation will bridge and ultimately eliminate political

[16] *Swords into Plowshares: The Problems and Progress of International Organization* (2nd ed. New York: Random House, 1959), p. 86. J. L. Brierly also takes this position. See: *The Law of Nations: An Introduction to the International Law of Peace* (4th ed.; London: Oxford University Press, 1949), pp. 280-283.

differences. Communists, on the other hand, regard these differences as implacable as long as capitalism continues to exist. Communists call for a radical transformation of society internally, while functionalists urge more international cooperation.

Because of the basic ideological difference, the Soviet Union could not have the same sort of commitment as the West (i.e., the states of Western Europe and Australia, Canada, New Zealand and the United States) to the League's economic and social activities or to those planned for the United Nations. If the USSR participated in such activities it was either because Soviet leaders thought that certain technical advantages would be gained from this course—the functionalists have a point after all in that some international collaboration in economic and social matters is a virtual necessity in the modern world—or because they decided that it would be tactically advantageous. The combination of unresolved issues between the USSR and the United States at the time that the Soviet Union agreed to the creation of the Economic and Social Council is instructive. This concession was probably made in the hope of obtaining equivalent concessions with respect to issues which the USSR regarded as more important, voting in the Security Council and separate representation for its autonomous republics.

There were also other reasons for the Soviet Union's lack of interest in the League's economic and social activities and in those planned for the United Nations. In practice most of these activities aimed at buttressing the existing economic and social system, a task which the USSR could hardly be expected to share with enthusiasm. Beyond this, most of the activities had greatest applicability for Western type economies and social structures. Their basic orientation was that of a relatively free economy and of a society in which private organizations played a major role. They tended to look to the individual rather than to class relationships for the causes of social problems and offered solutions which emphasized the individual. Furthermore, the internationalist implications of the activities—particularly of some of the tasks envisaged for the United Nations—might have violated the Soviet Union's closed system. Finally, reading the American plan, Soviet leaders could anticipate that the USSR would occupy a minority position in those UN organs which would deal with economic and social questions and that it would not have the protection of the veto there.

Despite its initial opposition to the inclusion of economic and social functions within the United Nations mandate, the USSR has always participated in these activities, although it has done so in its own manner and its participation has never extended to all of the activities. During the Chinese representation boycott in the first half of 1950, the only organ of the United Nations in which Soviet representatives continued to sit was one dealing with economic and social questions, the Economic Commission for Europe (ECE). It seems clear though that the same factors which were responsible for the USSR's original lack of interest in these activities have continued to affect its policy in varying degrees. The Soviet Union's actions and pronouncements have indicated that it has continued to regard the United Nations economic and social functions as subordinate to its political tasks, and of course the world organization as a whole has played only a minor role in the USSR's foreign policy.

Although it is important at the outset to put the UN's economic and social activities in their proper perspective in the over-all framework of Soviet foreign policy, doing so should not lead to an underestimation of the significance of these activities for the USSR or of the impact of Soviet participation on this aspect of the United Nations. Given the importance of economic and social questions in the years since the end of the Second World War, the Soviet Union has inevitably had to devote at least some attention to the UN's consideration of these issues. At first, the United Nations economic and social activities dealt primarily with problems which grew out of the war, and in many cases the USSR's interests were directly involved. Then the task of stimulating and aiding economic development was pressed to the fore. Since a large part of the Soviet-American conflict came to be a contest for the alignment of the underdeveloped countries, the USSR found that it could not afford to ignore the UN's activities in this field.

If for no other reason than the Soviet Union's great power status, its policies were bound to have an important effect on the United Nations institutions and functions. Beyond that, Soviet ideology claimed to have a special understanding of the very economic and social problems with which the UN was to deal. Even though communist beliefs ruled out an intrinsic interest in these activities as they were originally defined, once the USSR decided to participate, Soviet spokesmen were certain to advance and to try to gain acceptance for their particular ideological interpretation. Further, Soviet ideology commits believers to use all means to advance communist goals, and it was inevitable that the USSR would attempt to use the UN's economic and social activities for this purpose. To be sure, all states try to promote their national interests as they see them through international organizations, but few define their national interests in such broad and yet exclusive terms as are imposed by communist ideology. Finally, the political tensions generated by the Soviet-American clash were bound to have wide repercussions affecting all segments of the UN.

The USSR's policies concerning the United Nations economic and social activities can be divided into four relatively distinct periods. The first covered the stage of planning for the UN and lasted until the opening of the General Assembly's first session in January 1946. During this period, Soviet policy was marked first by opposition and then, after the Dumbarton Oaks Conversations, by passive acquiescence. Vyacheslav M. Molotov alone of the foreign ministers of the five great powers failed to mention economic and social functions in his opening speech at the San Francisco Conference. In all but a few instances, Soviet delegates played only a minor role in drafting those sections of the UN Charter which dealt with economic and social questions. Their part in planning the UN's economic and social activities in the Preparatory Commission later in 1945 was equally minute.

The second period began with the opening of the first Assembly session in January 1946. It became apparent then that vital Soviet interests—the fate of refugees and displaced persons and of relief and reconstruction assistance—would be affected by decisions taken in the United Nations. The Soviet Union worked actively to protect and to promote its interests. By the end of 1946, however, the USSR's position on both these major problems had been decisively rejected, and Soviet policy entered a new phase.

The third period, which began during the winter of 1946-1947, lasted until the winter of 1952-1953. During these six years Soviet participation in the United Nations economic and social activities was sharply limited. The USSR was active in the plenary and committee sessions of the General Assembly and in the Economic and Social Council and its committees and commissions. It was also a member of three specialized agencies: the Universal Postal Union (UPU), the World Meteorological Organization (WMO), and the International Telecommunications Union (ITU). These three had the most narrowly defined functions of all of the specialized agencies, and participation in their work was almost a necessity for a mid-twentieth century great power. The Soviet Union joined the World Health Organization (WHO), but withdrew from active participation in 1949, a few months after the organization began to function. The USSR did not become a Contracting Party to the General Agreement on Tariffs and Trade (GATT), which was negotiated under United Nations auspices, nor did it engage in the work conducted under this treaty. It did not participate in the remaining specialized agencies, the UN's program of assistance to refugees and displaced persons, nor in most of the important technical committees of the Economic Commission for Europe. The USSR refused to contribute to the UN's Expanded Program of Technical Assistance (EPTA) and to the United Nations Children's Fund (UNICEF). In sum, the Soviet Union largely abstained from the United Nations concrete work in the economic and social fields, its participation was confined, almost exclusively, to taking part in general discussions. In these, Soviet delegates were usually vituperative, attacking the institutions and policies of the capitalist West and sometimes even the United Nations, especially those programs in which the West played a leading role. At the same time, they extolled the advantages of the USSR's system and praised its policies.

The Soviet Union's policy with regard to the United Nations economic and social activities underwent a final change in the winter of 1952-1953. Starting then, the USSR began to participate in the UN's concrete economic and social work and to moderate its tactics in the general discussions. The Soviet Union joined or rejoined several of the specialized agencies which it had previously boycotted. By 1959 the USSR was an active member of seven specialized agencies: UPU, WMO, ITU and, in addition, the World Health Organization, the International Labor Organization (ILO), the United Nations Educational, Scientific and Cultural Organization (UNESCO) and the Inter-Governmental Maritime Consultative Organization (IMCO). The Soviet Union had also joined the International Atomic Energy Agency (IAEA), which, although technically not a specialized agency, was established under the aegis of United Nations and maintained a close relationship with it. In 1953 the USSR began to contribute to the Expanded Program of Technical Assistance, and the following year it announced that it would participate in all of ECE's technical committees. In 1955 it began contributing to UNICEF. Soviet delegates became more moderate and cooperative in general discussions in the Assembly and ECOSOC. Even with these changes, however, the USSR still did not participate in all of the UN's economic and social activities. As of July 1963, the Soviet Union did not belong to six of the UN's thirteen specialized agencies: the Food and Agricultural Organization (FAO), the International Monetary Fund (IMF), the International Bank for Reconstruction and Development (IBRD), the International Finance Corporation (IFC), the International Development Association (IDA), and the International Civil Aviation Organization (ICAO), and it had not signed the General Agreement on Tariffs and Trade. The USSR continued to have little to do with the UN's refugee work. Moreover, although Soviet delegates were less truculent in debates than they had been, their behavior still had various distinctive features.

Viewing the background of planning for the United Nations and the record of the USSR's participation in the UN's economic and social activities, even as sketched in this brief outline, stimulates a number of basic questions on a variety of levels. First, what is the meaning of the various changes in Soviet policy? How significant are they, and how can they be explained? Does there appear to be an underlying rationale, or does Soviet policy represent merely a series of unrelated *ad hoc* decisions?

Secondly, what impact has Soviet participation had on the UN's institutions and functions? What have been the effects of the actions of this state, so different in its ideology, governmental structure, and political goals, from the majority of the UN's member states? Have the differences mattered or not? To what extent have the differences affected the possibilities for fruitful cooperation? What effects have the changes in Soviet policy had, and how have these changes been related to the development of the UN's structure and tasks? Since the planners in the United States insisted that the United Nations should engage in economic and social activities, presumably they thought that a potentially universal international organization with a broad mandate was the best vehicle for efforts to achieve their objectives. Has this expectation proved valid? In particular, has the USSR's membership proved useful in terms of their values? Or would it have been better to have accepted the Soviet preference for a UN devoted entirely to political functions, leaving international economic and social cooperation as the exclusive province of separate organizations, many of which probably would have had considerably more restricted memberships than the UN?

Finally, the record of Soviet policy in the economic and social activities of the United Nations clearly has implications for the theory of functionalism. To what extent does the record support the contentions of the functionalists and the authors of the Bruce Report? Has collaboration concerning economic and social issues occurred despite the cold war? Has such collaboration as has occurred had any effect on the political differences between East and West? Does functionalist theory aid in understanding the changes in Soviet policy, or are other explanations more to the point?

None of these questions can be answered simply, and definitive and precise answers are probably impossible. However, insights can be gained and tentative and proximate answers found through a detailed analysis of Soviet policy, reactions to it and the resulting interaction.

2: CONSTITUTIONAL ISSUES

IN THE EARLY YEARS OF THE UNITED NATIONS A GREAT DEAL OF attention was devoted to what can be termed constitutional issues. A framework had to be elaborated for the conduct of economic and social activities, organs had to be created, powers delimited and relationships defined. In the process concrete meaning was given to the sometimes vague provisions of the UN Charter, and the outline which they provided was filled in. Although such issues came up less frequently as the years went on, they continued to be important. Questions, once settled, were occasionally reopened and new tasks frequently brought new constitutional problems.

Some of the constitutional issues concerning the economic and social activities of the United Nations cannot be separated from their substantive context; the links are too tight. This applies particularly to jurisdictional issues, concerning whether the UN could or could not undertake a certain task. These issues will be considered later, along with the substantive problems which were involved. Other constitutional issues, however, had a more or less independent existence, and they can be examined here.

THE ECONOMIC AND SOCIAL COUNCIL

According to the Charter, the Economic and Social Council is the basic organ for the conduct of the UN's economic and social functions. Comprised of eighteen states elected by the General Assembly for three-year terms, ECOSOC has broad powers to initiate studies and reports, make recommendations, prepare draft conventions and convene international conferences. Although it

CONSTITUTIONAL ISSUES   17

operates under the authority of the General Assembly, the Council has its own subordinate committees and commissions, and in addition shares responsibility with the Assembly for coordinating the activities of the specialized agencies.

Soviet Bloc Representation on ECOSOC[1]

The USSR has always held a seat on the Economic and Social Council, as have France, the United Kingdom and the United States. In the first election for ECOSOC in early 1946 three other Eastern European states (i.e., Albania, Bulgaria, Byelorussia, Czechoslovakia, Hungary, Poland, Romania, the Ukraine, the USSR, and Yugoslavia) also gained membership. Later that year in the second election, however, largely because of actions of Latin-American and Arab delegates,[2] this seemingly favorable ratio of representation was reduced by one. From 1947 through 1952 the Soviet bloc held three seats in ECOSOC. Then, in October 1952 at the General Assembly's seventh session, after twelve inconclusive ballots, Yugoslavia was elected to the Council over Czechoslovakia, the state which the USSR had backed.[3] Three years later Yugoslavia was elected to a second term. Although the USSR did not oppose Yugoslavia's re-election, there were many times during the six years when that state failed to vote with the Soviet Union in ECOSOC. Thus from 1953 through 1958, the effective Soviet bloc in the Economic and Social Council consisted of only two states. The Soviet bloc's representation was restored to three in the fall of 1958 with the election of Bulgaria at the Assembly's thirteenth session, but three years later it dropped back to two once more, when Yugoslavia again was elected.

[1] When the Soviet bloc in the UN began and what it consisted of at that point is at least partly a matter of definition. In his study, Thomas Hovet, Jr., lists 1947 as the date of its formal constitution and includes among its members then: the Byelorussian SSR, Poland, the Ukrainian SSR, the USSR, and Yugoslavia (*Bloc Politics in the United Nations* [Cambridge: Harvard University Press, 1960], pp. 47 ff.). According to Hovet, Czechoslovakia joined the bloc in February of 1948 and Yugoslavia left it in the summer of that year. The bloc's membership remained at five until December 1955, when Albania, Bulgaria, Hungary and Romania were admitted to the UN, increasing the size of the bloc to nine. The next increase came in October 1961, when Mongolia was admitted to the UN.

[2] See: the *New York Times*, November 20, 1946.

[3] See: UN, General Assembly, Plenary Meetings, *Official Records* (7th Session), pp. 172-177; and the *New York Times*, October 24, 26, 28, 1952.

The USSR's Preference for Other Organs

With the exception of the period from 1953 through 1958, the Soviet bloc's position has been proportionately more favorable in numerical terms in the Economic and Social Council than in the General Assembly. Even during the period from 1953 through 1958 the Soviet bloc's position in the Council was just about the same as it was in the Assembly. However, in most cases the General Assembly has proved the more receptive of the two bodies to Soviet proposals. It has also usually been easier for the Soviet Union to block or blunt Western proposals which it disapproved in the Assembly than in the Council. These generalizations apply especially to the General Assembly's Social, Humanitarian and Cultural Committee (Third Committee). Although all member states are represented on all of the Assembly's main committees, each committee has developed a special character. States have tended to appoint delegates to the Third Committee who have perhaps been somewhat less tough-minded than many of their colleagues on other committees, and, because of the nature of the subject matter considered there, the instructions for these delegates have often been written in a less rigid fashion. However, these generalizations also apply to the Assembly's Economic and Financial Committee (Second Committee), its other committees and its plenary sessions. The most important explanation for this difference is that, in terms of the UN's total membership, the West has always been overrepresented in ECOSOC, and increasingly so as the UN's membership has grown. Western states have never held less than six, or one-third of the seats on the Council. Moreover, Latin-American states, which have often been somewhat more sympathetic to Western positions concerning economic and social issues, especially if they have had cold war overtones, than other non-Western states (in the Soviet view because of their economic dependence on the United States), have consistently won four positions on the Council. Since all decisions in ECOSOC require only a simple majority of those members present and voting, in contrast to the Assembly where a two-thirds majority is required for decisions on "important questions," it has been considerably easier for the Western point of view to carry the day in the Council. Putting it in a different manner, the USSR has been more successful in the General Assembly than it has in the Economic and Social Council because

African and Asian states, which have been the most receptive of the various groups in the UN to Soviet overtures, have been underrepresented in the latter body.

Soviet proposals have also frequently met greater success in some of ECOSOC's subordinate bodies than they have in the Council itself. The Economic Commission for Europe has been a notable although exceptional example, since Soviet bloc representation has been proportionately higher in ECE than in any other United Nations organ dealing with economic and social questions. As of 1963, nine (or ten if Yugoslavia is included) of the thirty states represented on this Commission were members of the Soviet bloc. The explanation for the Soviet Union's relative success in various other subordinate bodies of ECOSOC has probably been in the nature and caliber of representatives on these organs. Western states have frequently appointed as delegates individuals who have not been professional diplomats and who therefore have not always been attuned to the nuances of Soviet tactics. Further, representatives on these bodies have often had only vague instructions.

Aware that its proposals would fare better elsewhere, the USSR has sought to de-emphasize the Economic and Social Council, and to enlarge the role of the General Assembly and that of certain of ECOSOC's commissions. As a corollary to these efforts, Soviet spokesmen strenuously objected to Western moves in the mid-nineteen fifties to restrict the freedom of the Council's commissions.[4] To some extent the Soviet Union's policy has succeeded, although this success is only partly attributable to Soviet actions. Since several underdeveloped states became increasingly dissatisfied with ECOSOC, particularly as the UN's membership expanded after 1955 and the Council became more and more unrepresentative, the General Assembly came to play an ever more prominent role in the United Nations economic and social activities. Because of the opportunities for concrete work presented by ECOSOC's regional commissions, increasing emphasis also came to be placed on them. Starting in 1960, this movement received formal approval and further impetus with the passage of a series of resolutions in the Economic and Social Council and the General Assembly directed toward decentralizing the UN's economic and social activities and strengthening the regional commissions. While the Soviet Union

[4] See for example: UN, ECOSOC, *Official Records* (18th Session), p. 256.

did not initiate these resolutions, it strongly supported them and has been one of the most forceful exponents of their implementation.

Proposals to Enlarge ECOSOC

Dissatisfaction with the Economic and Social Council has led to various proposals for its reform. One of the most significant of these involved increasing the Council's membership, a step which would require amending the Charter. Although various figures have been mentioned, twenty-four is the one most frequently suggested. Argentina first proposed enlarging ECOSOC in 1947, and it was considered then. Several states revived the proposal in 1956 and continued to press it in the following years.

The first time that the proposal was debated, Soviet delegates argued that an increase in ECOSOC's membership was not necessary to increase its representativeness; they maintained that instead strict attention should be paid to the principle of geographical representation.[5] However, earlier the USSR had objected to an Indian proposal that the Assembly should define precisely the geographical distribution of the Council's seats.[6] No doubt the Soviet position was at least partially determined by the fact that the proposed definition gave Eastern Europe only two seats. To the USSR, the principle of geographical representation apparently meant primarily that there should be no reduction in the number of seats assigned to the Soviet bloc.

When the proposal to expand the Economic and Social Council was raised again in 1956, after the United Nations membership had increased considerably, it was backed by the major Western powers, which previously had been opposed. In the debates that year, and each of the following years through 1959, Soviet delegates argued that even though an increase in the Council's membership might be desirable to provide greater representation for new member states, no revision of the Charter could be contemplated without the participation of the People's Republic of China. Since according to Article 108, any amendment to the Charter would require the USSR's consent, as a permanent member of the Security Council, and since the West adamantly refused the Soviet condition, an impasse re-

[5] UN, General Assembly, Joint Second and Third Committee, *Official Records* (3rd Session), pp. 77-78.

[6] UN, General Assembly, Joint Second and Third Committee, *Official Records* (2nd Session), p. 40.

sulted. In 1960, when the UN's membership jumped from eighty-two to ninety-nine, the matter seemed especially pressing, and forty-five states proposed that the Assembly adopt an amendment to the Charter, increasing ECOSOC's membership from eighteen to twenty-four, and urge its ratification. At this point, the Soviet Union interjected a second condition. It hit at the "predominant position" of capitalist states on the Council and its subordinate bodies and argued that any reorganization would have to provide for the equal representation of socialist, neutralist and imperialist states,[7] a demand which stemmed from Nikita S. Khrushchev's September 23 attack on Secretary-General Hammarskjold and the "troika" proposal, and which permeated all aspects of Soviet policy in the UN. The USSR opposed the amendment, announced that it would not participate in a proposed committee with the mandate of finding a solution for the impasse, and even refused to approve a proposal sanctioning a redistribution of seats on ECOSOC. The USSR's stand was a major factor in the Assembly's inability to achieve a majority for any resolution. As a consequence of this stalemate, the Assembly informally began to redistribute Council seats. Among other things, in 1960, for the first time, the Republic of China failed to be elected to ECOSOC. When the question came up again in 1963, the USSR continued to make its consent to any enlargement of ECOSOC conditional on a satisfactory settlement of the Chinese representation issue.

In the discussions with regard to enlarging the Economic and Social Council, quite apart from the issues which were immediately involved, the USSR exhibited great reluctance to allow any revision of the Charter. Probably it feared—with some justification—that if any change were allowed, attempts would also be made to alter other sections of the Charter, such as those dealing with the veto or the composition of the Security Council.

Seemingly a larger ECOSOC would offer greater opportunities for Soviet influence since presumably more African and Asian states would hold seats. On the other hand, a more representative ECOSOC might also have greater stature and authority in relation to the General Assembly, and it is doubtful whether an expanded ECOSOC would be as favorable an arena for Soviet policy as the Assembly. In reality therefore, the West would probably gain more from increasing the size of the Council than the Soviet Union.

[7] UN, General Assembly, Special Political Committee, *Official Records* (15th Session), pp. 56-57.

Then too, the USSR probably has not been displeased with the impasse concerning this question. The resulting tendency to push matters to the Assembly has not affected it adversely. Although some underdeveloped countries have been disappointed by the Soviet Union's stand, the principal argument upon which the USSR has based its position has enabled it to shift to the United States at least a part of the onus for the stalemate, and has also given it an instrument for use against the United States in the struggle concerning the representation of China.

NON-GOVERNMENTAL ORGANIZATIONS

From the point of view of increasing its own influence, the USSR probably saw its greatest opportunity, and certainly made its greatest effort, in connection with the participation of non-governmental organizations (NGO's) in the economic and social activities of the United Nations. The extent to which NGO's have been brought into the UN's work is one of the organization's significant structural innovations. Initially, they were formally recognized in Article 71 of the Charter, which gives ECOSOC the right to make "suitable arrangements" for consultation with them. While defined in differing ways during different periods, consultative status under this article has, subject to various conditions, always included the right to participate in the debates of ECOSOC, its commissions and committees, and to propose items for inclusion in the provisional agenda of these bodies.

THE WORLD FEDERATION OF TRADE UNIONS

Soviet policy was in part responsible for this development, and the USSR constantly sought to exploit the opportunities that it provided. Soviet demands at the San Francisco Conference for privileges for the newly created, communist-controlled World Federation of Trade Unions (WFTU) were a contributing factor in the decision to include Article 71, although the original impetus came primarily from non-governmental observer groups attached to the American delegation. The initial definition of Article 71 resulted primarily from the interaction of pressures by the Soviet Union and the WFTU and the Western response.

Responsibility for the creation of the WFTU may be traced largely to the Soviet Union. During the inter-war period most of the world's labor movements had been affiliated with the International Federation of Trade Unions (IFTU), an organization from which the Soviet trade unions had been excluded despite their several attempts to join. The American Federation of Labor (AFL) had been instrumental in perpetuating this exclusion. At the close of the Second World War there was a move to bring the Soviet unions into the IFTU, but their leaders demurred. Instead they demanded the creation of a new organization.

Those Latin-American and French trade unions which were communist-controlled supported this demand, as did the American Congress of Industrial Organizations (CIO). The latter, because of a rule barring representation of more than one organization from any State, also had been excluded from the IFTU. When confronted with such strong support, opposition to the creation of a new organization withered, and the WFTU was established. The AFL was the only large trade union organization that did not affiliate. Its decision was based on its traditional rivalry with the CIO and on its fear that the WFTU would be dominated by communists. This fear was well grounded. Probably one purpose of the Soviet Union's insistence on the creation of a new organization was to facilitate its securing, as it did, a dominant position for the trade unions under its control. After its formation, the WFTU became more and more obviously an instrument of Soviet foreign policy. Because of this, the major trade unions of the West left the WFTU in 1949 and with the AFL formed a new group, the International Confederation of Free Trade Unions.

Even before its constitution had been completed, the WFTU demanded the right to participate in the San Francisco Conference. Despite Soviet sponsorship and the support of China, France, and New Zealand, this request was not granted. The technical committee concerned with drafting the provisions for economic and social cooperation decided almost unanimously to admit the WFTU as an observer, but the following day the Steering Committee voted 33 to 10 to overrule this decision.[8] These developments nonetheless clearly contributed to the support given the American proposal to include Article 71.

[8] For the debate see: United Nations Conference on International Organization, *Documents of the United Nations Conference on International Organization* (New York: United Nations Information Organization, 1945-1955) [Hereafter cited as UNCIO, *Documents*.], V, 152-154, 207-212 and X, 16.

This Article provided a starting point for defining the relationship between non-governmental organizations and the UN, a process which took some time and allowed for considerable diplomatic maneuver. The WFTU took full advantage of the situation. With the USSR's support, it first demanded that it be given the right to participate on a permanent basis with full voting privileges in ECOSOC and in a consultative capacity in the General Assembly.[9] To grant such extreme demands would have placed the WFTU in a position with respect to ECOSOC that would have been superior to that of all of the member states of the UN, since no state has permanent membership on the Council.

While this demand was never completely renounced, it was soon reduced to the more modest request to participate permanently in an advisory capacity in the Economic and Social Council. Soviet delegates presented this demand several times during the negotiations and proposed its implementation.[10] Even this would have put the WFTU in a position superior to that of the specialized agencies, although the Charter would seem to imply that the opposite should be the case. But this was probably what the USSR desired, for during the same period Soviet representatives also attempted to limit the rights granted to specialized agencies, particularly those of the International Labor Organization. The WFTU also would have been in a stronger position than that of those member states of the UN which were not members of the Council, for they could participate without vote only in Council proceedings which were of special concern to them.

The demands of the WFTU provoked counter-demands. The American Federation of Labor and the International Cooperative Alliance (ICA—a confederation of national cooperative organizations founded in 1895), with the support of the United States and the United Kingdom, both requested that they be given rights equal to those granted to the WFTU. In the negotiations, Soviet delegates sought to block these requests and at the same time to secure maximum privileges for the WFTU.

They were not alone in the latter desire. Several labor groups within

---

[9] See the letter from Walter Citrine and Louis Saillant, President and General Secretary of the WFTU, to the President of the Preparatory Commission: UN Document A/BUR/8.

[10] UN Document A/C. 1/15, p. 4; E/NGO/10, p. 3; E/C. 2/10, p. 3; and UN, ECOSOC, *Official Records* (2nd Session), pp. 108-109.

Western states also appear to have shared such an ambition. Some, it is true, were under communist discipline, but many others were simply strongly attached to the symbol of labor unity. While several factors contributed to the disillusionment of the latter group, the communist attack on the Marshall Plan was one of the most important, and it signalized the split within the labor movement. Prior to that, noncommunist support of the WFTU and advocacy of its position in the UN made Western opposition to these demands more difficult. Sidney Hillman was one of the most active supporters of the WFTU.[11] Leon Jouhaux, who was also a member of the French delegation to the UN, was another.[12] During the first year of negotiations on this subject, France, Belgium, and some Latin-American and Middle Eastern states frequently voted with the Soviet bloc.

In spite of this support, Soviet tactics met with little success in terms of gaining special treatment for the WFTU, which was always included merely as one of several non-governmental organizations. Collectively, however, non-governmental organizations were granted extensive privileges, and because of its pressures on behalf of the WFTU, the USSR was at least partially responsible. These privileges were concretely developed first in ECOSOC Resolution 3 (II). Under the terms of this resolution there were three types of consultative status for NGO's depending on their character, and admission to such status was by *ad hoc* decision of the Council. Greatest privileges were accorded to organizations placed in what was called category "A." To be eligible for this category organizations must "have a basic interest in most of the activities of the Council," and must be "closely linked to the economic or social life of the areas which they represent." Once granted category "A" status, an organization could have an observer attend all public sessions of the Council and could submit written statements which would be circulated as Council documents. It could also consult with a standing committee of five members of ECOSOC—the NGO Committee—and, on recommendation of that body, could address the Council. In recognition of the political importance of the NGO Committee, the Council has always elected those permanent members of the Security Council in ECOSOC to membership. Category "A" NGO's could also con-

[11] See his letters to the President of ECOSOC: UN Documents E/50 and E/55.
[12] See his letter to the President of the Assembly: UN Document A/C. 2 and 3/2.

sult directly with all of ECOSOC's commissions. Organizations placed in the second and third categories were granted lesser privileges. On the basis of an Assembly recommendation, the Council placed in category "A" the WFTU, the ICA, and, despite Soviet objections, the AFL as well.

In spite of the extensive privileges granted in Resolution 3 (II), neither the WFTU nor the USSR was satisfied. The new demands of the WFTU were twofold: it desired the rights (1) to make verbal statements without having to receive the prior approval of the NGO Committee; and (2) to submit questions for inclusion in ECOSOC's agenda in accordance with the provisions applicable to specialized agencies.[13]

The first demand was never granted; the second, however, met with a more favorable reception. Agenda privileges were eventually extended to the WFTU, although at Western insistence they were given to all NGO's in category "A" and they were restricted.[14] A newly established Agenda Committee was given the power to examine the provisional agenda and to make recommendations on it to the Council, including suggestions for the adoption or deferment of items and on the order of debate. The Agenda Committee was obviously intended to prevent propagandistic abuses of the NGO's new privileges. During the negotiations Soviet delegates continually argued against granting equal treatment to all organizations in category "A" by maintaining that the WFTU was unique and therefore merited preferential treatment.

Even after this decision, which was taken in the spring of 1947 and which represented the full initial definition of the meaning of the term "consultation" under Article 71, further attempts were soon made to gain special status for the WFTU.[15] Specifically, the WFTU desired to eliminate the NGO Committee as "intermediary" in certain cases and to win the right to convene special sessions of the Council. Both demands involved privileges that distinguished the specialized agencies from NGO's. From the support of these moves by the Soviet Union and its concurrent attack on the International Labor Organization, it may be inferred that the USSR hoped to have

---

[13] See the letters from Louis Saillant and Leon Jouhaux and the draft resolution submitted by the Soviet Union: UN Documents E/C. 2/1; A/C. 2 and 3/2; and A/C. 2 and 3/10/Rev.1.

[14] See: ECOSOC Resolution 57 (IV).

[15] See: UN Document E/C. 2/48.

the WFTU supplant ILO as the most important spokesman on labor problems in UN counsels.

In reality, however, there was little chance of displacing ILO. The West, through its long participation in the agency, had developed a trust and respect that led it to firmly support the organization. Thus, not one of the new requests pressed by the WFTU in the summer of 1947 was granted, or even seriously considered. The point had been reached beyond which ECOSOC would not go.

During this period, the USSR also made a concerted but unsuccessful attempt to obtain special status for the WFTU in the Council's commissions, particularly the Social Commission and the regional economic commissions.[16] In addition to sponsoring these moves, the Soviet Union has constantly sought to bring the WFTU into the substantive work of the UN. Various methods have been used including: proposals to insert provisions for mandatory consultation with the WFTU on the terms of reference of commissions, committees and study groups; proposals to require the Secretariat to consult with this organization when preparing reports and surveys; and even proposals to refer questions to it. At times these moves have been successful, but only when phrased to cover all NGO's in category "A."

Not only was the WFTU unable to expand its privileges after the spring of 1947, but these were later actually reduced. As the nature of its participation became clear, a demand arose within the Council to restrict non-governmental organizations. Western delegates were particularly critical, but even an Indian delegate commented that the WFTU used its privileges not to promote worker's interests, but to "expatiate on various political problems which were outside its competence."[17] This movement reached its height in 1950. The Council then unanimously decided—in the absence of the Soviet bloc—to limit the length of written statements from NGO's and to allow only one oral statement per agenda item.[18] The right to propose items for inclusion in the provisional agenda, which the WFTU had frequently utilized, was also limited. To be included,

[16] See: UN Documents E/260, p. 24; E/AC. 7/7/Rev. 1, p. 9; E/ECE/12; E/CN. 11/SR. 39, pp. 2-3; and UN, ECOSOC, *Official Records* (6th Session), pp. 360-361.

[17] UN, ECOSOC, *Official Records* (10th Session), p. 212.

[18] ECOSOC Resolution 288 B (X). The NGO concerned had the choice of making the oral statement before either the Council or one of its committees.

items first had to be approved by the NGO Committee. This Committee's decision was final and could not be questioned in plenary session. Thus the automatic publicity given to any item proposed by an NGO and supported by a member of ECOSOC was eliminated. Further, communist representation on the NGO Committee was in effect reduced when its membership was increased to seven; while the USSR continued to be elected, no other communist country was ever chosen to fill one of the additional positions. This resolution, which a Soviet representative later characterized as a "policy of persecution," [19] represented the final definition of Article 71.

Soviet Attitudes Toward Other NGO's

Except for its support of the WFTU, Soviet policy was relatively unimportant in terms of the total fabric of relationships established between non-governmental organizations and the UN. Over 300 NGO's have been accorded consultative status. In addition to the WFTU, six communist-controlled organizations sought this privilege. Four of these succeeded: the Women's International Democratic Federation, the World Federation of Democratic Youth, the International Association of Democratic Lawyers, and the International Organization of Journalists. All were notable mainly for their repeated attempts to improve their status. The first two organizations were originally given second category privileges, despite Soviet protests that they merited category "A." Each Council session thereafter was confronted with a Soviet-sponsored application for placement in the first category until finally ECOSOC adopted a rule imposing a two-year limit on the frequency of such requests.[20] In 1950, during the absence of the Soviet bloc, the Council withdrew third category privileges from the last two organizations and transferred the World Federation of Democratic Youth from the second to the third category. Four years later, after an acrimonious debate which centered on the organization's activities in connection with allegations of germ warfare in Korea, the Council also withdrew privileges from the Women's International Democratic Federation. Soviet delegates sought on almost every possible occasion to have the privileges originally granted these organizations restored or to gain a more favorable position for them, but such attempts always failed.

[19] UN, General Assembly, Joint Second and Third Committee, *Official Records* (5th Session), p. 11.
[20] ECOSOC Resolution 133 C (VI).

Although it has supported fully the claims of organizations that were communist-controlled, the USSR has generally followed an opposite course with regard to other non-governmental organizations. In dealing with requests for admission to consultative status, it has usually been the most conservative member of the Council NGO Committee. At one point the USSR's delegate on the Committee renewed an earlier Soviet attempt to limit consultative status to "international" organizations, and thereby attempted to exclude the British Howard League for Penal Reform, the Carnegie Endowment for International Peace, and the United States National Association of Manufacturers. On another occasion the USSR's representative sought to exclude the International Criminal Police Organization, claiming that it was too specialized. Soviet delegates argued on other occasions that too many requests for consultative status had been granted, and frequently they voted against or abstained on applications giving no reason for their action.

The USSR's efforts to limit the granting of consultative status only succeeded in two instances. First, the Soviet Union successfully argued that no world government group should be given consultative status, since the UN Charter was based on the principle of the sovereign equality of its members.[21] The USSR's position was consistent with communist opposition to world government theories and proposals.[22] Secondly, the USSR was also successful—but to a lesser degree—in arguing that organizations which had contacts with Franco Spain should be excluded. Although a sweeping Soviet proposal which would have excluded even the Red Cross was rejected, the proposal which ECOSOC adopted, one introduced by the United States as a milder alternative, was quite restrictive. This ban, embodied in Council Resolution 57 (IV), remained in effect until 1951.

Further evidence that the Soviet Union's interest in the relationship between the Economic and Social Council and non-governmental organizations was specific rather than general was provided in 1950 when the UN adopted rules allowing the Council to convene conferences of NGO's. The USSR protested this decision and argued that it violated the Charter.[23] It held that ECOSOC could legally convene only conferences of states.

[21] UN Documents E/C. 2/SR. 38, pp. 11-12; and E/C. 2/SR. 52, p. 7.
[22] See: Elliot R. Goodman, "The Soviet Union and World Government," *Journal of Politics*, XV, no. 2 (May 1953), 231-253.
[23] UN, General Assembly, Sixth Committee, *Official Records* (5th Session), p. 277.

Starting in 1961 there have been indications that the USSR's restrictive policy might shift, at least in certain respects. At ECOSOC's thirty-first session that spring, after noting and regretting that no African non-governmental organization held consultative status, and that there were no national organizations on the list from socialist, Arab or Latin-American states, but that they were principally from the West, the USSR proposed that the Council initiate a review of the list of NGO's.[24] The following year the Soviet Union strongly supported the attempts of Senegal and India, respectively, to gain consultative status for the United Towns Organization—a group devoted to promoting cooperation between the peoples of Eastern and Western centers of population—and for the Afro-Asian Organization for Economic Cooperation. These moves were partially successful, in that, in 1962 the NGO Committee inaugurated a broad review of NGO's having consultative status, and at its thirty-third session ECOSOC granted the Afro-Asian Organization for Economic Cooperation category "B" status.

One other aspect of Soviet policy with regard to non-governmental organizations deserves mention. On several occasions after passage of the McCarran-Walter Immigration and Naturalization Act, United States immigration authorities refused to grant visas to representatives of the World Federation of Trade Unions and the Women's International Democratic Federation to enable them to attend meetings of the General Assembly, the Economic and Social Council, and the Social Commission. These incidents, which began in the fall of 1950 and were not finally settled until 1954, afforded excellent opportunities for Soviet criticism of the United States and its policies. Soviet delegates charged that in refusing to grant the visas the United States was attempting to exclude from UN proceedings spokesmen for important and representative views and postulated that this policy could conceivably be extended to representatives of member states. In the USSR's view, the American actions constituted a violation of the Headquarters Agreement defining the relationship between the United Nations and the United States. Soviet delegates and their colleagues from other bloc countries proposed resolutions which condemned the United States and which would have forced the Secretary-General to become the advocate for the excluded NGO representatives.[25] Although the Soviet-sponsored resolutions were never

[24] UN, ECOSOC, *Official Records* (31st Session), p. 20.
[25] UN Documents A/C. 6/L. 229; E/L. 372; and E/L. 493.

adopted, the Secretary-General was instructed to negotiate with the United States, and the incidents, and Soviet charges concerning them, appear to have created a profound sense of disquiet among UN delegates.

This attack on United States immigration practices, however, was peripheral to the USSR's main policy with regard to non-governmental organizations; that is, to gain extensive and exclusive privileges for the World Federation of Trade Unions. Gaining privileges for other communist-controlled and left-leaning non-governmental organizations was probably the USSR's second most important objective. That the USSR feels it has been less than totally successful in its efforts is reflected in a comment in a Soviet text on international law by S. B. Krylov, a noted scholar and the first Soviet citizen to serve on the International Court of Justice. He charged that one of the principal defects of ECOSOC is that "the majority of its members show no desire to consult with organizations representing democratic public opinion." [26] However, at least partly because of Soviet pressures, particularly for the WFTU, non-governmental organizations generally have received an unprecedented position in the United Nations. The impact of Soviet policy on the UN therefore must be measured not only by the use which the WFTU made of these privileges, and the political disputes which it and, in reaction, rival labor organizations injected into UN proceedings which will be examined later,[27] but also by the actions of the many other non-governmental organizations which have been granted consultative status.

ECOSOC'S FUNCTIONAL COMMISSIONS

While the effect of Soviet policy with regard to non-governmental organizations was that of leading the Economic and Social Council away from the concept of governmental representation, the effect of Soviet policy on the composition of the Council's functional commissions was exactly the opposite. In the League such bodies were generally composed of individuals with expert knowledge who in theory were appointed in their private capacity, rather than as gov-

[26] Academy of Sciences of the Union of Soviet Socialist Republics, Institute of State and Law, *International Law* (Moscow: Foreign Languages Publishing House, 1960), p. 344.

[27] See: Chapter VI, and also Harold Karan Jacobson, "Labor, the UN and the Cold War," *International Organization*, XI, no. 1 (Winter 1957), 55-67.

ernmental representatives, although in practice Whitehall and the Quai d'Orsay often played an important role. Some felt that because of this method of appointment these individuals could and would be impartial and that in a sense they could represent the international community, something conceived as being above and superior to national policies.[28] The technique was in accord with the theory of functionalism, which by placing emphasis on functional collaboration by and among technical experts sought to avoid "the complicating network of political and diplomatic censors."[29] The Dumbarton Oaks Proposals recommended a system of appointment for the United Nations similar to the League's, but this recommendation was not included in the Charter, and the issue was left for subsequent settlement.

During the ensuing negotiations, which began in the meetings of the Preparatory Commission and continued through the Economic and Social Council's second session, Soviet delegates insisted, at first against majority opinion, that the Council's functional commissions should be composed of governmental representatives rather than experts. They argued that since governments alone made agreements, only governmental representatives could accomplish useful work. In their view, commissions composed of individuals appointed in a private capacity would become mere discussions groups. Despite the opposition of the United Kingdom, the United States and others, ECOSOC ultimately accepted the Soviet position.

After the crucial vote on principle at the Council's second session, a euphemistic compromise was developed in an effort to preserve elements of a system of private appointment. The compromise provided that the Council would elect states to membership on its commissions; then these states would select, in consultation with the Secretary-General, individuals whose nomination would be confirmed by ECOSOC. The USSR consented to this arrangement only on the condition that it be purely "formal and procedural."[30] It has been that. The principle that the Council's functional commission should be composed of governmental representatives has been firmly established in the Council's procedure. Whenever it has been challenged, as it was during the discussions of the right to appoint alternates,

[28] See: Walter Schiffer, *The Legal Community of Mankind* (New York: Columbia University Press, 1954), pp. 247 ff.
[29] David Mitrany, *A Working Peace System*, p. 27.
[30] UN, ECOSOC, *Official Records* (2nd Session), p. 134.

methods of preventing the too frequent use of alternates, and the level of competence of appointees, Soviet delegates have always argued that the governments of the states which had been elected to membership on the functional commissions had an unqualified right to appoint whomever they chose, and in the end, this position has always triumphed.

There are several explanations for the Soviet Union's stand. The USSR obviously desired to ensure its own membership on the Council's functional commissions. Conceivably, if the commissions were composed of individuals chosen as private experts, the USSR could be overlooked, but if instead the commissions were composed of governmental representatives a great power could not be ignored. The Soviet Union probably also desired to avoid the possibility of its nationals being selected for assignments without its consent, a situation which no totalitarian government could contemplate with equanimity. In addition, the Soviet position reflected the communist belief that questions can only be decided on political bases. Communist ideology could hardly accept the Western concept of a group of experts "objectively" studying a problem and agreeing to a recommended solution for presentation to the Council. Communist views on this issue were later pungently expressed by Nikita S. Khrushchev during his attack on Secretary-General Hammarskjold in his phrase, "there are no neutral men." This is, as Alexander Dallin has pointed out, "a fundamental Bolshevik conception."[31] In a sense, the USSR was justified in its mistrust of groups of experts, for such groups in the UN have usually been predominantly Western, and they have seldom recommended the solutions advocated by the Soviet Union. The USSR's position was also consistent with communist opposition to world government schemes. To create technical bodies which would operate with minimal political supervision from states would be a step, however slight, in the development of supranational institutions. Finally, the USSR probably simply preferred to deal with governmental representatives, as Soviet delegates so frequently stated. The distinction between private and public capacities probably seems bothersome and also false to a state where it hardly exists. Moreover, in the communist view, it does not in reality exist in capitalist systems.

The impact of the adoption of the principle of governmental repre-

[31] Alexander Dallin, *The Soviet Union at the United Nations: An Inquiry into Soviet Motives and Objectives* (New York: Frederick A. Praeger, 1962), p. 161.

sentation on the Council's functional commissions has been variously estimated, although there is consensus that it has led to a rivalry for positions. The USSR and others have often proclaimed the need for adequate geographical representation on these organs and have vociferously objected when they thought their area was underrepresented. The Soviet concept of adequate geographical representation has not involved a mere reflection of the UN's total membership, but rather a reflection of the forces in world affairs, as the USSR has seen them. In 1948, the USSR objected to a suggestion for a scheme of rotation that would have divided the seats on the functional commissions among all UN member states, on the ground that the commissions could only accomplish significant work if the great powers were represented on all of them.[32] In 1961, when ECOSOC decided to increase the size of the functional commissions to provide more opportunities for the representation of new member states, the USSR argued that in view of the economic and social changes that had taken place throughout the world, the commissions ought in addition to be reorganized so as to provide equal representation for "the socialist countries, countries which were members of various blocs created by the West, and neutral countries." [33]

So far as the impact on the work of the commissions is concerned, a former official of a national delegation to the UN has noted that the principle of governmental representation has had the beneficial result of facilitating "the efforts of each government to assume mutually consistent positions" in the various organs.[34] On the other hand, a former member of the League Secretariat argued that adoption of the principle opened the commissions to "the full blast of power politics," and was one of the main reasons for the unsatisfactory character of their work.[35] Commission members have possessed varying degrees of technical expertise, depending on the body and their state. The Statistical Commission, the Population Commission

[32] See: UN: General Assembly, Joint Second and Third Committee, *Official Records* (3rd Session, 1st Part), pp. 35-36.

[33] UN Document E/AC. 24/SR. 219, p. 8.

[34] Robert E. Asher, in Robert E. Asher and others, *The United Nations and Promotion of the General Welfare* (Washington, D. C.: The Brookings Institution, 1957), p. 1030.

[35] A. Loveday, "Suggestions for the Reform of the United Nations Economic and Social Machinery," *International Organization*, VII, no. 3 (August 1953), 325-341, p. 327. See also his earlier article, "An Unfortunate Decision," *International Organization*, I, no. 2 (June 1947), 279-290.

and the Commission on Narcotic Drugs have always included several individuals with technical training. Other commissions, however, have been composed principally of diplomats on the staff of national missions to the UN, and instead of providing reservoirs of technical knowledge, these bodies have more frequently served as preliminary forums for a debate which has been repeated later in the Economic and Social Council and then in the General Assembly.

Few have been satisfied with the performance of the Council's functional commissions. In the early years of the United Nations, Western delegates frequently claimed that because of the adoption of the principle of governmental representation disproportionate emphasis was placed on "political" issues. This criticism lost at least some of its force after 1953, for with the broad changes in the USSR's policy, Soviet representatives on these bodies, who in Western eyes were most guilty of introducing such considerations, gradually became more cooperative and less prone repeatedly to press contentious points. However, Western delegates continued to argue that the principle of governmental representation was to some extent responsible for the commissions' unsatisfactory record. They claimed that governments often failed to appoint properly qualified specialists as representatives.

To obtain the technical advice which the commissions have been unable to supply, the Economic and Social Council has with increasing frequency resorted to the appointment of *ad hoc* groups of experts. The West was responsible for the initiation of this development. Interestingly, the USSR's objections to the creation of such bodies have diminished with the passage of time, and occasionally it has even argued for the appointment of groups of experts. No doubt this has partly been a result of the increasing availability of Soviet technicians and their growing world recognition. The USSR may also have gained some confidence in the United Nations, at least to the extent of feeling that the appointment of a group of experts to study an economic or social problem would not inevitably lead to actions inimical to Soviet interests.

In contrast to the West, the Soviet Union has argued that the unsatisfactory performance of the functional commissions was attributable to departures from the principle of equitable geographical distribution in the composition of these bodies—alluding usually to reductions in the strength of the Soviet bloc—and, more importantly to the commissions' concentration on secondary issues. Soviet commentators have also applied this criticism more broadly to ECOSOC.[36] In a general discussion of the work of the Council's functional commissions in 1951, the USSR's representative argued that too many commissions with trivial functions had been established and suggested that the Fiscal Commission, the Population Commission, the Statistical Commission, the Sub-Commission on Statistical Sampling, the Commission on Narcotic Drugs and the Transport and Communications Commission should be abolished.[37] Although this suggestion was not accepted, the Soviet Union subsequently partially achieved its goal. Three years later the Economic and Social Council decided to terminate the Fiscal Commission and the Sub-Commission on Statistical Sampling and to de-emphasize the activities of three of the other four commissions which the Soviet Union had attacked. Then, in 1959 the Council abolished the Transport and Communications Commission. Paradoxically, the USSR objected to this decision.[38] By that time Soviet policy had changed, and the USSR had discovered that the Transport and Communications Commission was a useful place for efforts to advance elements of its new policy; in particular to argue that more international tourism was needed and to present a variety of proposals designed to achieve this goal.[39] Furthermore, the United States had introduced the proposal to discontinue the Commission and several underdeveloped countries were opposed to the suggestion. Whatever its own attitude, the stand which the Soviet Union took had certain tactical advantages.

By these actions and others the USSR has clearly indicated that it has little interest in those of ECOSOC's commissions which have the most technical functions. If the Soviet Union developed a genuine interest in the Transport and Communications Commission, it was not because of the organ's technical work, but rather because it offered potentialities to advance new Soviet policies. Those commissions in which the USSR has shown the greatest interest are those with the broadest terms of reference: the Social Commission, the Economic, Employment and Development Commission (inactive since 1951), and the Commission on International Commodity Trade. The Soviet Union also strongly supported the attempts of the

[36] See: Academy of Sciences of the USSR, *International Law*, p. 344.
[37] See: UN, ECOSOC, *Official Records* (13th Session), p. 707.
[38] UN Document E/AC. 6/SR. 266, p. 10.
[39] See, for example: E/CN. 2/SR. 81, pp. 3-4.

underdeveloped countries to have the Economic and Social Council establish a Commission on Industrialization. The Soviet Union's claim that these commissions were concerned with some of the most significant problems was valid. It was also true though that because of their subject matter these commissions offered the greatest opportunities for publicity and for divisive attacks against the West.

The commissions in which the Soviet Union has shown least interest, and which have either been discontinued or de-emphasized, worked in the areas in which the League scored its greatest successes. Perhaps by mid-century further work was no longer needed in these areas, the basic tasks may have been accomplished. On the other hand, it may be that cooperation concerning relatively technical economic and social issues presupposes a measure of agreement on fundamentals. Certainly there was far greater consensus on economic and social issues in the League than there has been in the United Nations. With the special insights which are often the property of a dissenter, the Soviet Union saw this from the outset.

There appears to have been a definite connection between the USSR's policy toward the composition of ECOSOC's functional commissions and its attitude concerning the relative importance of these bodies. Both have reflected what might be called a political conception of the Council's functions. The original attitude of the West toward these questions reflected a very different conception. The Soviet Union was interested in creating organs which would be appropriate for discussion of and argument about fundamental questions concerning economic and social structure and organization. The West desired to create organs which could facilitate working out detailed arrangements for international economic and social cooperation. The USSR envisaged debate about the ends, the West assumed that these were given. The UN's record and the gradual change in the attitude of the West indicates that the Soviet theory fitted reality somewhat better. At the same time, it is important to recognize that a major factor shaping this reality was the nature of the Soviet Union's participation in the economic and social activities of the United Nations.

RELATIONS WITH SPECIALIZED AGENCIES

In early Western conceptions of the United Nations organizational structure, the functional commissions were to serve mainly as advisory bodies for the Economic and Social Council; operations were to be carried out by the specialized agencies. These agencies would be brought into relationship with the United Nations through the agreements which were provided for in Article 63 of the Charter, and the General Assembly and the Economic and Social Council would harmonize and coordinate their work and integrate it with that carried on by the United Nations itself. Although this relationship and division of functions may have been clear in theory (and probably it was never very precise), in practice it has often proved difficult to implement. It was never easy to separate the tasks of ECOSOC's subordinate bodies from those of the specialized agencies, and the problem was made more difficult with the establishment of the Council's regional economic commissions. Institutional loyalties have been a complicating factor, as has the fact that the United Nations and the specialized agencies have had differing memberships. Questions concerning the relationship between the UN and the specialized agencies were brought into sharpest focus in the debates concerning the drafting and approval of the formal agreements under Article 63, but they have been raised on other occasions as well.

Collaboration between the UN and Specialized Agencies

Until 1954, when its boycott of many of the specialized agencies began to be lifted, the Soviet Union generally did not favor a close or highly developed relationship between the UN and the agencies. In late 1946 when the General Assembly discussed and approved several agreements between specialized agencies and the United Nations, the Soviet Union objected to giving these bodies—particularly ILO—the right to participate without vote in the meetings of ECOSOC and the Trusteeship Council, the privilege of presenting their views to the General Assembly, and the right to request advisory opinions from the International Court of Justice.[40] The USSR would have preferred that the specialized agencies have contact only with the Economic and Social Council.

The fact that the Soviet Union was not a member of most of these agencies was clearly the major factor determining its attitude. The USSR's position also was probably a result of its concern for

[40] See: UN, General Assembly, Joint Second and Third Committee, *Official Records* (1st Session, 2nd Part), pp. 52-62; and UN, General Assembly, Sixth Committee, *Official Records* (1st Session, 2nd Part), pp. 136-150.

CONSTITUTIONAL ISSUES 39

the relative status of the World Federation of Trade Unions. Even as early as the San Francisco Conference the Soviet Union sought to define the term specialized agencies so that the WFTU could be included.[41] The Soviet attempts to gain extensive privileges for the WFTU have already been recounted; minimizing the privileges accorded to the specialized agencies was another method of elevating the WFTU's relative status.

The Soviet Union opposed all attempts to work toward the development of a consolidated budget for the United Nations and the specialized agencies and also all attempts to establish joint administrative services. While a consolidated budget was never seriously considered, some joint administrative services were established. Although Soviet efforts to prevent the latter development were without avail, the USSR did succeed in having the United Nations share of the costs of these services reduced. The Soviet Union also opposed transferring United Nations property to the specialized agencies. In sum, the USSR sought to avoid providing, through its contribution to the United Nations, finanical support for specialized agencies in which it might not participate.

Until 1954 the Soviet Union strongly opposed substantive cooperation with the specialized agencies. The USSR protested against the creation of joint working groups from the regional economic commissions and the Food and Agricultural Organization. It opposed the decision to allow the specialized agencies to participate in intergovernmental conferences convened by the Economic and Social Council. It viewed with disfavor the adoption of procedures under which the United Nations Secretary-General could consult the specialized agencies and obtain their views concerning ECOSOC agenda items which might involve their services. It vigorously objected to the practice of referring problems which had been introduced and considered in the UN to the specialized agencies for solution. The USSR's protests were particularly vehement in the case of items which had originally been raised in the United Nations by members of the Soviet bloc. It regarded this practice as a device for excluding most members of the Soviet bloc from participating in further consideration of an issue. Until the middle nineteen-fifties the practice had this effect, and there can be no question that it was often used for this purpose. Finally, the USSR opposed the establishment of formal machinery to coordinate the work of the

[41] UNCIO, *Documents*, X, 121.

specialized agencies, particulary the establishment of the Economic and Social Council's Coordination Committee.

THE SOVIET ATTACK ON SPECIALIZED AGENCIES

Not only did the Soviet Union oppose close liaison between the United Nations and the specialized agencies, during the years prior to 1954; it also engaged in a vitriolic attack against several of them.[42] This attack was conducted within and outside the United Nations.

The International Labor Organization was one of the agencies which the USSR severely criticized.[43] Soviet opposition to ILO had deep roots. During the 'twenties, perhaps with some justification, the USSR appears to have viewed the organization as a capitalist attempt to blunt the class consciousness of the workers. Later, as a result of its policy of cooperation with the Western states—specifically its membership in the League of Nations—the Soviet Union actually became a member of ILO. However, its participation was minimal and there was no indication that its basic view of the organization had changed.

At the San Francisco Conference the USSR's hostility toward ILO broke into the open again. Primarily because of Soviet opposition a British proposal explicitly to provide for cooperation between the UN and ILO was withdrawn. This launched a Soviet attack which was continued until the USSR rejoined ILO in 1954. Even since then, the USSR has often been quite critical of ILO's activities. Part of the Soviet attack consisted of attempts to have the UN undertake functions which properly fell within ILO's mandate. Another part consisted of criticism of ILO's work, especially of action taken by the agency in connection with matters which had been introduced in the UN by members of the Soviet bloc. The core of the Soviet criticisms was the charge that the International Labor Organization did not pay sufficient attention to workers' interests, and as a consequence accomplished little of value. The following comment, taken from a standard Soviet text, published in 1960, shows that Soviet views have at most only been moderated.

[42] For a concise presentation of this attack see: N. Yevgenyev, "What Some International Bodies Are Really Doing," *New Times*, no. 13 (March 29, 1950), pp. 10-14; and "Why the U.S.S.R. Is Not a Member of Certain U.N. Specialized Agencies," *News*, no. 10 (November 30, 1951), pp. 6-9.

[43] For a more detailed account see: Harold Karan Jacobson, "The U.S.S.R. and ILO," *International Organization*, XIV, no. 3 (Summer 1960), 402-428, pp. 402-405.

Despite the seemingly extensive scope of its work, the practical results of the activities of the ILO are not great, insofar as many of the conventions drafted by the Organisation have either remained unratified or been ratified only by a small number of States, excluding furthermore the most important industrial States. Nor do the "recommendations" of the ILO exert any real influence.[44]

Although there is some truth to the specific allegations contained in the passage, probably a fundamental ideological issue is at stake, whether or not real progress can be made in improving the conditions of workers without the establishment of communist regimes. On the whole, the Soviet attack on the International Labor Organization has been ineffective: the confidence of noncommunist governments and labor leaders in ILO appears to have diminished little, if at all.

The International Bank for Reconstruction and Development and the International Monetary Fund were other agencies which the Soviet Union severely criticized. The USSR charged that both were instruments of Western imperialism and monopolies. For a time, the onslaught against these agencies probably reflected Eastern Europe's dissatisfaction at being unable to obtain credits from them. In addition, there were deeper reasons for the Soviet Union's hostility. Both agencies were basically Western institutions; their mandate directed them toward the financial problems of the West; their structure insured Western control (e.g., the United States holds about one third of the voting power on the Board of Governors of each), and as a consequence the solutions which they advocated were predominantly Western. A description of various UN bodies in a Soviet journal published in August 1960 asserted that IBRD "is fully controlled by U. S. capital" and that IMF "is controlled by the United States."[45] The Soviet attack against these bodies was affected even less than that against ILO by the broad changes in Soviet policies in the mid-nineteen fifties. Indeed, the attack was extended to cover the International Finance Corporation and the International Development Association, agencies established in 1956 and 1960 and closely affiliated with IBRD. Although many of the Soviet Union's criticisms mirrored those advanced by other states, the over-all effects of the attack appear to have been negligible.

[44] Academy of Sciences of the USSR, *International Law,* p. 355.

[45] V. Demidov, "The United Nations," *International Affairs* (Moscow), VI, no. 8 (August 1960), 72-80, p. 78.

States which desperately needed capital were not in a position to reject the services of these institutions, and the Soviet criticisms failed to present an alternative.

The USSR's attack on ILO and on IBRD and IMF provided two exceptions to its general policy of not favoring a tightly integrated relationship between the United Nations and the specialized agencies. In 1948 the Soviet Union proposed that ECOSOC recommend that the structure of ILO should be changed so that workers' representation in the Conference and Governing Body would be increased from 25 to 50 per cent.[46] ILO has a tripartite system of representation whereby employers and workers as well as governments are represented and have separate votes in most of its organs. Soviet trade unions had raised this proposal as early as April 1944,[47] and the USSR had broached it informally at San Francisco and later in various UN debates. The Soviet Union raised it again when it rejoined ILO. The suggestion was never seriously considered.

During the debates concerning the agreements between the UN and IBRD and IMF, the Soviet Union protested against the special status given to these agencies.[48] The USSR objected to the fact that the UN did not have the right to examine their administrative budgets, to make recommendations to them without prior consultation, to make recommendations concerning individual loans, or to be represented at all of their meetings. The Soviet Union apparently desired to gain greater opportunities to influence the operations of these agencies, especially their credit activities, than were provided in the agreements. Although several other states also had reservations about the looseness of the connection between the UN and these agencies, the Soviet Union was unable to force renegotiation of the agreements.

OTHER ASPECTS OF SOVIET POLICY CONCERNING
THE SPECIALIZED AGENCIES

In addition, there were two other exceptions to the Soviet Union's general policy concerning the relationship between the UN and the specialized agencies. One involved applications for membership in

[46] UN Document E/973.
[47] Academy of Sciences of the USSR, *International Law*, p. 354.
[48] See: UN, ECOSOC, *Official Records* (5th Session), pp. 269-276, *passim*; and UN, General Assembly, Joint Second and Third Committee, *Official Records* (2nd Session), pp. 12-36, *passim*.

CONSTITUTIONAL ISSUES   43

the United Nations Educational, Scientific and Cultural Organization and in the International Civil Aviation Organization. Until 1962 the agreement between the UN and UNESCO provided that applications for membership by non-members of the UN must be approved by the Economic and Social Council; and that between the UN and ICAO, by the General Assembly. Most states have regarded these requirements as formalities. The Soviet Union on the other hand has frequently utilized the opportunity which they provided for attacks on the applicants and on colonialism. It is interesting that when the USSR was active in the World Health Organization, it opposed including a similar provision in the agreement with that agency.[49]

Soviet actions in ECOSOC's Coordination Committee provided another exception. Once this Committee was established, the USSR did not hesitate to use it to attempt to impose its conception of priorities of work on the specialized agencies. The USSR's first proposal of this nature was advanced in 1951 and several others have been introduced in the succeeding years. Only a few of the Soviet suggestions have been adopted, and those that have, have been greatly modified.

After 1954 Soviet policy toward the specialized agencies changed. The USSR became less critical of the agencies, even those in which it did not participate, and somewhat more willing to refer problems to them. Although the Soviet Union did not join the Food and Agriculture Organization, it participated in the joint working parties established by this agency and the regional economic commissions and also in certain joint FAO/UNICEF bodies. The USSR raised no objections to the agreements between the United Nations and the International Finance Corporation and the International Development Association despite the fact that they were very similar to those between the UN and IBRD and IMF. The Soviet Union was a co-sponsor of the resolution approving the agreement with the International Atomic Energy Agency. It is significant though that during the negotiations the USSR had insisted—and had won its point—that IAEA should have a status different from that of the specialized agencies, that it should have a special and direct relationship with the General Assembly and the Security Council.[50]

[49] See: UN Document E/C. 1/SR. 37, p. 3.
[50] See for example the note of October 1, 1955, from the Soviet Ministry of Foreign Affairs to the American Embassy: United States of America, Department of State, Press Release No. 527, October 6, 1956, p. 22.

On the other hand, the USSR continued to introduce and support proposals that would have assigned tasks which properly fell within the mandate of a specialized agency to the General Assembly or to the Economic and Social Council or one of its subordinate bodies. Apparently the USSR still regarded the United Nations as a more favorable arena for its efforts than the specialized agencies. There was some justification for this attitude. Most of the specialized agencies were created to deal with problems which were basically Western and their structure was such that Western influence was predominant. It is of course impossible to estimate the extent to which the West would have gained a dominant position in the specialized agenices had the Soviet Union participated in all of these bodies from the outset—the initial advantages certainly favored the West. However, the Soviet Union's boycott only served to insure this outcome.

Despite the general ineffectiveness of Soviet policy in the UN concerning the specialized agencies, the Soviet Union's impact in broad terms on the relationship between the UN and the specialized agencies was probably rather great. Certainly the Soviet-American clash affected the distribution of tasks between the UN and the specialized agencies. At least partly as a result of this clash calculations concerning the different patterns of influence in the various bodies came to be an important element in decisions relating to the division of functions. Then too, the fact that there were different patterns of influence in the UN and in the specialized agencies complicated the problem of coordination. Perhaps, though, the USSR's greatest impact was negative; by refusing to participate in the work of several of the specialized agencies it shattered the dream of postwar collaboration.

PROCEDURAL AND REPRESENTATIONAL QUESTIONS

Although the Soviet Union appears to have regarded the United Nations as a more propitious environment for its efforts than the specialized agencies, this could only have been a relative judgment. The Soviet bloc has always been a fairly small minority in the United Nations, and the USSR's efforts to compensate for this and to buttress its position have not been particularly successful. Indeed, most of the decisions which have been taken concerning procedural and representational questions have had the effect of diminishing

Soviet influence in the UN's economic and social organs rather than that of increasing it.

RULES OF PROCEDURE

The USSR has been unable to prevent the gradual tightening of the Economic and Social Council's rules of procedure and the imposition of restrictions on debate; it could only defeat the most extreme proposals. The Soviet Union has not even been able to secure the adoption of Russian as a working language in ECOSOC (though it did gain this in ECE), something probably desired as much for prestige as for convenience. Nor has the USSR been successful in its efforts to have extensive accounts of minority views included in the Council's published reports and those of its subordinate bodies.

ECOSOC's REGIONAL COMMISSIONS

The Soviet Union has not fared any better in relation to ECOSOC's regional economic commissions. At an early stage the USSR sought to exploit its relative strength in the Economic Commission for Europe by proposing that all decisions "on important questions" should require a two-thirds majority. This proposal was defeated both times that it was introduced. Before the impasse concerning admission to the United Nations was broken in December 1955, several states which were not members of the UN—both from Eastern and Western Europe—participated in the work of ECE in a consultative capacity. The Soviet Union proposed several times that all of these states should be given full voting privileges, a move which would have favored the Soviet bloc since its strength would have been disproportionately increased. Although these proposals were never adopted, ultimately it was decided to grant such states voting privileges in ECE's technical committees. The significance of this concession, however, was limited, since votes were almost never taken in the technical committees. Later, in 1954, despite bitter Soviet protests, the Economic and Social Council declared that all noncommunist states which participated in the work of ECE, but were not members of the UN—except Switzerland, which preferred its consultative status—were eligible for full membership in the Commission. The following year the Federal Republic of Germany was also declared eligible to become a member of ECE. Again Soviet protests were without avail. After 1955 then, Switzerland and the

German Democratic Republic were the only European states which did not have full membership in the Commission. Several Soviet proposals to accord this status to the latter failed of adoption; instead the German Democratic Republic's role in the Economic Commission for Europe continued to be confined to having representatives participate in a consultative capacity in the work of ECE's subsidiary bodies, a role which it refused to accept after 1959.

The Soviet Union's position with reference to the Economic and Social Council's other regional economic commissions was considerably less favorable. Until 1962 the USSR was the only communist state represented on the Economic Commission for Asia and the Far East. Its efforts to gain some form of representation in ECAFE for the Democratic People's Republic of Korea, the Democratic Republic of Viet Nam, the Mongolian People's Republic and the People's Republic of China all failed, but of course when Mongolia was admitted to the UN in 1961 it automatically became a member of ECAFE. The USSR was unable to gain a seat for itself on the Economic Commission for Latin America (ECLA) and the Economic Commission for Africa (ECA), and had an Economic Commission for the Middle East ever been created, the Soviet Union would not have been represented on that body either.

If broader standards of measurement are used, however, one Soviet tactic concerning the Economic Commission for Asia and the Far East may have been relatively successful. Although the proposal was not adopted, the USSR may have gained some propaganda advantages. The issue concerned associate memberships, a device used to bring non-self-governing territories into the Commission's work. When ECAFE's terms of reference were being formulated in 1947, the USSR proposed that such territories should be allowed to apply directly to the Economic and Social Council for associate membership in ECAFE, rather than through the intermediary of their metropolitan country, and that associate membership should carry with it the right to participate fully in all activities of the Commission.[51] These proposals were defeated each of the five times that they were introduced. The Economic and Social Council decided instead that applications for associate membership for non-self-governing territories would have to be made through the metropolitan countries responsible for their administration and that the privileges of associate membership would include voting rights in ECAFE's sub-

[51] See: UN Document A/C. 2/113/Rev. 1.

CONSTITUTIONAL ISSUES   47

sidiary bodies but not in the plenary session. The USSR's proposals were clearly part of its general attack on colonialism. Later, in the course of each discussion of an application for associate membership Soviet delegates inveighed against imperialism.

When the terms of reference of the Economic Commission for Africa were discussed a decade later, the Soviet Union did not attempt to modify the procedural arrangements concerning associate members, even though they conformed to the pattern established by ECAFE. By then Soviet tactics were generally more moderate, and the USSR concentrated its efforts in the negotiations concerning ECA on trying to get a seat for itself.

RULES FOR THE CONVOCATION OF CONFERENCES

Problems concerning the rights to be accorded to states which were not members of the United Nations and to non-self-governing territories also had to be faced in 1949 when the UN adopted rules governing the convocation of intergovernmental conferences by the Economic and Social Council. The USSR's position in the discussions concerning these rules paralleled that which it had held in connection with ECOSOC's regional economic commissions.[52] The Soviet Union proposed that voting privileges in the conferences should be extended to all states which participated, even though they might not be members of the UN. This time the proposal carried. The USSR also suggested that ECOSOC should be empowered to issue invitations directly to non-self-governing territories. This suggestion was not adopted. Both proposals were probably designed among other things to strengthen Soviet influence in conferences, and the latter was clearly a part of the USSR's general onslaught against colonialism.

Broader issues were raised in the discussions of these rules also. The original draft provided that under certain circumstances United Nations funds could be used to finance the conferences and that the participants in any conference would be bound by any decisions which ECOSOC might make relating to the conference. The USSR strongly objected to both provisions and succeeded in having the latter eliminated. Both issues involved sovereignty. As in the case of the specialized agencies, the Soviet Union was clearly unwilling to provide, through its obligatory contribution to the UN, financial support for activities in which it might not participate. The issue

[52] UN Document A/C. 6/L. 72.

of the binding nature of ECOSOC's decisions was probably the more crucial of the two for the USSR, particularly in view of the position of the Soviet bloc as a permanent minority in the Council. That its proposal on this issue was adopted was not surprising—other states also jealously guarded their sovereign rights. As this case illustrates, in controversies concerning procedural and representational questions, the Soviet Union was usually able to protect its minimal rights—they also involved the rights of others—but it could do little beyond that.

IMPLEMENTATION

The dispute about the effect of ECOSOC's decisions on intergovernmental conferences which it convened was related to a fundamental controversy concerning the extent to which states were obliged to implement recommendations of the United Nations on economic and social issues.

The first discussion of the question of implementation occurred at the San Francisco Conference in connection with Article 56 of the Charter. According to this Article UN member states "pledge themselves to take joint and separate action in cooperation with the Organization" to achieve the broad economic and social objectives outlined elsewhere in the Charter. The Soviet Union was partially responsible for the existence of this Article. Australia and several small states desired to include a "pledge" in the Charter, but the United States strongly resisted their pressures. Finally the Australian and American delegates reached an impasse. At this point the Soviet representative, Amazasp A. Arutiunian, whose association with the United Nations economic and social activities continued until 1959, assumed the role of mediator and facilitated drafting a compromise article. The USSR appeared not to take the "pledge" too seriously. When he intervened, Mr. Arutiunian stated that he thought that "the English language was rich enough to find words to satisfy all parties," and that if it were not, he could draft an article in Russian.[53]

Nevertheless, and despite its general concern for sovereignty, the USSR and other countries in the Soviet bloc were the first to claim that member states were obliged to implement the UN's recommendations concerning economic and social issues. In the fall of

[53] UNCIO, *Documents*, X, 140.

1947, at the General Assembly's second session, Poland proposed a draft resolution, which the Soviet Union seconded, requesting that member states "carry out all recommendations of the General Assembly passed on economic and social matters." [54] It was clear that this resolution was intended primarily as an attack against the United States European Recovery Program (ERP), or Marshall Plan. During the debate, members of the Soviet bloc charged that under the Marshall Plan economic assistance was being used for political purposes and that this violated the terms of General Assembly Resolution 48 (I). In spite of the motives which prompted it, the Polish proposal fitted the purposes of those states such as Australia which wanted to enlarge the UN's role in the economic and social area. Consequently, after it had been stripped of the features which were an obvious attack on the United States and its policies, the resolution was adopted.[55] In addition to containing a broad exhortation to member states, it requested that the Economic and Social Council report annually on the steps which member states had taken to implement the UN's recommendations concerning economic and social matters.

The latter provision provoked a searching examination of the question of implementation. This review was conducted mainly in ECOSOC and in an *ad hoc* committee which it created. In these discussions, the Soviet Union retreated from the unqualified dicta that it had offered at the Assembly's second session. One Soviet delegate sought to develop a theory of differential obligations. He argued that although the Charter made it mandatory for governments to cooperate in the international field, this was not the case with regard to internal measures which fell within the domestic jurisdiction of states.[56] He asserted that: "It was the prerogative of governments of the member states to apply the resolutions if and when they saw fit. They had to take their national legislation into account." [57] Under this interpretation, the USSR could legitimately allege that the Marshall Plan violated a United Nations resolution and at the same time not create a precedent which might lead to intervention in the USSR's internal affairs. This position was neither accepted nor rejected; it was simply ignored. Most states ap-

[54] UN Document A/C. 2/108.
[55] General Assembly Resolution 119 (II).
[56] UN Document E/AC. 31/SR. 3, p. 8.
[57] UN Document E/AC. 31/SR. 9, p. 2.

peared to assume that there was a general moral obligation to attempt to implement the UN's economic and social recommendations, and the discussions dealt primarily with the practical implications of this obligation; namely, the question of checking on measures of implementation.

The debate focused on Article 64 of the Charter. This article states that ECOSOC may "make arrangements" with member states "to obtain reports" on the steps which they have taken "to give effect to" the UN's recommendations concerning economic and social matters. The USSR's position with regard to this article was completely negative. The Soviet Union first argued that there was no need to send requests for information to member states; if any reports were to be prepared they could be compiled by the Secretariat on the basis of information which it had.[58] Then the USSR took the position that member states were not obliged to provide information to the United Nations on the steps which they had taken to implement recommendations. It held, in spite of the fact that this interpretation had been rejected at the San Francisco Conference,[59] that since Article 64 stated that ECOSOC could "make arrangements," the Council would have to negotiate individual agreements with each member state to obtain reports, just as it had with the specialized agencies.[60]

Despite Soviet opposition, the Economic and Social Council ultimately established, in Resolution 283 (X), an elaborate procedure for periodically obtaining information from member states on the steps which they had taken to implement the UN's economic and social recommendations. The USSR did little to facilitate the carrying out of the provisions of this resolution. When it did reply to questionnaires, its statements were seldom to the point. It should be recognized, however, that many of the UN's recommendations had little meaning for a communist country. Nor were the USSR and the other Soviet bloc states the only ones which failed to submit significant information.

On the whole, the elaborate system established in Resolution 283 (X) did not work well, and in 1952 ECOSOC voted to abandon it. At the same time the Council decided that in the future pro-

[58] UN, ECOSOC, *Official Records* (9th Session), pp. 127-128.
[59] See: UN Document E/1567, p. 2.
[60] UN Document E/AC. 31/SR. 2, p. 2.

visions for checking on measures of implementation should be included within substantive resolutions. Even though the USSR no longer openly questioned the principle that the United Nations could request information from member states on implementation, it voted against this decision. The Soviet delegate argued that the suggestion in the resolution that time limits should be established violated national sovereignty; "governments should be absolutely free to submit information under the conditions most convenient to themselves." [61]

In practice, since 1952, there have been few attempts to ascertain the extent to which member states have implemented the United Nations economic and social recommendations. In a sense then, the Soviet Union's position has triumphed; states can talk about the obligation to carry out the UN's recommendations, but hardly anything is done to enforce this obligation. This is what the USSR desired and apparently is the Soviet concept of how international organizations should function.[62]

THE SECRETARIAT

Nikita S. Khrushchev's September 23, 1960, speech attacking Secretary-General Hammarskjold and advocating the reorganization of his office signaled a final aspect of Soviet policy, the attack on the composition of the United Nations Secretariat. Although Chairman Khrushchev's attack and subsequent Soviet actions were touched off by the Secretary-General's actions in the Congo crisis, and were broadly aimed at the Secretariat, they had ramifications for the UN's economic and social activities. In addition to demanding the reorganization of the Secretary-General's office, Soviet policy hit at the predominant position of the West in the Secretariat and insisted that the entire Secretariat should be made more representative. Actually, starting in the late nineteen fifties, the USSR had begun to push for a greater number of posts for Soviet bloc nationals in the UN Secretariat; thus Soviet policy after Chairman Khrushchev's speech was a continuation and expansion of this earlier move.

The broad Soviet criticisms included attacks on the composition

[61] UN, ECOSOC, *Official Records* (14th Session), p. 708.
[62] See K. Y. Chishov's discussion of The Universal Declaration of Human Rights: Academy of Sciences of the USSR, *International Law*, pp. 138-139.

of those sections of the Secretariat dealing with economic and social activities. On the day of Chairman Khrushchev's address, *Izvestia* carried a story which pointed out that "all nine of the leading positions in the department of economic and social affairs belong to representatives of the major imperialist powers . . ." [63] The most detailed Soviet critique was given one year later in the Assembly's Fifth Committee. The USSR's delegate reviewed the composition of the Department of Economic and Social Affairs:

> . . . which had a staff of 250 and was headed by a French national. Of the 7 directors in the Department, 5 were United States nationals and not one was from a socialist country. The Director of the Bureau of Technical Assistance Operations, the Director of the Statistical Office, the Director of the Division of General Economic Research and Policies, the Director of the Bureau of Social Affairs were United States nationals, who thus held the most important posts. The same applied to the Special Fund, the Managing Director and Deputy Managing Director were United States nationals, who had established a monopoly over the management and supervision of the Fund's activities. The Technical Assistance Board was headed by a United Kingdom national; 5 of the Board's thirteen senior officials came from the United States, 5 were nationals of countries allied to the United States, and there again no socialist country was represented. Those examples clearly showed that the Secretariat was not organized on an international basis.[64]

In substantive debates Soviet delegates criticized various UN reports dealing with economic and social matters and attributed their alleged lack of objectivity to the biased composition of the Secretariat. The Soviet position was an attack on the basic Western belief that an impartial international civil service was a feasible and desirable component of an international organization. It was related to the stand that the USSR had taken with respect to the composition of ECOSOC's functional commission. To the extent that the United Nations began to decrease the role of citizens of the West in the Secretariat, and to employ more nationals from other areas, including the Soviet block, Soviet policy was successful, although by mid-1963, there were only sixteen citizens of the USSR in the Department of Economic and Social Affairs.

[63] *Izvestia*, September 23, 1960, as contained in *The Current Digest of the Soviet Press*, XII, no. 39 (October 26, 1960), 17.

[64] UN, General Assembly, Fifth Committee, *Official Records* (16th Session), p. 128.

CONCLUSIONS

There is no adequate single explanation for Soviet policies concerning these constitutional issues, which have been significantly rather consistent. The USSR frequently utilized these issues for efforts to advance broad Soviet objectives; for example, increasing the prestige and stature of the World Federation of Trade Unions, or weakening colonial relationships and embarrassing the West. Admittedly, many states framed their policies concerning constitutional issues in terms of extrinsic goals, but the Soviet Union was more blatant in its efforts. Some Soviet proposals had two purposes; they were designed both to influence public opinion and to affect the distribution of power. Even when such proposals were rejected, they may well have adequately served Soviet propaganda interests.

In the realm of intrinsic objectives, one consistent motivation for Soviet policies was a desire to maintain and improve its position within the United Nations economic and social organs, and to insure that its views would receive a full airing. Since the structure of power in different United Nations organs varied, this meant trying to mold the processes of decision-making so that the most crucial decisions would be made in the organs where the Soviet Union's position was relatively strongest, where the Soviet bloc had greatest representation and where there were the most opportunities for alliances with others. In addition, it meant attempting to insure that there would be ample opportunity to present and publicize dissenting views.

The Soviet Union also constantly sought to protect its sovereignty. Whether the issue was the composition of the Council's functional commissions, the creation of a common budget for the UN and the specialized agencies, the convocation of conferences, or the obligation to implement recommendations, the Soviet view always implied that states were supreme and that nothing should be done which might violate this supremacy. This reflected basic Soviet doctrines concerning international law. The USSR's position also stemmed from the fact that the Soviet bloc was always in a minority position and was separated from the majority by a wide ideological chasm.

However, the Soviet bloc's minority position was partially self-imposed. Cooperation could only occur if all parties believed it was feasible and desirable, and the USSR did not appear to hold this view. Its approach to constitutional issues appears to have been based on quite different assumptions. It no doubt distorts the position of all parties to say that the Soviet Union's approach to constitutional issues was that the UN's economic and social institutions should be arenas for combat rather than centers for cooperation, but there is some truth to the statement. Again, although the differences between Soviet policies and those of other states may have been only matters of degree, they were crucial differences.

Even though the USSR's proposals concerning constitutional issues were seldom adopted and its objections seldom heeded, the total impact of Soviet policies with reference to these matters was quite significant. Some of the Soviet proposals which were adopted dealt with basic issues. Then too, the USSR's policies affected the general atmosphere in which the UN's economic and social activities were conducted. One effect of Soviet policies was to ward off encroachments against state sovereignty. Most of the Soviet proposals which gained acceptance concerned this issue. Another impact, which resulted partly from the adoption of Soviet proposals and partly from the USSR's general attitude toward constitutional issues, was to give emphasis to political rather than technical considerations in the UN's economic and social work. The extrinsic issues which the Soviet Union introduced into the consideration of constitutional problems were usually highly controversial political matters. Granting extensive privileges to the World Federation of Trade Unions certainly served to bring political issues to the fore. The decision that ECOSOC's functional commissions should be composed of governmental representatives meant that political considerations would be stressed in their work. The decisions on implementation also fitted this pattern. Rigid checks on the measures which member states had taken to implement the UN's economic and social recommendations would be appropriate if these were fairly precise and dealt with technical subjects. Otherwise the sanction of public opinion would be more appropriate. As a matter of strategy and tactics, once one state started to emphasize political considerations, others had to do so also. This is not to argue that only the USSR stressed political considerations and that in each case it was the initiator, but simply to say that it did this more frequently and with greater consistency than the other states and therefore must bear the greatest responsibility.

That Soviet policies concerning constitutional issues had such a significant impact is instructive. For one thing it indicates that the USSR was not alone in its concern to protect its autonomy and in its desire to enlarge the sphere of its influence. Other states, especially Asian, African and Latin-American countries shared these objectives. Soviet proposals were not only vehicles for the attainment of its own purposes; intentionally or not they served those of others as well. And the increasingly dominant role of the General Assembly in the United Nations economic and social activities perhaps indicated among other things that many states felt that the political aspects of questions were the most important; certainly a body as large as the Assembly was hardly the best place for the consideration of technical problems.

Had the United Nations followed the spirit of the recommendations of the Bruce Report, or even more those contained in the writings of the functionalists, in deciding these constitutional issues, the outcome would have been quite different. Technical rather than political aspects would have been emphasized and gradual, but major inroads made on state sovereignty. That the UN did not take this course was partly the result of the participation of the Soviet Union. Perhaps this indicates that a considerable degree of political consensus is required before the kind of economic and social collaboration envisaged by the authors of the Bruce Report and the functionalists can occur, and that the relationship between an international organization's work in the political and in the economic and social fields is much tighter and more complex than they foresaw.

3: REFUGEES AND DISPLACED PERSONS

EVEN BEFORE ITS STRUCTURAL FRAMEWORK HAD BEEN COMPLETED, the United Nations was confronted with a substantive problem of immense proportions, and one which intimately involved the USSR's interests. Although there are no completely accurate figures, at the close of the Second World War at least 8,000,000 persons found themselves irregularly outside of their countries of origin. Most of them were in this position as a result of the actions of Nazi Germany or other developments which had occurred during the course of the war, though some, such as the Nansen Refugees and the Spanish Republicans, owed their status to earlier events. Repatriation of these individuals began with the cessation of hostilities, but in some cases the process was slow, and not all were willing to return to their countries of origin. Moreover, population movements generally attributable to the Second World War continued even after the fighting ceased. By the beginning of 1947, even though some 6,500,000 individuals had been returned to their homelands, 1,500,000 or more, the majority of whom were from Eastern Europe, remained unsettled. These people vitally needed assistance. Those who were willing to be repatriated needed temporary aid until they could return to their countries of origin, and the others needed longer-term care and help in resettlement. Although several organizations were working in this field, for various reasons none of them was equipped to provide the necessary assistance. It was clear as early as 1945 that this problem would emerge, and as time went on, the need for a solution became increasingly apparent and urgent.

Attempting to provide a solution became the first major substantive task of an economic or social character which the United Nations undertook. Consideration of the issue began in the Preparatory Commission, and it became one of the most time consuming items on the agendas of the General Assembly and ECOSOC during the UN's first year.

It was impossible to solve this problem quickly, and the unsettled conditions of the mid-twentieth century have produced a steady and occasionally—as during the Hungarian crisis of 1956—tumultuous flow of new refugees. Consequently, the UN has continuously had to deal with such issues, and over the years it has devoted considerable attention to them. Soviet interests, however, have usually not been as directly involved as they were in the problem which resulted from the Second World War.

UN action with regard to refugees and displaced persons has taken various forms. The first step was the creation of a temporary specialized agency, the International Refugee Organization (IRO), to deal with the immediate postwar problem. When IRO's mandate expired in 1951, the Office of the United Nations High Commissioner for Refugees (UNHCR) was created to take over some of that agency's functions and also to undertake certain new tasks. The UN also created, in 1949 and 1950, two institutions to deal with these problems in special geographical areas, the United Nations Relief and Works Agency for Palestine Refugees in the Near East (UNRWA) and the United Nations Korean Reconstruction Agency (UNKRA). With the exception of the Office of the High Commissioner all of these institutions have been financed completely outside of the UN's regular budget, and most of the UNHCR's funds have come from special contributions. In addition, the United Nations adopted recommendations and drafted declarations and conventions, and it declared 1959-1960 World Refugee Year.

The USSR's participation in the UN's activities with regard to refugees and displaced persons was greatest in the negotiations concerning the drafting of the IRO Constitution. It has not participated in any of the concrete work which the United Nations has conducted in this field, nor has it made any financial contribution other than that involved in its contribution to the UN's regular budget. However, the Soviet Union has often taken a stand on these issues in the General Assembly and the Economic and Social Council.

DRAFTING THE IRO CONSTITUTION

The question of what action the United Nations should take with regard to refugees and displaced persons was first discussed seriously during the meetings of the Preparatory Commission in the fall of 1945. By then the outlines of the developing problem were fairly clear. An individual who is outside of his country of origin has essentially three alternatives: repatriation, integration in the area where he is located, or resettlement in some other area. The agreements which the USSR, the United Kingdom and the United States signed at Yalta, February 11, 1945, assumed general acceptance of the first alternative,[1] and the mandate of the United Nations Relief and Rehabilitation Administration (UNRRA), the institution with the largest operational program in this field, was confined to providing temporary care for displaced persons and returning them to their native countries. However, by the summer of 1945—and probably even earlier—it was apparent that not all would be willing to return to their countries of origin. Further, in August 1945 the UNRRA Council voted that the Administration should terminate its activities in early 1947: thus it might not even be able to finish its task. Although the Inter-Governmental Committee on Refugees (IGCR) had been established in 1938 for the express purpose of facilitating resettlement—especially the resettlement of Jews who fled from Germany and Austria—it would not be able to cope with the emerging problem without fundamental alterations in its financial and constitutional structure. Integration was not a very feasible solution at that time, either in economic terms or in terms of the personal feelings of many of the individuals involved. Therefore, there was great pressure for the United Nations to take some action.

Negotiations concerning the subject continued for an entire year; the final decision was not taken until December 15, 1946. In retrospect, the outcome seems to have been predetermined. The West, with its belief in free choice, and despite the wartime agreements with the USSR—or perhaps because of the experience in applying

---

[1] See: United States of America, Department of State, *Foreign Relations of the United States: The Conferences at Malta and Yalta, 1945* (Washington, D. C.: Government Printing Office, 1955), pp. 985-987. The agreement which the Soviet Union and France signed June 29, 1945, was similar.

them—was committed to having the United Nations in some way provide support for the resettlement of large numbers of refugees, most of whom would be from Soviet bloc countries. The USSR was unalterably opposed to this. Once the issue was raised, a serious clash could not be avoided, and since the West at that time had little difficulty in mustering a majority in the UN, its view was bound to prevail. But although this stark sketch is basically correct, it neither does justice to the complexity of the problems nor adequately portrays the policies of the various states involved, especially those which the Soviet Union pursued. A more detailed analysis is needed.

Consideration in the Assembly

The USSR's initial position was that the United Nations should not concern itself with the problems of refugees and displaced persons. In the meetings of the Preparatory Commission, the Soviet Union argued against including the subject in the agendas of the General Assembly and the Economic and Social Council.[2] The USSR took the same position during the first stages of the discussion in the General Assembly. It strongly supported a resolution proposed by Yugoslavia which stated that the problem had ceased to be important since the defeat of the Fascist countries permitted all displaced persons to return to their native states.[3] The resolution recommended the conclusion of bilateral agreements to facilitate the repatriation of displaced persons and the apprehension of war criminals. Under the terms of the Yugoslav proposal the UN would consider giving assistance only to the Spanish Republican refugees.

This position was in accord with that which the USSR had taken previously in other international organizations. In the nineteen twenties the Soviet government had cooperated with Fridtjoff Nansen in work which he carried out under League auspices.[4] However, the USSR's cooperation concerned programs which involved repatriation to the Soviet Union or resettlement there. After the USSR joined the League of Nations it fought against the organiza-

[2] Preparatory Commission of the United Nations, Committee 1, *Summary Records of Meetings* (London, 1945), p. 41; Committee 3, *Summary Records of Meetings* (London, 1945), pp. 15-16.
[3] UN Document A/C. 3/7.
[4] See: K. W. Davis, *The Soviets at Geneva*, pp. 27-43.

tion's efforts to assist "White Russian" refugees.[5] The USSR participated in the work of UNRRA and IGCR: it joined both agencies in 1943. But neither organization did what it was obvious that the United Nations would have to do—resettle large numbers of persons from Eastern Europe. This was beyond UNRRA's competence and as a practical matter beyond IGCR's also, since it could only resettle citizens of member states with the consent of the state involved. The Soviet Union fought attempts in both organizations to alter their mandates so that they could deal with the emerging postwar problem.[6]

Although the USSR's position may have been a logical extension of that which it had taken elsewhere, it was totally unacceptable to the majority in the United Nations. As this became apparent in the Assembly discussions in January and February 1946, Soviet policy shifted. The USSR submitted a resolution which referred the problem to the Economic and Social Council and outlined a number of principles to guide ECOSOC in its work.[7] According to this proposal the UN's "main task" concerning refugees and displaced persons should be "to give all possible help in facilitating their return to their native countries." Some individuals, providing that they were not "quislings, traitors, or war criminals," could be resettled *if* their country of origin agreed. No propaganda against repatriation should be allowed in the camps where the refugees and displaced persons were assembled, and the personnel of those camps should consist principally of citizens of the countries of origin. A specialized agency should be established to assist the countries concerned in carrying out joint measures for repatriation. No protection should be given to "quislings, traitors, or war criminals"; instead, such individuals should immediately be returned to their home countries. Finally, Germans who were being transferred from other countries or who had fled to other states from Allied troops should not be entitled to protection.

On the basis of this proposal, it is possible to infer that the USSR was willing to participate in a temporary specialized agency which

[5] See: George Ginsburgs, "The Soviet Union and the Problem of Refugees and Displaced Persons, 1917-1956," *The American Journal of International Law*, LI, no. 2 (April 1957), 325-361, pp. 341-342.

[6] John George Stoessinger, *The Refugee and the World Community* (Minneapolis: The University of Minnesota Press, 1956), pp. 53-54.

[7] UN Document A/C. 3/19.

would have had the task of facilitating the repatriation of displaced persons; one which would register such individuals and provide care for them during the interval prior to their repatriation.[8] However, the agency would have had few functions beyond that. Resettlement activities, even though allowed under the resolution, would have been severely restricted. Eligibility would have depended on how broadly war crimes were defined, and the USSR made it clear that it favored a sweeping definition. The provision requiring the permission of the countries of origin could have created difficulties for those few individuals who were eligible. The requirement that almost all personnel in the camps should be citizens of the countries of origin would have given those states considerable control over the entire operation. Thus, the shift in the Soviet position was actually not too great. The proposal implied only that the USSR was willing to participate in a temporary specialized agency which would have roughly the same mandate as UNRRA had had.

Although most member states had a different and considerably broader conception of what the United Nations should do, at this stage the differences could be composed or glossed over. After some debate, on February 12, 1946, a compromise resolution was adopted. This resolution, 8 (I), referred the problem to the Economic and Social Council for detailed examination and listed a series of principles which the Council should take into account in its consideration. Several of these were almost identical to those which were contained in the Soviet proposal; the UN's "main task" was held to be repatriation and various Germans and "war criminals, quislings and traitors" were excluded. However, the resolution said nothing about propaganda against repatriation, nor did it make any recommendation concerning the administration of the refugee camps. Beyond that, the resolution held that the problem was "international in scope and nature," and it clearly stated that no refugees or displaced person who, after having received "full knowledge of the facts" including "adequate information" from his country of origin, still expressed "valid objections" to repatriation, should be "compelled" to

---

[8] An American who participated in the negotiations, E. F. Penrose, reached the same conclusion. See: "Negotiating on Refugees and Displaced Persons, 1946," in Raymond Dennett and Joseph E. Johnson (eds.), *Negotiating with the Russians* (Boston: World Peace Foundation, 1951), pp. 139-168. His account, which has been corroborated by other participants, is an invaluable supplement to the documentary record.

return to his native state. This was the most important difference between the Soviet proposal and the resolution which the Assembly adopted. Despite this provision, and the defeat of several Soviet amendments,[9] the USSR voted for the resolution, which nonetheless provided a broad enough framework to allow the possibility of a satisfactory solution from the Soviet point of view.

THE DETAILED NEGOTIATIONS

The test would come in the detailed application of the principles which were outlined in the resolution. Although negotiations began immediately, more than ten months elapsed before these issues were finally decided. Four days after resolution 8 (I) was adopted, on February 16, 1946, the Economic and Social Council established a Special Committee on Refugees and Displaced Persons. The twenty states which were appointed to the Special Committee included all six Eastern European states which were then UN members: Byelorussia, Czechoslovakia, Poland, the Ukraine, the USSR and Yugoslavia. The USSR was therefore in a relatively favorable position. The Special Committee met in London from April 8 through June 1, and prepared a report which included a draft constitution for an International Refugee Organization. The draft constitution was considered at ECOSOC's second session in June, circulated to all UN member states for their comments, examined again in the light of these comments at the Council's third session in the fall, and debated finally at the second part of the first session of the General Assembly in November and December. In addition, the financial arrangements for IRO were considered by another specially appointed committee which met in July. In the Economic and Social Council and in the General Assembly there were always at least two discussions; first in a committee and then in the plenary meetings. The process was extremely thorough, though repetitive, arduous and time-consuming. The meetings of the Special Committee were the most important phase, for this was where the IRO constitution was first formulated in concrete terms. Although it was amended many times thereafter, the basic structure remained intact.

Throughout the negotiations the USSR fought hard to secure acceptance of its views, but in the main it did not succeed. The draft constitution which the Special Committee prepared was unaccepta-

[9] UN Document A/C. 3/23.

ble to the Soviet Union, and its subsequent attempts to modify this document by and large failed. Although various compromises were made, in the end the gap between the USSR and the UN's majority could not be bridged. The final vote in the General Assembly on the IRO constitution was 30 to 5, with 18 abstentions. The Eastern European states voted against the constitution, except Czechoslovakia, which abstained.

In the negotiations, Byelorussia, the Ukraine and Yugoslavia provided a solid core of support for the USSR. At times, Yugoslavia took an even more extreme position than the Soviet Union. Poland also almost always voted with this group and Czechoslovakia usually did. In addition to providing two extra votes, the separate representation of the two Soviet Republics enhanced the USSR's tactical flexibility. Arguments could be repeated in a slightly different key and amendments proposed several times. Among other things, the latter technique enabled the Soviet Union to establish "fall back" positions.

Near the end, when the pressure of time was great, because, among other things, UNRRA was definitely scheduled to cease its operations as of June 30, 1947, the negotiations almost took on the character of a war of attrition, and full use was made of these devices. During the final consideration of the IRO constitution in the General Assembly the countries of origin proposed fifty-four amendments, not one of which was new.[10] A case could be made that by the fall of 1946, the USSR was principally interested in delaying the proceedings and preventing the creation of IRO.

Of the major Western powers, France was the most sympathetic to the Soviet position. One explanation for this was that the problems of recovery which France faced were similar to those of the Eastern European states. The strength of the French communist party and its participation in the government were also factors. Significantly, the USSR would have preferred Paris rather than London as a site for the meetings of the Special Committee, and Paris rather than Geneva for IRO's headquarters. Other Western countries which had been occupied by Germany during the Second World War and a few Latin-American and Middle Eastern states also occasionally supported the Soviet position.

In the prolonged negotiations three central issues emerged. The first was determining the nature of the problem; how many refugees and displaced persons were there, what were the conditions where

[10] UN Document A/C. 3/77.

64   The USSR and the UN's Economic and Social Activities

they were located, and what were their desires for the future. The second involved deciding what concrete action the United Nations should take and what institutional arrangements should be made. The third issue consisted of defining who would be eligible for UN assistance.

DETERMINING THE NATURE AND SCOPE OF THE PROBLEM

ECOSOC's Special Committee on Refugees and Displaced Persons decided that its first task was to determine the nature and scope of the problem presented by the refugees and displaced persons. Of course, the broad outlines were known. Most of the people who would be of concern to the United Nations were receiving assistance from one or another international organization or from the American, British and French armies, and as a consequence a considerable amount of data concerning them was available. The Special Committee used this data as a basis for its conclusions without conducting any further investigation.[11] It did not attempt to be precise, but simply concluded that there were over a million and a half refugees and displaced persons and that many of these individuals would not want to be repatriated. It also concluded that at some point there would have to be a formal registration.

There were two major controversies between East and West on these points. One concerned the way in which the registration should be conducted. Soviet representatives maintained that personnel from the countries of origin should participate in the registration and that the information which was obtained should be communicated to these states for verification.[12] The West feared that this would allow communist countries to bring pressure on the refugees and displaced persons and held that the registration should be conducted by the local officials of the authorities which were responsible for the administration of the camps.[13] The Special Committee adopted the recommendation favored by the West.

The second controversy involved the alleged existence of obstacles to repatriation. Soviet bloc delegates claimed that the large number of

[11] UN, ECOSOC, *Official Records* (2nd Session), Special Supplement No. 1, "Report of the Special Committee on Refugees and Displaced Persons," pp. 42-45, 63-64. Hereafter cited as "Report of the Special Committee."
[12] *Ibid.*, pp. 9 and 64.
[13] See: E. F. Penrose, "Negotiating on Refugees and Displaced Persons," p. 152.

refugees and displaced persons who apparently were not willing to be repatriated could be explained by the presence in the camps and the activities of quislings, traitors and war criminals.[14] They claimed that in some camps these groups were actually in control and that in others they were free to carry on propaganda against repatriation and terroristic activities. These delegates also maintained that their government could not obtain information concerning their nationals. UNRRA investigated the specific complaints made during the meetings of the Special Committee concerning camps under its administration and reported that all were without foundation.[15] The Special Committee was willing to include in its report a statement that the presence of quislings, traitors and war criminals in displaced person camps would impede speedy repatriation, but it refused to go beyond that and state that such individuals actually were present in the camps.

Delegates from the Eastern European countries repeated their allegations when the report of the Special Committee was discussed in the Economic and Social Council and later in the final debate in the General Assembly. In ECOSOC, Yugoslavia proposed that a fact-finding commission composed of France, Poland, the USSR, the United Kingdom, the United States and Yugoslavia should be appointed to investigate conditions in the camps and obstacles to speedy repatriation.[16] This proposal was rejected by a vote of seven to nine, with two abstentions.[17] The USSR introduced a similar proposal in the General Assembly, which also was rejected, this time by a larger margin.[18]

It is impossible to state whether the USSR's position was motivated by sincere conviction or simply by a desire to erect a defense against a politically embarrassing situation. Partly the accuracy of the Soviet charges depended on how the terms quislings, traitors, and war crimi-

[14] See: "Report of the Special Committee," pp. 45-58.
[15] *Ibid.*, pp. 55-58.
[16] UN Document E/70.
[17] UN, ECOSOC, *Official Records* (2nd Session), p. 131. The division was: *In favor:* Chile, Cuba, Czechoslovakia, Peru, Ukrainian SSR, USSR, Yugoslavia; *Against:* Belgium, Canada, China, Colombia, Greece, India, Lebanon, United Kingdom, United States; *Abstained:* France, Norway.
[18] UN Document A/C. 3/62; UN, General Assembly, Third Committee, *Official Records* (1st Session, 2nd Part), p. 271. The vote was 9—21—9. France, Egypt and Norway joined the Eastern European states in voting for the investigation.

nals were defined. If the terms were defined so as to include persons who opposed the communist regimes which were being established in Eastern Europe, some of the Soviet allegations were in that sense correct. Some of the refugees and displaced persons in the camps openly argued against repatriation. The United States and the United Kingdom and other Western states regarded this as a legitimate exercise of individual freedom. Whether the actions of these persons ever went beyond the stage of argument was not clear. The Soviet allegations were always denied, but to allow the Soviet bloc to participate in an investigation would have permitted these countries to identify their nationals.

Determining the UN's Role

The second major issue which arose in the negotiations in the United Nations during 1946 concerning refugees and displaced persons was that of determining what action the UN should take and what institutional arrangements should be made. First, there was the question of whether the machinery which was to be created should be an integral part of the United Nations or an autonomous body, linked with the UN. The United Kingdom argued for the first alternative, while the Soviet Union sided with the United States and favored the latter. At an early stage, the Special Committee decided to take the second course and to recommend the creation of a temporary specialized agency, the International Refugee Organization.

When it came to determining what this agency should do and what its institutional structure should be, divisions followed a more typical East-West pattern. Although there was general agreement that the functions of IRO should be broadly defined, so that in principle they would include repatriation, integration and resettlement, the emphasis to be placed on each of the solutions was a matter of controversy. The Soviet bloc sought to give greatest stress to repatriation, while the West tried to maintain freedom of choice for the individuals concerned. Concessions were made to the Soviet bloc, largely in matters of nuance, but the IRO constitution clearly allowed all three solutions.

Perhaps the concession which had the greatest practical consequences was the decision that IRO should provide some material assistance and a three months' supply of food rations for those individuals who chose repatriation. This decision was made in response to the Soviet argument that many displaced persons did not desire repatriation because of economic reasons; their homelands were devastated, but the countries where they might be resettled were not, and, in any case, they would be given financial help in resettlement. Some observers have held that this argument had some validity, while others have argued that the UN's decision amounted to a "ration bribe." [19] During the negotiations, the United States and the United Kingdom maintained that the decision in effect meant that those who chose repatriation would be given a bonus. On the other hand, France and Belgium were rather sympathetic to the Soviet position, and both introduced proposals concerning this matter. Belgium's suggestion that IRO supply repatriates with three months' food was adopted at the second session of ECOSOC, and at the following session of the Council, as a result of a Ukrainian proposal, this commitment was expanded into its final form.

The controversies concerning the structure of the International Refugee Organization and the way in which it should be financed were considerably more involved. One of these controversies concerned membership in IRO. The USSR argued, albeit unsuccessfully, that only UN member states should be eligible to join IRO.[20] Had the Soviet position been adopted Sweden and Switzerland, two countries which had often played an important role in the solution of refugee problems, would have been excluded from IRO. The Soviet Union argued that if Sweden and Switzerland were allowed to join IRO, they would be able to make financial contributions that would entitle them to significant influence in the Organization and that, because of their status during the Second World War, they should not have such influence.[21]

The USSR's efforts to shorten the period of notification required for the termination of membership from one year to six months also failed,[22] as did its attempts to increase the number of ratifications

[19] Marvin Klemme, an UNRRA official, took the former position in his book, *The Inside Story of UNRRA* (New York: Lifetime Eds., 1949), p. 142. John Stoessinger stated the opposite viewpoint in *The Refugee and the World Community*, p. 68.

[20] At one stage in the negotiations, the Soviet delegate stated: "If a state is not a member of the United Nations, it is because its 'peace-lovingness' is held in doubt" (UN Document E/87, p. 6).

[21] "Report of the Special Committee," p. 35.

[22] *Ibid.*, p. 82.

necessary before the IRO constitution could enter into force from fifteen states to twenty-six UN member states.[23] The proposals on notification were no doubt designed to protect the USSR's position should it decide to join IRO. A broader effect, though, of both sets of proposals and of those limiting eligibility for IRO to members of the UN, would have been to make the Organization's existence precarious. As it was, only eighteen states joined the International Refugee Organization, one of which was Switzerland.

In the discussions relating to the internal structure of IRO, the USSR sought to concentrate power in the Executive Committee, a nine-member body which would be elected by the General Council. The United States and the United Kingdom, on the other hand, favored giving greater authority to the General Council, which would include all members of the Organization, and to the Director-General. In reality each side sought to maximize its influence. The Eastern European states, as the countries of origin of most of the refugees, were certain to have proportionately greater strength in the Executive Committee than in the General Council. On the other hand, the West, because of the size of its financial contribution, would hold a predominant position within the administration. The three men who held the post of Director-General were all Americans and the Deputy Director-General was a citizen of the United Kingdom.

The provisions of the IRO constitution relating to the internal division of power were changed more than any others during the course of the negotiations. The Soviet Union won its greatest victories in the Special Committee. At its second session, ECOSOC reduced the authority of the Executive Committee, but at its next session, the Council reversed itself and restored some of the Committee's power. In the end, the Executive Committee was certainly more powerful than the West would have preferred, but it was not as strong as the USSR desired.

In the final draft the Executive Committee was empowered to make policy decisions of an "emergency nature" and generally to perform such functions as were necessary "to give effect to the policies of the General Council." The version approved by the Special Committee, which the Soviet Union preferred, allowed the Executive Committee to "perform all the functions of the General Council" and to "issue directives on policy to the Director-General" and to

---

[23] UN Document E/AC. 13/4, p. 7.

"exercise control over his activities." [24] The USSR sought to have the Executive Committee organized so that it could function continuously.[25]

In the Special Committee a Soviet proposal was accepted which provided that the Executive Committee should organize commissions including representatives of the countries of origin to visit the refugee camps and other centers which were under the control of the Organization. On the basis of these investigations, the Committee was to give instructions to the Director-General. The Western powers opposed this provision. As in the case of the Soviet proposals concerning registration, they feared that the visits would be used to apply pressure on the refugees.[26] During the course of the negotiations, as a result of Western efforts, this provision was modified so that in the end, the visits were optional rather than mandatory, and the composition of the inspecting groups was not specified.

Had the Soviet Union had its way, the Executive Committee would have been in a position to determine the day-to-day operations of IRO. Just to insure the strength of their influence, the Eastern European countries sought to write into the IRO constitution the requirement that "adequate representation" be given to the countries of origin on the Executive Committee.[27] As it was, the Executive Committee had extensive powers, and had they chosen to join IRO, the Eastern European states would have been certain of obtaining a number of seats.

The Soviet position with respect to financing the International Refugee Organization was that the costs of resettlement should be borne by the receiving countries, Germany should be responsible for the costs of repatriation, and the administrative budget should be prorated among the membership, with special consideration being given to those countries which had suffered enemy occupation.[28] The effect of these proposals would have been to make the Soviet contribution almost nothing. Although the USSR's position was not adopted, under the final arrangements, its financial commitment would have been relatively small. The IRO budget was divided into

---

[24] "Report of the Special Committee," p. 76.
[25] *Ibid.*, p. 83.
[26] See: E. F. Penrose, "Negotiating on Refugees and Displaced Persons," p. 151.
[27] "Report of the Special Committee," p. 83.
[28] UN, ECOSOC, *Official Records* (3rd Session), pp. 94, 95.

three categories: administrative, operational (mainly temporary care and repatriation), and large-scale resettlement. Contributions to the last category were voluntary, thus, the countries of origin could not have been forced to subsidize the relocation of their political enemies. In the provisional budget for the first year the USSR's allocation—including that of the two Soviet Republics—was set at 7.4 per cent of the administrative expenses and 5.47 per cent of the operational expenses. The total would have amounted to slightly over $8,500,000. This figure was, however, several times greater than the USSR's annual contribution to the UN budget during that period. After the first year, allocations had to be approved by a two-thirds vote of the General Council.

ESTABLISHING CRITERIA FOR ELIGIBILITY

The third issue in the negotiations, and perhaps the most important, consisted of defining the terms "refugee" and "displaced person," and spelling out the conditions under which such persons would become, and cease to be, the concern of the Organization. As finally approved, these provisions were quite broad. A large number of individuals were clearly eligible for IRO assistance, regardless of whether they chose repatriation, integration or resettlement.

There was some agreement between East and West concerning these sections. For example, the general principles which more or less restated the early resolutions of the Assembly and Economic and Social Council were accepted without much controversy. Both sides agreed that IRO should aid those refugees and displaced persons who desired repatriation. Both sides also agreed that IRO should aid the Spanish Republicans, and that these individuals should not be forced to return to Spain. The Soviet Union only mildly objected to including in IRO's mandate persons who had held the status of refugee prior to the Second World War, even though this meant that the "White Russians" among the Nansen refugees would be eligible to receive assistance from the Organization.[29] There was general agree-

---

[29] The USSR made only one attempt to delete this provision (UN Document E/74, pp. 5-6). Interestingly, the USSR also adopted a series of decrees which allowed such individuals to obtain Soviet citizenship. These decrees did not require that the individuals who desired Soviet nationality should return to the USSR. (George Ginsburgs, "The Soviet Union and the Problem of Refugees," pp. 346-347).

ment that IRO should not aid: quislings, war criminals and traitors; ordinary criminals; persons who had voluntarily aided the enemy during the Second World War; or individuals who had participated in movements which had as their purpose overthrowing the government of a member state of the United Nations by armed force.

The areas of disagreement, however, were far greater, and in the negotiations the sections relating to definitions caused the greatest controversy. The USSR attempted to shape IRO's mandate so that the Organization would not be able to aid political dissidents from Eastern European countries. The West, on the other hand, insisted that the Organization should have this competence.

The Soviet Union sought to exclude from the definition of the term "refugee":

> . . . a person, other than a displaced person . . . who is outside of his country of nationality or former habitual residence, and who, as a result of events subsequent to the outbreak of the Second World War, is unable or unwilling to avail himself of the protection of the Government of his country of nationality or former nationality.[30]

This provision was designed, *inter alia*, to allow IRO to aid individuals from the Baltic states. This group comprised about 17 per cent of the refugees and displaced persons, and almost without exception they refused to return to their countries, which now were part of the USSR.[31] The Soviet Union also proposed that only individuals who left their countries prior to the cessation of the Second World War should be eligible for IRO assistance.[32] The obvious purpose of this was to exclude those who might flee Eastern Europe as a consequence of the imposition and tightening of communist rule. During the negotiations, representatives from the USSR and other Eastern European countries frankly stated that they could not agree to an international organization's having the power to aid their political enemies.[33] The only exception to this was that the Soviet

[30] "Report of the Special Committee," pp. 16, 70. In cases where the USSR made the same proposal several times, only the first action will be cited. For a comprehensive list of the Soviet proposals see UN Document A/C. 3/70.

[31] E. F. Penrose, "Negotiating on Refugees and Displaced Persons," pp. 146-147.

[32] "Report of the Special Committee," pp. 19, 70.

[33] *Ibid.*, p. 16. See also E. F. Penrose, "Negotiating on Refugees and Displaced Persons," p. 147.

Union was willing to allow Jewish people to leave Poland and did not object to their being eligible for IRO assistance.[34]

Other Soviet proposals aimed at expanding the list of persons who would not be eligible for IRO assistance. The USSR attempted to exclude people who had fled to Spain and other countries to avoid falling into the hands of Allied armies.[35] It argued that such a provision was necessary to bar "lesser quislings." The Soviet Union also sought to rule out persons who had served in the military or civil service of a state other than their country of origin.[36] Among others, this proposal would have excluded those who had served in General Ander's and General Vlasov's armies. The most extreme Soviet proposal was to exclude all persons who, since the end of the Second World War, "have engaged in hostile activities directed against the government of their country of origin, being a Member of the United Nations, or against the principles of the United Nations." [37] This would have precluded practically all political dissidents.

The USSR followed a similar policy when it came to spelling out exactly which refugees and displaced persons would be eligible for assistance from the International Refugee Organization. There was general agreement that the Organization should aid both those who chose repatriation and those who, after having received "full knowledge of the facts," expressed "valid objections" to returning to their homelands. The controversies concerned the details. The Soviet Union objected to including as valid reasons for rejecting repatriation: "Objections of a political nature," and fear of persecution because of "race, religion, nationality or political opinions." [38] Again, the question was whether or not IRO should aid political *emigrés*.

Soviet delegates also argued that a realistic description of the situation in the countries of origin could be given only by representatives of the governments of those countries or by individuals acceptable to them.[39] Their position had elements of validity, for some of the individuals in UNRRA camps who had responsibility for ex-

[34] See: E. F. Penrose, "Negotiating on Refugees and Displaced Persons," pp. 149-150; and Patrick Murphy Malin, "The Refugee: A Problem for International Organization," *International Organization*, I, no. 3 (August 1947), 443-459, p. 451.
[35] "Report of the Special Committee," pp. 23-24, 71.
[36] *Ibid.*, pp. 24-26, 71.
[37] *Ibid.*, pp. 26-28, 71.
[38] UN Document A/C. 3/70, p. 8.
[39] "Report of the Special Committee," pp. 70-71.

plaining conditions in Poland were representatives of the London government, who could hardly be expected to be ardent advocates of repatriation. A similar situation prevailed with regard to Yugoslavia.[40] For the West, though, the question again involved the fear that if representatives of the countries of origin were allowed to enter the camps, they might use the opportunity to apply pressure on the inmates.[41]

One of the most difficult problems involved unaccompanied children who were war orphans or whose parents had disappeared. The West was willing to concede that in most cases children under sixteen years of age should be repatriated if their nationality could be determined. The Soviet Union, on the other hand, wanted a blanket commitment to repatriation.[42]

Although concessions were made to the Soviet position, they were largely in matters of phraseology. In no case did the USSR gain the substance of its demands. Had the Soviet proposals been adopted, IRO's mandate would have been severely restricted. The Organization would have been able to assist those refugees who chose repatriation and only a few others. The West wanted, and achieved a much broader mandate. The decisions relating to the third issue in the negotiations clearly meant that the Organization would be able to aid political *emigrés* and to facilitate their resettlement or their integration in the areas where they were presently located. Probably these decisions were the most important in determining the USSR's opposition to the International Refugee Organization.

The Negotiations in Retrospect

On an abstract level, Soviet participation in the negotiations had a substantial impact on the IRO constitution. Compromises were made to the USSR's point of view on various occasions. The Executive Committee was given greater powers than the Western states would have desired. In many places the phrasing was blurred, and as a consequence difficult problems of interpretation could have arisen.[43] However, since the Eastern European states did not join IRO, and therefore could not exploit these opportunities, the practical con-

[40] See the speech of Fiorello H. LaGuardia, Director-General of UNRRA: UN, ECOSOC, *Official Records* (3rd Session), p. 21.
[41] E. F. Penrose, "Negotiating on Refugees and Displaced Persons," p. 151.
[42] UN Document E/135, p. 19.
[43] See: John Stoessinger, *The Refugee and the World Community*, pp. 86-89.

sequences of Soviet participation in the negotiations seem to have been negligible.[44]

It seems unlikely that the USSR could have been induced to join or even tacitly to sanction an international agency which had among its functions aiding large numbers of political *emigrés* from Eastern Europe, and the West apparently realized this from the outset.[45] Probably the maximum concessions which the USSR was willing to make were defined in the proposal which it submitted to the General Assembly in January 1946. This proposal was clearly the model for all subsequent Soviet suggestions. The USSR not only was opposed to subsidizing its political enemies, for the decisions concerning the IRO budget would have minimized this, but it was opposed to participating in any way in an organization which would protect and aid *emigrés* from communist countries. The USSR's decision in July 1946 to withdraw from the Inter-Governmental Committee on Refugees when that agency began to engage in activities which were aimed at the resettlement of displaced persons from Eastern Europe provided additional evidence of this attitude. Though not praiseworthy, the Soviet position is certainly understandable. Probably few if any states would have taken a different position had they been in similar circumstances.

In view of the Soviet attitude, it is difficult to see what point there was in having the IRO constitution drafted within the framework of the United Nations. It is true that the decisions of the United Nations provided a moral vindication for the Western position, but beyond that it is questionable whether the ultimate handling of the problem was significantly affected by the fact that the IRO constitution was drafted within the UN. On the other hand, the negotiations involved the United Nations in a very serious controversy at an early stage in its existence. Admittedly, though, the controversy was less serious than it would have been, had responsibility for operational activities in this field been given to the UN itself rather than to a specialized agency. Apparently one of the major factors determining Western policy was a desire to gain as much financial support for IRO as possible,[46] but it would be difficult to prove that the UN's

[44] This is the position taken by E. F. Penrose, "Negotiating on Refugees and Displaced Persons," pp. 166-167. James B. Reston, on the other hand, maintained that the compromises significantly weakened IRO, "Negotiating with the Russians," *Harper's Magazine*, CXCV, no. 1167 (August 1947), 97-106.

[45] Louis K. Hyde, Jr., *The United States and the United Nations*, p. 58.

[46] *Ibid.*

validation had much effect in this regard. The principal contributors to IRO were those Western states which had also provided the greatest financial support for UNRRA and IGCR. At the London session of the Special Committee on Refugees and Displaced Persons, it was suggested that IRO's functions might be limited to repatriation, and that a special conference of receiving states could be convened to consider problems of resettlement. Such an approach might have had some advantages, but it was never formally explored on an international level.

THE SOVIET ATTACK ON IRO

Certainly the fact that the United Nations approved the IRO constitution and periodically sanctioned the Organization's activities did not prevent the USSR from attacking the agency. Soviet hostility was evident from the moment that the constitution was approved and it continued without cessation. No member of the Soviet bloc joined IRO, and they had little contact with the agency. These countries had insisted on including in the IRO constitution a statement that the staff should include an "adequate number of persons" from the countries of origin, but they did not press this point later. Out of a total of 2,571 staff members, only two were from the USSR and 63 from other countries of Eastern Europe.[47] These states sent repatriation officers to IRO camps, but they were extremely unpopular and caused outbursts by the inmates. In 1949, the United States ordered the Soviet Repatriation Mission to leave the American zone of Germany and by the end of the year, all repatriation officers had left IRO assembly centers.[48] That same year, Czechoslovakia, Poland and Yugoslavia expelled the IRO liaison offices which had been maintained in those countries.[49]

At every session of the General Assembly and the Economic and Social Council the Soviet Union and its satellites attacked the International Refugee Organization through speeches and proposals. The main theme of the attack, which was also carried on outside the United Nations, was that the agency failed to carry out its basic

[47] Louise E. Holborn, *The International Refugee Organization: A Specialized Agency of the United Nations: Its History and Work, 1946-1952* (New York: Oxford University Press, 1956), p. 100.
[48] John Stoessinger, *The Refugee and the World Community*, p. 111.
[49] *Ibid.*

task, repatriation.⁵⁰ Soviet delegates constantly argued that IRO ignored General Assembly Resolution 8 (I), which in their view, made repatriation mandatory in almost all cases. They claimed that quislings, war criminals and traitors had improperly been given assistance. They charged that IRO had become an instrument for recruiting cheap labor; that the agency discouraged repatriation through the use of threats and that the refugees who were resettled suffered ruthless exploitation by Western monopolies. They also alleged that IRO was used to recruit soldiers for service in Western military and paramilitary units and agents for Western intelligence services. The Western states were berated for their alleged failure to carry out in IRO their wartime agreements concerning repatriation. Soviet proposals were almost always defeated, and on the few occasions when they were not, they were adopted only after drastic modification. The most that could be said for the Soviet charges is that they were sometimes caricatures of real problems which IRO faced.⁵¹

THE UNITED NATIONS
HIGH COMMISSIONER FOR REFUGEES

As the expiration of IRO's mandate drew near, it became apparent that a number of refugees would remain unsettled after the Organization ceased operations. The final figures showed that IRO repatriated approximately 73,000 persons and resettled over 1,000,000. There were about 400,000 individuals, however, for whom no solution could be found by the end of 1951. The United Nations began to consider this so-called "hard core" problem in 1949, and the following year, at its fifth session, despite Soviet opposition, the General Assembly established the Office of the High Commissioner for Refugees. The High Commissioner's Statute was broadly defined, so that the competence of the Office included both the "hard core" and new refugees.

After its creation, UNHCR became the object of the Soviet attack which previously had been directed at IRO. This attack was on occa-

⁵⁰ For a summary statement of the basic elements of this attack see G. Mikhailov, "Who Needs IRO, and For What," *New Times*, 1950, no. 3 (January 18, 1950), pp. 11-14.

⁵¹ John Stoessinger describes some of these. See: *The Refugee and the World Community*, pp. 121-139. See also: George Ginsburgs, "The Soviet Union and the Problem of Refugees," pp. 356-357.

sion aimed at the first High Commissioner personally, Dr. G. J. van Heuven Goedhart and members of his senior staff. For a number of years Soviet opposition to UNHCR was so intense that the USSR had no contact with the Office, refusing even to cooperate in the few cases when refugees desired repatriation. The Soviet Union especially opposed UNHCR's provision of aid to refugees who had fled to Hong Kong from the People's Republic of China. In terms of the adoption of proposals, the Soviet attack continued to be ineffectual. The broader impact on public opinion is more difficult to gauge, but it also seems to have been negligible.

Although the USSR continued to criticize UNHCR, starting in the mid-nineteen fifties its attitude toward the Office began to soften. The shift in the Soviet attitude was part of the broader transformation in the USSR's policy toward the UN's economic and social activities. In addition, the appointment of a new High Commissioner helped to facilitate the change, once it had begun. Dr. van Heuven Goedhart died in 1956. He had been dedicated to the cause of refugees and had felt that the USSR was largely responsible for their plight. Furthermore, he had been angered by the Soviet attack. His speeches in UN sessions took on the character of a heated rebuttal. Dr. van Heuven Goedhart's successor, Auguste Lindt, took a different approach to the position, emphasizing its humanitarian aspects. Also, as the former Deputy High Commissioner has put it, in contrast to his predecessor, Dr. Lindt "took pains to have the Office play a positive role in the voluntary repatriation of refugees." [52] Among other things this meant establishing a budget for this purpose and in some instances providing financial assistance to those who sought repatriation, especially from distant overseas areas. His approach made it easier for the Soviet Union to change its policy. The transformation in the USSR's attitude, however, should not be overemphasized. Soviet delegates continued to insist that repatriation was the only correct solution for Eastern European refugees—although they stressed that they also had in mind "voluntary repatriation"—and they continued to submit proposals trying to mould the UN's activities in this direction.[53]

As part of its more moderate policy, in 1956 the USSR began to abstain rather than to oppose resolutions dealing with the Office of

[52] James M. Read, "The United Nations and Refugees—Changing Concepts," *International Conciliation*, no. 537 (March 1962), p. 22.
[53] See for example: A/C. 3/L. 697.

the High Commissioner except for those concerning the Chinese refugees in Hong Kong. Moreover, since the issue first came up in 1958, the USSR has consistently voted for resolutions praising UNHCR for its work in connection with Algerian refugees in Tunisia and Morocco.

Some Eastern European states went even further. As early as 1953, Yugoslavia, which was originally even more intransigent than the USSR, began to support UNHCR. In 1956, it granted asylum to some 19,000 Hungarians, and cooperated with the High Commissioner in seeking a permanent solution for these individuals. Two years later, Yugoslavia was elected to the Executive Committee of the High Commissioner's Programme. The split even extended to Hungary and Poland. Both states appear to have been satisfied with UNHCR's handling of the refugee problems which resulted from the Hungarian crisis, even though many of the refugees were resettled. The speeches of the delegates from the two states reflected this, and in 1957 Hungary split with the rest of the Soviet bloc and voted for two resolutions: one prolonging the Office of the High Commissioner until December 31, 1963, and the other concerning international assistance to refugees within the High Commissioner's mandate.[54] The determining factor in the Hungarian action was the High Commissioner's efforts to encourage and facilitate the repatriation of Hungarian refugees, especially unaccompanied minors. Hungary did not want to jeopardize the possibility of continuing cooperation in these matters.

When the question of the future of the Office of the High Commissioner was considered again in 1962, the nature of the refugee problem had changed considerably from what it had been previously. During the year from April 1, 1961, until March 31, 1962, the Office of the High Commissioner provided emergency assistance to some 300,000 new refugees in Africa. Africans had come to be one of the principal groups receiving assistance from UNHCR. In July 1962, the USSR announced that it supported the continuation of the Office of the High Commissioner, despite the fact that as recently as the previous fall Soviet delegates had argued that it should be abolished, and at the seventeenth session of the Assembly in December 1962, the USSR voted to extend the mandate of UNHCR through 1968. Also, starting in 1961 the USSR began to argue that the same

[54] See the Hungarian delegate's explanation of his votes: UN, General Assembly, Third Committee, *Official Records* (12th Session), pp. 237-238.

principles of geographic distribution which were supposed to be applied to the United Nations Secretariat should also be applied to UNHCR. The implication of this was that the Soviet Union sought posts for its nationals on the High Commissioner's staff, which previously did not contain any citizens of Soviet bloc countries.

The reason for the change in Soviet policy was the changing nature of the refugee problem. In announcing the USSR's new attitude with respect to the continuation of the Office of the High Commissioner, the Soviet delegate stated that the African refugees "were refugees in the fullest sense, refugees from the persecution they had suffered for their participation in national liberation movements." [55] Obviously, it was quite a different proposition for the USSR to countenance an international organization which provided emergency aid to refugees from Algeria or Angola during a nationalist uprising, than an international organization which provided aid to refugees from Soviet bloc countries in Eastern Europe. However, it should be pointed out that the solution which the Algerians and the Angolans themselves desired was repatriation (though to a new regime), not resettlement.

How far the new Soviet policy would extend was not clear. The Soviet Union still did not contribute to any of the voluntary funds established to support the High Commissioner's work, and it continued to object to his activities in connection with the Chinese refugees in Hong Kong.

OTHER UN ACTIVITIES

The Soviet Union has not pursued an especially active policy with regard to other activities of the United Nations concerning refugees and displaced persons and related matters. The USSR voted against the Convention Relating to the Status of Refugees and refused to sign that instrument. It objected to attempts to draft a Convention on Statelessness, arguing that there would be no problem if its proposals for repatriation were adopted. It boycotted the Conference on the Elimination or Reduction of Future Statelessness which was held in 1959 and 1961. Soviet authorities on international law regard the convention which was prepared there as a serious departure from the generally recognized principles of international law on the ground

[55] UN, ECOSOC, *Official Records* (34th Session), p. 201.

that it treats questions of citizenship which in their view lie exclusively within the internal jurisdiction of states.[56] The Soviet Union opposed all attempts to regularize the legal situation caused by the presumed death during the Second World War of missing persons, claiming that this was a matter of domestic jurisdiction. It strongly opposed the adoption of an Assembly resolution which recommended, albeit in veiled terms, that the USSR should return whatever prisoners of war it still held. Even though the Soviet Union in principle favored the UN's action in 1951 concerning survivors of Nazi concentration camps it abstained from voting on the resolution because it objected to the Organization's dealing with the Federal Republic of Germany. Two years later, the USSR opposed accepting the Federal Republic's accession to the Convention on the Declaration of Death of Missing Persons. The USSR opposed the designation of 1959-1960 as World Refugee Year.

The Soviet Union did not participate in any way in the work of the United Nations Korean Reconstruction Agency, and its attitude toward the Agency reflected its general attitude on the Korean question. The USSR has not participated in nor contributed funds for the work of the United Nations Relief and Works Agency for Palestine Refugees in the Near East. For a long time the USSR pursued an especially quiescent policy concerning UNRWA. Soviet delegates seldom participated in the annual Assembly debates concerning UNRWA's work and they always abstained from voting on the relevant resolutions. The Soviet Union apparently desired to remain aloof from a complicated and confused situation. Participation in any form would have risked alienating some groups, and, in any case, local communists could exploit the Arab refugee's discontent. Starting in the late nineteen fifties, however, the USSR began to support the position of the Arab states. The first sign of this was that representatives of some of the Soviet bloc states began to argue that repatriation was the most appropriate solution in this case also and that those who did not desire repatriation were entitled to compensation for their lost property. In 1959, the USSR also took this line.[57] In that year the entire Soviet bloc voted for the continuation of UNRWA and since then the Soviet bloc has consistently sided with the Arab states on questions relating to this issue. As early as April

[56] See: Academy of Sciences of the USSR, *International Law*, pp. 23, 150-151.
[57] UN, General Assembly, Special Political Committee, *Official Records* (14th Session), p. 154.

1960 Anastas I. Mikoyan, visiting Baghdad, sought to make political capital of this stand.[58]

CONCLUSIONS

Perhaps the most striking feature of Soviet policy with regard to the activities of the United Nations concerning refugees and displaced persons, is the limited extent to which the USSR has been involved. There has been almost no cooperation between the Soviet Union and the major Western states in this aspect of the UN's work. It is true that in the late nineteen fifties, the Soviet position began to shift somewhat, but at most this meant the USSR's representatives were more moderate and occasionally voted for a resolution in ECOSOC and the Assembly. The USSR and its bloc continued to have virtually nothing to do with the conduct and financing of the UN's practical work concerning refugees and displaced persons.

Given the limited extent to which the USSR has been involved in this aspect of the activities of the United Nations, its policy has had almost no positive impact. Since its inception, the UN's work with regard to refugees and displaced persons has been Western in orientation and has been controlled and financed principally by Western states. The USSR's policies had some impact on the IRO constitution, but it would be difficult to prove that this affected IRO's functioning. Since 1959, Soviet support may have made it easier for the Arab states to muster a majority for their position concerning the refugee problem in the Middle East. Beyond that, the Soviet Union's impact has been negative; that is, the UN has not been able to do what it might have, had the USSR chosen to participate fully.

This outcome was probably predetermined, given the nature of the UN's first problem in this area. The clash concerning the drafting of the IRO constitution set the tone for future proceedings. This clash has often been described in terms of one side favoring free choice and the other compulsion. To some extent it was that. The USSR clearly gave the impression that it preferred repatriation as the principal solution, and it is not difficult to find economic and political reasons for this preference. However, a case could be made that so far as the UN was concerned, the Soviet Union's objective

[58] See the transcript of his news conference in Baghdad: *Pravda*, April 18, 1960, as contained in *The Current Digest of the Soviet Press*, XII, no. 16 (May 18, 1960), 17.

was merely to prevent an international organization from being able to protect and aid political *emigrés* from Eastern Europe. Probably few Western states would have been very magnanimous in this regard had similar numbers of their nationals been involved. It would have been most embarrassing for the Soviet Union to agree that IRO should aid Balts and Ukrainians who refused to return to the USSR, as well as those individuals who would not return to the new communist states which were being established in Eastern Europe.

John Stoessinger has written persuasively on the difficulties which universal international organizations have when they attempt to deal with refugee problems.[59] It is significant that after the experiment with IRO, the West chose to rely more heavily on instrumentalities which were outside of the framework of the United Nations—the Intergovernmental Committee for European Migration and the United States Escapee Program—for handling the problem of refugees from Eastern Europe. Actually, Soviet delegates in the United Nations have not criticized these programs as much as they did IRO. Had the UN's first problem in this area been that of the Algerian refugees in Morocco and Tunisia, or the Angolan refugees in the Congo (Leopoldville), and had the subsequent problems been of this nature, perhaps there would have been more East-West cooperation. As it was, the clash was inevitable. It is difficult to determine whether or not this controversy spilled over and affected other areas of the economic and social activities of the United Nations. Clearly an acrimonious atmosphere was introduced into ECOSOC and the Assembly's Third Committee at an early stage.

There is a danger, however, of carrying this interpretation of Soviet policy too far. Even when its own interests were not directly involved, as in the case of the Arab refugees in the Middle East, the USSR has shown little willingness to cooperate. There has been little evidence that the Soviet Union shares the humanitarian concern for refugees which is so widely felt in the West. The USSR's verbal support of certain programs starting in the late nineteen fifties appears to have been motivated primarily by a desire to strengthen its position with the African and Asian states, and large-scale resettlement was not an issue in these cases. Thus, the most that could have been hoped for in this area probably would have

---

[59] *The Refugee and the World Community.*

been a temporary convergence of interests between East and West which would have allowed cooperation on a few modest programs. To have achieved more would have required a broader consensus on values.

4: RELIEF AND RECONSTRUCTION

DURING THE FIRST YEARS OF THE UNITED NATIONS, PROBLEMS OF relief and reconstruction were just as pressing as those posed by refugees and displaced persons, and the Soviet Union had an equal interest in them. The Second World War brought immense devastation to large parts of Europe and Asia, and the Eastern European states, including the USSR, were among the most severely damaged. The devastated states were desperately short of food and fuel, and they confronted the enormous task of rebuilding their economies and social structures. Large-scale economic assistance was probably the most essential ingredient for the solution of both their immediate and longer-range problems. In addition, some international cooperation was needed to facilitate the allocation of supplies, to aid in the restitution of displaced industrial equipment, and to plan reconstruction on a regional and global basis. Most of the relief and reconstruction problems which resulted from the Second World War were solved by 1950, but the Korean War, natural disasters, and the chronic food shortage in certain areas continued to draw international attention to problems of this nature from time to time thereafter. David Mitrany saw in these problems one of the primary indications of the need for functional collaboration and also one of the principal opportunities for such activities.[1]

The United Nations role with regard to problems of relief and reconstruction, however, has been extremely limited and has mainly been confined to providing a framework for international cooperation and to adopting resolutions on general policy. Only in the program of the United Nations Korean Reconstruction Agency,

[1] See: A *Working Peace System*, pp. 23-25.

which lasted from 1950 through 1959, has the UN been charged with responsibility for large-scale economic assistance. Economic assistance directed toward the solution of problems which arose out of the Second World War was handled first by the United Nations Relief and Rehabilitation Administration, and then through a national program, the United States European Recovery Program (ERP—the Marshall Plan), and an exclusively Western institution, the Organization for European Economic Cooperation (OEEC). OEEC probably became, in addition, a more important agency for international cooperation concerning these problems than the UN. The East also developed an exclusive, albeit smaller, aid program in a series of bilateral agreements between the USSR and other Eastern European states and its own international agency, the Council for Mutual Economic Assistance (CMEA). This body, though, while formed in January 1949, held only three sessions prior to 1954, and did not become effective until after the reconstruction period.

The advent of the cold war and the consequent desire of the United States to retain a high degree of control over its major aid programs were the prime reasons why the UN's role was so restricted. Policies in the United Nations largely reflected those which each state pursued in the broader arena of world politics. To the limited extent that events in the UN served a causal function, however, Soviet policy there may well have been a factor in narrowing the organization's role with regard to relief and reconstruction problems.

As an indication of their urgency, three relief and reconstruction problems were considered at the first part of the General Assembly's first session: ways of providing economic assistance to devastated countries; the definition of the role that the UN should play; and, measures to relieve and mitigate the effects of the world food shortage. Consideration of these three items continued to be an important feature of Assembly and Economic and Social Council sessions during the next few years, and the last, the world food shortage, was still an important item on the UN's agenda in 1963.

In contrast to its attitude concerning refugees and displaced persons, the USSR did not object to these problems being brought before the United Nations. It was even partially responsible for the introduction of one of them and played an active role in all three debates. Nevertheless, the Soviet Union was then and has since been unwilling to go much beyond this. Its participation in the UN's concrete work in this field has always been severely limited. It had nothing to do with the Korean program, and although it has supported resolutions concerning relief measures to alleviate the problems caused by natural disasters, it has never initiated such action nor made a significant contribution.

ECONOMIC ASSISTANCE

The first relief and reconstruction problem which was considered at the first part of the General Assembly's first session concerned economic assistance for the devastated countries. At that time economic assistance was handled on a multilateral basis by the United Nations Relief and Rehabilitation Administration.

UNRRA

Since UNRRA was such an important element in the early UN discussions of this problem, it may be useful briefly to consider the nature of that agency and certain aspects of the USSR's policy concerning it. UNRRA fitted Soviet desiderata with respect to relief and reconstruction rather well, as it did in the case of refugees and displaced persons. It dispensed aid on a "non-political" basis, and almost half of the commodities which it distributed were given to Eastern European countries.[2] Receiving countries incurred minimal financial obligations, and even those were reduced in the case of the Ukrainian SSR and the Byelorussian SSR.[3] Further, the USSR was able to exercise considerable influence in UNRRA and to utilize the agency's aid to advance its own objectives in Eastern Europe.[4]

But UNRRA was not perfect from the Soviet viewpoint; it deviated in many important respects from the USSR's original plan for relief activities.[5] This plan provided for the establishment of an

[2] George Woodbridge, *UNRRA: The History of the United Nations Relief and Rehabilitation Administration* (3 vols.; New York: Columbia University, 1950), III, 428.

[3] See: *ibid.*, I, 377-378; and II, 64-65.

[4] See: M. Klemme, *Inside Story of UNRRA*, pp. 144, 240-241; and Jack N. Behrman, "Political Factors in U.S. Financial Cooperation, 1945-1950," *The American Political Science Review*, XLVII, no. 2 (June, 1953), 431-460, pp. 440-442.

[5] The original Soviet proposal is contained in Cable No. 327 from Ambassador Winant in the United States Embassy in London to the Secretary of State, dated January 22, 1942. This cable is available in the archives of the Department of State. For accounts of the negotiations concerning the formation of

Inter-Allied Committee on Post-War Requirements, which would first estimate the needs of the devastated countries and the resources which they had available to meet these needs, and then would endeavor to secure the supplies necessary to fill the gap. In addition, the Committee would have some responsibilities for allocation and the duty of preventing speculation in the needed commodities. There were several differences between this projected Committee and UNRRA: its mandate included reconstruction, while UNRRA's was limited to relief and rehabilitation; it did not include the United States, which was mentioned only as a supplier of food and raw materials, while in UNRRA the United States played a major role; it could give aid only to Axis-occupied countries, while UNRRA also aided others; its decisions required unanimity, while UNRRA's required a simple or qualified majority depending on the issue; it could take no decision unless it was endorsed by the country concerned, while UNRRA had greater although not unlimited powers. The USSR's plan was clearly designed to secure maximum freedom of action for itself, and Soviet policy in UNRRA with regard to organizational problems also seemed to be oriented toward this goal.[6] This early Soviet plan is significant because many of the USSR's policies and actions in the UN were reflections of it.

AIDING UNRRA

UNRRA's shortage of funds prompted the discussion of economic assistance at the first part of the Assembly's first session. In an effort to aid UNRRA, the United Kingdom proposed that the Assembly should recommend that the states which had signed the UNRRA Agreement make a further contribution of one per cent of their national income, as the UNRRA Council had recommended in August 1945, and that other "peace-loving" states, which had not already done so, join UNRRA.[7] The USSR submitted an alternative draft which limited the appeal for contributions to states which had not suffered enemy occupation and the appeal to join UNRRA to

---

UNRRA see: Ernest F. Penrose, *Economic Planning for the Peace* (Princeton: Princeton University Press, 1953), pp. 146-167; and George Woodbridge, *UNRRA*, I, 3-24.

[6] See: Robert H. Johnson, "International Politics and the Structure of International Organization: The Case of UNRRA," *World Politics*, III, no. 4 (July 1951), 520-538.

[7] UN Document A/C. 2/2.

UN members.[8] Both features were incorporated in the compromise resolution which the Assembly unanimously adopted: the last by using the Soviet phraseology and the former by deleting the direct appeal and instead establishing a committee of eleven states, including Poland and the USSR, to consult with members of UNRRA concerning further contributions.[9] Although there was no desire to force Eastern European countries to contribute, the West did not want to preclude contributions from such states as France which had also suffered enemy occupation.

The *ad hoc* committee which was established by this resolution conducted its negotiations and reported to the second part of the Assembly's first session in the fall of 1946. The USSR's participation in the committee was marked by its opposition to efforts to obtain information on the progress made toward economic rehabilitation in states which received UNRRA assistance and to requiring these states to send full reports to the Secretary-General on UNRRA's work.[10]

Post-UNRRA Assistance

When the Assembly reconvened in October 1946, however, its original resolution, and the activities of the *ad hoc* committee, had little relevance to the current situation. During the interim, it had been decided to terminate UNRRA's activities by June 30, 1947, and UNRRA's Council had recommended that the United Nations should establish or designate an agency to review the basic needs of the devastated states which were receiving UNRRA aid and to make recommendations concerning the economic assistance which they would require in the future. ECOSOC had endorsed this resolution and had recommended that the Assembly take immediate action. Thus, the broad question of the nature of future economic assistance for relief and reconstruction purposes was placed before the second part of the Assembly's first session. The central issue was whether economic aid should be distributed on an international or a bilateral basis. The United States and the United Kingdom, the principal donors, desired more control over the use of their funds than they had had in the past, among other reasons so they could

[8] UN Document A/C. 2/4.
[9] General Assembly Resolution 6 (I).
[10] See: UN, General Assembly, Second Committee, *Official Records* (1st Session, 2nd Part), p. 188.

avoid aiding communist countries, and consequently were opposed to the continuation of UNRRA or the creation of a new world-wide agency. Canada, Denmark and Norway, and Fiorello H. LaGuardia, UNRRA's Director-General, were the most vocal proponents of the opposite view. Curiously, the USSR and the other Eastern European states, which were among the principal recipients of UNRRA assistance, played only a minor role in the discussions.

At first, the Soviet Union argued that UNRRA should be continued in 1947, but its activities should be limited to supplying food and other essentials. This suggestion found little support. Greatest support was given to Director-General LaGuardia's proposal that a United Nations Emergency Food Fund should be created. This Fund, which he estimated would require at least $400,000,000, would be financed through voluntary contributions in money or goods, and the resources which were collected would be used for the distribution of food and other essential commodities. The Soviet Union supported this proposal on the condition that the Fund be based on the same international principles as UNRRA had been and announced that it would be willing to make a small contribution.[11] The United States and the United Kingdom, however, were opposed, and their opposition was determining.

The Assembly finally adopted Resolution 48 (I) which essentially left the problem of economic assistance to be met through bilateral arrangements, though it also contained a few international features. It established a Special Technical Committee, composed of representatives of ten states, to survey the minimum import needs of countries which might require assistance and their ability to meet these needs. The difference was to be reported to the Secretary-General, who in turn would transmit this information to UN member states. Member states were urged to furnish relief assistance where needed, and the Secretary-General was instructed to provide all facilities that might be necessary, including arrangements for information, consultations and technical assistance. The resolution affirmed the principle:

> . . . that at no time should relief supplies be used as a political weapon, and that no discrimination should be made in the distribution of relief supplies because of race, creed, or political belief.

This was one of the few provisions which pleased the Soviet Union.

[11] See: UN Documents A/C. 2/85, pp. 5-6, and A/C. 2/90, p. 2.

90   The USSR and the UN's Economic and Social Activities

The Special Technical Committee held thirty meetings from January 3 to January 23, 1947. Of the ten members, two, Poland and the USSR, were from Eastern Europe. The Committee examined the situation in all countries which had received UNRRA assistance except Byelorussia and the Ukraine, neither of which replied to the Secretary-General's request to present its requirements.[12] On the basis of this examination the Committee decided that six European states (Austria, Greece, Hungary, Italy, Poland, and Yugoslavia) would need $583,000,000 in credits during 1947, 43 per cent of which the Committee felt should be allocated to the three communist countries.[13] Even though the Soviet representative voted for this allocation, a special statement of dissent signed by another Soviet representative and dated January 28, 1947, was attached to the report, and Soviet delegates protested against the allocations whenever they were considered in UN meetings. The essence of the Soviet complaint was that the allocations discriminated against Eastern Europe.

THE MARSHALL PLAN

Neither the Soviet complaints nor the Committee's report, though, had much impact, for in 1947 the United States inaugurated the Truman Doctrine and the Marshall Plan, and thereafter the United Nations had little to do with the main economic assistance programs. Not all were pleased with the UN's exclusion. In an effort to prevent this exclusion, Secretary-General Trygve Lie publicly offered the use of the Economic Commission for Europe for the European Recovery Program, and ECE's Executive-Secretary, Gunnar Myrdal, made various attempts to involve ECE. However, at no stage in the significant negotiations concerning ERP in June and July 1947 did the United States, the other Western powers, or the Soviet Union suggest a major role for the United Nations. British Foreign Minister Ernest Bevin wanted to avoid the UN because of the USSR's membership. He was convinced that the Soviet Union "would prove unco-operative in any scheme backed by American aid and that anyway Congress would not vote this aid if the Russians were among the recipients."[14] M. Georges Bidault, the French For-

[12] UN Document E/269, p. 8.
[13] Ibid., p. 27.
[14] David Wightman, *Economic Co-Operation in Europe: A Study of the United Nations Economic Commission for Europe* (New York: Frederick A. Praeger, 1956), p. 32.

eign Minister, shared these views, and apparently so did several individuals within the American government.[15] Although earlier in 1947, as will be discussed in the following section, various Soviet proposals had implied that ECE should itself engage in or should be an agent for multilateral economic assistance programs, the Commission was accorded at most a minimal role in the proposals which the USSR advanced in June and July.

At first the Soviet Union made no effort to obscure its position. In July 1947, at ECE's second session, France, the United Kingdom and the USSR all gave their account of the recently concluded Paris Meeting of Foreign Ministers where Secretary of State Marshall's offer of assistance had been discussed.[16] The Soviet delegate stated that the Soviet Union had proposed that a Committee of Cooperation should be established to ascertain the needs of European states.[17] This would be done on the basis of statements supplied by the several governments. Aid would be limited to states which had suffered German occupation and which had assisted in the Allied victory. After establishing the requirements, the Committee would pass these on to the United States, with the assumption that the United States would furnish the needed supplies. The similarity between this plan and the earliest Soviet plan for postwar relief is striking. The only mention made of the United Nations was that the Committee would be instructed to establish relations with ECE.[18]

It is apparent from the plan that the USSR was no more interested in creating a strong international organization to supervise relief operations in mid-1947 than it had been in earlier years. Nor was the Soviet Union interested in joint planning for reconstruction. If the United Nations had been involved, it is likely that efforts would have been made to carry out reconstruction on an all-European basis. There were great pressures in the Economic Commis-

[15] See the story by Thomas Hamilton: *New York Times*, September 30, 1954.

[16] For the full record of the Paris Meeting see the French White Paper: France: Ministère des Affaires étrangères: *Documents de la Conférence des Ministres des Affaires étrangères de la France, du Royaume-Uni, de l'URSS tenue à Paris du 27 juin au 3 juillet 1947, et pièces rélatives aux négociations diplomatiques engagées à la suite du discours prononcé par le Général Marshall, Secrétaire d'Etat des Etats-Unis, le 5 juin 1947* (Paris: Imprimerie Nationale, 1947).

[17] UN Document E/ECE/SR. 2/3, pp. 5-12.

[18] During the Paris Meeting, on June 29, 1947, Radio Moscow stated quite explicitly that the Soviet proposals did not envisage ECE having an important role (David Wightman, *Economic Co-operation in Europe*, p. 43).

sion for Europe for regional planning. Had such plans been put into effect, in addition to infringing on the USSR's own economic planning they would have interfered with the consolidation of Soviet control in Eastern Europe. Quite apart from the pressures which would have come from the UN side, it is known that some groups in Eastern Europe regarded cooperation in the United Nations as a way of working against Soviet domination.[19] Moreover, had the UN been involved, it might have been more difficult for the Soviet Union to bar the Eastern European states from participation.

Surely the interest which some Eastern European states showed in General Marshall's offer must have alarmed the Soviet Union. As an example of this interest, at ECE's Second Session, on July 7, 1947, the Polish delegate spoke favorably about the idea of a joint recovery program and the positive statements made by the United Kingdom and France, while he ignored the USSR's statement.[20] He went so far as to ask that the discussion be postponed until he could receive instructions from his government. Outside ECE, Poland and Czechoslovakia went even farther. Both indicated that they might participate in the European Recovery Program, but both subsequently recanted.

THE SOVIET ATTACK ON ERP

By the time of the General Assembly's second session, which opened in September 1947, the Soviet Union was in a firmer position with regard to its Eastern European satellites. The Cominform, first announced in *Pravda* on July 6, was in process of formation, and other devices were being used to draw these states closer to the USSR. The entire Soviet bloc cooperated in a full-blown attack on the Marshall Plan which was led by Andrei Vyshinsky. He charged that the principles of the United Nations were being violated in that relief was being used as a political weapon in contradiction to Resolution 48 (I).[21] He also alleged that aid was being given to avert a depression in the United States, and that its acceptance would place European countries under the direct economic and

---

[19] See Trygve Lie's account of some of his discussions with Jan Masaryk: *In the Cause of Peace: Seven Years with the United Nations* (New York: Macmillan, 1954), pp. 230-234.

[20] UN Document E/ECE/SR. 2/3, p. 19.

[21] UN, General Assembly, Plenary Meetings, *Official Records* (2nd Session), pp. 86-87.

political control of the United States. He claimed that the Marshall Plan was an attempt to split Europe into two hostile camps (conveniently ignoring previous Soviet actions which had this effect and the USSR's general unwillingness to have Europe treated as a unit).

In the Second Committee the Polish delegate, Oskar Lange who had received part of his education in the United States, had taught in several American universities, and had even taken out United States citizenship, submitted a resolution, which was seconded by the USSR, and which asked member states to carry out all UN recommendations on economic and social matters and to use the UN's machinery in settling all fundamental economic issues.[22] The resolution advised member states "not to establish for such purposes any machinery outside of the United Nations." It also requested the Secretariat to prepare periodic surveys of world economic conditions, which "should contain analyses of the major dislocations of needs and supplies in the world economy and recommendations as to the appropriate measures to remedy them." This phraseology was probably designed to emphasize the needs of Eastern Europe and the fact that no aid would be provided for this area under the European Recovery Program. Finally, the resolution instructed the Secretary-General to report annually on the steps taken by member states to give effect to UN recommendations. In view of the USSR's position at the Paris Meeting of Foreign Ministers, it is interesting that the main criticism implicitly contained in the resolution involved the fact that ERP was conducted outside the United Nations. The Soviet attack, however, for which the resolution served as a point of departure, was much broader. Despite its obvious propaganda features, the resolution had several constructive aspects, and parts of it were similar to an Australian proposal for periodic reports on world economic conditions and trends.

At the conclusion of the debate, the representatives of Australia and Poland submitted a joint proposal on reports on world economic conditions and trends, which included several points contained in the original Polish draft, although stripped of their prejudicial phraseology. After the rejection of two curious amendments proposed by the USSR—one would have deleted the request to ECOSOC to make recommendations on the basis of the reports and the other would have prohibited ECOSOC from considering such reports more than once a year—the resolution was adopted

[22] UN Document A/C. 2/108.

unanimously.[23] The annual United Nations World Economic Surveys partially owe their origins to it.

The General Assembly also adopted a resolution on the implementation of United Nations economic and social recommendations.[24] It consisted of all the relevant sections of the original Polish draft except the recommendation that member states should use United Nations machinery for the settlement of all fundamental economic problems and the admonition against using extra-United Nations machinery. The United States proposed this deletion, and only the Soviet bloc opposed the suggestion.[25] Although the Soviet bloc supported the resolution, its result, the attempt to give meaning to the provisions of Article 64,[26] must have been very different from that originally intended. It certainly did little to embarrass the United States.

Soviet polemics against the Marshall Plan were repeated at every possible opportunity in succeeding United Nations debates. Fresh charges were added to those which had already been made. The USSR alleged that the European Recovery Program aimed at the restoration of German war potential, caused unemployment in Europe, ruined small and medium-sized concerns, and created international tensions. Soviet delegates charged that the Marshall Plan was a device for dumping useless surplus goods from the United States. They also claimed that the United States was using the Marshall Plan to steal Europe's colonies. They continually asserted that it made no contribution to the economic restoration of Western Europe. Opportunities for these polemics were provided by the general debates in the Economic and Employment Commission, the Economic Commission for Europe, the Economic and Social Council and the General Assembly. The effect of this attack is difficult to measure. After the General Assembly's second session, the United Nations never again adopted a resolution which owed its origins to the Soviet attack on ERP. However, there can be no question that the UN provided an excellent forum within which the Soviet Union could voice its attack. Of course, the United States and the West had an equal opportunity to reply.

[23] General Assembly Resolution 118 (II).
[24] General Assembly Resolution 119 (II).
[25] UN, General Assembly, Second Committee, *Official Records* (2nd Session), pp. 65-66.
[26] See above, pp. 49-51.

Beyond this vituperation, what is perhaps most striking about Soviet policy with regard to economic assistance is the limited extent to which the USSR was willing to submit to international control, even though a small measure of international cooperation might have meant gaining substantial benefits. At times the Soviet Union gave the impression that it wanted to obtain aid for itself and other Eastern European states through the United Nations, but the price which it was willing to pay was extremely low. In fact, with its desire to consolidate control over Eastern Europe, the USSR may well have preferred that the United Nations should have as little to do with the problems of rebuilding this area as possible.

THE UN'S ROLE—ECE AND ECAFE

Reluctance to allow the United Nations to undertake significant tasks in Eastern Europe was also evident in Soviet policy with regard to the second item concerning relief and reconstruction which was discussed at the first part of the Assembly's first session, determining what role the UN should play. The ultimate outcome of this discussion was the establishment of two of ECOSOC's regional economic commissions, the Economic Commission for Europe and the Economic Commission for Asia and the Far East. Poland introduced the question by proposing a draft resolution on the Reconstruction of UN member states, which appeared to be a thinly veiled appeal for economic aid from the United Nations.[27] However, since it only committed the Assembly to discuss the problem again in the fall of 1946 and asked ECOSOC to consider the issue in the interim, it found universal support. The United States delegate, though, felt compelled to state that in voting for the resolution, he in no way committed his country to direct or indirect assistance in any particular case.[28]

The Temporary Sub-Commission on Economic Reconstruction of Devastated Areas

ECOSOC's initial response to this resolution was to establish a Temporary Sub-Commission on Economic Reconstruction of Devastated Areas, consisting of twenty states, five of which were from

[27] UN Document A/22.
[28] UN, General Assembly, Plenary Meetings, *Official Records* (1st Session, 1st Part), p. 335.

Eastern Europe. This body was instructed to investigate the nature and scope of the problem of reconstruction and the progress which had been made, and to recommend international measures to facilitate and accelerate this progress. At the USSR's insistence the Sub-Commission was allowed to conduct on-the-spot investigations only "with the agreement and collaboration of the government concerned," and reparations were excluded from its terms of reference.[29] The Soviet Union also sought to limit the investigation to member states of the United Nations, but this attempt failed.[30] The Sub-Commission was granted permission to consider reconstruction problems in neutral countries as well as UN member states, and in addition, with the consent of the occupying authorities, it could examine certain aspects of the economies of the ex-enemy countries. Had the Soviet position been adopted, the Sub-Commission would have been forced to plan recovery on a partial basis: it could not have included Sweden, Switzerland, Finland, Austria, Italy and Germany. Several of these countries desperately needed assistance and two, Italy and Austria, had received UNRRA aid. Conversely, the Sub-Commission would have been compelled to give greater emphasis to the needs of Eastern Europe. The Soviet Union also failed in its attempt to have the Sub-Commission base its analyses solely on material which was submitted by the governments concerned and to require that all sections of the Sub-Commission's report which pertained to a particular government be approved by that government.[31]

The Temporary Sub-Commission on Economic Reconstruction of Devastated Areas met from July 29 through September 13, 1946. Most of its efforts were focused on Europe and Africa, although it also considered in less detail some of the problems of reconstruction in Asia and the Far East. The two Soviet Republics, Byelorussia and the Ukraine, were quite uncooperative. Both refused to give the Sub-Commission permission to visit their territories, and the data which they supplied consisted merely of extracts from public documents concerning the USSR's first postwar five-year-plan. Other Eastern European states, however, took a different attitude. Czechoslovakia, Poland and Yugoslavia allowed the Sub-Commission to

[29] See: UN Document E/EMP/12, pp. 2-3.
[30] See: UN Document E/JC/2, pp. 8 ff; UN, ECOSOC, *Official Records* (2nd Session), pp. 118 ff, and, the *New York Times*, June 6, 1946.
[31] UN, ECOSOC, *Official Records* (2nd Session), p. 120.

conduct on-the-spot investigations and also supplied previously unpublished statistical information.

The Sub-Commission's report, which was presented to ECOSOC's third session in the fall of 1946, contained an estimate of the extent of devastation and of the progress which had been achieved toward reconstruction, analyses of plans of governments, and recommendations for international cooperation. The Soviet delegate criticized the report on the grounds that it made no provision for "material assistance to the devastated areas," and was "limited to general recommendations."[32] Perhaps the Ukrainian delegate expressed most clearly what the USSR would have desired when he stated that "the primary need . . . was for specific and concrete proposals regarding, for example, how long-term credits on favourable terms could be secured for devastated countries, and how technical and industrial equipment was to be made available." [33] The Soviet charges, which ignored the fact that the Sub-Commission's terms of reference had not mentioned direct relief, but instead had emphasized international cooperative measures, may have reflected a genuine desire to obtain aid through the United Nations. On the other hand, they may also have been chosen as an appealing focal point for an attack motivated by other reasons.

Several of the recommendations contained in the report envisaged European reconstruction on a continental basis. For example, with regard to electric power the Sub-Commission recommended:

> . . . that an agency designated by the Economic and Social Council, with the aid of technical advisers shall study and prepare plans for the co-ordinated development of European power resources, the construction of hydro-electric plants; and the establishment of an international grid for the economic distribution of electric power in all European countries.[34]

Others were equally international in conception. Soviet delegates objected to these recommendations and alleged that they were directed against the independence of the smaller European countries.[35] To use the same example, Soviet delegates argued that it would be better to help each country rebuild its own electric power plants, that to do this would insure their economic independence.

[32] UN Document E/AC. 14/2, p. 2.
[33] UN Document E/AC. 14/3, p. 3.
[34] UN Document E/156, p. 99.
[35] See: UN Document E/AC. 14/3, p. 3.

The Soviet attitude probably reflected fear of the ties which might be developed between Eastern and Western Europe and also a desire to maintain its own freedom of action. At the same time, it is true that in the first decade after the Second World War most planning in Eastern Europe seems to have been done almost on a basis of national autarky.[36]

The Sub-Commission's most important recommendation was that an Economic Commission for Europe should be created. Poland, the United Kingdom and the United States had jointly proposed that such a body should be established to facilitate the reconstruction of Europe and later the expansion of European economic activity. Although this suggestion won enthusiastic support from the majority of the Sub-Commission—among other things, many hoped that ECE might provide a vehicle for bridging the growing chasm between East and West—it was the recommendation which the USSR appeared least willing to accept. At ECOSOC's third session the Soviet delegate claimed that it "had no connection with the problem of extending aid to the devastated areas" and that such a body was not needed as Europe was not an economic unit.[37] The USSR obviously feared the creation of an organ which might interfere with its efforts to consolidate its control over Eastern Europe. David Wightman, the author of the most authoritative analysis of ECE, has speculated that the Soviet Union "may well have regarded the idea of ECE as another move, beginning with economic cooperation, to undo the understandings reached at Yalta,"[38] which in the Soviet view—as he understands it—placed this area within the USSR's sphere of political influence. If the Temporary Sub-Commission's recommendations were a sample, ECE would take an international and all-European approach to problems of reconstruction. The Soviet Union clearly viewed with concern the support which some Eastern European countries gave to the Sub-Commission's recommendations, and it must have been alarmed by the fact that Poland was a co-sponsor of the recommendation to establish ECE.

[36] See: Zbigniew K. Brzezinski, *The Soviet Bloc: Unity and Conflict* (Cambridge: Harvard University Press, 1960), pp. 124-128; and, Gunnar Myrdal, *An International Economy: Problems and Prospects* (New York: Harper and Brothers, 1956), pp. 147-148.
[37] UN Document E/AC. 14/2, p. 2.
[38] *Economic Cooperation in Europe*, p. 23.

RELIEF AND RECONSTRUCTION 99

Although several delegations at ECOSOC's third session strongly desired to establish ECE immediately, Soviet opposition led the Council to resolve only to consider the matter again at its next regular or special session. Various states, however, reserved the right to raise the question at the forthcoming Assembly meeting.[39] The other substantive recommendations in the Temporary Sub-Commission's report were also postponed.

THE CREATION OF ECE

Despite the pessimism engendered by the USSR's negative stand in the ECOSOC debate, at the second part of the General Assembly's first session, Norway proposed that the Council should be directed to create an Economic Commission for Europe. At China's insistence this recommendation was broadened to include an Economic Commission for Asia and the Far East as well. Although the USSR protested that the peoples of the devastated areas "expected real, concrete assistance and not the adoption of yet one more resolution,"[40] it voted for the proposal, which was adopted unanimously.

Terms of reference for the Economic Commission for Europe were put in final form and adopted at ECOSOC's fourth session in February and March 1947. In these negotiations, and in the earlier discussions of this issue, the Soviet Union's policy was characterized by an overriding desire to protect its freedom of action in Eastern Europe. In January 1947, when the Economic and Employment Commission attempted to draft principles which could serve as a basis for ECE's terms of reference, the USSR was able to gain the deletion of the statement that the Commission should work toward "integration of the European economy."[41] The Soviet Union also secured the inclusion of the principle that the Commission should not take any action without first obtaining the consent of the government concerned.[42] This restriction was later included in the first paragraph of ECE's terms of reference. The USSR succeeded in deleting from the terms of reference specific mention of problems of European inland transport, although the exclusion did not pre-

[39] ECOSOC Resolution 5 V (III).
[40] UN, General Assembly, Second Committee, *Official Records* (1st Session, 2nd Part), p. 105.
[41] UN Document E/CN. 1/SR, 13, p. 2.
[42] *Ibid.*, p. 8.

clude the Commission's working in this area. In this case, the Soviet Union was concerned about the regime of the Danube River.

One of the central issues throughout the negotiations was the position of the United States. At first the Soviet Union questioned the majority's desire to have the United States be a member of ECE.[43] But once it was clear that the United States would receive a seat on the Commission, the Soviet Union successfully insisted that the Commission's jurisdiction should extend to all of its members, not just to those in Europe, which was the way the American proposal read.[44] Understandably, a commission on which both the United States and the USSR were represented, but which could only make recommendations to the latter, would be intolerable for the Soviet Union. Moreover, if the Soviet bloc hoped to use ECE as an instrument for putting pressure on the United States to obtain economic assistance, this body would have to have power to make recommendations to the United States.

Several Soviet proposals concerning ECE failed. Many of these were directed against the specialized agencies.[45] The USSR sought to delete a provision from the terms of reference which stated that ECE could not establish subsidiary bodies without prior consultation with the specialized agencies in the field. It opposed the requirement that effective liaison be established with the specialized agencies. These positions were consistent with the Soviet Union's non-participation in the specialized agencies and its hostility toward them. The USSR also opposed the provision for consultation with other intergovernmental agencies. In addition, the Soviet Union objected to the requirement that the Commission should report to the Council on its plans as well as its accomplishments—a forerunner of later Soviet policies which sought to emphasize the Economic Commission for Europe and downgrade the Council. The Soviet Union opposed extending ECE's competence to European states which were not members of the UN, and the provision that such states could be admitted to the Commission in a consultative capacity. Later it took a different position on this issue.[46] However, it

[43] UN Document E/AC. 14/2, pp. 2-3.
[44] See: UN Documents E/CN. 1/SR. 14, p. 10; UN Document E/CN. 1/SR. 15, p. 4; E/AC. 17/1, p. 11; E/AC. 17/4, pp. 2-4; and E/AC. 17/5, pp. 4-7.
[45] See UN Document E/AC. 17/5, *passim*, and UN, ECOSOC, *Official Records* (4th Session), pp. 200-205.
[46] See above, pp. 45-46.

desired to grant consultative rights to the representatives of the Allied Control Authorities, rather than just allowing consultations with them. Finally the Soviet Union proposed giving the "governments concerned" veto powers over all ECE recommendations which might affect them.

Perhaps because of the rejection of these amendments, the USSR abstained from voting on the ECOSOC Resolution which established the Economic Commission for Europe.[47] The resolution created a potentially strong agency. ECE was "empowered to make recommendations directly to its Member Governments, Governments admitted in a consultative capacity . . . and the specialized agencies concerned." Prior approval by the Council was necessary only if a recommendation would have "important effects on the economy of the world as a whole." Three tasks were assigned to the Commission: first, to initiate and participate in measures designed to facilitate concerted action for the economic reconstruction of Europe, for raising the level of European economic activity, and for maintaining and strengthening the economic relations of the European countries both among themselves and with other countries of the world; secondly, to undertake or sponsor investigations and studies of economic and technological problems and of economic developments within Europe; and finally, to collect, disseminate, and evaluate whatever economic, statistical and technological data it deemed appropriate or to sponsor such action. In its initial stages the Commission was instructed to give "prior consideration" to measures to facilitate economic reconstruction in the devastated areas of the European members of the United Nations. The Commission's headquarters were to be in Geneva and it was to have its own secretariat. Gunnar Myrdal, a dynamic Swedish economist and one firmly committed to the proposition that reconstruction could only be accomplished effectively on an all-European basis, became ECE's first Executive Secretary.

The Soviet abstention, however, cast doubt on the contribution which ECE would make toward all-European cooperation, and this apprehension increased when the USSR gave no indication of whether or not it would participate in the Commission until shortly before the first session, which opened in May 1947.[48] A year and a half elapsed before the Soviet Union responded to Mr. Myrdal's

[47] ECOSOC Resolution 36 (IV).
[48] See: *New York Times*, May 2, 1947.

request that a Soviet citizen be approved for appointment as Deputy Executive-Secretary, and then, instead of approving the man he had wanted, the USSR nominated one of lesser stature.[49]

Soviet Participation in ECE's Early Activities

Soviet tactics at ECE's first session provided further grounds for pessimism. One facet of the USSR's policy then was an attempt to use the Commission as a device for gaining aid, or if this proved impossible, for criticizing Western assistance policies. During the general discussion of ECE's future work, the Soviet delegate suggested that the Commission should give priority to considering ways and means of aiding the Allied countries which had suffered enemy occupation.[50] At the same time, he argued that the Commission should insure that there would be no infringement of the principle of state sovereignty and no interference in the internal affairs of states. The USSR apparently hoped to bring pressure on the United States. In these terms, its optimal goal was probably the recreation in ECE of UNRRA or the establishment there of a similar agency, although one which would more closely approximate the Soviet ideal. If this failed, as it obviously would at that time, the criteria which the USSR suggested would provide a convenient basis for criticism of Western and especially United States policies. Not even this was gained, however, except in the sense that the Soviet statement was written into the record. Perhaps because it was clear that they would be defeated, no formal Soviet proposals were ever presented.

A second facet of Soviet policy was the attempt to strengthen its position within the Commission. The USSR's proposals for a two-thirds majority rule in ECE have already been recounted.[51] In addition, the Soviet Union sought, albeit vainly, to have an Eastern European, Jan Masaryk, chosen as President.

The third facet of Soviet policy at ECE's first session was an attempt to erect a further restriction on the Commission's power. The USSR proposed to insert in the rules of procedure a provision that the Commission could only make recommendations to a state if the government concerned agreed.[52] According to ECE's terms

[49] *Ibid.*, September 21, 1948.
[50] UN Document, E/ECE/SR. 1/3, p. 3. See also the account by Michael L. Hoffman: *New York Times*, May 6, 1947.
[51] See above, p. 45.
[52] UN Document E/ECE/SR. 1/13, p. 7.

of reference, consent was necessary only for action and not for recommendations; the Soviet proposal was a revival of its earlier attempt to gain veto powers. This proposal was defeated; the rules of procedure as adopted followed the Commission's terms of reference.

Forcing delay was the final facet of Soviet policy. Perhaps one reason for this was the knowledge that the minor peace treaties would soon become effective, and then Bulgaria, Hungary, Romania and Finland—assuming they were admitted to the UN—would be eligible for full membership in ECE, thus giving the Eastern European and Scandinavian states a clear majority. Since the Scandinavian states seldom opposed the Soviet bloc, the USSR's position would have been significantly improved. Earlier Soviet attempts to limit the rights of non-members were consistent with this explanation.

Another reason for this tactic may have been that the USSR wanted to prevent ECE from taking action. The principal business of the Commission's first session was arranging for the absorption or termination of the activities of three emergency bodies which had been established to deal with European economic problems: the Emergency Economic Committee for Europe (EECE); the European Coal Organization (ECO); and the European Central Inland Transport Organization (ECITO). The USSR participated only in the last body. Some Eastern European states participated in ECITO and also in the European Coal Organization, but EECE was composed solely of Western states. The Soviet Union proposed termination dates which would have effectively ended the activities of these three organizations, as they would have preceded the date on which ECE would have been prepared to assume their functions.[53] Further, the Soviet Union's refusal to indicate whether or not it would pay its pledge of $380,000 to ECITO cast doubt on the ability of this organization to continue. Forcing delay fitted this pattern of action. However, despite Soviet objections, the Commission decided to discuss EECE's functions at its second session and set the termination date for this agency's functions forty-five days after the close of that session; it took similar action with regard to ECO; and it called a meeting of transport experts to discuss the future of ECITO. Soviet opposition to these three agencies, which was demonstrated elsewhere in the UN as well, stemmed from the fact that they were

[53] UN Document E/ECE/SR. 1/12, pp. 3-5.

Western-oriented and aided Western recovery and, perhaps more importantly, they interfered with the USSR's ability to exercise sole control in Eastern Europe—particularly ECITO through its activities concerning the Danube.

At the second session of the Economic Commission for Europe in July 1947, a number of so-called Technical Committees were established to assume the work of the three emergency bodies. These became the focal points for ECE's concrete work concerning reconstruction and rehabilitation.[54] On the basis of the recommendations of the *ad hoc* meeting of Transport Experts, an Inland Transport Committee was established. Soviet interests in the Danube were protected by the provision in the Committee's terms of reference prohibiting recommendations "in respect of the regimes of the international waterways of Europe." [55] The Soviet Union would have preferred and fought for a stronger formulation, arguing quite frankly at one point that any recommendation concerning the international waterways would have "political implications." [56] A Coal Committee was established to replace ECO. And, in order to continue the functions of EECE the Commission established: a Committee on Electric Power; a Committee on Industry and Materials, which had sub-committees on Timber, Fertilizers, and Alkalis; and a Panel on Housing. Later a Manpower Committee and a Steel Committee, and several other sub-committees, were established.

The Soviet Union and its two Republics, the Ukraine and Byelorussia, did not participate in the work of any of these Technical Committees during the period that they were concerned with reconstruction.[57] During this time, the Soviet Union participated in only two of ECE's subsidiary bodies, the Committee on Agricultural

---

[54] See: David Wightman, *Economic Cooperation in Europe*, and also UN Document E/ECE/291, "ECE: The First Ten Years, 1947-1957."

[55] UN, ECOSOC, *Official Records* (5th Session), Supplement No. 3, "Report of the Economic Commission for Europe," p. 23.

[56] UN Document E/ECE/TR/SR. 5, p. 3.

[57] The USSR, however, did occasionally send observers to the sessions of the Inland Transport Committee and the Bid Acceptance Meetings. The latter negotiated the flow of European traffic through the occupied zones of Austria and Germany. See: UN Document E/ECE/SR. 3/4, p. 8; UN, ECOSOC, *Official Records* (6th Session), Supplement No. 10, "Interim Report of the Economic Commission for Europe," pp. 5-15; and Walt W. Rostow, "The Economic Commission for Europe," *International Organization*, III, no. 2 (May 1949), 254-268, p. 260.

RELIEF AND RECONSTRUCTION

Problems and the Committee on the Development of Trade; both were created as the result of Soviet proposals, and neither was directly concerned with reconstruction. It was 1953 before the USSR and its two Republics began to join in the work of the other committees, and a year later before they participated fully. Since the USSR was a major producer of several important commodities, its nonparticipation hindered ECE's work. Other Eastern European countries were somewhat more cooperative. Yugoslavia became deeply involved. Until 1950, Czechoslovakia, Hungary and Poland were also active in a number of the Technical Committees, and this led to several instances of mutually fruitful cooperation between these states and Western Europe.

This may explain the force of the Soviet attack on ECE's Technical Committees. A year after their creation, at ECE's third session in April 1948, Amazap Arutiunian launched an attack which was continued into the early nineteen fifties. He charged that the Committees had "greatly exceeded their terms of reference." [58] He claimed they had attempted "to interfere with the domestic affairs of states." His allegations were capped with the statement that the United Kingdom and the United States were attempting to shape the work of the Commission's Technical Committees so as to aid their plans for "seizing European markets and for subordinating the economy of European countries" to their "political, military and strategic interests." All these charges contained indications of the USSR's fear of the implications of the collaboration of Eastern European countries in the Commission's activities.

This fear, and the desire to cut off Western influence in Eastern Europe, were probably among the principal reasons for the USSR's own abstention from ECE's Technical Committees; it would make it easier to urge others not to participate. In addition, the Soviet Union probably felt that it could gain little from participation—no concrete economic assistance was involved—and to participate actively would have required the divulgence of then secret economic data. Moreover, it would have exposed the state of Soviet technology to the world's gaze.

One other aspect of Soviet policy in the early sessions of the Economic Commission for Europe deserves mention. When the Commission assumed the functions of EECE, ECITO and ECE, some

---

[58] See his speech: UN Document E/ECE/SR. 3/4 Corr. 3, pp. 1-3.

arrangements had to be made for consultation with the Allied Control Authorities in Germany. The Soviet Union violently opposed and continually sought to reverse a decision which allowed the Executive Secretary to establish separate liaison with each zone, arguing that Germany had to be treated as an economic unit, and that liaison could only be established through the Allied Control Council in Berlin. Given the prevailing political situation, the Soviet solution would have precluded the establishment of an effective relationship with Germany.

The Soviet Union's participation in ECE thus did little to involve it in the United Nations concrete work concerning relief and reconstruction. Since from 1948 through 1952, this participation was limited almost exclusively to the plenary sessions, it consisted solely of statements and proposals made in the general debates. During this period, Soviet policy in ECE consisted primarily of attacks on the West and sometimes even the Commission itself. These attacks seldom led to the adoption of Soviet-sponsored resolutions, but they may have had some impact on public opinion in Europe, how much, though, is impossible to measure. The ardent hope and desire which many had for all-European cooperation meant that there was fertile ground for Soviet propaganda.

THE ECONOMIC COMMISSION FOR ASIA AND THE FAR EAST

The USSR's policy with regard to the establishment of the Economic Commission for Asia and the Far East, which was created at the same time as ECE, was similar to that which it pursued concerning the Economic Commission for Europe. The Soviet Union proposed many similar amendments, but just as few were adopted.[59] ECAFE's original terms of reference were identical to those of ECE except for the difference in geographical area and the absence of operating emergency organizations whose functions the Commission could assume. The USSR also abstained from voting on the resolution which established ECAFE.

Once ECAFE began operations, some important variations in Soviet policy became evident. These derived from the facts that ECAFE's tasks were somewhat different and the USSR's interests in the area were very different. The Soviet Union could not expect direct aid from ECAFE, nor did it have important interests similar

[59] See: UN Documents E/30/Rev. 1, *passim*, and E/AC. 18/SR. 2, *passim*.

to those in Eastern Europe which it needed to protect. Therefore Soviet policy tended to be less defensive. It consisted mainly of an attack on colonialism and the colonial powers.[60] Soviet tactics with regard to associate memberships in the Commission have already been discussed. Instead of arguing that the Commission's task was that of giving aid to devastated countries, Soviet delegates at an early stage supported a broader concept. They maintained that the Commission's primary mission was to bring political and economic independence to the area.[61] In early sessions the Soviet Union unsuccessfully fought to secure the establishment of field teams composed of governmental representatives to investigate conditions in member states. This was a reversal of the position which the Soviet Union had maintained during the drafting of ECAFE's terms of reference and it contradicted Soviet policies elsewhere. According to the Soviet proposals these teams would start by investigating conditions in India and China. The USSR probably hoped that these investigations would prove embarrassing to the Western powers and might be useful propaganda instruments.

Some of the Soviet Union's tactics, however, were similar to those which it pursued in ECE. The USSR sought to prevent contact with Japan in ECAFE. Barring this, it sought to have the ECAFE establish contact with the Allied Council rather than the Office of the Supreme Commander. All these attempts failed, and when Japan was finally admitted in a consultative capacity in 1952 the USSR joined in the unanimous vote. The USSR's attempt to prevent contact with the British Commander in Southeast Asia also failed. As in ECE, the Soviet Union refused to participate in most of ECAFE's Technical Committees during the period prior to 1954, and thus was excluded from the Commission's concrete work. This exclusion did much to blunt the effectiveness of the Soviet attack upon colonialism and the colonial powers.

THE WORLD FOOD SHORTAGE

The third problem involving relief and reconstruction discussed at the first part of the General Assembly's first session, the world

[60] See: Alvin Z. Rubinstein, "Soviet Policy in ECAFE: A Case Study of Soviet Behavior in International Economic Organization," *International Organization*, XII, no. 4 (Fall, 1958), 459-472.
[61] See, for example, UN Document E/CN. 11/AC. 2/SR. 2, p. 6.

food shortage, is the only one which the United Nations has continued to consider on a regular basis since then. The USSR's policy concerning this problem can be divided into three phases. For a while during 1946 the Soviet Union was one of the leaders in the UN's discussions. Then, from the winter of 1946-1947 through 1953, the USSR did little beyond criticize the UN's ongoing activities and the West. Starting in 1954, these criticisms were softened somewhat, and the Soviet Union assumed a slightly more active role.

1946

In February 1946, the USSR, in cooperation with China, France, the United Kingdom and the United States, requested that the world shortage of cereals be included in the Assembly's agenda. The five great powers also jointly proposed a resolution which the Assembly unanimously adopted and which inaugurated the UN's activities in this field.

In pursuance of this resolution, 27 (I), the Food and Agriculture Organization convened a Special Meeting on Urgent Food Problems in Washington in May 1946, which resulted in the establishment of the International Emergency Food Council (IEFC). The main function of this temporary agency was to recommend allocations for the international distribution of the available export-import supplies of food during the emergency period. FAO also began to consider various longer-range activities, including the creation of a World Food Board, which would have the purpose of allaying both agricultural shortages and surpluses. Despite its sponsorship of the original Assembly resolution, the Soviet Union did not participate in the Special Meeting in Washington, IEFC, or FAO. The USSR had joined in the wartime drafting of the Food and Agriculture Organization's constitution, but had never ratified that document.

Other Eastern European states followed a different policy. Czechoslovakia, Hungary and Poland attended the Washington meeting and cooperated actively with IEFC. In addition, these three states and Yugoslavia joined FAO.

When the activities which had been undertaken as a result of Resolution 27 (I) were reviewed at the Second Part of the Assembly's First Session in the fall of 1946, Ambassador Gromyko hit at IEFC's allocation policies, claiming that it had assigned too much to Belgium, the Netherlands and the United Kingdom, and too little to Eastern Europe. Although the draft resolution which he submitted contained a number of points which were included in proposals introduced by other states and some on which there apparently was general agreement, it also included a number of distinctive and controversial features.[62] It made no mention of the international action which had been undertaken to that point, it contained an implied criticism of United States agricultural policies, and it included a plea for aid for Eastern Europe. Some concessions were made to the Soviet position: a mild indirect criticism of the United States was written into the resolution which the Assembly finally adopted, and there was no direct reference to IEFC and FAO. Perhaps because of this, the USSR voted for Resolution 45 (I). The unanimity achieved on this resolution, however, was at best contrived and temporary.

1947-1953

After this, the differences between East and West concerning international action with respect to the world food shortage became more pronounced, and for roughly seven years almost every discussion of this issue in the United Nations was characterized by a sharp clash between the cold war protagonists.

The Soviet Union continued to abstain from the UN's concrete work, most of which was conducted under the auspices of the Food and Agriculture Organization. Although other Soviet bloc states participated in some of the activities and in FAO, gradually they withdrew, so that by 1952 the boycott was complete.

Most UN debates on the world food shortage were based on reports of the Food and Agriculture Organization. In these discussions, until 1954, Soviet delegates exhibited great hostility toward FAO. The reasons for this hostility are not clear. Perhaps the Soviet Union feared that FAO might contribute to solving some basic Western problems, and that the agency might tend to preserve and cement ties between the underdeveloped countries and the major western industrial states. The USSR may also have feared that through cooperation in FAO some Eastern European countries might perpetuate their connections with the major Western states. The fact that as late as August 1948 the Soviet bloc split on an ECOSOC resolution concerning FAO—Poland supported it while Byelorussia and the USSR abstained—would support such fears.[63]

[62] UN Document A/C. 2/49.
[63] UN, ECOSOC, *Official Records* (7th Session), p. 782.

Significantly, the Soviet attack on FAO reached its height in 1949 and that same year the Eastern European states began to withdraw from FAO.

The explanation of the USSR's refusal to participate in the work of the Food and Agriculture Organization was probably that it wished to preserve complete freedom of action in matters involving its internal production of and external trade in agricultural commodities. It apparently preferred to pursue whatever policies it chose in this area, rather than to attempt to shape international action. It may also have been embarrassed about its record with respect to agricultural production.

The USSR's policies toward other UN activities concerning agricultural matters were also characterized by a desire to protect its sovereignty. For example, at the Council's ninth session in 1949, the Soviet Union strongly opposed an Indian proposal that ECOSOC recommend that the principal food-producing countries should enter into bilateral and multilateral agreements to facilitate the economic disposal of surpluses and that they should avoid restrictionism in their future production of food, on the ground that such matters were the exclusive prerogative of the states concerned.[64] The USSR was willing to sacrifice the opportunity to attack United States policies, which the recommendation offered, in order to defeat the proposal.

However, this was one of the few such opportunities passed over. Most were exploited to the fullest possible extent. At ECOSOC's sixth session in 1948, during the first discussion in the United Nations of the world food shortage since 1946, the Soviet delegate submitted an amendment which charged that certain states, "as for example the United States," had failed to comply with the provisions of Assembly Resolution 45 (I) and had allowed unwarranted price increases.[65] Only the Soviet bloc supported the amendment.

Later that year, at the Assembly's Third Session, Poland, with the USSR's support, introduced an item entitled "the problem of wasting food in certain countries." This served as a springboard for a blatant attack on United States policies. Ultimately, the Assembly adopted a resolution which incorporated many features which had been proposed by members of the Soviet bloc, although these states did not succeed in making it a condemnation of the United States. The

[64] UN Document E/AC. 6/SR. 53, p. 5.
[65] UN Document E/AC. 6/20, p. 2.

resolution had constructive features in that it helped to focus attention on longer-range aspects of the world food shortage and eventually led to a number of studies by FAO.

Perhaps it was the USSR's exclusion from the UN's concrete work —the result of its refusal to join FAO—that led to the most important Soviet initiative with regard to food problems. In 1948 the Soviet Union proposed that the Economic Commission for Europe establish a Committee on Agricultural Problems, and it insisted that FAO should not be involved. A year later the Commission established the Committee. Some statesmen and Secretariat officials felt that it might be a useful instrument, *inter alia*, for facilitating the development of East-West trade in Europe, but Soviet tactics in the first two sessions in 1949 and 1950 created such doubts about the probability of fruitful cooperation that four years elapsed before the third meeting was convened. In the initial sessions the USSR insisted that the Committee should study methods of assisting "small and medium peasants." As there were few if any who could be included in these categories in the USSR and its satellites, it appeared that the Soviet Union hoped to use this to embarrass the West and, to whatever extent possible, to sow discontent.[66] ECE's Committee on Agricultural Problems was not the only place where Soviet delegates raised this question; they also mentioned it frequently in Assembly and ECOSOC debates, but with little success. In addition, the USSR attempted to use the Committee on Agricultural Problems as a device to develop pressure against Western controls on the export of strategic goods.

After 1950 the UN's work concerning the world food shortage began to be based on a longer time perspective. At first, there was little change in Soviet policy. The USSR continued to abstain from the UN's practical work in this field and to attack the West in the general discussions. On one occasion, in 1951, the Soviet Union vainly sought to append strictures against the arms race to an Assembly resolution dealing with food and famine.[67] A year later, the USSR opposed a resolution, introduced by India and Indonesia, which among other things linked the food shortage with population growth. Soviet delegate Georgy P. Arkadev argued that: "The shortage was actually attributable to capitalist ideas of economics and the remedy

[66] See: David Wightman, *Economic Cooperation in Europe*, p. 149.
[67] UN Document A/C. 2/134.

was to take specific action, such as land reform, and to apply to agricultural production the modern methods which had proved their merit in socialist countries." [68]

1954-1962

As the USSR's general policy changed, however, its attitude toward these questions also shifted. The Soviet Union's new course was characterized by moderation and somewhat more extensive participation in the UN's activities.

In 1954 Soviet delegates played an active and constructive part in the third session of ECE's Committee on Agricultural Problems, and their conduct at subsequent sessions of the Committee followed this pattern.

That same year, at the General Assembly's ninth session, the USSR supported a resolution which requested that FAO examine the question of establishing a world food reserve which could be used to relieve emergency situations and to counteract excessive price fluctuations.[69] Since the United States opposed the resolution, there was some political capital to be gained from this action. The split between the majority and the United States continued in ECOSOC and Assembly discussions of the problem during the next two years. In these debates the Soviet Union sided with the majority, and voted for the resolutions which that group favored. In 1956 the Soviet Union even voted for a resolution which the United States proposed concerning international cooperation in the establishment of national food reserves, and in 1960, although it protested that the proposal was a device to gain votes for the Eisenhower Administration, and despite the defeat of several Byelorussian amendments,[70] it voted for an American-sponsored resolution on the provision of food surpluses to feed deficient peoples through the United Nations system. However, the following year, when the World Food Program began to take definite shape as an experimental, three-year joint UN/FAO project for the multilateral utilization of surplus food, financed through voluntary contributions which it was hoped would total $100,000,000, the USSR abstained from voting on the relevant resolu-

[68] UN, General Assembly, Second Committee, *Official Records* (7th Session), p. 317.
[69] UN, General Assembly, Second Committee, *Official Records* (9th Session), p. 229.
[70] UN Document A/C. 2/L. 468.

tions in ECOSOC and the Assembly. It has followed this course since then, even though on one occasion, at the thirty-third session of the Economic and Social Council, Poland voted for the resolution under consideration. In the debates, the USSR has raised various doubts about the program, but it has given as the reason for its abstention, the fact that it was not a member of FAO and therefore was not intimately familiar with the project.

As can be inferred from several of these actions—since many of the resolutions involved FAO—in the period since 1953 Soviet hostility toward the Food and Agriculture Organization has lessened considerably. Moreover, the Soviet bloc's boycott of the agency has been discontinued. In 1957 Poland resumed membership and four years later Romania joined the agency. In 1957 Hungary also asked if it could resume its membership and the Ukrainian SSR applied for admission, but both states requested that the consideration of their applications be postponed. The Soviet Union itself, though, has made no move to join the Food and Agriculture Organization, although it did begin to supply information on its agricultural production directly to the FAO Secretariat. Apparently the USSR still prefers unfettered freedom with regard to its domestic and external agricultural policy to whatever benefits it might gain from increased international cooperation. At the same time, if the Ukrainian SSR were to join the agency, the USSR conceivably could receive many of the benefits of membership with few of the costs.

Until the Soviet Union achieves a more active connection with FAO, its role in this aspect of the UN's work is bound to be peripheral. Since 1954 the USSR has gained something through its new policies. In particular, it has probably ingratiated itself with the underdeveloped countries by supporting their position concerning the world food reserve, but the restricted nature of its participation has been obvious to all, and this has circumscribed its gains.

CONCLUSIONS

The most distinctive feature of Soviet policy with regard to the UN's work concerning relief and reconstruction problems has been the limited extent to which the USSR has been willing to become involved in international cooperation. Although after the Second World War the Soviet Union apparently would have liked to have received economic assistance from the United Nations, the price which it was willing to pay in terms of involvement in UN activities was extremely small. The USSR seemed hyper-cautious about giving the UN, or any international organization, significant power. Probably the most important reason for this was the Soviet desire to consolidate its position in Eastern Europe. A desire to protect its own sovereignty and closed system was another basic factor. A profound suspicion of the West and of the UN and a deep sense of the Soviet Union's uniqueness were also important ingredients in the Soviet position. In addition, at that time the USSR was preoccupied with the problems of rebuilding its own society. The Soviet Union had suffered heavy damage during the war—much more than many in the West realized—and domestic reconstruction clearly had first priority on the USSR's available resources. The Soviet Union could spare little for the UN's work. Any Soviet contribution at that time would have been dwarfed by that of the West. The Soviet Union has frequently demonstrated great sensitivity concerning its relative status and has often shown extreme reluctance to become involved in any situation where invidious comparisons might be possible. The Soviet Union may have participated in the United Nations activities to the extent that it did only to placate its Eastern European satellites, which in the immediate postwar period evidenced considerable interest in international cooperation. Had it not been for this, the USSR's role might have been even smaller.

The impact of the Soviet Union on the United Nations work concerning relief and reconstruction has essentially been negative. It was limiting first in that the USSR's general political demeanor immediately after the Second World War including its policy in the UN, contributed to the Western decisions to choose other channels for the major postwar economic assistance programs. The impact has also been limiting in that the Soviet refusal to participate in the concrete work which the United Nations has undertaken has given this work a less than global orientation.

It is impossible to measure the impact of Soviet attacks against the West and the United Nations. After the first few sessions, the USSR was unable to influence the course of the UN's activities. Few in the UN seem to have been impressed by the Soviet charges and protestations of good will; the USSR's refusal to participate in the organization's concrete work was all too evident. Those outside the UN who were not as familiar with the actual situation, however, may have been more impressed. Soviet polemics made good copy for journalists and were as widely reported as any feature of this segment of the UN's work. The general impact on public opinion, however, must have been small; it seems to have done little to alter the course of events.

It is interesting to speculate about what would have happened had either side chosen to place greater emphasis on the United Nations in the years immediately after the Second World War. Had the Soviet Union been a more willing participant, the United Kingdom and the United States probably would have found it more difficult to avoid channeling at least a portion of their major economic assistance programs through the world organization, and this might have led to the USSR's receiving some aid. Whether the price of this aid would have been as high as the Soviet Union apparently feared is an open question. Certainly the United Nations did not become an extremely powerful economic and social agency. Nevertheless, there is evidence that noncommunist groups in Eastern Europe viewed cooperation in the UN as a means of buttressing their position internally.[71] Allowing the world organization to assume a greater role, therefore, might have made the consolidation of Soviet power in Eastern Europe more difficult. The divisions which occurred among the Eastern European states on UN votes concerning relief and reconstruction problems are certainly evidence of some centrifugal forces. Perhaps it would have been in the interest of the Western powers to place greater emphasis on the UN in order to exploit these tendencies. Realistically, though, the results of such efforts probably would not have been of major importance, for greater emphasis on the United Nations would not have affected the basic factors which allowed the USSR to achieve a dominant position in Eastern Europe.

All of this, however, remains only speculation. The United Nations' real role in aiding the devastated states of the Second World War was limited, and what activities there were, came to be conducted almost exclusively among noncommunist states. The latter part of the generalization applies broadly to the UN's activities concerning relief and reconstruction.

The record clearly indicates that activities and work in this area cannot be approached on an apolitical basis, as the functionalists would have it, for they almost inevitably have political overtones and could have profound political consequences. Aiding a devastated area

---

[71] See: David Wightman, *Economic Cooperation in Europe*, p. 16.

is not only a humanitarian gesture, it also carries with it an opportunity to shape the future. The USSR's refusal to become deeply involved in the UN's relief and reconstruction activities signifies, among other things, its rejection of the largely Western image of the future implicit in these activities.

5: SOCIAL WELFARE

ARTICLE 55 OF THE CHARTER DIRECTS THE UNITED NATIONS *inter alia* to promote "conditions of . . . social progress"; "solutions of international . . . social, health and related problems; and international cultural and educational cooperation." The activities which have been undertaken as a result of this mandate are numerous and range widely. Some, particularly in the early years, were primarily relief operations. Other UN activities have involved attempts on an international level to combat such social evils as drug addiction. Still other UN activities have attempted to analyze basic social problems and to facilitate progress in such areas as housing, community development and family and child welfare. As the United Nations generally became increasingly oriented toward underdeveloped areas, so did its social welfare activities. This changed the focus of several programs and also led to the inauguration of new activities. In addition to the social welfare functions that have been undertaken by the United Nations itself, two specialized agencies, the World Health Organization and the United Nations Educational, Scientific and Cultural Organization (although most aspects of their work are beyond the scope of this study) have developed extensive programs in this area.

ADVISORY SOCIAL WELFARE SERVICES

One of the first things which the UN did in this field was to assume responsibility for the continuation of the United Nations Relief and Rehabilitation Administration's advisory social welfare functions. UNRRA's social welfare work included: the training of personnel, aid in the rehabilitation of the physically handicapped, aid in the restoration of social welfare institutions and activities, and coordination of the activities of voluntary agencies. When it became clear that UNRRA's mandate would soon expire, the UNRRA Council authorized the transfer of these functions to the UN. Negotiations in the United Nations to achieve this began at the third session of the Economic and Social Council in the fall of 1946 and were completed that December with the adoption of General Assembly Resolution 58 (I). The Soviet Union played an active role only in the last stage; that is, in drafting the Assembly resolution.

At first, the USSR argued that the transfer of these functions to the UN could serve no useful purpose; advice was of secondary importance to the devastated countries, their most pressing need being that of obtaining material assistance.[1] Other Eastern European states, however, took a different view. Poland, for one, supported the proposal that the United Nations should assume these functions. Perhaps because of this, the USSR modified its position and eventually voted for the transfer, though Soviet delegates continued to contest the details of the program.[2]

The Secretary-General received a flood of applications for assistance under the Advisory Social Welfare Services Program. Several of the requests came from Eastern European states, as perhaps was to be expected, since they had been among the largest recipients of UNRRA's program in this field. Even the Ukrainian Soviet Socialist Republic submitted a request for: four fellowships in the United States to study prosthetic aid; prostheses models of all kinds; equipment and tools for the manufacture of prostheses; and general literature on the subject. This request was approved and all aspects of it were carried out except the fellowship program. Despite repeated appeals from the UN Secretariat, the Ukrainian government never forwarded nominations for the fellowships. On the other hand, during the early years, the USSR was willing to allow its nationals to participate as experts. In 1947, one of the twenty-four experts in the field under this program was a Soviet national, and the following year, two of the twenty-one were citizens of the USSR.

Because of the number of requests for assistance, ECOSOC soon had to create a system of priorities. Soviet bloc delegates unsuccessfully sought to establish the principle that first consideration should

---

[1] See: UN Documents A/C. 3/Sub. 1/6, pp. 4-5, and A/C. 3/Sub. 1/7, p. 4.
[2] See: UN Document A/C. 3/Sub. 1/10, p. 5; and UN, General Assembly, Fifth Committee, *Official Records* (1st Session, 2nd Part), pp. 257, 259.

SOCIAL WELFARE 119

be given to UN member states which had been victims of Fascist aggression and had received UNRRA assistance.[3] Instead, in March 1947, the Council decided that the sole criterion should be need. This meant that Latin-American and Asian states as well as such countries as Austria and Italy could receive equal consideration with those which had previously been favored.

That decision was the first step toward putting the Advisory Social Welfare Services Program on a more permanent basis and de-emphasizing its relief aspects. The United Nations moved further in this direction in the fall of 1947. Discussions were launched then which implied that the program would become a regular feature of the work of the United Nations. The negotiations, which lasted over three years, concerned details rather than the principle.

Although the USSR did not object to this program's being given permanent status, until 1950 it argued with dogged persistence that the program should be financed so that it would not constitute a charge on the regular UN budget. The suggestion which it advanced most frequently was that the expenses should be borne principally by the governments which requested assistance.[4] Soviet delegates argued that the quality of the services would be improved if the recipients had to meet the costs, that "efficient" experts would be chosen then. This position found no support. The Western states wanted to re-orient the program toward the underdeveloped countries. Its value for such states, or for the war-devastated states for that matter, would be greatly reduced if the recipients had to pay the costs of the services. Since it was one of the few operating programs which the UN had undertaken under the terms of Article 55, there was strong pressure to preserve its integrity. In an important vote in the Social Commission in September 1947, even Czechoslovakia, Poland and Yugoslavia—the other Eastern European states represented on the Commission—opposed a proposal which the USSR submitted concerning this matter.[5] Their position was understandable; at that time they were among the principal beneficiaries of the program.

Because of the rejection of its position on financing, in 1949 the

[3] See: UN Document E/CN. 5/SR. 20, pp. 4-8.
[4] See: UN Documents E/AC. 7/SR. 17, p. 4; E/CN. 5/SR. 31, pp. 6-8; E/CN. 5/SR. 36, pp. 3-4; E/AC. 7/SR. 25, pp. 6-7; E/CN. 5/SR. 61, p. 6; E/AC. 7/SR. 47, pp. 12-13; E/CN. 5/SR. 86, pp. 5-6; and, E/AC. 7/SR. 84, pp. 5-6.
[5] UN Document E/CN. 5/SR. 36, p. 5.

Soviet Union voted against the ECOSOC resolution which recommended that the General Assembly should place the Advisory Social Welfare Services Program on a continuing basis, and when the Assembly took this action at the fourth session, it abstained. Despite the earlier split, the Soviet bloc voted as a unit on these decisions. The following year, at the Assembly's fifth session, when terms of reference for the program were finally approved, the Soviet Union abstained again, but this time only because the resolution (418 [V]) allowed for the possibility that increased funds might be needed.[6]

When the program was next reviewed in 1959, Soviet policies had changed, and the USSR voted for an ECOSOC resolution which recommended that the funds for this work, which over the years had been increased from $670,186 to $925,000 per year, be increased still further to meet the growing needs of underdeveloped countries, especially in Africa. The Soviet Union followed a similar course in 1961 and, in addition, suggested that a greater share of the funds should be utilized for on-the-spot training of national social welfare personnel.[7] This recommendation, which was adopted in a modified form, represented the first Soviet effort to influence the character of the program. It was analogous to proposals which the USSR advanced in other areas emphasizing the training of national cadres. Another Soviet suggestion, which was introduced simultaneously and which also was incorporated in the final resolution, implied that the USSR wanted to have some of its nationals chosen to serve as experts under the program. None had been chosen since 1948. Moreover, since the reconstruction period, only two recipients of fellowships under the program had elected to study in the USSR, one each year in 1959 and 1960.

Whether or not these moves presaged significantly increased Soviet participation in the Advisory Social Welfare Services Program was not clear. For a time, the Eastern European states had discontinued all connections with this work. However, after its break with the Soviet bloc, Yugoslavia resumed participation. In 1957 a program of aid to Poland was reinaugurated and the following year the list of experts included one Polish citizen. These two countries have continued to be actively involved since then, both as recipients and as sources of assistance. In 1962 Czechoslovakia also served as a host

[6] UN, General Assembly, Third Committee, *Official Records* (5th Session), p. 22.
[7] E/CN. 5/L. 255.

country for two fellows. In 1961 and 1962 one Soviet expert was chosen to serve under the program. In addition, in the latter year five recipients of fellowships elected to study in the USSR. While these figures were extremely small in terms of the total numbers involved in the program (in 1962 there were 160 experts and 350 fellowships), at least the Soviet bloc was more engaged than it had been. However, there was little evidence that the USSR had reevaluated the intrinsic merits of the program; rather, the changes in its attitude seemed to have stemmed from the broader changes in Soviet policies.

THE UNITED NATIONS CHILDREN'S FUND

At the same time that the United Nations considered the question of assuming responsibility for the continuation of UNRRA's advisory social welfare services, it also examined the issue of continuing UNRRA's other activity in this area, its program of assistance to children. The paramount importance of continuing this aid was generally recognized, and the UNRRA Council had passed a separate resolution recommending that the UN create an International Children's Emergency Fund and providing for the allocation of UNRRA's residual assets to such an organization. As in the case of the advisory social welfare services, negotiations began in ECOSOC in the fall of 1946 and were completed shortly thereafter at the second part of the General Assembly's first session. Here too, the Soviet Union played an active role only in the Assembly discussions.

Soviet efforts were mainly directed toward the structure of the new organization. The USSR sought to restrict the power of the administrative authority, the Executive Director, in relation to the political body, the Executive Board. The latter was to consist of twenty-four states which were named in the resolution, including the six Eastern European states which were then members of the UN (later the Board became an elective body and its size was increased to thirty). The Soviet Union's position was consistent with its general attitude toward organizational questions, and over the years it has continued to advance similar proposals.[8] The USSR's efforts on this occasion, though, were without avail; United States proposals with the opposite effect were adopted. And an American, Maurice Pate, a former invest-

[8] See: UN Document E/ICEF/SR. 195, p. 5.

ment banker, was immediately chosen as Executive Director, and he has served in that capacity since then.

Despite its defeat on the structural questions, the USSR voted for the establishment of the United Nations International Children's Emergency Fund, or UNICEF as it came to be known. Perhaps it was influenced by the attitude of other Eastern European states. They were much more enthusiastic than the USSR. Poland even joined the United States in co-sponsoring an amendment to broaden UNICEF's activities to include "child health purposes generally" as well as relief and rehabilitation. It may have done this because Mrs. Franklin D. Roosevelt clearly indicated in the debate that her government would be more willing to contribute to an organization with broader functions. Or perhaps it was because of the personality of the Polish representative, Dr. Ludwik Rajchman, a former director of the League Health Organization, who later became Chairman of UNICEF's Executive Board.

The interests of the Eastern European states were well protected under the terms of reference contained in the resolution which the Assembly adopted, 57 (I). In fact, their position was even more favorable than it had been in UNRRA, and during UNICEF's first two years of operations these states received almost half of the available funds. This was the result of a general consensus on the vast needs of children in these countries, rather than Soviet pressures. The terms of reference provided in Resolution 57 (I) remained in effect until 1950, when the Assembly, by passing Resolution 417 (V), took the first step toward putting the Fund on a permanent basis. This process was completed three years later with the passage of General Assembly Resolution 802 (VIII). At that time, the organization's name was shortened to United Nations Children's Fund, although for the sake of euphony the more frequently used initials were not changed.

After its establishment UNICEF's most pressing problem was to obtain funds. The program was to be, and has been, financed outside of the UN's regular budget. An initial contribution of $550,000 was made from UNRRA's Emergency Food Collection Fund. This money had been donated by voluntary agencies and private individuals in the United States. UNRRA's ultimate contribution, the entire sum of its residual assets, finally amounted to more than $32,200,000. Voluntary contributions from governments, however, have become the most important source of funds. In 1961 the United States contributed over 40 per cent of UNICEF's income of $27,900,000, and in the early years its contribution was proportionately even higher. Of the Soviet bloc, Bulgaria, Hungary, Poland, Czechoslovakia, and Yugoslavia donated money during the first few years. However, all but Yugoslavia discontinued their contributions during the early nineteen fifties. The USSR did not contribute anything until 1955. Its initial contribution signaled the resumption of general Eastern European financial support for UNICEF. From 1955 through 1960, the USSR made an annual contribution of two million unconvertible rubles, or $500,000 at the official rate of exchange then in effect. The constancy of the USSR's contribution during this period stood in contrast to the increases in those of almost all other states, unless the new contributions of 300,000 rubles ($75,000) from the Ukraine and 150,000 rubles ($37,500) from Byelorussia in 1958 should be credited as an increase in the Soviet Union's. During these years the United States contribution grew from $9,000,000 to $12,000,000. In ECOSOC and the Assembly, the USSR successfully opposed all phrases in resolutions concerning UNICEF which might be interpreted as urging it to enlarge its contribution. However, in 1960 at the fifteenth session of the Assembly, the Soviet Union dropped this position, and in 1961 the total contribution for the USSR, the Ukraine and Byelorussia was increased by 41 per cent to $862,500. The three contributed the same amount in 1962 and 1963. Interestingly, Poland and Bulgaria increased their contributions in 1960, before the USSR did. Despite the fact that the Soviet contribution must be spent in the USSR, there have not been any serious problems concerning its utilization.[9]

In addition to governmental contributions, UNICEF has also benefited from private funds. Individual donations have always been possible, and in 1948, 1949 and 1950 world-wide solicitations were conducted under the United Nations Appeal for Children (UNAC). Czechoslovakia, Poland and Yugoslavia were the only Eastern European countries to participate in UNAC, or to allow private donations, and the bulk of the money collected in these three countries was used for relief programs within their own borders. The USSR's delegates abstained from voting on resolutions concerning UNAC.

In spite of its limited financial participation, the USSR has always been a member of UNICEF's Executive Board and has served on

[9] See the interesting Profile of Maurice Pate, "At the Heart of UNICEF," *The New Yorker*, December 2, 1961, pp. 69-112, pp. 102, 105.

some of the Board's most important committees, though it has not made extensive use of these positions. In the early years, Soviet delegates sought to emphasize the needs of Eastern Europe. They opposed attempts to diminish the priority given to "invaded" countries and also a British appeal for assistance for Hong Kong, Singapore, Malaya, Northern Borneo, Sarawak and Brunei, claiming that there was not even enough money available to satisfy the need of countries which had "suffered from Fascist aggression." [10] In addition, Soviet delegates sought to insure that each side would receive its "proper" share of the funds allocated to states in which conditions of civil war existed.[11] Concretely, this meant giving aid to children in the areas of China and Greece held by the local communists and in those areas of the Netherlands East Indies held by the Republicans. On numerous occasions UNICEF's Executive Director affirmed his intention to be impartial in the distribution of aid, if at all possible, but these statements never satisfied Soviet delegates, and they occasionally succeeded in securing the adoption of resolutions instructing the Executive Director to be impartial.

Gradually Eastern European states began to lose their favored position in UNICEF's allocations. This was the result of a variety of factors. Probably the most important was the feeling among the principal contributors that the most pressing needs of children there had been met, and that the limited funds available could more profitably be used to help children in the chronically poor underdeveloped countries. The West also had political motives for the shift in emphasis. As cold war tensions heightened, the desire to help states in the Soviet orbit rapidly diminished. Assistance to Hungary was terminated in 1949 because the government violated its UNICEF agreement by exporting powdered milk, a commodity included in the program. Aid to Albania ceased in 1950 because it proved impossible to agree on a mission chief and his staff. By 1952 all aid to Soviet bloc countries had ceased. Yugoslavia, however, continued to receive UNICEF assistance, and in 1958 a small program for Poland was re-inaugurated. This program has been continued, and in 1962 Poland was the only European country to receive UNICEF assistance.

[10] See: UN Document E/ICEF/SR. 12, p. 9.
[11] See: UN Documents E/ICEF/SR. 11, p. 7; E/ICEF/SR. 12, pp. 5, 9; E/ICEF/SR. 15, pp. 12, 14-15; E/ICEF/SR. 30, p. 4; E/ICEF/SR. 38, pp. 7-8; and, E/ICEF/SR. 53, p. 8; and, UN, General Assembly, Third Committee, *Official Records* (2nd Session), p. 125.

Soviet delegates protested the de-emphasis as it occurred, particularly the cessation of aid to Hungary and Albania.[12] They denounced the Fund for its "discriminatory policy" and called it "a mere tool of the Anglo-Saxon bloc." They claimed that UNICEF had violated its terms of reference and the fundamental policies which the General Assembly had set for it. Outside the UN, the attack was conducted in even more vituperative tones. One commentator, writing in a Soviet journal in March 1950, characterized UNICEF as:

> . . . an organ that furthers the ends of the warmongers and abets the imperialist plotters against the freedom and welfare of the peoples and, primarily, against a happy future for the children.[13]

He accused UNICEF mission personnel in the People's Democracies of engaging in subversive activities. The Soviet attack, however, had no perceptible effect. The initial decisions putting the Children's Fund on a permanent basis were adopted during its most virulent period.

Soviet delegates have always been alert to connections between UNICEF activities and the USSR's general policies, attempting to prevent actions which might contravene these policies, or conversely, to utilize Fund activities to advance Soviet objectives. Thus they objected, albeit unsuccessfully, to UNICEF's aiding children in Germany on a zonal basis, claiming that the only correct approach was through the Allied Control Council in Germany, and that Germany must be treated as a unit.[14] They also argued that the request for aid in Japan should have emanated from the "Allied Command in Japan" rather than "the United States Department of the Army." [15] Later, when the Soviet Union sought to gain recognition

---

[12] See: UN Documents E/ICEF/SR. 33, p. 3; E/ICEF/SR. 37, p. 2; E/ICEF/SR. 60, pp. 11-14; E/ICEF/SR. 61, p. 13; E/ICEF/SR. 62; E/ICEF/SR. 72, p. 6; E/ICEF/SR. 76, pp. 6, 13; E/CN. 5/SR. 151, pp. 15-16; E/AC. 7/SR. 182, p. 10; E/ICEF/SR. 78, pp. 6-7; E/ICEF/SR. 81/Add. 1, pp. 14-15; and, E/AC. 7/SR. 198; and also, UN, ECOSOC, *Official Records* (9th Session), p. 459; UN, General Assembly, Third Committee, *Official Records* (4th Session), p. 169; UN, ECOSOC, *Official Records* (12th Session), pp. 335-336; and, UN, ECOSOC, *Official Records* (13th Session), p. 246.

[13] N. Yevgeyev, "What Some International Bodies Are Really Doing," p. 14.

[14] See: UN Documents E/ICEF/SR. 15, pp. 7 ff.; E/CN. 5/SR. 59, p. 6; E/ICEF/C. 1/SR. 51, p. 3; E/ICEF/C. 1/SR. 52, p. 5; E/ICEF/SR. 36, p. 7; and, E/ICEF/SR. 73, p. 4.

[15] UN Document E/ICEF/SR. 46, p. 6 and UN, ECOSOC, *Official Records* (8th Session), pp. 646-647.

of the German Democratic Republic and the People's Republic of China, the USSR's delegate sought to prevent an amendment to UNICEF's terms of reference which would limit the Executive Board to members of the UN or specialized agencies.[16] On another occasion, in September 1957, the Soviet delegate used an Executive Board meeting to expatiate on the dangers to children caused by the testing of nuclear weapons.[17] The Soviet Union also attempted that year and in 1958 to have Russian made a working language of the Executive Board, but without success. As in the case of a similar attempt with regard to ECOSOC, prestige and recognition probably ranked equally with convenience as motivating factors. Consistent with its general policy toward the UN Secretariat, in 1961 the USSR began to criticize the distribution of posts in the upper levels of UNICEF's staff and to urge the appointment of more citizens from Soviet bloc countries.[18] Soviet delegates argued that the same principles concerning geographic distribution that were applied to the UN Secretariat should be applied to the UNICEF staff.

Many UNICEF activities—actually the greatest share since 1950—have had no direct implications for the USSR or the Soviet bloc. The Soviet Union has not pursued a particularly active policy with regard to these matters. In line with the USSR's general attitude, Soviet delegates have constantly stressed the need to minimize UNICEF's administrative expenses and to increase the proportion of funds allocated to the provision of supplies.[19] The Soviet Union unsuccessfully argued against the inauguration of a program of technical assistance in milk conservation, maintaining that the available money should simply be given to the governments concerned for the purchase of cattle. It also unsuccessfully opposed allocations for medical personnel in the BCG anti-tuberculosis program, claiming that the funds should be used for the purchase of syringes, needles, tuberculin and vaccine.

In 1948 and 1949, Soviet delegates welcomed the first signs of the trend in UNICEF to devote increasing attention to the needs of

[16] UN, ECOSOC, *Official Records* (21st Session), pp. 114, 116.
[17] UN Document E/ICEF/SR. 182, pp. 11-12.
[18] UN Documents E/ICEF/SR. 258, p. 14, and E/ICEF/SR. 263, p. 12.
[19] See: UN Documents E/ICEF/SR. 12, p. 5; E/CN. 5/SR. 40, p. 5; E/ICEF/SR. 51, pp. 13-14; E/ICEF/SR. 54, pp. 9-10; and, E/ICEF/SR. 72, pp. 6-7; and also, UN, ECOSOC, *Official Records* (5th Session), pp. 32, 34; UN, ECOSOC, *Official Records* (8th Session), pp. 646-647; and, E/ICEF/SR. 258, pp. 13-14.

children in underdeveloped areas. They asserted that the child health and welfare problems revealed in various UNICEF reports were striking evidence of the neglect and exploitation of colonies by metropolitan states.[20] But when the decisions were taken to accelerate this trend, and to put UNICEF on a permanent basis with the understanding that its work would primarily be directed toward children in underdeveloped areas, Soviet delegates did not follow this lead. They were absent from some of the crucial negotiations because of the Chinese representation boycott, and when they were present, their efforts were devoted to protesting the cessation of programs in Eastern Europe. To emphasize their objections Soviet delegates even voted against an ECOSOC resolution dealing with UNICEF in 1951.[21] These protests were without avail, however, and the costs of opposing such a popular program were high. In recognition of this, the following year Soviet policy was that of abstention, and by 1953 unanimity on UNICEF was restored, even though Soviet delegates remained silent when this subject was discussed in ECOSOC and the Assembly.

Since 1955, when the USSR made its first contribution to the Fund, Soviet delegates have missed no occasion to state the USSR's support for UNICEF and its programs. In addition, after 1955 Soviet delegates on the Executive Board became more active than they had been previously, although their role has remained relatively minor. They have stressed the importance in this field of action by national governments, as opposed to private individuals and voluntary agencies. Among other things, this has provided opportunities for fervid descriptions of the USSR's progress with respect to these matters. Soviet delegates have also stressed the importance of training indigenous personnel instead of dispatching consultants and have argued that these people should be trained at home rather than abroad.[22] Beyond this, interventions by Soviet delegates—who often seem to have been hampered by vague or late instructions—have mainly been limited to supporting programs which were favored by underdeveloped states.

This support is probably indicative of the most important motivation for Soviet policy concerning UNICEF since the early nineteen

[20] UN Documents E/ICEF/SR. 34, p. 3; E/ICEF/SR. 36, p. 3; E/ICEF/SR. 38, p. 5; and, E/ICEF/SR. 51, p. 9.
[21] UN, ECOSOC, *Official Records* (12th Session), pp. 335-336.
[22] See: UN Documents E/ICEF/SR. 263, p. 12; and, E/ICEF/SR. 268, p. 10.

fifties. The Soviet Union probably began to contribute to this program because of its interest in influencing the underdeveloped states. The size and relative constancy of the Soviet contribution do not indicate great enthusiasm for the program. Yet it can no longer be said that the USSR does not contribute to UNICEF. In internal negotiations, Soviet backing has helped the underdeveloped states and has cost the USSR virtually nothing. At the same time, it has created a new pressure for the West. A similar explanation might also be advanced for earlier Soviet policies; that is, the USSR may well have been forced to support UNICEF to the limited extent that it did because of the program's popularity with other Eastern European states.

SOCIAL DEFENSE

The United Nations legacy in the social welfare area extended far beyond UNRRA's activities, even though these certainly were the most urgent tasks. By the time the UN came into being, many steps had been taken on an international level to combat social evils. Developments in modern technology were partially responsible for this, for it had become impossible to work effectively on a purely national level. Numerous conventions establishing measures of international cooperation and control and pledging national action had been negotiated, signed and ratified, some under League auspices, and others earlier. After attempting to meet the immediate relief needs, the United Nations began efforts to bring these conventions within its purview and to develop a broad program in the field of social defense.

THE SUPPRESSION OF TRAFFIC IN PERSONS AND OBSCENE PUBLICATIONS

In 1947 negotiations were begun concerning the assumption by the United Nations of the League's activities with regard to the suppression of traffic in persons and obscene publications. Three Conventions were involved,[23] each of which contained an article, which was

[23] The Convention for the Suppression of the Traffic in Women and Children of September 30, 1921; the Convention for the Suppression of the Traffic in Women of Full Age of October 11, 1933; and the Convention for the Suppression of the Circulation of and Traffic in Obscene Publications of September 12, 1923. At that time the USSR had ratified only the last convention, it ratified the first two subsequently.

SOCIAL WELFARE 129

customary in international law, permitting signatory states to adhere separately for each of their dependent territories. It allowed such territories to exercise a measure of self-government and to decide for themselves which international obligations they wished to assume. It was difficult for colonial powers—especially the United Kingdom— to adhere to international conventions which did not contain these so-called colonial application clauses. In the Assembly debate, Soviet delegates charged that this was actually an "escape clause" which permitted colonial powers to maintain illicit traffic in their dependent territories, and they submitted an amendment proposing that the clauses should be deleted from each convention before the UN would agree to assume the functions involved.[24] Debate was heated and emotional and at times confused and ill-informed. Protestations by the metropolitan states did little to dampen anticolonial feelings. Nor did the United Kingdom delegate's statement that the treaties were applied to all British colonies have any perceptible effect. The Soviet amendment was ultimately adopted by a small margin.

The Soviet Union pursued a similar policy in 1948 when the General Assembly considered assuming functions previously exercised by the French government under agreements negotiated in the early years of the twentieth century concerning the suppression of the white slave trade and of the circulation of obscene publications.[25] The USSR proposed that the application of the treaties should be extended "to all the territories in regard to which a signatory state performs the functions of the governing and administering authority."[26] On this occasion the Soviet proposal was rejected; perhaps because the issue was considered in the Assembly's more conservative Sixth (Legal) Committee rather than in the Third Committee.[27]

[24] UN, General Assembly, Third Committee, *Official Records* (2nd Session), pp. 92-93; UN, General Assembly, Plenary Meetings, *Official Records* (2nd Session), pp. 346-348; and, UN Document A/C. 3/165.

[25] The International Agreement of May 18, 1904, for the Suppression of the White Slave traffic, the International Convention of May 4, 1910, for the Suppression of the White Slave Traffic, and the Agreement of May 4, 1910, for the Suppression of the Circulation of Obscene Publications.

[26] UN, General Assembly, Sixth Committee, *Official Records* (3rd Session, 1st Part), p. 513; and, UN Document A/C. 6/274.

[27] States tend to assign delegates with legal backgrounds to the Sixth Committee. The Third Committee, on the other hand, usually contains the largest number of women. These differences in composition have had an impact on some of the detailed decisions, on matters probably not covered by broad instructions.

Having so many treaties on related subjects proved cumbersome; consequently, in 1948 work was begun in the United Nations on a new, comprehensive convention on the suppression of the traffic in persons and of the exploitation of the prostitution of others. Throughout the negotiations on this new convention, which were completed at the General Assembly's fourth session in the fall of 1949, Soviet policy concentrated on four clearly defined goals.

First, Soviet delegates attempted to eliminate the colonial application clause and to make the convention applicable to all territories governed and administered by a signatory state.[28] They succeeded. Secondly, Soviet delegates sought to block United States and French moves to insert a non-self-executing clause in the convention which was intended to facilitate signature by federal states.[29] They attacked the proposed article as "a colonial clause for federal states," and again, were successful. Third, Soviet delegates attempted to broaden the definition of procuring.[29a] Western delegates wanted to make the offense punishable only if it had been committed for purposes of gain. They held that without this concept, the definition of procuring would be legally obscure and might well lead to anomalies in prosecution. Soviet delegates argued, on the other hand, that prostitution was "incompatible with the elementary principles of morality and a crime offensive to public decency," and they held that those characteristics remained whatever "the motives of those who encouraged that disgraceful profession." The USSR was also successful in this instance. Finally, Soviet delegates sought to replace the provision that disputes under the convention should be referred to the International Court of Justice with a simple requirement of arbitration.[30] This was their sole failure.

[28] See: UN Documents E/CN. 5/SR. 70, p. 10; E/CN. 5/SR. 74, pp. 7, 11-12; E/AC. 7/SR. 82, pp. 11, 12; and, UN, General Assembly, Third Committee, *Official Records* (4th Session), pp. 41, 71; UN, General Assembly, Sixth Committee, *Official Records* (4th Session), pp. 391-392; and, UN, General Assembly, Plenary Meetings, *Official Records* (4th Session), pp. 469-471.

[29] See: UN Document E/CN. 5/SR. 76, p. 5; and, UN, General Assembly, Sixth Committee, *Official Records* (4th Session), pp. 390, 405-406, 407, 411, and 417-418.

[29a] See: UN Documents E/CN. 5/SR. 91, pp. 4, 5; E/AC. 7/SR. 81, p. 21; and UN, General Assembly, Third Committee, *Official Records* (4th Session), p. 22; UN, General Assembly, Plenary Meetings, *Official Records* (4th Session), pp. 462-464, and 471.

[30] See: UN Documents E/CN. 5/SR. 74, p. 5; and E/AC. 7/SR. 82, p. 11; and UN, General Assembly, Third Committee, *Official Records* (4th Session), p. 59.

In the negotiations on the Convention for the Suppression of the Traffic in Persons and of the Exploitation of the Prostitution of Others, the Soviet Union scored its successes in the Assembly's Third Committee and Plenary Sessions. Not once did the Soviet position prevail prior to this. The USSR gained a tactical advantage when the Anglo-American proposal to refer the Convention to the Sixth instead of the Third Committee was rejected, and it was decided to use the Sixth Committee only as a source of legal advice. As it was, the Sixth Committee expressed reservations concerning the legal implications of some of the Soviet amendments.

The negotiations provided several opportunities for Soviet attacks on capitalism. For example, in the Assembly's Third Committee, the Soviet delegate charged that the root of the evil of prostitution "lay in unemployment and improper living conditions." [31] The Soviet Union sought to pose as the protector of the downtrodden. Its task was made easier by the fact that because of the adoption of the Soviet amendments, the major Western powers, France, the United Kingdom and the United States felt they could not vote for the Convention nor ratify it. Subsequently, the Soviet bloc sought to exploit this situation.

The Soviet Union ratified the Convention in 1954. In doing so it made the formal declaration that in the USSR "the social conditions which give rise to the offences covered . . . have been eliminated." [32] It stated that it completed the ratification only because it recognized the international importance of suppressing the offenses which were involved. The USSR's ratification was also accompanied by a reservation concerning the jurisdiction of the International Court of Justice. Several other Soviet bloc countries ratified the Convention in the following years, and Poland had done so in 1952.

When the Convention and progress in this area were discussed in the spring of 1959 at the twelfth session of the Social Commission, the Soviet delegate noted that the problem was still "wide-spread, particularly in capitalist countries," and that many states including France, the United Kingdom and the United States had not yet ratified the Convention.[33] He urged them to follow the USSR's lead, and Czechoslovakia, with full Soviet support, submitted a draft resolution urging all states to ratify the Convention. Both the Commission

[31] UN, General Assembly, Third Committee, *Official Records* (4th Session), p. 40.
[32] UN, *Treaty Series*, Vol. 196 (1954), p. 349.
[33] UN Document, E/CN. 5/SR. 294, p. 5.

and the Economic and Social Council ultimately adopted this resolution, but only after it was amended so that it was an exhortation to governments to ratify the convention or to "attempt to implement its principal provisions." Although this amendment protected the legal position of the Western powers, it did not erase the subtle barbs interjected into the debate.

The Soviet Union has always brushed off questions concerning prostitution or traffic in persons in the USSR with the assertion that because of fundamental changes in the social system such problems do not exist. No other reply has ever been given to the UN. Poland and Hungary have been more candid.[34]

The impact of Soviet policy on opinion is difficult to measure, but the adoption of several Soviet proposals in the United Nations would indicate at least a degree of success. In the General Assembly, where the anticolonial forces were strongest, Soviet proposals found a receptive audience. The impact on the UN's work is somewhat clearer. Emotion was introduced into what previously were regarded as technical matters, and measures of legal control were so altered that several Western states with the highest social standards felt that they could no longer participate.

The Prevention of Crime and the Treatment of Offenders

In contrast to the situation with regard to other matters of social defense, very little work had been done at an international level in the field of the prevention of crime and the treatment of offenders. The International Penal and Penitentiary Commission (IPPC) had been established in 1872, but it was the only international agency working in this area until the UN began its activities.

In 1948 the USSR strongly opposed the inauguration of a UN program concerning the prevention of crime and the treatment of offenders. It argued that a program in this area would constitute an infringement of national sovereignty.[35] Later that year, the Soviet Union proposed that the UN's activities in this field should be restricted to questions on which international agreements already existed, such as genocide, warmongering, slavery, narcotics, prostitution and obscene publications.[36] Only the Soviet bloc supported this suggestion.

[34] See: UN Document ST/SOA/SER. M. 13, *International Review of Criminal Policy*, No. 13 (October 1958).
[35] UN Document E/CN. 5/SR. 64, pp. 2-4.
[36] UN Documents E/AC. 7/SR. 48, p. 15 and E/AC. 7/W. 33.

SOCIAL WELFARE   133

Instead ECOSOC authorized the Secretariat to begin a modest, though comprehensive, program of activities, including the convocation of a number of regional conferences. The program also included the assumption of the functions of the International Penal and Penitentiary Commission.

The USSR has never shown much interest in these activities. Soviet legal doctrine continues to hold the view that "the campaign against crime is an internal matter." [37] The Soviet Union has never participated in any of the technical conferences of the European Consultative Group, nor has it appointed an individual correspondent to keep the Secretariat informed of developments in this field in the USSR. The Soviet Union did not participate in the First United Nations Congress on the Prevention of Crime and the Treatment of Offenders in 1955, but it did send a delegation to the Second Congress in 1960. The fact that problems of underdeveloped countries were given emphasis at the Second Congress perhaps explains the USSR's attendance. In addition, starting in 1957, the Soviet Union has occasionally voted for resolutions in this field. Its policy, however, has appeared almost quixotic, for quite similar resolutions have alternately been condemned as violating domestic jurisdiction or supported without any apparent rationale.

THE INTERNATIONAL CONTROL OF NARCOTIC DRUGS

ASSUMING THE LEAGUE'S FUNCTIONS

As in the case of activities concerning the suppression of traffic in persons and obscene publications, the United Nations first task with respect to the international control of narcotic drugs was that of assuming the functions which had been exercised by the League of Nations. This involved arranging for the transfer of powers which had been assigned to the League of Nations under several international agreements, conventions and protocols.[38] In the negotiations concerning the protocol of transfer, which were completed in December 1946, the USSR concentrated on only one goal, the exclusion of

[37] Academy of Sciences of the USSR, *International Law*, p. 167.

[38] These were: The Hague Convention of January 23, 1912; The Geneva Convention of February 19, 1925; the Limitation Convention of July 13, 1931; the Convention for the Suppression of the Illicit Traffic of June 26, 1936; the Geneva Agreement of February 11, 1925, on Opium Smoking; and, the Bangkok Agreement of November 26, 1931, on Opium Smoking. The Soviet Union was a signatory to all but the Conventions of January 23, 1912, and June 26, 1936.

Fascist Spain.³⁹ Notwithstanding protests from international officials and members of national delegations that the proposed exclusion would weaken the international control of narcotic drugs, the Soviet Union achieved its goal. Spain was excluded completely until the Assembly removed the ban on its participation in UN activities in 1950, and in many respects the exclusion continued until 1955, when ECOSOC adopted a special resolution inviting Spain to become a party to the Protocols of 1946 and 1948.

One of the conventions had provided for the creation of the Permanent Central Opium Board (PCOB), an independent control body. The protocol of transfer provided the PCOB should continue as a United Nations organ. In negotiations in 1947 concerning the details, the USSR objected to the requirement that persons appointed to the Board could not hold any office which would place them in a position of direct dependence on their government.⁴⁰ Soviet delegates claimed that this provision would make it impossible for individuals from socialist states to serve on PCOB. At one point the USSR even suggested that all members of the Board should be governmental representatives. Finally, the Economic and Social Council, to which PCOB was responsible, adopted an interpretation of the relevant article which in effect allowed individuals who held governmental positions to be members of the Board.⁴¹

The League's system of enforcement was badly in need of revision by the time that the United Nations took it over. Modern pharmacology and chemistry had developed many new synthetic drugs since the last convention had been adopted and new control measures were urgently needed. Accordingly, in 1947 ECOSOC began work on a new protocol which would cover all harmful synthetic drugs, both those in existence and, it was hoped, those yet to be discovered. On the basis of the Council's instructions, the Secretary-General prepared a draft protocol. When this was discussed in 1948 in the Commission on Narcotic Drugs, ECOSOC, and the Assembly, the Soviet Union's sole contribution was to insist on the elimination of the colonial application clause.⁴² In this case the Soviet proposal was

---

³⁹ See: UN Documents E/AC. 12/4, pp. 2-3; and E/AC. 17/7, pp. 2-3, 5, 6-7, 8; and, UN, ECOSOC, *Official Records* (3rd Session), pp. 57-58, 59.

⁴⁰ See: UN Documents E/AC. 7/2, p. 5, and E/AC. 7/SR. 36, p. 2; and also, UN, ECOSOC, *Official Records* (6th Session), pp. 66-67, 71-72.

⁴¹ ECOSOC Resolution 123 D (VI).

⁴² See: UN Documents E/CN. 7/155, pp. 42, 102, 107-108, 224; E/AC. 7/SR. 43, pp. 9, 12; and also UN, ECOSOC, *Official Records* (7th Session),

SOCIAL WELFARE   135

rather redundant, for the Protocol and the Convention of 1931, on which it was based, were written so that the control measures tended to apply to all states, whether or not they were signatories. Perhaps this explains why the several Soviet proposals were rejected. Nevertheless, in the Assembly's Third Committee a Soviet amendment was adopted which urged that all signatories should take as soon as possible the necessary steps in order to extend the application of this Protocol to territories for which they have international responsibility.[43]

THE 1953 PROTOCOL

As in the work with regard to the suppression of traffic in persons and obscene publications, the United Nations soon began an attempt to prepare a single convention which would replace the several international instruments concerning illicit traffic in narcotic drugs. This task, which was started in 1948, was not completed until 1961.

In view of the slow progress and the difficulties involved in preparing a single convention, several members of the Commission on Narcotic Drugs, particularly the United States, came to feel that it might be desirable to prepare an interim agreement limiting the production of opium to medicinal and scientific needs. Two methods of achieving this goal were discussed in the early nineteen fifties: one involved the creation of an international opium monopoly; the other, control through national agencies which would have monopoly powers over the production of, and international and wholesale trade in, opium. ECOSOC finally chose to proceed on the latter basis, and in 1953 convened a conference for the purpose of preparing a special protocol. The USSR opposed every decision which was taken with respect to the proposed interim agreement, refused to participate in the United Nations Opium Conference and has not ratified the Protocol which was completed there.[44] Soviet delegates held that nothing should stand in the way of work on the Single Convention. They also argued that an international monopoly would be beyond

---

pp. 213-214; UN, General Assembly, Third Committee, *Official Records* (3rd Session, 1st Part), pp. 9-10, 20, 22; and, UN, General Assembly, Plenary Meetings, *Official Records* (3rd Session, 1st Part), pp. 352-354.

[43] UN, General Assembly, Third Committee, *Official Records* (3rd Session, 1st Part), p. 26.

[44] The Protocol for Limiting and Regulating the Cultivation of the Poppy Plant, the Production of, International and Wholesale Trade in, and Use of Opium (1953).

the UN's jurisdiction and that any other measure would represent no improvement over the existing situation. Further, although this was never stated, the Soviet Union probably objected to the control features of the 1953 Protocol, which are the strongest ever to be included in treaty concerning this subject. In addition to the extensive system of national control and licensing involved, on an international level, the Permanent Central Opium Board is authorized to arrange a local inquiry into a country, with the express consent of the government, if it has reasons to assume that a gravely unsatisfactory opium situation exists, and PCOB is also authorized to recommend or impose an import and/or export embargo on opium. It is difficult to estimate the effects of Soviet opposition to the Protocol. The USSR has traditionally been a major producer of opium, but with the Soviet system, its production has been tightly controlled, and there appears to be little addiction within the Soviet Union. Because of these facts the control features of the 1953 Protocol probably seem unnecessarily burdensome to the USSR, as they do to various other European countries which do not have major narcotics problems and which also cultivate poppy for purposes other than opium. The USSR is one of the seven states which according to the 1953 Protocol are allowed to produce opium for export. The others are: Bulgaria, Greece, India, Iran, Turkey and Yugoslavia. Three of these states were required to ratify the Protocol before it could come into effect. Bulgaria and Yugoslavia (although the latter attended the 1953 Conference) have taken basically the same attitude as the USSR. Because of the opposition of these three states, the prospects for the Protocol appeared dim. India and Iran ratified the Protocol fairly early, but for several years it seemed as if a third ratification would not be gained from the states authorized to produce opium for export. Finally, however, Greece—which was included in the seven even though it was not actually an opium producer—took this step, and the Protocol came into force on March 8, 1963. Many features of the Protocol are designed to apply to all states and territories, whether or not they are parties. However, one official of the UN Division of Narcotic Drugs has stated that the Protocol cannot be "fully effective" without the participation of Bulgaria, the USSR and Yugoslavia.[45]

[45] Adolf Lande, "The Single Convention on Narcotic Drugs, 1961," *International Organization*, XVI, no. 4 (Autumn 1962), 776-797, p. 780.

The Single Convention on Narcotic Drugs

During the negotiations on the Single Convention on Narcotic Drugs, which culminated in a conference of plenipotentiaries in early 1961, the Soviet Union's concern for its sovereignty and basic conservatism in matters of international law, which probably were the fundamental sources of its opposition to the 1953 Protocol, came to the fore significantly. The USSR objected to proposals to give the new International Narcotics Control Board (INCB)—a body which eventually will replace PCOB and other organs—the power to conduct local inquiries in cases of suspected violations and to impose a mandatory embargo if it decided that a state had failed to carry out its obligations under the Convention.[46]

Although PCOB had been given such powers by the 1953 Protocol, they failed to receive the necessary two-thirds majority at the 1961 Conference, and thus were not included in the Single Convention. INCB was, though, given the traditional power to recommend an embargo, and this was expanded to include export as well as import embargoes. The Soviet Union successfully opposed provisions, similar to those contained in the 1953 Protocol, restricting the number of states which would be allowed to produce opium and poppy straw for export and empowering INCB to stipulate the maximum stocks of opium and poppy straw which signatory states could hold.[47] The USSR also sought to insure that signatory states to the Single Convention would not be required to submit more data than they had under previous arrangements other than the 1953 Protocol.[48] To some extent it gained its point. Finally, in keeping with its general attitude, the Soviet Union opposed compulsory submission of disputes under the treaty to the International Court of Justice[49] To mollify the Soviet Union and others, states were allowed, as a matter of course, to reserve their position on this article.

Other aspects of the USSR's policy in the negotiations concerning the Single Convention also reflected broader Soviet attitudes. The USSR sought to ensure that "the principle of equitable geographical distribution" would be taken into account when ECOSOC elected the eleven independent members who would comprise INCB.[50] A re-

[46] UN Document E/CONF. 34/1, pp. 84, 86, 89.
[47] *Ibid.*, pp. 115, 120.
[48] *Ibid.*, pp. 93, 94, 97.
[49] *Ibid.*, p. 173, and UN Document E/CONF. 34/L. 21.
[50] UN Document E/CONF. 34/1, p. 71.

quirement to this effect was written into the relevant article. The USSR also submitted an amendment which, had it been adopted, would have complicated the requirements for the Convention's entry into force and would have given Eastern European states a greater voice in this matter, and consequently in determining the content of the treaty.[51] The Soviet Union argued, albeit unsuccessfully, that the section of the Single Convention which dealt with the treatment of addicts should include an admonition to signatory states to "raise the material welfare and cultural level of the population and to improve the medical service."[52] Soviet delegates have always maintained that drug addiction, like other social problems, is primarily a product of capitalist conditions. Although Soviet delegates came to state this less frequently than they did in the UN's early years, this proposal and the USSR's reports to the UN indicated that it remained a firmly held Soviet dogma.[53]

The USSR's greatest efforts were in connection with the article of the Single Convention defining the states which would be eligible to sign. It strongly opposed limiting eligibility to states which were: members of the UN, or of a specialized agency, or parties to the Statute of the International Court of Justice, or specially invited by ECOSOC.[54] As a practical matter, this provision would exclude Communist China, East Germany, North Korea and North Vietnam. In this case, expert opinion provided considerable support for the Soviet position, for many who were professionally associated with this work agreed with one commentator who stated that the exclusion of these states would "greatly limit the effectiveness of the control regime."[55] The USSR also argued that it was unjust to allow INCB to exercise control measures over states which were not parties to the Convention.[56] Because these provisions were not changed—although states were allowed to enter reservations concerning the ar-

[51] UN Document E/CONF. 34/L. 20.

[52] UN Document E/CONF. 34/1, p. 158.

[53] For example, the USSR's 1958 report began with the statement: "As a result of general social and economic conditions . . . the number of drug addicts in the U.S.S.R. is very insignificant." (UN Document E/NR. 1956/ Summary, Commission on Narcotic Drugs, "Summary of Annual Reports Relating to Opium and Other Narcotic Drugs," p. 54.)

[54] UN Document E/CONF. 34/1, pp. 162-163.

[55] Leland M. Goodrich, "New Trends in Narcotics Control," *International Conciliation*, no. 530 (November 1960), pp. 181-242, p. 221.

[56] UN Document E/CONF. 34/1, p. 82, p. 163.

SOCIAL WELFARE 139

ticles giving INCB powers over non-parties—the entire Soviet bloc abstained from the final vote approving the Single Convention. Bulgaria, Byelorussia, Czechoslovakia, Poland, the Ukraine and the USSR, seven of the nine Soviet bloc states which attended the conference (the others were Albania and Romania), eventually signed the new treaty. Yugoslavia did also. However, as of April 1963 no communist country, other than Cuba, had ratified the Single Convention. Actually, only seventeen states had taken this action; forty must before the Convention will come into effect.

The Submission of Statistics

International control measures against illicit traffic in narcotic drugs depend for enforcement primarily upon the submission of statistics by the signatory states to the several international conventions and agreements. During and immediately after the Second World War, the USSR and other Soviet bloc states ceased submitting data almost completely.[57] In 1948, ECOSOC attempted mildly to reprimand these states, as well as several others which had failed to meet their international obligations, but Soviet delegates succeeded in blunting this criticism.[58] A year later the USSR resumed submitting practically all the required information to the Permanent Central Opium Board, an important step in view of the Soviet Union's rank among the top five producers and consumers of opium. But even though it sent this data to PCOB, for some time the Soviet Union would not send essentially the same information to the Commission on Narcotic Drugs, and several years elapsed before the USSR submitted complete data. During this period, the Soviet Union was especially reluctant to submit additional information which the UN requested either to explain the required material, or to supplement it. Eventually, however, the USSR became more cooperative, and since the middle nineteen fifties it has complied fully with the requirements. Since 1956, the Soviet Union has even submitted detailed information on drug addiction within its borders. According to these statistics, in 1960 there were only 249 known addicts in the USSR.[59]

[57] See: UN, ECOSOC, *Official Records* (6th Session), Supplement No. 2, "Report of the Commission on Narcotic Drugs," p. 47.
[58] See: UN Document E/AC. 7/SR. 17, p. 2, and ECOSOC Resolution 123 A (VI).
[59] UN Document E/CN. 7/404, p. 8. The United States reported 45,391 addicts, while the United Kingdom reported 454 (*ibid.*, pp. 6, 8).

The UN Narcotics Laboratory

To facilitate the control of illicit traffic in narcotic drugs, the General Assembly decided in 1954 to establish a United Nations Narcotics Laboratory. When this subject was first discussed a year earlier, the Soviet delegate stated that "such functions were entirely foreign to the Organization and had nothing to do with the Purposes and Principles of the Charter."[60] "He wondered whether it was intended to transform the United Nations into an academy of minor sciences. . . ." But in 1954 Soviet opposition was modified to mere abstention, and in 1958, after the USSR had established its own laboratory for work in this field, it announced its willingness to collaborate with the UN laboratory. Three years later, in 1961, the Soviet Union was one of the strongest supporters of the UN laboratory and had nothing but praise for its work.[61] Fiscal considerations seem to have been partially responsible for the initial Soviet opposition. The fact that the original proposal provided that the laboratory would be established in the United States may have also been important. Even in these matters the Soviet Union appears to have been greatly concerned about protocol, and the decision to establish the UN laboratory in Geneva may have been a factor in the Soviet shift from opposition to abstention.

Technical Assistance

Most of the United Nations work concerning narcotic drugs is of a control nature, but the organization has on occasion acted in an advisory capacity. In 1949 the Economic and Social Council acceded to a request from Peru and Bolivia, and established a Commission of Enquiry to investigate the effects of chewing coca leaves, a traditional habit among the indigenous population of several Latin-American countries. Throughout the negotiations, Soviet delegates maintained that such a commission was superfluous, as the effects were known to be harmful.[62] In addition, Soviet delegates argued, as they had with regard to the Advisory Social Welfare Services, that the two countries concerned, rather than the United Nations, should

---

[60] UN, ECOSOC, *Official Records* (15th Session), p. 55.
[61] See: UN Documents E/CN. 7/SR. 471, p. 2; and, E/CN. 7/SR. 477, p. 17.
[62] See: UN Documents E/CN. 7/155, p. 186; and, E/CN. 7/SR. 119, pp. 2-3.

SOCIAL WELFARE 141

pay the costs of the Commission.[63] Because this position on financing was never adopted, the Soviet Union either opposed or abstained from voting on all resolutions dealing with this subject. These Soviet arguments, however, were not heard in 1956 when ECOSOC authorized the use of technical assistance to help Iran enforce a ban on opium production, nor in 1959 when the General Assembly voted to establish a continuing program of technical assistance on narcotics control. The USSR supported both resolutions. By that time, the general Soviet position toward technical assistance and UN operational programs in the economic and social fields had changed.

THE PEOPLE'S REPUBLIC OF CHINA AND THE DRUG TRAFFIC

The one exception in this area, since the mid-nineteen fifties, to the USSR's policy of cooperation and accommodation concerns the People's Republic of China. The controversy with respect to this state during the drafting of the Single Convention on Narcotic Drugs has already been mentioned. In addition, starting in 1950 both the Republic of China and the United States have brought complaints against Communist China to the Commission on Narcotic Drugs, alleging that it was the source of a large illicit traffic, and in 1951 the Economic and Social Council adopted a resolution condemning the revival of the opium trade in China. Soviet delegates strongly protested all such complaints. The argument continued into 1963. Despite its willingness to raise the complaints, the United States, because of the recognition issue, has not been willing to allow the People's Republic of China to participate in the UN's enforcement activities. Soviet delegates have frequently pointed out this contradiction.

By and large the USSR's involvement in this aspect of the work of the United Nations has been limited. After some lapses in the early years, the Soviet Union has generally cooperated with the UN's efforts. The USSR has been sensitive about its sovereignty, but so have other states. The Soviet Union has not been a leader in these activities; on the other hand, illicit traffic and drug addiction do not seem to have been serious problems in the USSR. To be sure, Soviet delegates have used debates on these matters to advance their ideological views, but such statements have gradually been toned down. It is impossible to say whether or not they have had much effect,

[63] See: UN Documents E/AC. 7/SR. 35, p. 10; E/AC. 7/SR. 54, p. 18; and also, UN, ECOSOC, *Official Records* (6th Session), pp. 66-67, 71.

but Soviet policy generally appears to have had little impact on the UN's work.

ADVANCING SOCIAL WELFARE

The other activities of the United Nations in the social field are vast in number and variety. They may be grouped together by their purpose, advancing social welfare. Although inhibitions concerning domestic jurisdiction do not seem to have been a significant factor in Soviet policies concerning these activities, the USSR's role has nevertheless been peripheral. The Soviet Union has never exercised a dominant influence in determining the course of these activities, and its policy has seldom been concerned with the central problems which have been involved. These generalizations, though, have gradually lost some of their force, for the USSR has increasingly sought to become more actively engaged.

THE WORLD HEALTH ORGANIZATION

One of the first steps which the United Nations took in this broad area was to establish the World Health Organization. The only Soviet contribution in the negotiations in the UN which led to the convocation of the World Health Conference was to insist that the World Federation of Trade Unions should be allowed to send an observer to the Technical Preparatory Committee. Although the USSR did not participate in this Committee, it did attend the later World Health Conference and joined WHO. All of the Eastern European states took the latter step at the same time, Soviet delegates successfully opposed a UN grant of funds to the new organization.[64]

The Soviet Union's active membership in WHO was short-lived. It ceased participation in early 1949 and did not resume active membership until 1957. Although several Eastern European states participated for a short time after the Soviet withdrawal, and Yugoslavia never disrupted its connection, the entire Soviet bloc boycotted WHO from 1950 until the USSR resumed participation. In 1957 all Soviet bloc states, except Byelorussia, Hungary and the Ukraine, returned to WHO. As of mid-1963, these three states still remained inactive members of the agency.

[64] UN, General Assembly, Third Committee, *Official Records* (1st Session, 2nd Part), pp. 191-193.

SOCIAL WELFARE 143

The officially stated reasons for the USSR's withdrawal were that the World Health Organization was too expensive and that its swollen administrative machinery accomplished little concrete good. The Soviet Union also held that Anglo-Americans dominated the Organization and that its questionnaires were of a spying nature. In March 1950, a Soviet commentator even asserted that WHO was being "used to whip up war hysteria and popularize the use of the bacteriological weapon." [65] However, the USSR's criticisms of WHO were in general much milder than those leveled against several other specialized agencies, and the only perceptible effect of the withdrawal on Soviet policy in the UN was that the USSR abstained from voting on resolutions dealing with WHO, rather than supporting them, as it did earlier and later.

On various occasions both during its absence from the World Health Organization and after it resumed active participation, the Soviet Union has sought to have the United Nations initiate work which would properly fall within WHO's jurisdiction. In 1951 the USSR proposed that the Social Commission should study and formulate recommendations on the problem of making adequate medical attention available to all without discrimination.[66] This proposal, although repeated frequently, was always summarily rejected. In 1958 the Ukrainian SSR introduced a more concrete proposal.[67] It suggested that the UN should instruct WHO to organize an International Public Health and Medical Research Year. After the resolution was amended so that it merely asked WHO to consider the idea, it was adopted unanimously, an event which a Soviet journalist hailed as evidence of the influence of advocates of peaceful co-existence on international affairs.[68] WHO, however, ultimately rejected the suggestion. The following year Byelorussia introduced a resolution for a United Nations program of prizes to encourage research into the control of cancerous disease.[69] Again, this proposal was adopted after modification. Although the Ukrainian resolution clearly mentioned the World Health Organization, the Byelorussian proposal in its original form did not, perhaps because of the

[65] N. Yevgenyev, "What Some International Bodies Are Really Doing," p. 13.
[66] See: UN Document E/CN. 5/1. 139.
[67] UN Document A/C. 3/L. 698.
[68] V. Alexandrov, "Some Results of the 13th General Assembly," *International Affairs* (Moscow), V, no. 2 (February 1959), 44-47, p. 46.
[69] UN Document A/C. 3/L. 722.

experience of the former, and both implied criticisms of the work of this specialized agency. The introduction of the two resolutions in the Assembly probably insured that they received the greatest possible publicity.

UNESCO

The Soviet Union has pursued a similar policy with regard to the other specialized agency working in this field, the United Nations Educational, Scientific and Cultural Organization. UNESCO was founded almost simultaneously with the UN, but the Soviet Union did not become a member until 1954.[70] Czechoslovakia and Poland, however, were among the agency's original members, and Hungary and Yugoslavia joined in 1948 and 1950 respectively. As in the case of WHO, the entire Soviet bloc boycotted UNESCO during the early nineteen fifties, but when the USSR became a member, other bloc states resumed participation and still others joined the agency.

During the period of its boycott, the Soviet Union was sharply critical of UNESCO. The agency was held to have "come under the thumb of the American imperialists," and to have become "an auxiliary of the U. S. State Department." [71] UNESCO personnel allegedly engaged in spreading American propaganda and espionage. The agency's publications were excoriated. A pamphlet entitled "The American Way of Life," was termed "an utterly fraudulent piece of advertising." [72] Although their criticisms of UNESCO have been moderated since 1954, Soviet commentators have continued to emphasize the dominant role of the United States and its "voting machine" in the agency.[73]

The USSR has often sought to have the United Nations undertake tasks which clearly fall within UNESCO's mandate. The same resolution which the USSR introduced in 1951 asking the Social Commission to consider problems of medical care, in addition asked

[70] For an analysis of Soviet policy toward UNESCO until the time that it joined the agency see: John A. Armstrong, "The Soviet Attitude Toward UNESCO," *International Organization*, VIII, no. 2 (Spring 1954), 217-233.

[71] N. Yevgenyev, "What Some International Bodies Are Really Doing," p. 11.

[72] There is a certain parallel between these Soviet criticisms and the more recent American condemnations of the UNESCO publication, *Equality of Rights Between Races and Nationalities in the U.S.S.R.* (Paris: 1962).

[73] See the account of the 11th General Conference of UNESCO by S. Lapin, *Izvestia*, December 28, 1960, as contained in *The Current Digest of the Soviet Press*, XII, no. 52 (January 25, 1961), 25-26.

SOCIAL WELFARE 145

it to study and formulate recommendations on the problems of the availability of education without discrimination and the introduction of free compulsory education.[74] This suggestion was also rejected each time that it was introduced. In 1958, at the twenty-sixth session of the Economic and Social Council, the USSR introduced a resolution requesting that the Secretary-General prepare a survey of recent international exchanges in the field of science, culture and education.[75] Resolutions on this same subject had been introduced by Czechoslovakia at the previous two Assembly sessions, but amendments had insured that responsibility would generally be left with the specialized agencies, particularly UNESCO. This happened again with regard to the Soviet proposal. It was adopted, but only after rephrasing so that it was apparent that primary responsibility rested with UNESCO. The Soviet Union also proposed at ECOSOC's twenty-sixth session that a convention on the principles of international cooperation in the field of science, culture and education should be prepared, but nothing came of this suggestion.[76]

These Soviet proposals clearly reflected the emphasis in the USSR's general foreign policy on exchanges of personnel and information. They, and the proposals concerning medical subjects, also reflected the USSR's progress in the fields of science, education and medicine. Even in earlier years, Soviet delegates in the Social Commission, ECOSOC, and the Assembly's Third Committee, always described their country's progress in these fields in glowing detail. Gradually these statements were buttressed with increased data for UN reports and proposals such as the above. However, the introduction of these proposals in the United Nations rather than the specialized agencies, their tendency to de-emphasize the agencies, and their semi-political rather than technical character indicates that Soviet policy concerning these subjects, although more active than previously, still was considerably different from that of the majority of UN member states.

POPULATION PROBLEMS

A similar gap between Soviet concepts and those of other states has been apparent in the UN's work with regard to the social aspects

[74] See: UN Document E/CN. 5/L. 139.
[75] UN Document E/AC. 24/L. 138.
[76] UN Document E/AC. 24/L. 139.

of population problems. The USSR has disagreed with the premises of much of this work. Soviet delegates have argued that the only correct solution to problems of rapid population growth is to raise economic levels, and they have condemned suggestions that birth rates should be lowered.[77] This position has deep roots in Marxist theory and communist ideology.[78] Furthermore, in the UN's early years, the USSR regarded the Population Commission's work concerning internal migration as a violation of domestic jurisdiction, and its bias against international migration has always strongly colored its views with respect to this aspect of the Commission's activities.

In 1953 the Soviet Union sought to influence the orientation of the Secretariat's studies in this field, proposing that more attention should be paid to: the demographic characteristics of various social and ethnic groups; demographic factors in unemployment; economic and social factors responsible for migration; and living conditions in Trust Territories and non-self-governing territories.[79] The bulk of the resolution appeared to most other delegates to be more an attempt to obtain international support for preconceived Soviet ideas than an attempt to further scientific research into demographic problems. For this reason, only the first part of the suggestion was adopted. At subsequent sessions of the Population Commission, Soviet delegates have continued to expound the same ideas and also to ask for data to support them, but no new formal proposals have been introduced.

Here as elsewhere Soviet policy has gradually shifted over the years. In this case, the move was from abstention to support. In addition, with the approach of the USSR's first post-Second World War census in 1959, Soviet delegates became increasingly interested in the Population Commission's technical work. Their enthusiasm continued after 1959. In 1961, when ECOSOC decided to convene a Second World Population Conference in 1964 or 1965, the USSR showed considerable interest, although it had only sent a token delegation to the first Conference in 1954. The USSR also became more interested in the UN's program of technical assistance in this

[77] See: UN Documents E/CN. 9/SR. 113, p. 7; E/CN. 9/SR. 123 [February 12, 1959], p. 7; and, E/CN. 9/SR. 136, pp. 6-7.
[78] For a detailed statement of the official Soviet interpretation of Marx's views on population problems, see: UN Document E/CN. 9/SR. 78, pp. 3-8.
[79] UN Document E/CN. 9/L. 49.

SOCIAL WELFARE

field, volunteering the services of Soviet experts.[80] It stressed, though, that the emphasis should be on the training of national staff.

OTHER SOCIAL PROGRAMS

Many of the UN's activities in this area have dealt rather specifically with such problems as housing, community development, urbanization, and family and child welfare. A large proportion of these activities have been conducted within the Expanded Program of Technical Assistance (EPTA). The Soviet Union has not been responsible for the initiation of any of these activities, and its contribution has been restricted. When conferences in the field of housing and town and country planning were first discussed, Soviet delegates insisted that they should be limited to exchanges of technical information and that the participants should be responsible for the costs. There was agreement on the first suggestion and it was accepted, but the second, like other similar Soviet proposals, was not. For a time Soviet delegates unsuccessfully attempted to utilize discussions of the UN's child welfare work in the Social Commission as an instrument to increase pressure for the repatriation of Soviet children who were abroad as a result of the Second World War. The data gathered under this program, and under others including the *Report on the World Social Situation* (especially when it has dealt with education, housing and medical care), has been used by Soviet delegates as a point of departure for harangues on capitalism and laudatory descriptions of social conditions in the Soviet Union. With the shift in Soviet policy, the harangues have been tempered somewhat, and the descriptions made more concrete. They also came to be accompanied by offers of technical assistance in the various fields.

Occasionally the USSR has made extremely broad proposals concerning this aspect of the UN's work. At the Social Commission's second session in 1947, the Soviet delegate proposed that the Commission regard as its primary task:

> . . . urgent study of all aspects of the social conditions of the colonial population and populations of under-developed dependent territories and of territories under trusteeship, with a view to preparing such proposals, as will lead to improvement of social conditions of the people in these territories without regard to race, sex, language or religion.[81]

[80] UN Document E/CN. 9/SR. 155, pp. 8-9.
[81] UN Document E/CN. 5/SR. 32, p. 3.

His statements in the debate made it even more apparent that this was intended as an attack on colonialism. Nevertheless, the proposal was amended to apply to underdeveloped areas generally, and it led to several United Nations studies and programs concerning social problems in underdeveloped areas. Subsequent Soviet attempts to limit these to dependent and Trust Territories were without success and gradually these efforts were abandoned. In 1959 the Soviet Union even introduced a resolution in the Social Commission on UN assistance for national social service programs which was phrased in terms of underdeveloped areas generally.[82]

The USSR submitted proposals in 1951 and 1952 which would have completely re-oriented the United Nations' work in this field. Soviet delegates charged that the Social Commission had ignored the "major problems" and suggested that it should abandon its current activities and embark on a new five-point program. In addition to points relating to medical care and education which have already been mentioned, this program included consideration of: unemployment insurance and care of the families of the unemployed; measures relating to maternity, infant and child care; and social measures against sickness, old age and disability.[83] Only the point relating to maternity, infant and child care was incorporated into the UN's program, since the majority in the Social Commission felt that the programs of the specialized agencies adequately covered the other problems. This rebuff and others like it may well have been a factor in the Soviet decision to increase its participation in the activities of the specialized agencies. By this time underdeveloped countries were becoming increasingly interested in these activities, from which the Soviet Union was isolated. As the USSR was not able to alter the UN's program, participation in the specialized agencies was the only way in which it could become involved.

In 1957 the Soviet Union again sought broadly to influence the UN's work in the field of social welfare. It submitted two resolutions at ECOSOC's twenty-fourth session: one recommended international exchanges of doctors, teachers, social welfare workers, child welfare workers and other specialists in the social field; and the other, the cessation of nuclear weapons tests.[84] The former was

[82] UN Document E/CN. 5/L. 227. Again no mention was made of the specialized agencies in this proposal.
[83] See: UN Document E/CN. 5/L. 139.
[84] UN Documents E/L. 748 and E/L. 759.

SOCIAL WELFARE 149

adopted in a modified form, the latter, rejected twelve votes to six. Despite the remoteness of nuclear weapons tests from the UN's work in the social field, Egypt, Finland, Indonesia and Yugoslavia joined Poland and the USSR in voting for the resolution.

This resolution on nuclear weapons tests in many ways illustrates the Soviet attitude toward this aspect of the United Nations activities. Despite the fact that Soviet delegates to the Social Commission have generally been of a high caliber, the USSR does not seem to have been terribly interested in this work, nor does it appear to have comprehended all of it. This ignorance was illustrated at the Social Commission's twelfth session in 1959 when the Soviet delegate asked for clarification on the precise function of social workers.[85] Soviet delegates appear to understand UN activities with regard to housing, education and medical care and perhaps social security but they do not seem truly to understand the others.

Even with regard to those activities which it does understand, the Soviet Union's attitude is so different from that of the majority of the UN's members that there are great barriers to effective cooperation. This was illustrated by a resolution submitted by the USSR at the twenty-eighth session of the Economic and Social Council in July 1959.[86] This proposal recommended that governments of member states:

> . . . take measures for systematically increasing State appropriations for the social needs of the people, paying particular attention to such important questions as the extension of education, the reduction of cost of medical services, the expansion of housing construction and the lowering of rents, and the development of social security and social insurance systems.

The aims of this proposal were unexceptional, but several delegates objected to the techniques which were involved. For one thing, many of them felt that the resolution violated domestic jurisdiction. Clearly—and ironically in light of the USSR's usual stand—it implied a very broad concept of the competence of an international organization. For another, by this time there was considerable impatience with exhortatory resolutions concerning these matters and a desire to concentrate on practical activities. Finally, not all delegates agreed that the role of the state in these matters should be as large as was implied in the resolution. The Soviet proposal found

[85] See: UN Document E/CN. 5/SR. 284, p. 13.
[86] UN Document E/L. 838.

little support, and ultimately it was withdrawn without a vote being taken.

Since then Soviet tactics have concentrated on supporting measures favored by the underdeveloped states, proclaiming Soviet achievements and offering advice. Soviet support, however, did not extend to being willing to vote for an enlargement of the Secretariat in this area. The USSR has shown some interest in the UN's programs for the exchange of information and has come to be more favorably disposed toward the programs of technical assistance. But basically, the Soviet Union's role in this aspect of the UN's activities has remained almost peripheral.

CONCLUSIONS

It appears therefore that profound ideological barriers continue to bar effective cooperation between East and West in the work of the United Nations with regard to social welfare. The premises which the Soviet Union brings to this work seem to be fundamentally different from those of the majority of the UN's members. In the Soviet view, social problems are the result of economic factors, and they can only be cured by basic transformations in economic structure. The role of the government in any action program is central. The West, on the other hand, frequently tends to treat social problems as such, and Western governments, although increasingly important in social welfare work, still do not dominate the scene.

Soviet statements in general debates on social welfare, which condemn the capitalist West in strong or moderate terms depending on the political dictates of the moment, while vividly praising communist achievements, sound so strange to Westerners that they have often been dismissed as mere propaganda. While it is no doubt true that many of the Soviet statements have been made mainly for their anticipated effect on public opinion (as many UN speeches are), they also seem to have reflected firmly held theories and at least some elements of the Soviet image of reality. Soviet statements have been intimately related to the USSR's voting record and to the initiatives which it has proposed. All seem to have stemmed from a similar *weltanschauung*.[87]

[87] For detailed analyses of this *weltanschauung*, see: Frederick C. Barghoorn, *The Soviet Image of the United States* (New York: Harcourt Brace, 1950); Herbert Marcuse, *Soviet Marxism* (New York: Columbia University Press, 1958); and, Gerhart Niemeyer, with the assistance of John S. Reshetar, Jr., *An Inquiry into Soviet Mentality* (New York: Frederick A. Praeger, 1956).

In addition to this ideological gap the ties of common interest with regard to this aspect of the United Nations work have been extremely nebulous. Because of its tightly centralized and controlled governmental organization, the USSR has not had the same need for the UN's control activities involving social evils and narcotic drugs as have many member states. To the extent that these matters have been problems within the USSR, they could be controlled from within. Even with regard to the early relief activities in the social field, the USSR's direct interests were limited. The fact that other Eastern European states showed some enthusiasm for this work may well have blocked any Soviet curiosity concerning these programs. As in the case of the UN's other relief activities, the development of extensive cooperation between Eastern Europe and the United Nations could possibly have been detrimental to plans for consolidation of the Soviet bloc. Of course this did not prevent the Soviet Union from attempting to gain maximum benefits for the Eastern European states closely associated with it once the work began. Not to have made this attempt could only have diminished Soviet influence. Finally, Soviet concepts of domestic jurisdiction have limited still further the areas of common interest.

For all these reasons Soviet participation in the United Nations social welfare work has been peripheral. It has never been willing to contribute financially unless absolutely necessary. Without a fundamental commitment to this work, the Soviet Union has been free to concentrate on other goals regardless of their impact on the matter at hand. It was no doubt more important to the USSR to have its stature among the anticolonial groups increased by its sponsorship of amendments to delete colonial application clauses, than it was to preserve intact the legal framework of the control system. The same may be said with regard to the exclusion of Franco Spain. Of course the Soviet Union has not been alone in such tactics; the Western refusal to deal with the People's Republic of China has also weakened the international control system. The Soviet Union has probably pursued tactics which have had detrimental consequences for the UN's programs in this area more frequently than the West has, but both sides have done it as the occasion has demanded.

The fact that general Soviet policies came to call for increased cooperation with other states, especially the underdeveloped countries, has been reflected by increased cooperation in the UN's social welfare work. However, even with these changes, Soviet policy has differed considerably from that of other states. Its contribution to UNICEF, for example, must be viewed as token participation in a popular program, and even though the USSR has sought to introduce initiatives, these proposals have seldom dealt with the central problems involved in this part of the work of the United Nations.

The impact of Soviet policies on the UN's social welfare work as a consequence has been fairly restricted. By leading movements to bar Franco Spain and to delete colonial application and federal state clauses, the USSR has created legal difficulties for the UN's control activities. By constantly stressing the anticolonial theme, the Soviet Union may have induced the United Nations to direct greater efforts toward social problems in underdeveloped areas than might have been the case otherwise. And by always harping on social problems in noncommunist countries, the USSR has never allowed anyone in the UN to ignore these or to dismiss them lightly. Viewed in terms of the ideal of universal participation and application, the Soviet Union's reluctance to become deeply involved has severely limited the scope of the United Nations activities in this field.

The effects of Soviet policy upon public opinion are not as easy to ascertain. The fact that most Soviet initiatives, except those which emphasized anticolonial themes, have either been rejected or significantly modified, indicates that the impact of the USSR's policies on participants in the UN has not been great, and this probably indicates that the impact on those individuals and groups who follow these activities has also been rather small.

6: ECONOMIC WELFARE

SOCIAL WELFARE ACTIVITIES ARE ONLY A PART OF THE UNITED NATIONS mandate under Article 55. In addition, the organization is instructed to promote "higher standards of living, full employment, and conditions of economic . . . progress and development" as well as "solutions of international economic problems." The resulting activities have probably been of greater importance than those concerning social welfare, and they have certainly been more numerous. The UN's several economic programs can be divided into three broad categories: economic development; international trade; and economic welfare. In reverse order, they are the subjects of the next three chapters.

The United Nations itself has undertaken few practical activities with regard to economic welfare. In most cases where concrete action has been required, the International Labor Organization has assumed operational responsibility. Until 1954 this meant that the USSR was excluded. However, Albania, Bulgaria, Czechoslovakia, Poland, Hungary and Yugoslavia were members of ILO in the years immediately after the Second World War, and although Albania, Bulgaria and Hungary gradually became inactive, the other three states continued active participation even during the early nineteen fifties. When the USSR entered ILO, Byelorussia and the Ukraine did also, Soviet bloc states which had been inactive became active again, and, in 1956, Romania joined the agency. The UN's role in this field has generally been limited to adopting resolutions on broad policy, preparing studies, and carrying out occasional investigations. Nevertheless, discussions of economic welfare have been an important and sometimes explosive feature of General Assembly and

Economic and Social Council proceedings. These discussions have been used by each of the protagonists in the cold war to expound the virtues of its own economic system and to point out the defects in its opponent's. Generally, the USSR and its allies have been the attackers, and therefore they have been responsible for initiating many of the United Nations activities in this field. Because of the nature of their attacks, they have also been primarily responsible for the vehemence which has often characterized the UN's debates concerning economic welfare issues.

When the USSR rejoined ILO, the UN's role in this area was altered and in some ways diminished. Many proposals which the Soviet Union previously would have introduced in the UN, were now raised in ILO.[1] Since the West had always felt that these subjects belonged in ILO and could be handled most effectively there, it made no attempt to reverse this trend. Further, as a part of the general shift in Soviet policy which occurred at about the same time, Soviet attacks on the West and its economic system became less violent. Consequently, at least some of the rancor disappeared from UN discussions on economic welfare. The basic division between East and West, however, remained, and Soviet policy continued to consist primarily of criticisms of the West.

Although the USSR has generally sought to seize the initiative with regard to economic welfare issues, it was not responsible for introducing this aspect of the United Nations mandate. There was general agreement at San Francisco that the UN should have functions in the field of economic welfare. The Dumbarton Oaks Proposals provided substantial coverage in this area, and this was expanded at San Francisco. The words "full employment" were added to Article 55 on the basis of an Australian proposal. Soviet efforts at the Conference were mainly confined to supporting those who favored "full employment" instead of "high and stable levels of employment," the formulation offered by the United States.[2] The USSR and the Ukrainian SSR introduced a proposal to include in the Charter a "guarantee for all the working people of the right to work," but this was never pressed to a vote.[3] However, Foreign Min-

---

[1] For an account of Soviet moves in ILO see: Alfred Fernbach, *Soviet Coexistence Strategy* (Washington, D. C.: Public Affairs Press, 1960); and, Harold Karan Jacobson, "The U.S.S.R. and ILO."
[2] See: R. B. Russell, *A History of the United Nations Charter*, p. 784.
[3] UNCIO *Documents*, III, 633 and X, 27.

ister Molotov made use of it at his final press conference in San Francisco to demonstrate Soviet concern for the interests of the working classes,[4] and subsequent Soviet scholarship has credited the suggestion with providing at least a major portion of the impetus for Article 55.[5]

TRADE UNION RIGHTS

During its first year the Economic and Social Council was fully occupied with organizational matters and problems which resulted from the Second World War. Thus it was the spring of 1947 before the Council began to consider substantive problems in the field of economic welfare. The World Federation of Trade Unions touched things off. Utilizing its newly won right, it proposed that two items should be included in the agenda of the Council's Fourth Session: guarantees of trade union rights and equality of treatment between immigrant and indigenous workers.[6] The latter issue was postponed until the following session, but the former was considered immediately.

The debate which was precipitated then continued into 1963. Two issues ultimately were involved: (1) guaranteeing trade union rights generally, and (2) infringements of these rights. The first was a substantive problem on which world labor appeared to be fairly united, at least in principle. It had been considered frequently in labor groups, and the AFL also submitted a memorandum on the subject to the Fourth Session of ECOSOC.[7] However, even on this issue a division concerning procedure soon developed.

The second question was somewhat different. While it certainly had substantive aspects, it could also be used for propagandistic purposes. Although the WFTU and the Soviet bloc made several allegations concerning infringements in the early debates, the problem was not formally raised until June 1948. Then and in the course of the following winter, the WFTU submitted three memoranda stating that trade union rights were being violated in several West-

[4] See: The New York Times, May 8, 1945.
[5] See: E. A. Korovin, "The USSR and the Establishment of the United Nations Organization," International Affairs (Moscow), III, no. 9 (September 1957), 36-39, p. 37.
[6] UN Document E/C. 2/27.
[7] UN Document E/C. 2/32.

ern countries.[8] During the same period the major trade unions of the West left the WFTU because of its attack on the Marshall Plan and with the AFL formed the International Confederation of Free Trade Unions. The cold war also heightened in intensity. These factors were evidenced in the Economic and Social Council, for the WFTU memoranda set off explosive charges and countercharges that became a continuing feature of the debate.[9] Most of the WFTU's charges involved alleged discriminations against communists and against its own members. On the other hand, many of those submitted by the AFL and ICFTU centered on the Soviet Union and its satellites, with special reference to the "controlled status" of trade unions in those countries.

In the debate on trade union rights until 1954, the position of the WFTU and of the Soviet Union and other communist states, was that the item should be considered by the United Nations itself. The initial resolution submitted by the WFTU expressed this position quite clearly.[10] Couched in broad philosophical terms, it recognized trade union rights as inviolable prerogatives and condemned all contrary legislation as incompatible with United Nations principles. It also provided for the establishment of an ECOSOC committee for trade union rights. This body would permanently safeguard respect for trade union rights by investigating all alleged violations and by submitting recommendations to the Council on the necessary corrective measures. Later, the Soviet Union advanced similar suggestions;[11] however, none of these proposals received significant support. Their adoption could have served several purposes. They could have been used for attempts to protect communist trade union leaders in noncommunist countries, and they would have provided an excellent base for propaganda attacks against the West. But both of these purposes were also served to some extent simply by having the subject debated.

On the other hand, the position of the West generally was that the item should be referred for consideration to the competent specialized agency, the International Labor Organization. This position was determined partially by the conception that Western statesmen

[8] UN Document E/822 and Add. 1 and 2.
[9] See: UN Documents E/841; E/1095; E/1822 and Add. 1; E/1922 and Add. 1; E/2154; E/2333; E/2498; E/2587; E/C. 2/341; and, E/343.
[10] UN Document E/C. 2/28.
[11] UN Documents E/1264 and E/1478.

held of the role of ECOSOC—that it should be a coordinating but not an operating body. They also felt that this subject involved one of ILO's primary functions (the agency had done work in this field as early as 1928), and that it should be considered in a body in which the workers had direct representation. Further, with reference to the allegations of infringements of trade union rights, Western statesmen maintained that the Council was not empowered to assume judicial or arbitral functions and that these questions could be considered only in a body specially created for that purpose. Finally, Western statesmen were obviously aware that the effect of transferring the item to ILO, would be to bar the USSR from further deliberations concerning the matter.

The Soviet Union was bitterly opposed to referring the question to ILO. No doubt this opposition stemmed in part from the fact that until 1954 the USSR was not a member of ILO. But it was probably also a result of the general Soviet objective of detracting from the International Labor Organization and elevating the status of the WFTU.

Despite Soviet protests the Council and the Assembly adopted the West's proposals and on most occasions the USSR and its bloc stood alone in opposition. Ironically, one of the important decisions in this regard was based on a proposal submitted by Leon Jouhaux, a noted French trade unionist and also a Vice President of WFTU. This complicated the Soviet position. ILO was requested to assume responsibility for continuing work in the field of trade union rights, which began in the summer of 1947. The following year the International Labor Conference adopted the Freedom of Association and Protection of the Right to Organize Convention (No. 87), and in 1949 it adopted the Right to Organize and Collective Bargaining Convention (No. 98). In 1950 ILO established a Fact-Finding and Conciliation Commission to investigate specific complaints.

Shortly after the creation of this Commission, ECOSOC decided to make use of it. In doing so the Council formulated procedures for referring complaints to the new body. It was decided to forward all allegations concerning members of the International Labor Organization to the Governing Body of ILO for consideration as to referral to the commission. At first such action required a Council decision, but later the Secretary-General was authorized to act on his own initiative. With regard to charges against members of the United Nations which did not belong to ILO, the Council decided that before taking any action it would ask the consent of the government concerned to refer the allegation to the Commission. If consent were not granted, the Council agreed to give consideration to such refusal with a view to taking "any appropriate alternative action." [12] This decision, which the Soviet bloc, India, and to a lesser degree Egypt, opposed, implied an inherent bias against non-members of ILO (and thus until 1954 against the USSR) since it provided opportunity for giving greater publicity to complaints against such states than against ILO members.

This actually happened. Starting in 1950 most of the charges against Western countries were referred in a rather routine manner to ILO. The specialized agency investigated the complaints, but not in the manner originally envisaged. Since no government was willing to allow on-the-spot inquiries, the Fact-Finding and Conciliation Commission never functioned. Instead, allegations concerning violations of freedom of association in ILO member states were investigated by the Governing Body's Committee on Freedom of Association. In contrast, complaints against the Soviet Union and some of its satellites had to be discussed in ECOSOC. The Council adopted a number of resolutions directed at the USSR and Romania and inquiring as to their willingness to accept the services of the Fact-Finding and Conciliation Commission.[13] Neither ever replied affirmatively.

In debates in the General Assembly and the Economic and Social Council Soviet delegates were highly critical of ILO's activities. They argued that because of its tripartite structure the agency could not take effective action to protect worker's rights, and claimed that no practical action had been taken during the time that the Organization had been studying the problem. Soviet representatives alleged that in dealing with freedom of association rather than trade union rights, ILO discriminated against workers, for it put employers, who in the communist view needed no special protection, on an equal basis with workers. They argued that the principle which figured in one of ILO's early resolutions that there should be agreement between employers and workers on the exercise of trade union rights, gave the former a veto power. Consistent with general Soviet policy,

[12] ECOSOC Resolution 277 (X).
[13] ECOSOC Resolutions: 351 (XII); 444 (XIV); 474 B & C (XV); 503 (XVI); 523 A (XVII); and, 575 B (XIX).

ECONOMIC WELFARE

representatives of the USSR criticized the colonial application clause in the 1948 Convention.

When the Soviet Union rejoined ILO in 1954, the charges against it were immediately sent to the Governing Body, and similar action was taken, when it became possible two years later, with regard to the charges against Romania. Thus the debate on trade union rights in the United Nations was brought to an incongruously quiet close. However, it continued to rage in the International Labor Organization. The Soviet Union continued to use the issue to criticize the West, though it altered its tactics considerably. For instance, it ratified ILO's 1948 and 1949 Conventions and also the 1921 Right of Association (Agriculture) Convention. The West also continued to be critical of Soviet practices in this area. The results of the investigations of the ICFTU complaints against the USSR were published in 1956 and 1958.[14] Though couched in diplomatic language, these reports substantially confirmed the allegations. Since 1959 the Soviet Union has also been criticized in this matter by ILO bodies which check on the implementation of conventions.

On one level the result of this controversy in the United Nations would appear to be that a propaganda attack begun by the Soviet Union and its allies was eventually neutralized and to some extent even turned against the USSR. On another level, certain substantive achievements must be recognized. ILO adopted two conventions, it investigated numerous complaints, and in 1959 it inaugurated a far-reaching project involving on-the-spot surveys of freedom of association in various countries including the Soviet Union and the United States.[15] To the extent that Soviet initiatives led to these developments, the USSR must receive credit. However, the Soviet Union's role usually was that of a critic standing outside of the proceedings, goading those involved to action, rather than that of a true participant. The USSR also initiated an extremely bitter and hostile debate. The persistence of this debate indicates that more than propaganda issues—however important they may have been—were at stake. Fundamentally different conceptions of the role of trade unions in society were involved.

[14] See: ILO, *Official Bulletin*, XXIX, no. 4 (1956), 211-304; and, *Official Bulletin*, XLI, no. 3 (1958), 228-241.
[15] See: ILO, *The Trade Union Situation in the United States* (Geneva, 1960); and *The Trade Union Situation in the U.S.S.R.* (Geneva, 1960).

PROTECTION OF MIGRANT LABOR

The other item which the World Federation of Trade Unions proposed for inclusion in the agenda of ECOSOC's fourth session, equality of treatment between immigrants and indigenous workers, was not discussed until August 1947, and then not in the exact form that the WFTU suggested. It appeared on the agenda of the Council's fifth session as an item sponsored by the AFL and was entitled "Protection of Immigrant Labor." The AFL's supporting memorandum discussed the international migratory movement after the Second World War and the need for further migration to settle the remaining displaced persons.[16] To facilitate this and to protect migrants' rights, the AFL suggested that the Council should request ECE and ECAFE to promote the use of standards recommended by ILO and also that it should urge ILO to hasten reconsideration of its convention and recommendations concerning migrant workers.

After debate, and despite Soviet objections, the Council voted to refer the AFL's memorandum to ILO and to its own Population and Social Commissions for their consideration. The USSR's basic complaint was that the separate problems of immigration and refugees were merged in the AFL's memorandum; in the Soviet view the only solution for the refugee problem was repatriation.

Nonetheless, the same fusion occurred the next time that the problem arose, and then in a proposal advanced by a member of the Soviet bloc. At the General Assembly's third session in the fall of 1948 Poland proposed that action be taken against "discriminations Practiced by States against Immigrant Labour and Especially against Labour Recruited from the Ranks of Refugees."[17] This proposal was clearly part of the Soviet campaign against the resettlement of refugees and displaced persons. Because the agenda was overcrowded, consideration of this item was deferred until the Assembly's fourth session, the following year.

Soviet bloc representatives supported a draft resolution submitted by Poland which proclaimed that refugees and displaced persons who had been resettled had been discriminated against and recommended a series of specific measures which member states should

[16] UN Document E/454.
[17] UN Document A/614.

ECONOMIC WELFARE

apply in their treatment of immigrants.[18] These included the principle of nondiscrimination, the right to transfer savings to the immigrant's country of origin, and the right of repatriation at the expense of the country of immigration. The resolution also recommended that labor should be recruited, and working and living conditions determined, exclusively on the basis of bilateral agreements between the countries of origin and immigration. Finally, it asked the Secretary-General to transmit a questionnaire on the condition of immigrant labor to all member states where such individuals were employed. Among other things, this proposal, with its insistence on bilateral agreements, might well have blocked all resettlement. The Assembly, however, adopted an alternative resolution submitted by the United Kingdom which referred the problem to ILO and requested that ILO take all possible steps to hasten the adoption by its member states of the revised Convention on Migration for Employment (No. 97). This Convention, which was partly a response to the earlier ECOSOC resolution, had just been completed at the International Labor Conference in the summer of 1949, and it was designed to protect migrant workers in matters of health conditions, housing, wages, social security, and travel, and to prevent discrimination against them on grounds of race, sex or religion.

Thus the Soviet Union was again, because of its absence from ILO, unable to participate in the detailed consideration of an item which its supporters had introduced. It seems clear that the primary motive for raising this question was to work against the resettlement of the refugees and displaced persons. Since 1949, Soviet bloc delegates have not reintroduced the issue, except through occasional references in UN debates to the "wetback" problem in the United States.

EQUAL PAY FOR EQUAL WORK

A third item brought before ECOSOC by the WFTU was the question of "equal pay for men and women workers." At the Federation's request it was included in the agenda of the sixth session of the Council in the spring of 1948. In its supporting memoranda the WFTU outlined a number of principles which it felt members of the United Nations should implement.[19] These included recogni-

[18] UN Documents: A/C. 3/524, and A/1084.
[19] UN Documents E/627 and Add. 1.

tion of the necessity of providing maternity insurance and of reducing domestic tasks, as well as recognition of the importance of trade union rights for women. Other principles concerned occupational selection and guidance, apprenticeship and occupational training, and the rational assessment of the value of work. The WFTU stated in its memoranda that the Soviet Union was the only country in which these principles were being fully implemented, and during the discussion, Soviet delegates attacked the West for failure to implement the concept of equal pay, particularly in colonial and economically underdeveloped areas.

Again, the Council divided on the question of procedure. The Soviet block and the WFTU tried to keep the question within the UN. The USSR submitted broad general resolutions morally committing all member states to implement the principles involved.[20] The West, on the contrary, attempted to refer the problem to ILO. Although all Western representatives agreed on the theoretical validity of the principal of equal pay for equal work, some of them argued that there were technical difficulties involved in putting it into effect. They argued that ILO would be better equipped to cope with these difficulties, and that in any case it would be more appropriate to work on the basis of formal technical conventions. Moreover, this problem was also one concerning which the agency had done previous work; it was even mentioned in the ILO Constitution.

While some concessions were made to the East (for example, in affirming the principle of equal pay in general terms) ECOSOC substantially accepted the Western position.[21] The subject was referred to ILO. Only the Soviet bloc opposed this decision. In 1951, after three years' study, ILO completed its consideration of this question with the adoption of the Convention on Equal Remuneration for Work of Equal Value (No. 100).

During this period, Soviet delegates in ECOSOC criticized ILO's work and made several attempts to bring the problem back before the Council. In one debate on equal pay the USSR's representative charged that ILO "had done its utmost to obstruct the implementation of that principle." [22] The discussions provided numerous oppor-

[20] UN Documents E/657 and E/1148.
[21] See: ECOSOC Resolutions 121 (VI), 196 (VIII), 242 D (IX), 445 E (XIV), 504 G (XVI), and, 587 C (XX).
[22] UN, ECOSOC, *Official Records* (8th Session), p. 93.

ECONOMIC WELFARE

tunities for attacks on the West for failure to implement the principle of equal pay and for laudatory statements concerning communist practices. Curiously, though, the USSR did not reply to a UN questionnaire concerning actions which governments had taken in this field.[23] When the ILO Convention was completed the Soviet Union was extremely critical, and in 1952 when ECOSOC commended the Convention and recommended that all states introduce legislation in accordance with it, the USSR abstained.

As this action indicated, Soviet policy-makers probably found themselves in something of a quandary. Most states supported ILO's work and to oppose these steps might damage the USSR's efforts to appear as a leader in progressive causes. Again it seems that an attack against the West begun by the East was taken out of its hands through the mechanism of referring the question to ILO. Subsequently, by rejoining ILO in 1954 and two years later ratifying the Convention on Equal Remuneration the USSR did much to ease this predicament.[24] The success of Soviet policy as propaganda is another matter. The UN provided an ample forum for such efforts and Soviet delegates continued to use it to describe how well the principle of equal pay was implemented in their country and how poorly elsewhere. However, no new proposals have been introduced in the UN itself since 1949.

FORCED LABOR

Motivated at least partly by a desire to retaliate for the attacks of the East, the West, through the instrumentality of the AFL, raised the issue of forced labor in the spring of 1948 at ECOSOC's sixth session.[25] There were, however, many precedents for the Western action, and it should be interpreted in this broader context as

[23] UN Document E/1096.

[24] K. Y. Chizhov asserts, in an authoritative Soviet text, that the USSR was the first to ratify this convention (Academy of Sciences of the USSR, *International Law*, p. 142). In actual fact, ten states, including Bulgaria, Poland and Yugoslavia, had ratified the convention before the USSR took this action in April 1956.

[25] AFL officials publicly announced that the proposal was aimed at the Soviet Union and its satellites (*New York Times*, February 3, 1948), and the American delegate, Willard Thorp, admitted that the item "had been brought before the Council in a somewhat questionable way" (UN, ECOSOC, *Official Records* [6th Session], p. 13).

well as that of the cold war. Forced labor had frequently been a problem of humanitarian concern and there had been considerable international action in this area. For example, ILO had adopted a Convention on Forced Labour in 1930 (No. 29). The West's ultimate goal in raising this issue was to supplement and revise this Convention. It had been oriented primarily toward forced labor in dependent territories, and the West desired to broaden its application so that it would include systems of forced labor used as a means of political coercion or as a means of enforcing labor discipline. The introduction of this item provoked a heated debate which continued intermittently in the Council and the Assembly and later in ILO.

The initial memorandum submitted by the AFL made several allegations against the Soviet Union and other Eastern European states.[26] These allegations were supported in the debates which followed by delegates from the United States and the United Kingdom through the use of extracts from testimony by refugees from corrective labor camps in communist-controlled countries and of citations from the *Corrective Labor Codex* of the RSFSR and other Soviet legal documents.

In reply, the East attacked the motives of those who introduced and sponsored the item. On one occasion, a Soviet delegate claimed that the United States "wished to raise a hue and cry on that particular subject in order to divert the attention of the working masses in capitalist countries from their own status, which was no better than that of wage slaves."[27] On other occasions it was alleged that the item was introduced in order to divert attention from the aggressive plans of the NATO bloc. The crux of the Soviet counterattack, however, was an onslaught on the nature of capitalism. It was claimed that under capitalism forced labor is inevitable—that workers are economically dependent upon their capitalist employers who exploit them and who enjoy the fruits of their labor. The claim was also advanced that real freedom of labor could not exist side by side with unemployment.

The United States and the United Kingdom urged ECOSOC to refer the item to ILO and to have that body establish an investigatory commission—as suggested in the original AFL memorandum. It was planned that the information gathered by this commission would be used in revising and supplementing the 1930 ILO Con-

[26] UN Document E/596.
[27] UN, ECOSOC, *Official Records* (8th Session), p. 105.

ECONOMIC WELFARE

vention. The Soviet Union also favored an investigation, but by a very different type of commission. In the Soviet view, the investigatory commission should consist of from 110 to 125 members who would represent national and international trade unions.[28] Apportionment would be on the basis of one representative for every million trade unionists. This plan would have ensured communist control because of the large trade-union memberships claimed in Soviet bloc states. The proposed duties of the investigatory commission were: (1) to study the situation of the unemployed and the semi-employed in all countries where unemployment had not yet been eliminated; thus according to their claims, the USSR and the other Soviet bloc states would have been excluded from the survey; (2) to investigate working conditions in colonies and dependent territories; again Soviet bloc states would have been excluded by definition; (3) to collect as complete and objective information as possible on the basis of facts supplied by governments, trade unions, and other similar groups; and (4) to draw up reports and recommendations for the Council on the basis of the information received. The Council would have been pledged to give "wide publicity" to the obviously predetermined results of the commission's work.

The introduction of this item posed a dilemma for many members of the Council. While morally opposed to forced labor, they were decidedly reluctant to accept the political consequences of an official investigation. Their reaction throughout the debate was one of hesitancy and delay. It was a year before the Council decided to have the Secretary-General ask all governments if they were willing to submit to an investigation by an impartial commission.[29] The result could have been foretold. Those states against which the specific accusations were directed, the Soviet bloc, either replied that they were not willing, or they did not reply at all.[30]

During this same period, the USSR attacked ILO and sought to discredit in advance any investigation in which the agency might have a part. David A. Morse, ILO's Director-General and a United States citizen, was labeled "a representative of American business

[28] See: UN Documents E/1194; E/1222; E/1485; and, E/L. 165.
[29] ECOSOC Resolution 195 (VIII). Even this decision was a compromise. It resulted from the adoption of an Australian amendment which was designed to replace the American proposal for an immediate investigation. The vote on the amendment was 12 to 5, with 1 abstention (UN, ECOSOC, *Official Records* [8th Session], p. 464).
[30] UN Document E/1337 and Add. 1 and 2.

interests," and Soviet commentators asserted that the Anglo-American bloc had "succeeded in turning the ILO into a regular centre of propaganda against the Soviet Union and the democratic forces of the world." [31]

Further delay finally became impossible, and in 1951, at its twelfth session, the Council, after again rejecting the Soviet proposal,[32] voted to establish an *ad hoc* committee on forced labor in conjunction with ILO. All but the Soviet bloc supported this decision. Soviet opposition was carried to the Assembly's Fifth Committee, where the USSR attempted to prevent the allocation of funds for the new group. Three distinguished persons were chosen for membership on the commission: Pall Berg, former President of the Supreme Court of Norway; Enrique Garcia Sayan, former foreign minister of Peru; and as Chairman, Sir Ramaswami Mudaliar, an eminent Indian who had been President of the drafting committee on economic and social matters at San Francisco and subsequently President of ECOSOC. The stature of these three men gave added weight to the report of the committee, which was submitted to the Council in 1953.[33] The report contained *inter alia* a carefully documented substantiation of the charges made by the AFL, the United States and the United Kingdom. The Soviet bloc vehemently criticized this report.

Again there was delay, but eventually both the Council and the Assembly duly acknowledged the report and condemned forced labor.[34] On the basis of these resolutions and the report, the International Labor Organization began drafting a new convention on forced labor—a task which was completed in 1957 (No. 105). In these negotiations the Soviet Union pursued tactics similar to those which it had pursued in the UN; that is, it attempted to divert the debate into a consideration of broader issues, and, to a limited extent, it succeeded. The USSR voted for the Convention in ILO, but has not yet ratified it. Nonetheless, in 1962 an ILO committee criticized the USSR, asserting that Soviet practices contravened the Convention.[35]

[31] N. Yevgenyev, "What Some International Bodies Are Really Doing," p. 11.
[32] Reintroduced as UN Document E/L. 165.
[33] UN, ECOSOC, *Official Records* (16th Session), Supplement No. 13, "Report of the Ad Hoc Committee on Forced Labour." Also reproduced as UN Document E/2431.
[34] ECOSOC Resolution 524 (XVII) and General Assembly Resolution 842 (IX).
[35] See: ILO Conference, *Report III (Part IV)*, 1962 (46th Session), "Re-

Meanwhile, also as a result of the two resolutions, the Secretary-General of the UN and the Director-General of ILO jointly filed a supplementary report in 1955 which devoted considerable attention to forced labor in the People's Republic of China, a state not covered in the original survey.[36] This report was also strongly criticized by Soviet bloc delegations. But neither this, nor Soviet diversionary moves,[37] prevented the Council from again condemning "all forms of forced labor, wherever they exist." [38] A year's delay, however, ensued before the adoption of this resolution.

The result of the discussion of forced labor in the United Nations would seem to have been both a substantive gain through the adoption of ILO's new Convention and a damaging propaganda blow to the Soviet Union and its bloc, though this blow was weakened somewhat by the rather negative position which the United States took in ILO. For a while, because of its general policy concerning international conventions, it appeared that the United States would not even vote for the new Convention.[39] Ultimately the United States adopted a more positive stance, and the worker and government delegates voted for the Convention. The American employer delegate, however, abstained. He was the only delegate to the International Labor Conference not to vote for the Convention. Until 1963, when President Kennedy submitted the Convention to the Senate, the United States made no move to ratify.

SLAVERY

Although the problem of slavery is related to that of forced labor, the legal definitions of slavery used in international work create few dangerous implications for the USSR. Therefore, the Soviet Union has been able to support the UN's activities concerning slavery, and to use them as a vehicle to criticize the West, without fear of retaliation. In debates and negotiations involving this issue the USSR has generally sought to assume the most progressive position.

Belgium inaugurated the UN's consideration of slavery at the

---

port of the Committee of Experts on the Application of Conventions and Recommendations," pp. 193-245.

[36] UN Document E/2815.

[37] See the USSR's proposed amendments to the resolution adopted by ECOSOC: UN Document E/L. 714.

[38] ECOSOC Resolution 607 (XXI).

[39] See: Harold Karan Jacobson, "The USSR and ILO," p. 423.

Assembly's third session by proposing that the Economic and Social Council should be instructed to study this problem. There had been previous international work in this field; a Convention had been signed in 1926, and, on the basis of this, the League of Nations had performed certain functions. One question was how best to continue this past work, another was whether or not the functions should be increased. The Soviet Union joined the unanimous vote for the Belgian proposal.

This unanimity, however, was short-lived. Once more a division soon developed concerning procedure. The Soviet bloc sought to have the problem studied by groups appointed by the council—a method of appointment which presumably would ensure bloc representation —and to place emphasis on the problem of slavery in colonies and non-self-governing territories.[40] The West, on the other hand, felt that the problem should be studied by experts appointed by the Secretary-General and it opposed the emphasis suggested by the Soviet bloc. The Western view prevailed.

On ECOSOC's instruction, in 1949, the Secretary-General appointed an *ad hoc* Committee of Experts on Slavery, which consisted of four members, three from the West and one from Latin America.[41] In preparing the survey of "slavery and other institutions or customs resembling slavery," which the Council had requested, the Committee first sent a questionnaire to all governments. The USSR replied that "the problem of slavery . . . does not arise in the Soviet Union." [42]

After the Committee's report was submitted to the Economic and Social Council in 1951, the Secretary-General was asked to examine the matter in more detail, and then, in 1954, a Special Rapporteur, Hans Engen of Norway, was appointed to conduct further investigations. Meanwhile, the General Assembly, at its sixth session in 1953, adopted a special protocol which provided for the transfer to the UN of the functions which the League had exercised under the International Slavery Convention of 1926. The USSR has not ratified this Convention, nor has it signed the special Protocol. Soviet delegates termed the 1926 Convention weak and unsatisfactory, and they

---

[40] See: UN Documents E/1435; E/AC. 7/L. 108; and, E/AC. 7/L. 136.

[41] Moises Poblete Troncoso (Chile), Chairman and Rapporteur; Charles W. W. Greenidge (United Kingdom); Bruno Lasker (United States); and Mme. Jane Vialle (France).

[42] UN Document E/AC. 33/10/Add. 51, p. 1.

criticized ECOSOC's tendency to use it as a basis for further action.

Mr. Engen's report was considered at the Economic and Social Council's nineteenth session in 1955.[43] The Soviet Union was bitterly critical because it contained materials which alleged that slavery existed in the People's Republic of China.[44] After an acrimonious debate on this matter, the Council voted to establish a committee of ten governmental representatives—including one from the USSR and one from Yugoslavia—to prepare a draft text of a supplementary convention.

In the Committee's negotiations, which were held early in 1956, Soviet tactics concentrated on: (1) eliminating the word "progressively" from the declaration in Article 1 that slavery should be abolished "progressively and as soon as possible"; (2) eliminating the article prohibiting reservations; (3) eliminating the compulsory jurisdiction of the International Court of Justice in matters of treaty interpretation; and (4) eliminating the colonial application clause.[45] Although some Soviet drafting suggestions were accepted by the Committee, its substantive proposals were all rejected. Perhaps the fact that the United Kingdom prepared the text which the Committee used as a working document, and that this state had been one of the leaders in the movement to draft a new convention explains why the Soviet proposal to delete the colonial application clause failed. Even so, the strength of anticolonial sentiment was such that the clause as originally drafted was amended so as to provide an elaborate system of publicity for any case in which the treaty was not applied to a dependent territory of a signatory state. Soviet attempts to have its amendments reconsidered later at the Economic and Social Council's twenty-first session and the General Assembly's eleventh session met with failure.

Despite this, the Soviet Union attended the United Nations Conference of Plenipotentiaries on a Supplementary Convention on the Abolition of Slavery, the Slave Trade, and Institutions and Practices Similar to Slavery. The USSR signed the Convention which was completed there and in 1957 became the first state to ratify it. No reservations were attached. The stated motives for this action were similar to those offered with regard to the UN's work concerning the sup-

[43] UN Document E/2673 and Add. 1-4.
[44] See: *Izvestia*, March 30, 1955, as contained in *The Current Digest of the Soviet Press*, VII, no. 13 (May 11, 1955), 25-26.
[45] See: UN Documents E/AC. 43/L. 5 and E/AC. 43/L. 13.

pression of traffic in persons, obscene publications and narcotic drugs. During the sessions of the ten-member committee, in early 1956, the Soviet delegate said that "although the problem of slavery did not exist in the USSR," his state would "support any measure that might help to abolish slavery and related institutions and practices where they still exist." [46]

To the extent that Soviet policy showed distinctive characteristics, it was marked, especially in the early years, by attempts to embarrass others, especially the West. Its efforts in this direction, however, were generally thwarted. On the other hand, opportunities for such Soviet tactics have continued to exist. The United States, because of the attitude which it adopted toward such questions starting in 1953, refused to sign or ratify the Supplementary Convention of 1956, although previously it had signed the 1926 Convention and the 1953 Special Protocol. This action and the American refusal in 1960 to vote for a resolution urging states to adhere to the Supplementary Convention made invidious comparisons possible. There were signs, however, that this situation might change. In 1963, President Kennedy asked the Senate to give its consent to ratification of the Supplementary Convention.

UNEMPLOYMENT

Like slavery, unemployment is an issue concerning which the Soviet Union does not feel vulnerable. But this issue, with which the West itself has been seriously concerned, has provided greater opportunities for Soviet attempts to influence public opinion. The specter of the depression of the 1930's has figured prominently in many of the UN's economic debates. Soviet delegates have had only to play on these already existent fears. They have used the item to attack capitalism as an economic system, maintaining that it was "the root cause" of unemployment. The issue has also been invoked as a springboard for attacks on specific Western policies; notably, the Marshall Plan, controls on East-West trade, and rearmament and other military measures. These attacks have all reflected Soviet dogma and ideological interpretations. In addition, the Soviet Union has attempted to use the issue of unemployment to detract from some of the Western criticisms of conditions in the USSR. It is significant that the most vitriolic debates on trade union rights, forced labor and unemployment all occurred in 1949, and it will be recalled that the Soviet

[46] UN Document E/2824, p. 9.

Union's proposal for an investigation of forced labor would have focused on the situation of the unemployed and semi-employed.

In the early years of the United Nations, there was little unemployment, and the organization was primarily concerned with more pressing problems. During this period Soviet policy sought to keep the issue alive. In early sessions of the Economic and Employment Commission, the Economic Commission for Europe and the Economic and Social Council, Soviet representatives continually stressed the importance of full employment, and submitted proposals calling for studies and the adoption of hortatory recommendations to governments. While none of the proposals was adopted, these Soviet actions continued to direct attention to the problem of unemployment. However, even without these moves, the problem would not have been ignored. Most states in the UN were sufficiently concerned to keep it under continual advisement.

In late 1948 and 1949 unemployment figures began to rise significantly for the first time since the end of the Second World War, thus confirming the officially sanctioned communist analysis and belief in an imminent crisis in world capitalism.[47] The USSR took full advantage of the opportunities that this situation presented in discussions of the problem in April and May 1949 in ECOSOC's functional economic commissions.

The Economic Commission for Europe also met in May, and unemployment appeared on its agenda at the Soviet Union's request. In the general debate there, the Soviet delegate, Mr. Arutiunian, argued that although unemployment was a permanent feature of capitalist economic systems, it had been accentuated by the Marshall Plan.

> ... the difficulties with which industries producing manufactured products and machinery had to contend in industrialized countries were chiefly caused by the shrinkage of export markets. That shrinkage arose from the success of the United States monopolies in obtaining control of what had previously been export markets for the countries of Europe. This they had been able to achieve by the Marshall Plan, which put them in an advantageous position vis-a-vis Western European producers.[48]

Despite the flaws in fact, logic and analysis in this argument, it possibly had some popular appeal. The Soviet Union submitted a resolu-

[47] See: Marshall D. Shulman, *Stalin's Foreign Policy Reappraised* (Cambridge: Harvard University Press, 1963), p. 34.
[48] UN Document E/ECE/SR. 4/18, p. 8.

tion, which requested the Committee on Manpower to make recommendations toward ensuring full employment "by means of the all around development of the principal branches of national industry and expansion of trade between the countries of Europe on a non-discriminatory basis." [49] The Committee was instructed to carry out its task in consultation with "democratic organizations" such as trade unions—an obvious reference to the WFTU. In addition to focusing on the problem of unemployment, this resolution was a part of the USSR's campaign to break down the West's developing controls on the export of strategic goods. Only the Soviet bloc supported it. However, perhaps the Soviet purpose was served, for by common consent the debates attracted wide attention throughout Europe.

Perhaps to achieve the same result on a global basis, the World Federation of Trade Unions requested that "Unemployment and Full Employment" be placed on the agenda of the Economic and Social Council's ninth session which opened in July 1949. It would have been discussed in any case simply as a result of the prior work done by ECOSOC's commissions. However, the Soviet bloc thereafter hailed the WFTU as the initiator of the Council's consideration of the unemployment problem. The WFTU submitted a memorandum which discussed unemployment in agonizing terms and a draft resolution which Poland sponsored. This resolution, which was offered several times in varying forms by Soviet bloc delegates in subsequent debates, recommended that all member states suffering from unemployment should immediately adopt the following measures "to be elaborated and applied with the effective participation of the truly representative trade unions":

> (a) the introduction of a comprehensive system of unemployment insurance, guaranteeing a decent standard of living to all fully or partially employed workers and covering all wage-earners as soon as they become unemployed and throughout the entire unemployment period;
> (b) the prohibition of dismissals of workers without agreement with the representative trade union organization concerned;
> (c) the increase of purchasing power of wage-earners and the extension of the domestic market, particularly by an increase in wages and social allowances for workers of all categories;
> (d) the control of all activities, transactions, profits and utiliza-

[49] UN, ECOSOC, *Official Records* (9th Session), Supplement No. 12, "Report of the Economic Commission for Europe," p. 45.

tion of profits of trusts and monopolies, the reduction of these profits, and price control;
(e) the democratic reform of tax systems, the reduction of the proportion of revenue derived from indirect taxes, and the increase of taxes on profits;
(f) the reduction of working hours and of the intensity of work;
(g) the creation, development and extension of a broad system of vocational training;
(h) the initiation of large-scale programmes of productive public works for the purpose of raising the standard of living, and promoting the cultural development of peoples;
(i) the reduction of expenditures on armaments;
(j) the establishment and development of free trade relations between countries, based on equality of rights, respect for national independence and for the free economic and political development of each country;
(k) the establishment of a relationship between industrial prices, the prices of raw materials and agricultural prices, which shall be suitable having regard to the standard of living of urban and rural workers and of the underdeveloped and industrialized countries.[50]

Member states were to report to the Council on the steps that they had taken to implement this resolution, and the Council would review their replies and the whole problem of unemployment at forthcoming sessions in terms of the above recommendations. This proposal was carefully calculated to put ECOSOC members in an embarrassing position. It had elements which would appeal to several interest groups both within and outside the UN. Its vague statements of principle were difficult to vote against, yet many of them contained insidious Soviet attacks, and some, because of the amount of central control involved and the implied limitation on profits, would have had very serious consequences for capitalism as an economic system. Thus, the Council found itself in the anomalous position of allowing all of the specific provisions of the resolution to be adopted, with the majority of the members abstaining, and then of having to reject the proposal as a whole. Czechoslovakia reintroduced the resolution at the fourth session of the General Assembly that fall,[51] and this embarrassing sequence was repeated in the Second Committee and later, with minor variations, in the plenary meeting.

After rejecting the Soviet-backed suggestion, the Economic and Social Council accepted the Western interpretation that the rise in

[50] UN Document E/1332/Add. 2.
[51] UN Documents: A/C. 2/L. 16 and A/1081.

unemployment was the result of "sales difficulties," rather than of any basic structural problem, and asked the Secretary-General to publish material on measures taken by governments in this area and to appoint a group of experts to prepare a report on "national and international measures required to achieve full employment." [52] The Soviet Union opposed these decisions and also the Assembly's subsequent endorsement of them.

Because of the Chinese representation boycott, during the first seven months of 1950, the Economic Commission for Europe was the only UN forum in which the USSR could press its attack on unemployment.[53] Its intervention there, though, was of little significance, for the principal discussions occurred elsewhere and were based on the report of the group of experts, which was not even formally considered by ECE. The group of experts, all from the West, had met from October through December 1949 and had prepared a unanimous report entitled *National and International Measures for Full Employment*.[54] ECOSOC devoted much of its tenth and eleventh sessions to the problem of unemployment, and after considering the report of the group of experts and material prepared by the Secretary-General, adopted Resolution 290 (XI), which established guidelines for the UN's future work concerning this issue. The resolution made a number of recommendations for national and international action, established a continuing program of studies and work for the Secretariat, and insured periodic reviews of the problem in the Council.

The resolution also sanctioned and provided for the further development on an annual basis of the questionnaires which the Secretary-General had sent to governments acting under the authority granted to him by the Council the previous year. In these questionnaires governments were asked to supply detailed information on the current situation in their country and on the measures they had taken to insure full employment. Soviet replies always began with the assertion

[52] ECOSOC Resolution 221 E (IX).
[53] See: UN Document E/ECE/SR. 5/5, pp. 11-12.
[54] The group consisted of the following economists: John Maurice Clark, Professor of Economics, Columbia University, Chairman; Nicholas Kaldor, Fellow of King's College, Cambridge University; Arthur Smithies, Professor of Economics, Harvard University; E. Ronald Walker, Economic Adviser to the Australian Department of External Affairs; and, Pierre Uri, Economic and Financial Adviser to the Commissariat général du Plan, Paris. Their report was issued as: United Nations Publication, Sales Number: 1949. II. A. 3.

that unemployment did not exist in the USSR. This was generally followed by extracts from the USSR's most recent economic plan, or other similar documents.

When the Soviet Union resumed broad participation in the UN in the fall of 1950, there was little that it could do except criticize the Council's action. Soviet delegates, however, did this, and with considerable force. In addition, they took advantage of the debate in the General Assembly's fifth session to repeat their descriptions of the situation of the unemployed in capitalist countries, their analyses of the causes of this situation, and their glowing descriptions of workers' lives in the people's democracies. The crux of the Soviet criticism of ECOSOC's work was that, following the recommendations of the groups of experts, it emphasized international measures to combat unemployment. Soviet delegates argued that the only effective remedies lay in domestic measures along the lines suggested in the original WFTU memorandum. There were propaganda advantages to be gained from this position and it also was in accord with Soviet ideology. In addition, the Soviet position may have been partially determined by the USSR's relatively small role in international trade at that time. Later, when the Soviet Union was more interested in trade, it came to emphasize "nondiscriminatory" trade as a possible solution to unemployment. The Soviet bloc opposed the Assembly's resolution endorsing Council Resolution 290 (XI). It was clear at this Assembly session, and it became more obvious as time went on, that the Soviet Union was isolated from the mainstream of the UN's activities concerning the unemployment problem.

This isolation was the result of several things. Because of its absence from the important negotiations during the Council's tenth and eleventh sessions, the USSR had lost many opportunities to channel this work in a direction more favorable to it. But more important, the UN had passed the stage of adopting vague, general resolutions, the type that the Soviet Union preferred. Then, too, as the Council's work became more technical, it had to be based on a number of assumptions and invariably these were not those contained in Soviet ideology. Further, in the early nineteen fifties the Council adopted a number of organizational reforms, dropping the Economic and Employment Commission (by then renamed the Economic, Employment and Development Commission), restricting the role of NGO's and tightening the rules of procedure for debate. In addition, the regional economic commissions began to concentrate on rather specific cooperative tasks, and de-emphasized general discussions of such topics as unemployment. Soviet opportunities to use the UN as a forum were thereby constricted.

The next time that the Soviet Union attempted to play an active role in the UN's work on unemployment was at the Economic and Social Council's fourteenth session in the summer of 1952. The USSR submitted a draft resolution on measures to increase employment and combat unemployment. This resolution alleged that the armaments race initiated by the United Kingdom and the United States was responsible for unemployment and recommended that governments should cease their efforts to curtail civilian production and that they should undertake to ease the burdens of the unemployed.[55] This proposal was rejected, and the Soviet Union opposed those which were adopted.

The USSR's role was equally peripheral in the discussions of the problem of unemployment in the Economic and Social Council and the General Assembly during the next two years even though unemployment figures rose again. Soviet delegates submitted resolutions at ECOSOC's sixteenth and eighteenth sessions and at the Assembly's ninth session.[56] The first of these resolutions linked the abolition of "discriminations" in international trade to the solution of unemployment. The other two paralleled those which had been submitted previously, and in addition called for the convocation of a conference of trade union groups and other non-governmental organizations to exchange information on "the real state of affairs as regards unemployment" and "practical steps" to eliminate it. All three resolutions were rejected, but instead of opposing those which were adopted, the Soviet Union abstained.

When unemployment figures jumped once more in the winter of 1957-1958, the Soviet Union tried new tactics, but with little more success. The USSR submitted two resolutions to the Council's twenty-sixth session.[57] The first recommended the convocation of a Second United Nations Conference on Trade and Employment, and was one of a series of Soviet initiatives concerning international trade.[58] Employment received relatively minor emphasis in this proposal. The second resolution asked the regional economic commis-

[55] UN Document E/L. 388/Rev. 1.
[56] UN Documents: E/L. 531; E/L. 624; and, A/L. 188.
[57] UN Documents E/AC. 6/L. 217 and E/AC. 6/L. 219.
[58] See below: Chapter 7.

ECONOMIC WELFARE 177

sions "to devote attention to questions of employment" taking into account specific regional aspects of the problem and to make recommendations to the Council at its twenty-eighth session. This was clearly an attempt to have the unemployment problem considered in bodies which might be more receptive to Soviet proposals. As none but the Soviet bloc supported the first resolution, in accordance with the USSR's changed tactics, it was not pressed to the vote. The second proposal was rejected in ECOSOC's Economic Committee by twelve votes to two, with four abstentions. That it was not offered again in the plenary session provided further evidence of the changed Soviet tactics. Although the USSR abstained in the resolution which the Council did adopt, its introduction by Canada, Greece and the United States appeared to be, at least partially, a response to the Soviet move, and, to a limited extent, its phraseology reflected the Soviet proposal.

In the following years, the USSR's representatives continued to use UN debates on the unemployment problem to criticize capitalism and to praise communism. Outside the UN, Soviet commentators criticized Secretariat studies for allegedly glossing over the seriousness of the situation and implied that this was attributable to the nationality of those responsible for their preparation.[59] In 1961, the Soviet Union asked for a new study of unemployment so that the Economic and Social Council could consider this issue in detail again in 1962.[60] The preamble in the original version of the Soviet proposal proclaimed that as a result of rising unemployment "millions of workers have suffered increased hardship and want." It is significant that the USSR was willing to modify this and other similar references without argument and it is also significant that, with these changes, the resolution was adopted unanimously. When the study was presented in 1962, the USSR made no move to push the issue further, nor did it criticize the analysis, which among other things discussed the problem of underemployment in communist countries.[61] Perhaps the past failures of Soviet proposals for exhortatory resolutions had discouraged further attempts of this nature. It is also true, though, that Soviet proposals have usually coincided with increases in the number of unemployed, and 1962 was not such a year. The USSR's purpose in

[59] *Izvestia,* April 27, 1961, as contained in *The Current Digest of the Soviet Press.* XIII, no. 17 (May 24, 1961), 23.
[60] UN Document E/L. 907 and Rev. 1.
[61] See: UN Document E/3659 and Add. 1 and 2.

1962 appears to have been, as it was in the years immediately after the Second World War, merely to keep the issue in the forefront of public consideration.

It is almost impossible to measure the success of Soviet efforts to influence public opinion by means of its position concerning this issue. There can be no doubt, however, that unemployment remains a potent issue, and the fact that even though the Soviet Union has been isolated from most of the UN's activities, other members of the UN have felt that they have had to pay some attention to Soviet proposals and to modify their own accordingly, suggests that at least they have believed that the Soviet campaign has had some appeal. Clearly, this has been the USSR's most effective effort in this field, and Soviet efforts have indubitably had some impact on the UN's activities concerning this problem.

ARMAMENTS, DISARMAMENT AND THE STANDARD OF LIVING

Apparently hoping to raise an equally strong issue as unemployment, at the Economic and Social Council's twelfth session in 1951 the World Federation of Trade Unions requested consideration of the item, "Lowering of the Workers' Standard of Living: A Result of War Economy." At that meeting, and at various Council and Assembly sessions through 1957, the USSR and other Soviet bloc countries introduced resolutions which asserted that increasing expenditures on armaments entailed a considerable lowering of the standard of living of workers.[62] These resolutions recommended that governments should reduce their armaments budgets by various amounts up to 50 per cent, and that the funds thus released should be devoted to improving workers' standards of living and other appealing purposes, including promoting economic development. Similar proposals were introduced in the Council's regional economic commissions. None of these resolutions won majority support in its original form, though during this period various UN bodies did adopt resolutions on the relationship between arms expenditures and standards of living, and occasionally these incorporated features included in the Soviet proposals.

While the USSR's attack in the UN concerning unemployment reflected Soviet ideological views, in this case there was something

[62] UN Documents: E/L. 156; A/C. 2/L. 135; A/2079, and, E/AC. 6/L. 179.

of a dichotomy. Domestically, Soviet economists argued that the level of expenditures in the West had produced a "temporary stabilization of capitalism," and allowed Western states to maintain a high level of profits and employment. Nevertheless, the Soviet proposals served various purposes, including making good copy for *Pravda*.[63]

After having argued for several years that the arms race caused a deterioration of workers' standards of living in capitalist countries, in 1960 Soviet delegates began to argue that disarmament might have the same effect, a position more in accord with Soviet ideology. Taking their key from Nikita S. Khrushchev's address to the Assembly the previous fall and the proposals which he submitted, Soviet delegates at the twenty-ninth session of ECOSOC and the fifteenth session of ECE proposed that each body should study the economic and social consequences of general and complete disarmament.[64] Soviet bloc delegates argued that there was serious need to consider how the funds which would be released by disarmament could and would be spent, and in particular, how they could be used to increase assistance to underdeveloped countries. Although these proposals were rejected, or withdrawn, primarily because of the opposition of the United States,[65] a similar proposal introduced by Pakistan later that year at the fifteenth session of the General Assembly was adopted. As a consequence, a group of ten experts, including nationals of Czechoslovakia, Poland, and the Soviet Union, was appointed to undertake a detailed study of the issue.[66] This

[63] *Pravda*, July 9, 1955, as contained in *The Current Digest of the Soviet Press*, VII, no. 27 (August 17, 1955), 13-14.

[64] UN Document E/L. 861; and UN, ECOSOC, *Official Records* (30th Session), Supplement No. 3, "Economic Commission for Europe: Annual Report," p. 30. The USSR also raised the issue in ECAFE, but did not make a formal proposal; UN Document E/CN. 11/566, p. 84.

[65] At that time the United States opposed any UN analysis of the economic and social consequences of disarmament even though studies of this subject had been conducted within the U.S. government and a major research effort directed by Emile Benoit of Columbia University and under the sponsorship of the Center for Research on Conflict Resolution of The University of Michigan was then underway.

[66] The members of the group were: V. Y. Aboltin, Deputy Director, Institute of World Economics and International Relations, Academy of Sciences of the USSR; Mamoun Beheiry, Governor, Bank of Sudan; Arthur J. Brown, Head, Department of Economics, University of Leeds, England; B. N. Ganguli, Head, The Delhi School of Economics, India; Aftab Ahmad Khan, Chief Economist, Planning Commission, Government of Pakistan; Oskar Lange,

group met in August 1961 and January and February 1962, studied documents submitted by governments and international organizations, and prepared a report entitled *Economic and Social Consequences of Disarmament*.[67] Despite this ongoing analysis, in 1961, the USSR again unsuccessfully sought to have ECE study the matter.[68]

When the report of the group of experts was considered at the thirty-fourth session of the Economic and Social Council in July 1962, perhaps the most interesting feature of the Soviet presentation was the argument, which had also been advanced in the documentation submitted by the USSR to the experts,[69] that disarmament would not present any insuperable problems for capitalist countries, that its effects would be beneficial for all. The Soviet delegate, the same economist who had served on the group of experts, agreed "that it should not be difficult to maintain effective demand during the transitional period, particularly as real incomes would be rising." [70] Nonetheless, the USSR maintained that the principal emphasis in the UN's activities in this area should be placed on the capitalist, private-enterprise economies, since reconversion would present no problems in the socialist countries as it could be encompassed in the normal planning activities. Both the USSR and the United States joined Ethiopia, India, Poland and Yugoslavia in sponsoring the resolution which the Council unanimously adopted. It endorsed disarmament as a desirable objective, sought to publicize the report of the group of experts, and insured that the issue would receive continuing attention in the United Nations.

Once more, the Soviet Union had introduced an issue of signifi-

---

Chairman, Economic Council, Council of Ministers of the Government of the People's Republic of Poland; W. W. Leontief, Professor of Economics, Harvard University, United States; José Antonio Mayobre, Ambassador of Venezuela to the United States; Alfred Sauvy, Director, National Institute of Demographic Studies, Government of France; and, Ludek Urban, Economic Institute, Czechoslovakian Academy of Sciences. Jacob L. Mosak, Director of the Division of General Economic Research and Policies of the United Nations Secretariat, served as Chairman.

[67] United Nations Publication, Sales Number: 1962. IX. 1.

[68] UN, ECOSOC, *Official Records* (32nd Session), Supplement No. 3, "Report of the Economic Commission for Europe," p. 31.

[69] See: *Economic and Social Consequences of Disarmament: Replies of Governments and Communications from International Organizations*, United Nations Publication, Sales Number: 1962. IX. 2, pp. 172-189.

[70] UN, ECOSOC, *Official Records* (34th Session), p. 94.

cance and with popular appeal, which it was impossible to ignore. Clearly, the USSR had propagandistic motives, but in addition, the problems had substantive importance, and to the extent that they were considered in a meaningful way, the world probably gained.

CONCLUSIONS

The predominant motivation for Soviet policy concerning the United Nations work in the field of economic welfare can be broadly characterized as a desire to influence public opinion, to point out the flaws in the capitalist West and to glorify conditions under communism. There probably were other motivations as well; for example, the introduction of the question of trade union rights may have been prompted by a desire to gain protection for communist trade union leaders. But these seem to have been subordinate to the basic objective of propaganda. The draft resolutions submitted by the WFTU, the Soviet Union, or other Soviet bloc states all appear to have been designed with this purpose in mind. Their adoption or rejection probably made little difference to Soviet leaders, for it was equally useful to be able to demonstrate that the West, through its negative votes, opposed "progressive" measures. Certainly the statements made by Soviet delegates in the general debates, however much they may have reflected ideological convictions, seem to have been primarily oriented toward influencing public opinion. What other motives could the Soviet Union have when dealing with problems which it felt could exist only in the capitalist West?

The extent to which the Soviet Union attained its goal is subject to speculation. Many of its propagandistic proposals were removed from the UN arena by the device of referring the question to the International Labor Organization. The Soviet Union's re-entry into that organization in 1954 should probably be interpreted in this context. One of the attacks in the UN, that concerning trade union rights, was turned against the USSR. Further, a counterattack on the issue of forced labor was provoked which appeared to result in a resounding propaganda defeat for the USSR. Procedural revisions decreased the opportunities for Soviet propaganda efforts. On the other hand, it is evident that some of the Soviet attacks had considerable effect on the UN's work. It is perhaps not going too far to say that the Soviet Union served as a "gadfly" to the conscience of the United Nations. Through its attacks it stimulated substantive action which otherwise might not have been taken. That this occurred probably indicates that Soviet propaganda efforts had some success; the issues raised were important and sensitive, and provided fertile ground for the USSR's onslaughts.

These Soviet attacks, and the Western reaction, contributed to the "politicization" of ECOSOC and of the UN's economic and social work generally. This development has been viewed with apprehension by both statesmen and scholars. However, while the political character of much of the UN's proceedings concerning economic welfare issues may have caused delay and provoked tempers, disturbances which possibly spilled over to other aspects of the organization's work, it has also had beneficial effects. The injection of a sense of political reality into the debates has linked them with "the world that is." This development may also have accentuated the importance of the Economic and Social Council during its formative years, since it was in that body that much of the central ideological discussion took place. The debates on economic welfare clearly outlined the alternatives presented by the two conflicting ideological systems.

7: INTERNATIONAL TRADE

THE UNITED NATIONS MANDATE CONCERNING INTERNATIONAL TRADE IS as broad as it is vague. The Charter directs the UN to promote "solutions of international economic . . . problems," and at the same time it lists "higher standards of living," "full employment," and "economic . . . progress and development" as at least equally important objectives. No guidelines are given concerning the techniques which should be followed in implementing these objectives, nor are priorities assigned amongst them. National views concerning the appropriate methods have varied, and there have also been pronounced differences concerning which objectives should receive greatest emphasis.[1] The United States, which has provided greatest leadership in this aspect of the UN's activities, has generally interpreted the UN's mandate in terms of the Atlantic Charter and Article VII of the Mutual Aid Agreement which it negotiated with the United Kingdom during the Second World War; that is, it has assumed that the UN's goal should be the expansion of international trade on as free and as multilateral a basis as possible. In supporting this concept American planners in a memorandum which was prepared in 1943 held that its achievement would not only be valuable in itself, but that it would also be "essential to the attainment of full and effective employment in the United States and elsewhere, to the preservation of private enterprise, and to the success of an international system to prevent future wars."[2] They therefore saw little conflict between the

[1] See: Robert E. Asher, *The United Nations and Promotion of the General Welfare*, pp. 28 39, 240-241.

[2] "Summary of the Interim Report of the Special Committee on Relaxation of Trade Barriers," in *Postwar Foreign Policy Preparation, 1939-1945* (Washington, D. C.: Government Printing Office 1949), p. 622.

various objectives outlined in the Charter, and even thought that through these methods gains could be made in the security field as well. By and large the United States has not deviated from this view, and the major industrial states of the West have also generally accepted it, although they have occasionally given greater emphasis to "full employment." The underdeveloped countries, however, with their overriding interest in economic growth, have taken a very different position. Free trade has at best been a secondary objective with them, and sometimes they have even viewed it as an obstacle to the fulfillment of their ambitions.

Soviet attitudes toward the UN's activities in the field of international trade have varied greatly, at least on the surface. Before the conclusion of the Second World War, the USSR took part in many of the preliminary negotiations, although its contribution was limited and unenthusiastic. This participation ceased after the war was over, and the Soviet Union's role in the activities which the UN inaugurated then was extremely restricted. Since 1953, however, the Soviet Union has radically altered its policy concerning these functions of the United Nations. Soviet representatives began to participate in many UN organs which they previously boycotted, and they even attempted to seize the initiative through the submission of new, far-reaching proposals.

The limited nature of the Soviet Union's interest in the UN's activities in the field of international trade in the early years should not have occasioned surprise. The USSR could hardly have been expected to share either the direct or indirect objectives of the United States with regard to these activities. The role of foreign trade in the Soviet Union traditionally had been quite narrow and considerably different from that in other countries.[3] Communist doctrine had stressed the necessity of self-sufficiency, and much of the USSR's economic policy had been directed toward this end. The trade in which the Soviet Union had engaged had generally been aimed at securing imports necessary to implement economic development programs, or at gaining political advantages. Thus, the Soviet Union had

[3] See: Alexander Baykov, *Soviet Foreign Trade* (Princeton: Princeton University Press, 1946); Harry Schwartz, *Russia's Soviet Economy* (2nd ed., New York: Prentice-Hall, 1954), chapter 14; Willis C. Armstrong, "The Soviet Approach to International Trade," *Political Science Quarterly*, LXIII, no. 3 (September, 1948), 368-382; and, Willis C. Armstrong, "Soviet Use of Trade as a Weapon," in C. Grove Haines (ed.), *The Threat of Soviet Imperialism* (Baltimore: The Johns Hopkins Press, 1954), pp. 69-79.

exhibited little interest in the expansion of international trade *per se*, and its ends usually could best be achieved through bilateral rather than multilateral trade. Nor could the USSR have been sincerely committed to preserving private enterprise and maintaining full employment in the United States and other Western countries, two indirect goals which underlay the American desire for expanded multilateral trade. Further, the state monopoly of foreign trade, although it facilitated the attainment of the USSR's objectives, precluded Soviet interest in the UN's technical work in this field, which generally assumed very different conditions. The changes in Soviet policy were therefore perhaps more noteworthy than the Soviet Union's earlier disinterest.

Partially because of the UN's broad mandate and the diversity of views concerning it, the framework within which activities concerning international trade were conducted soon became exceedingly complex. Specialized agencies were established and others were planned. The Economic and Social Council set up its own subsidiary bodies, and both the Council and the General Assembly debated subjects in this area and inaugurated work programs. In addition, both sides in the cold war established exclusive institutions outside the UN; the West, the Organization for European Economic Cooperation—later the Organization for Economic Cooperation and Development—and other regional institutions; and the East, the Council for Mutual Economic Assistance.

Despite the many organs involved and the complexity of the structural framework, the inherent unity of the subject, as well as the General Assembly's overriding role, have served to tie the several activities together, at least in the UN. Because of this, and since Soviet policies have changed so markedly but have also been relatively consistent at any given time, a temporal framework provides a better vehicle for examining the USSR's role in this aspect of the United Nations activities than a division by structure or substantive problem.

CREATING A STRUCTURAL FRAMEWORK

The UN's first activities in the field of international trade dealt primarily with the creation of specialized agencies, which it was anticipated would conduct most of the actual work. In the American view, three specialized agencies were thought to be especially necessary: one to aid in stabilizing currencies; another to lend money for reconstruction and development purposes; and a third to regulate commercial policy and to work toward the reduction of tariffs and other barriers to trade. In addition, it was anticipated that the Food and Agricultural Organization, because of its concern with primary commodities, would have some functions in this area, as would, though to a much lesser extent, specialized agencies in the field of transportation.

Three of the specialized agencies were created even before the United Nations. The foundation for the Food and Agricultural Organization was laid at the Hot Springs Conference in May 1943. The USSR's participation in this conference and its attitude toward FAO have already been described.[4] The Charters for the International Monetary Fund and the International Bank for Reconstruction and Development were drafted at the Bretton Woods Conference in 1944. The USSR participated in this Conference and in earlier informal discussions. In these negotiations Soviet delegates appeared to have little interest in the broad objectives particularly of the Monetary Fund.[5] Instead, they were mainly concerned with matters which would directly affect the USSR: the cost of participation; the availability of credits; the extent of the organizations' control over the Soviet economy; and conversely, the extent of Soviet control over the organizations' activities. While concessions were made to the Soviet position, these did not affect the organizations' fundamental structures and purposes. Many in the West hoped that the USSR would ratify the Bretton Woods Agreements and become a member of IMF and IBRD, but it did not. Although Czechoslovakia, Poland and Yugoslavia joined the two agencies, Poland withdrew from membership in 1950, and Czechoslovakia was expelled in 1954 because of failure to comply with the Articles of Agreement. Since 1954, Yugoslavia has been the only communist country in IMF and IBRD.

An International Trade Organization was to have been the final—and many felt the most important—specialized agency in this field. As a result of an American initiative, steps were taken toward its creation at the first session of the Economic and Social Council in

[4] See above pp. 108-110, 112-113.
[5] See: Raymond F. Mikesell, "Negotiating at Bretton Woods, 1944," in Raymond Dennett and Joseph E. Johnson (eds.), *Negotiating with the Russians*, pp. 101-116.

the spring of 1946. The USSR supported the initial resolution which was passed then, but did not attend the subsequent conferences in London, Geneva, and Havana. Nor did Soviet delegates participate significantly in ECOSOC's step-by-step discussions of these conferences. Czechoslovakia and Poland were more active and attended the various conferences, though only the former signed the agreements which were drafted.

One authority maintains that because of the USSR's failure to take part in these negotiations some of the proposals concerning state-controlled economies were dropped from the ITO, or Havana, Charter and that the sanctions against non-members were reduced.[6] Neither the Soviet Union's abstention, nor its later attack on the Havana Charter, however, was a basic cause of the instrument's failure to obtain the necessary ratifications. Its nature as a complex, compromise document which fully satisfied no one and the lack of American support were chiefly responsible for this.

The Economic and Social Council's consideration of its own structural arrangements for work in the field of international trade provided further evidence of Soviet disinterest in such questions. Several Council members desired to establish a balance of payments subcommission as one of the subsidiary bodies of the Economic and Employment Commission. The USSR opposed this suggestion, arguing that such a sub-commission was not necessary and could serve no useful function.[7] The Soviet Union's lack of interest in the creation of the regional economic commissions, which would have important functions in this field, was another similar sign.

The traditional communist attitude toward foreign trade was probably one explanation for the USSR's disinterest in and abstention from the activities of the United Nation's in this field during this early period. Furthermore, membership in any of the specialized agencies might have involved some slight degree of outside control over Soviet economic policies and would have required the disclosure of then secret information. Then, too, the UN's activities, with their global orientation, might have interfered with attempts to unify the Soviet bloc. It is likely that the USSR participated in the Hot Springs and Bretton Woods Conferences and other wartime negotiations only

[6] Clair Wilcox, A *Charter for World Trade* (New York: Macmillan, 1949), pp. 101-102 and 162-164.
[7] UN Document E/150.

188   The USSR and the UN's Economic and Social Activities

to maintain the necessary inter-allied unity and perhaps in the hope of obtaining credits for postwar reconstruction. The development of the cold war made it clear that this hope would not be fulfilled.

THE COLD WAR PERIOD

The cold war increased in intensity during the period from 1948 through 1952, and it appeared to be the dominant factor motivating Soviet policy then. During these years the Soviet Union continued to abstain from most of the UN's activities designed to expand international trade. It did not participate in the International Civil Aviation Organization,[8] the negotiations to establish the Inter-Governmental Maritime Consultative Organization,[9] FAO, IMF, IBRD, the interim organizational arrangements established to work in the area planned for the ITO, or in most of the technical committees established by the Economic Commission for Europe which could have had a significant impact on intra-European trade. But this abstention did not preclude an active policy. On the contrary, the USSR was extremely active as it constantly used the UN as a forum within which to attack Western international trade policies. This attack had three main facets: one centered on the activities of the United Nations and the specialized agencies; a second concerned the policy pursued by the United States and other Western countries of limiting the export of strategic goods to the Soviet bloc; and a third, while having the same ultimate target as the second, concentrated on problems of East-West trade in Europe.

THE ATTACK ON THE UN AND THE SPECIALIZED AGENCIES

The Soviet attack on the Havana Charter illustrated the first facet of Soviet policy. When the report on the recently completed Charter

[8] The International Civil Aviation Convention was drafted at Chicago in 1944, and ICAO came into existence in 1947. Czechoslovakia and Poland attended the Chicago Conference, joined ICAO, and have been members of the agency ever since then. Yugoslavia joined ICAO in 1960. The USSR's unwillingness to attend the Chicago Conference and to join ICAO seems to stem from its desire to regulate air traffic on the basis of bilateral agreements and from its opposition to the requirements in the Chicago Convention that signatories must automatically extend certain overflight, landing and other privileges to all ICAO members. (See: Academy of Sciences of the USSR, *International Law*, pp. 244, 351-352.)

[9] Of the Eastern European states, only Czechoslovakia and Poland attended the 1948 Geneva Conference where the Convention for IMCO was drafted.

was discussed at the Economic and Social Council's seventh session in the summer of 1948, the Soviet delegate, Mr. Arutiunian, charged that the Havana Conference "had produced no useful results whatever for the development of international trade." [10] He argued that the Conference had failed because the industrially developed states had used it as a device to attempt to impose unfavorable trading conditions on underdeveloped countries, and because the United States had used it to assert its interests to the exclusion of those of all others. He claimed that the Charter's provisions against tariffs and quantitative restrictions would hurt underdeveloped countries, which needed these devices to protect their "infant industries," and maintained that the decisions to allow preferential agreements and export subsidies would benefit only the highly developed states of the West, and particularly the United States. He also argued that the Havana Charter was discriminatory against states with controlled economies and against non-members. Here, his comments may have been motivated by real fear, however slight, that the Charter, if put into effect, might have harmed Soviet interests. For contrast, Mr. Arutiunian gave a eulogistic description of the USSR's foreign trade policy, which he claimed always led to mutually advantageous trade and also "promoted friendly relations between nations and preserved peace."

There had been sufficient conflicts during the negotiations to make these charges have some appeal, and they were repeated by Soviet delegates on several occasions in the United Nations. Although the USSR's point of view was never reflected in any resolution adopted by the United Nations concerning the Charter of the International Trade Organization, Soviet attacks in UN debates may well have exacerbated the conflicts which were inherent in any endeavor of this nature and made ratification of the Charter more difficult to achieve.

Soviet delegates in the United Nations also attacked the International Monetary Fund and the International Bank for Reconstruction and Development. They alleged that both were "tools" of United States foreign policy and that both discriminated against underdeveloped and Eastern European countries.[11] They deplored the fact that the agreements with these agencies gave the UN so little power

[10] UN, ECOSOC, *Official Records* (7th Session), p. 322. The following section is based on his major address: *ibid.*, pp. 322-330.

[11] See, for example: UN, General Assembly, Plenary Meetings, *Official Records* (3rd Session, 1st Part), p. 692.

and argued that it should have the right to make recommendations concerning their credit activities so that the alleged discriminations could be corrected.

The USSR maintained that it did not participate in the technical committees of the Economic Commission for Europe because they had been subordinated to Anglo-American policies and consequently did not deal with the "fundamental tasks and aims" which had been assigned to them.[12]

The USSR voted against, or abstained on, all United Nations' resolutions dealing with the technical problems of international trade on the ground that they violated national sovereignty and were therefore *ultra vires*. These resolutions concerned the elimination of double taxation, the conclusion of a convention on customs treatment of samples and advertising, and the amelioration of problems involved in the movement of goods and persons across national frontiers. Soviet representatives refused to take part in the UN's efforts to deal with problems involved in the transport of dangerous goods and attacked these activities, charging that the problems would not exist were it not for the aggressive Anglo-American rearmament policy.

THE ATTACK ON THE WESTERN EMBARGO ON STRATEGIC EXPORTS

While the first facet of Soviet policy during the years 1948 through 1952 consisted of an attack on the activities of the United Nations and the specialized agencies, in reality it was aimed at the West. The second facet of Soviet policy was less circuitous. It was a direct attack on the West. Starting with the third session of the General Assembly in the fall of 1948, the USSR and other Soviet bloc states constantly raised the question of "discrimination in international trade." Their representatives maintained that the Western controls on the export of strategic goods to communist countries were the most important discrimination and, therefore, the chief factor limiting the expansion of international trade. They argued that greater East-West trade was not only necessary for reconstruction, but would also facilitate diplomatic and political cooperation.

These arguments were frequently capped with the introduction of resolutions condemning discrimination in international trade.[13] Although phrased in general terms, statements in the debates made it clear that these were aimed at the United States and its principal

[12] UN Document E/ECE/SR. 3/4. Corr. 3, p. 2.
[13] See: UN Documents A/C. 2/137 and E/1479.

allies.¹⁴ None of these resolutions was ever adopted. However, the United Nations often did adopt resolutions expressing the hope that trade would be expanded, and these usually stated that this should be done on a nondiscriminatory basis. But these resolutions were carefully phrased so that they could not be construed as a condemnation of the Western controls on strategic exports.

EAST-WEST TRADE IN EUROPE

The third facet of Soviet policy during this period was somewhat more successful. Although the ultimate target again seemed to be the Western embargo on the export of strategic goods, the immediate goal was the creation of special machinery in the Economic Commission for Europe to promote intra-European trade. This campaign was inaugurated at ECE's third session in the spring of 1948 when the USSR proposed that ECE should establish a committee to study and make recommendations on steps to facilitate an expansion of intra-European trade and also trade between Europe and other areas; on methods of obtaining long- and short-term credit for use in developing European trade; and on means of eliminating the after-effects of the war.¹⁵ This proposal fell on fertile ground, for many, including ECE's Executive Secretary, Gunnar Myrdal, thought that a revival of East-West trade would be an important contribution to solving Europe's economic problems.

The United States and the United Kingdom, however, were skeptical. They feared that the proposal might simply be an appeal for aid for Eastern Europe and an attempt to have ECE condemn the United States for channeling its relief and reconstruction aid outside the United Nations. The fact that it was linked with another proposal providing for the creation of a subcommittee "for the Maintenance and Development of those Branches of Industry which are most essential for the Economy of European Countries" strengthened their doubts.¹⁶ Despite the Anglo-American caution, though, there

---

[14] See, for example, Mr. Arutiunian's statement at the General Assembly's third session: UN, General Assembly, Second Committee, *Official Records* (3rd Session, 1st Part), pp. 213-223.

[15] UN Document E/ECE/79, Appendix B.

[16] *Ibid.* Others interpreted Soviet behavior more charitably and more optimistically. Walt W. Rostow, who at the time was Special Assistant to ECE's Executive Secretary, reviewing the USSR's conduct in this area through the spring of 1949 concluded that it seemed "to have been based at least as much upon serious economic considerations as upon political motives." ("The Economic Commission for Europe," p. 263.)

was sufficient support in the Commission to inaugurate negotiations on the establishment of a committee for the development of trade.

Before these negotiations began, at the Economic and Social Council's seventh session in the summer of 1948, the Soviet Union attempted to further its cause by proposing that the Council should adopt a series of principles which should serve as a guide for ECE in its future work.[17] According to the first principle ECE should encourage the extension of trade between all European countries and thereby "promote the liberation of the economy of Western Europe from one-sided dependence on the United States of America." The second held that assistance to European countries should be granted within the framework of the United Nations and that such assistance should not be conditional on demands for special political, military, or economic privileges (implying that extant programs were). The third stated that "discrimination in the sphere of foreign trade should cease." According to the fourth principle European countries should direct their efforts toward developing basic industries and steps should be taken to prevent these states from curtailing production because of competition with United States goods. The fifth directed ECE to assist European countries in the organization of cheap agricultural credits, with a view to removing "the abnormal dependence of Western European countries on the importation of agricultural commodities from overseas, which had been aggravated and strengthened by the Marshall Plan." The final principle was that European reconstruction "should be carried out in such a way as to promote a rise in the standard of living of the masses—the workers, artisans, farmers, intelligentsia and small owners." It also stated that "steps should be taken against the increase in unemployment brought about by the Marshall Plan." The entire resolution was a blatant attack upon the United States and its policies. It amply confirmed Anglo-American suspicions concerning Soviet motivations. Curiously, on paragraph by paragraph votes each of the principles was adopted; the Soviet bloc supported them while the rest of the Council abstained. However, the resolution as a whole was rejected, fourteen votes to three. Again, the Soviet bloc provided the sole support.

The actual negotiations for the establishment of ECE's Committee on the Development of Trade, as it was named, began in the fall of 1948 in an *ad hoc* committee appointed by ECE and were completed at the Commission's fourth session in the late spring of 1949.

[17] UN Document E/844 and Rev. 1.

Meetings of the *ad hoc* committee were held from September 27 through October 4, 1948, during the height of the Berlin crisis and concurrently with the opening of the General Assembly's third session. During the negotiations the USSR pursued three main tactics.

First, Soviet bloc delegates attempted to link the question of intra-European trade with that of economic development. They initially insisted, as they had at ECE's third session, that two committees should be established, one on trade and the other on economic development. The United States and the United Kingdom, on the other hand, initially contended that ECE's existing technical committees could perform all of the proposed functions. Finally, it was agreed that one new committee should be established. Most members of ECE agreed with the Anglo-American position that this committee's mandate should be limited to trade. The USSR's proposal that the committee "should also study and make recommendations on measures promoting restoration and development of the industries of European countries, especially those which have suffered from war and occupation," failed, receiving support only from the Soviet bloc.[18]

Secondly, the USSR attempted to secure full voting privileges for certain states which had consultative status with ECE: Albania, Bulgaria, Finland, Hungary, Italy and Romania. The Soviet proposals were discriminatory since they ignored four other states which had similar status: Austria, Ireland, Portugal and Switzerland. Had these proposals been adopted the USSR would have controlled ten—or nine, because of Yugoslavia's expulsion from the Cominform—of the twenty-four possible members. Since the Scandinavian states were often reluctant to oppose the Soviet Union, and since it was not certain that all eligible states would participate, the USSR would have been in especially powerful position. Again, the Anglo-American position triumphed, as voting privileges were restricted to ECE members.

Finally, on every possible occasion during the negotiations, either the Soviet Union or one of its satellites attacked the Western controls on the export of strategic goods. For example, the Soviet Union proposed that the *ad hoc* committee should "pronounce itself against the prohibitions and limitations imposed on trade of the countries of Western Europe by the Marshall Plan."[19] This suggestion was rejected, as were all similar proposals. Only the Soviet bloc supported them.

[18] UN Document E/ECE/83, p. 4.
[19] *Ibid.*, pp. 4-5.

The USSR's abstention on the final vote on the terms of reference of ECE's Committee on the Development of Trade reflected the general Soviet defeat. These terms largely followed the position of the United Kingdom and the United States.

The Committee on the Development of Trade held two meetings in 1949, even before its terms of reference were finally approved.[20] Despite Soviet protests these meetings were held in private. The two sessions ended in deadlock. The West held that the Committee's first task should be to establish a clear conception of the goods available for East-West trade and of the demand for these goods. Western representatives argued that only on the basis of such a preliminary exchange of information could plans be evolved for increased trade. Since the Soviet bloc at that time was not willing to supply any information beyond that which was already published, the West felt there was no point in continuing the discussions.

On the other hand, Soviet delegates maintained that the export licensing policy practiced by the Western countries rendered any effort to develop East-West trade futile. The USSR and other Eastern European states argued that the Committee's prime function should be to adopt resolutions against this alleged discrimination and to force the states involved to end it. As the West was not willing to do this, the deadlock was complete.

The most significant decisions resulting from these two sessions of the Committee on the Development of Trade were those which gave the Executive Secretary power to conduct studies and other activities exploring methods to expand East-West trade. On this basis Gunnar Myrdal continued work in this area even though no further meetings of the full Committee were held until 1954.

Mr. Myrdal first circulated memoranda containing suggestions for a multilateral trade agreement.[21] He thought that such an agreement might include: (1) relatively long-term purchasing agreements by Western countries for cereal (and possibly other goods from Eastern countries); (2) a Western commitment that the proceeds of these sales could be used for the purchase of goods on lists which would be established by mutual agreement; and, if desired, (3) arrangements for increased flexibility in payments. No government opposed these suggestions.

Therefore, in the fall of 1950, Mr. Myrdal convened an *ad hoc*

---

[20] See: UN Document E/ECE/114/Rev. 1, pp. 55-58.
[21] *Ibid.*, p. 57.

meeting to explore the possibility of implementing his proposals. Little came of this conference, and Mr. Myrdal himself characterized the results as "disappointing."[22] Soviet delegates blamed the failure on the Western European countries, alleging that they could not guarantee the delivery of goods because of the controls on strategic exports, and called for a meeting of the full Committee on the Development of Trade.[23] Western representatives, on the contrary, felt that the real responsibility lay with the countries of Eastern Europe which they claimed could not supply the needed grain. They agreed with Mr. Myrdal that the Committee should not be convened unless there was sufficient preliminary agreement, and this position prevailed.

The following year, Mr. Myrdal organized an informal meeting of trade experts from Denmark, France, Poland, the USSR, and the United Kingdom in the hope—which proved illusory—that some trade agreements might eventually develop from bilateral talks started there. After this, he decided that it might be useful to have another consultation of trade experts in September 1952, and circulated an *aide memoire* suggesting such a meeting. Although fourteen Western countries replied affirmatively, the Soviet bloc states failed to reply. Therefore, the Conference was not held.

The onus for the breakdown of the talks thus fell clearly on the Soviet bloc. It was apparent that the USSR was not interested in increasing trade within the existing framework, although there were some signs that Soviet policy perhaps was in the process of changing. For example, Soviet initiative in calling the International Economic Conference in Moscow in April 1952, and the relative absence of polemics on the part of Soviet representatives there,[24] indicated that

[22] UN Document E/ECE/SR. 6/1, p. 5.

[23] Outside the UN, Soviet commentators were even more vituperative. See the description of ECE's 1950 session, the only UN meeting in which the USSR participated during the first seven months of that year: *Pravda*, June 11, 1950, as contained in *The Current Digest of the Soviet Press*, II, no. 24 (July 29, 1950), 43-44. The article concluded: "Observing the work of the latest session of the Economic Commission, the peoples of Europe had one more opportunity to convince themselves that the Soviet Union is really seeking to consolidate the U.N. and to develop normal economic relations between countries, while the Anglo-American bloc is driving a sap under the U.N., disorganizing and destroying the economy of West European countries, subjugating it to the selfish interests of American monopoly capital."

[24] See: Peter Calvocoressi, *Survey of International Affairs, 1952* (London: Oxford University Press, 1955), pp. 180-182, 343-344; and, Richard P. Stebbins, *The United States in World Affairs, 1952* (New York: Harpers, 1953), pp. 42-46. Oskar Lange served as Chairman of this Conference.

the USSR might be embarking on a new course. Moreover, as early as May 1950 Joseph V. Stalin had told Secretary-General Trygve Lie that "the charter of the International Trade Organization was a good one, and that, with a few changes, it might well be ratified by a number of countries which had not yet done so, including the Soviet Union." [25] Nevertheless, the period closed with East-West trade at an extremely low level and with a complete deadlock on these questions in the Economic Commission for Europe. What constructive work the United Nations carried on concerning international trade was the result of cooperation solely among the non-Soviet bloc states. Soviet abstention from these activities was complete. Moreover, the USSR's onslaught against the West appears to have had little success, for during this period the effectiveness of the Western ban on strategic exports had increased. In addition to other developments, the United States adopted the Battle Act, and fifteen Western countries (Japan and all North Atlantic Treaty States except Iceland) established the Consultative Group and its subsidiary body, the Coordinating Committee (COCOM), to implement a multilateral system of trade controls against the Soviet bloc.

THE ERA OF SOVIET INITIATIVES

As the Economic Commission for Europe had been the focus of the deadlock between East and West on international trade, it was a logical place for the USSR to introduce its new policy of cooperation, and for some time this new policy had its greatest impact in ECE. However, the new Soviet policy has had broader aspects as well. It has also been oriented toward the trade problems of underdeveloped countries and toward the organization of global machinery to facilitate the conduct of international trade. In addition, the USSR has become more willing to participate in the UN's technical activities in this field.

THE SOVIET TRADE OFFENSIVE IN ECE

The first evidence of the change in Soviet policy came on January 17, 1953, when the USSR finally replied to Mr. Myrdal's *aide memoire* of the previous fall suggesting another trade consultation. The USSR agreed to participate, and this signaled the end of the deadlock in ECE. As a result, a meeting of trade experts was held

---

[25] Trygve Lie, *In the Cause of Peace*, p. 302.

in August 1953. The technique of simultaneous bilateral negotiations was given its first large-scale test at this meeting. The ECE Secretariat had long advocated this device as a possible means of improving the system of strictly bilaterally negotiated trade agreements which prevailed in postwar Europe. During these talks Soviet representatives are said to have adopted a "business is business" attitude and apparently never mentioned the Western export restrictions.[26] The meeting was generally judged a success, and it was agreed that another similar session should be held in 1954.

Since then such consultations have been a regular feature of ECE's work. Although few actual trade agreements have resulted from these negotiations, the general discussions of trade matters have probably been useful for smaller countries with minimal diplomatic facilities. The meetings have also provided a means of contact for countries which have not had diplomatic relations or whose normal trade relations have otherwise been interrupted. In addition, some settlements of trade problems seem to have been arranged in these meetings.

Further evidence of the new Soviet policy of cooperation was given at ECE's ninth session in the spring of 1954. The Soviet representative announced then that his government would participate in all of the Commission's technical committees,[27] and by the end of that year this promise had been fulfilled. This vastly increased the potential range of ECE's activities. These committees covered a variety of fields, and their work consisted of technical collaboration on problems of mutual interest, exchanges of information and experience, and the preparation of studies. Because of their East-West composition, all, in varying degrees depending upon the subjects with which they dealt, were concerned with questions of intra-European trade.

At ECE's ninth session, the Soviet delegate also proposed that the Committee on the Development of Trade should convene in 1954 and consider "(a) the removal of obstacles to foreign trade; (b) the conclusion of long-term and multilateral trade and payments agreements; (c) the convening of meetings of experts on trade questions; (d) the arranging of meetings of representatives of business circles;

---

[26] See: UN Document E/ECE/166; and, Michael L. Hoffman, "Problems of East-West Trade," *International Conciliation*, no. 511 (January 1957), pp. 259-308, p. 296.

[27] UN Document E/ECE/SR. 9/2, p. 11.

198   The USSR and the UN's Economic and Social Activities

(e) the publication of a special bulletin on foreign trade questions; (f) the organization of international trade fairs."[28] In the debate, this proposal was used as a springboard for an attack on the Western restrictions on trade with communist countries. Despite this, the Soviet record in the 1953 trade consultation and the subject's natural appeal provided sufficient inducement for most Western delegates, and the Soviet resolution was adopted in a modified form.[29]

The Committee on the Development of Trade convened in the fall of 1954, and this group has also held regular meetings since then. In addition to making an annual survey of developments and problems in intra-European trade, it has concentrated on such matters as: facilitating trade fairs; drafting standardized sales contracts; examining arrangements for international commercial arbitration; developing improved payments relations whereby the need for strict bilateral balancing of accounts would be eliminated; and establishing long-term trade agreements.[30] Although few concrete accomplishments appear to have resulted from the Committee's discussions, a limited multilateral clearing system has been established and the ground work has possibly been laid for future action.

At the same time that this new Soviet policy of cooperation was inaugurated in the Committee on the Development of Trade and in ECE's subsidiary organs, in the Commission's public plenary sessions Soviet delegates continued their attack on the Western embargo on strategic exports. At ECE's tenth session in 1955, after a long harangue against the controls, the USSR's representative proposed that the Executive Secretary should give special attention to these restrictions in preparing documentation for meetings of the Trade Committee.[31] The fact that only the Soviet bloc supported

[28] UN Document E/ECE/SR. 9/6, p. 20.

[29] See: UN, ECOSOC, *Official Records* (18th Session), Supplement No. 3, "Economic Commission for Europe: Annual Report," p. 26.

[30] This work is described in: UN, DPI, *In the Service of Europe*, pp. 34-38, and in ECE's annual reports which are published as supplements to the *Official Records* of ECOSOC's even-numbered sessions. Two non-official accounts are also of interest: Peter Benjamin, "The Work of the Economic Commission for Europe in the Field of International Commercial Arbitration," *The International and Comparative Law Quarterly*, VII, Part 1 (January 1958), 22-30; and Raymond F. Mikesell and Jack N. Behrman, *Financing Free World Trade with the Sino-Soviet Bloc* (Princeton: International Finance Section, Department of Economics and Sociology, Princeton University, 1958), pp. 55-61.

[31] UN, ECOSOC, *Official Records* (20th Session), Supplement No. 3, "Economic Commission for Europe: Annual Report," p. 44.

this proposal perhaps explains why Soviet tactics were modified still further.

The transformation in Soviet policy in the Economic Commission for Europe was finally completed in 1956, and Soviet tactics at the Commission's eleventh session established a pattern which has been followed since then. Although Soviet delegates continued to attack the Western controls on the export of strategic goods in general debate, this onslaught was comparatively mild, and it was accompanied by the submission of several seemingly new and far-reaching proposals. The USSR proposed the initiation of negotiations concerning an all-European economic agreement; the creation of an ECE subsidiary organ to deal with peaceful uses of atomic energy; and the elaboration of recommendations for developing business contacts between countries of Eastern and Western Europe.[32] The Commission did not act on the substance of the first two proposals; it merely asked the USSR to expand them and requested that the Executive Secretary solicit the views of member states concerning these suggestions. The USSR's third proposal concerning business contacts was adopted, but in a broadened form covering increased contacts generally. The Soviet press treated these proposals, and ECE's disposal of them, in such a straightforward and technical manner that the story verged on being dull, a procedure which has been followed since then, but which stood in marked contrast to the polemical accounts of Soviet moves in ECE in the late nineteen forties and early nineteen fifties.[33]

Since 1956 the USSR has continued to stress these themes in ECE's plenary sessions. In the spring of 1957, at the twelfth session of the Commission, in addition to elaborating its proposal for an all-European economic agreement and the creation of an ECE subsidiary organ to deal with atomic energy, the USSR introduced new proposals which it held would further develop intra-European cooperation. Although separate, these proposals were related and suggested collateral actions.[34] They emphasized the energy shortage in Western Europe—this was the year after the Suez Crisis—and recommended that this be met by all-European efforts which might

[32] UN Document E/ECE/243.
[33] *Izvestia*, April 22, 1956, as contained in *The Current Digest of the Soviet Press*, VIII, no. 16 (May 30, 1956), 15.
[34] See UN Documents E/ECE/270, Part I, pp. 4-11, Part III; E/ECE/272; and, E/ECE/280 and Add. 1.

involve atomic energy, electric power or other energy sources. Far-reaching steps were suggested such as the joint construction of petroleum and gas pipe-lines, electric transmission lines and possibly even large hydro-power stations. In some ways these proposals were similar to those which had been discussed a decade earlier when the Commission was being established. The Soviet proposals also contained provisions concerning trade and *inter alia* suggested that the Commission should study the possibility of wider application of the most-favored nation principle and of "agreements concerning the removal of embargoes and restrictions of a noneconomic nature." None of the Soviet proposals was adopted. The West argued that some would involve the duplication of functions performed by extant institutions; for example, the then newly-established International Atomic Energy Agency and ECE's own technical committees. Others, it was held, suggested actions which were not feasible under existing conditions. After discussion, substantive action on all of these proposals was either formally or informally postponed. The following year, the Soviet Union added to this list of proposals by suggesting that ECE convene a conference at the ministerial level to consider problems of increasing intra-European trade and technical exchanges.[35] Eventually, the suggestion was withdrawn because of lack of support.

The Soviet Union continued to advance similar proposals through 1962.[36] In particular, it pressed for a conference of ministers of trade and for the creation of an all-European regional trade organization. Also, in 1962, having enacted a new tariff schedule the previous year, the USSR proposed that ECE should elaborate an agreement on the reciprocal reduction of tariffs. In formal terms, the Soviet Union did not achieve its goals; only a few of the USSR's proposals were

[35] UN, ECOSOC, *Official Records* (26th Session), Supplement No. 3, "Economic Commission for Europe: Annual Report," pp. 34-35.

[36] See: UN Documents E/ECE/348; E/ECE/385; E/ECE (XVII)/L.7; E/ECE (XVII)/L. 8; E/ECE (XVII)/L. 11; and E/ECE (XVII)/L. 29. Starting in the late nineteen fifties, Soviet initiatives become increasingly difficult to trace because an informal East-West good offices committee was created in ECE to consider draft resolutions before they were tabled and to try to arrange compromises so that the proposals would command unanimous support and could be jointly sponsored by countries from both East and West. Occasionally, the USSR violated the understanding and tabled its proposals without reference to the committee and for a time at the seventeenth session in 1962 the committee was inoperative.

INTERNATIONAL TRADE 201

adopted, and these were adopted only after considerable modification. On the other hand, in 1960, at the fifteenth session of the Economic Commission for Europe, the Executive Secretary proposed that the Commission should convene periodic meetings of high-level senior government advisers, and that work should be started on drafting "a set of multilateral principles and procedures which could be applied in relations between countries having different economic systems." [37] With some modification, both proposals were adopted, and a meeting of high-level government advisers was held in March 1961. The meeting proved so successful that the Commission authorized the Executive Secretary to convene other similar meetings, and to make them a regular feature of ECE's work. A second meeting was convened in November 1962. In a sense then the Soviet Union at least partially gained its objectives.

Starting in 1956, the USSR has also sought to expand the work of ECE's technical committees. Soviet delegates in the Commission's plenary sessions have introduced a variety of proposals for new work for these bodies, and have even suggested the creation of new committees. In the committees themselves, Soviet participants have become much more active and have sought to stimulate increased exchanges of information and personnel.[38] In fact, the USSR has become so active that, in contrast to earlier periods, since 1955, the West has frequently been in the position of attempting to ward off Soviet initiatives in and concerning ECE's technical committees. The Soviet suggestions for increased exchanges have appeared to some to be attempts at industrial espionage, and in other cases the West has felt that they have implied a measure of governmental control of economic life which does not exist in Western economies. The United States in particular has felt unable to push its businessmen to participate.

Since the mid-nineteen fifties, there have only been two major exceptions to the USSR's generally moderate conduct. The attempted Cuban invasion occurred during the course of ECE's sixteenth session in 1961. When the news broke, Soviet bloc delegates launched a bitter attack against the United States. The other exception is more germane to the Commission's activities. Starting in

[37] UN Document E/ECE/386.
[38] For an indication of how active the USSR has been in ECE's technical committees see: UN, ECOSOC, *Official Records* (30th Session), Supplement No. 3, "Economic Commission for Europe: Annual Report," pp. 1-22.

1960 the USSR began to severely criticize the work of the Research and Planning Division of ECE's Secretariat. The attack was broadly aimed at the contents of publications of the Division and also at the Director personally, F. Strauss, an American citizen, on leave from the United States Department of Commerce. The USSR alleged that the reports distorted developments in both East and West, and suggested that consultation with experts of the governments concerned should become a mandatory feature in the preparation of publications. It is hard to estimate what effect the Soviet attack has had. The Executive Secretary has defended the Division generally and the Director personally, and the Soviet suggestions have not been accepted. However, for personal reasons, in 1962 Mr. Strauss returned to the Department of Commerce and was replaced by a Norwegian. Whether or not in the long run ECE's publications will become increasingly bland cannot be foretold.

Clearly as a consequence of the transformation in Soviet policy, in 1957 Oskar Lange of Poland was elected Chairman of the Economic Commission for Europe, and in 1961 and 1962 Gheorghe Radulesco of Romania was chosen for this post. They were the first delegates from Soviet bloc countries to head ECE. Presumably, as long as the Soviet bloc continues its moderate and active tactics, its delegates can expect to hold the top position in the Commission with some regularity. It perhaps should also be mentioned that in 1961 a Yugoslav, Vladimir Velebit, was appointed Executive Secretary.

One of the motivations responsible for the transformation of Soviet policy in ECE appears to have been a desire to construct a more effective attack against the Western embargo on the export of strategic goods to the Soviet bloc. Soviet delegates have always dwelt on this subject in ECE's plenary sessions and it has been the target of both blatantly open and since 1956 somewhat more subtle proposals. As popular feeling in Western Europe against these controls has increased and as COCOM has twice, in 1954 and again in 1958, reduced the list of prohibited articles, these new tactics appear to have been somewhat more effective than those which the USSR previously used. However, other factors outside the UN, such as the general relaxation of tension which occurred prior to 1960, have also been important. Further, the reduction of the list has in part merely reflected technological developments.

Another motivation for the changed Soviet policy may have been a desire to block progress toward integration in Western Europe, or to capitalize on some of the problems which have accompanied this progress. Western European integration can be interpreted as having adverse consequences for the Soviet bloc, both politically and economically. Two of the Soviet proposals introduced in 1956 covered exactly the same areas as the treaties for a European Economic Community (ECE—Common Market) and a European Atomic Energy Community (EURATOM), and since they were introduced at the same time that these treaties were being prepared, they must have been posed as alternatives. The Soviet proposal in 1959 for creation of an all-European regional trade organization was an obvious attempt to capitalize on the developing difficulties between the Common Market countries and the "outer seven" states, or the members of the European Free Trade Association (EFTA). In 1960 the USSR advanced the suggestion that it should be invited to join the negotiations concerning the Organization for Economic Cooperation and Development (OECD), and in 1961 and 1962, it proposed that it should be invited to become a member of this organization. In stressing energy problems, Soviet delegates have sought to emphasize European dependence upon outside sources, particularly the United States, and to suggest the alternative of European self-sufficiency based on East-West trade. All of these Soviet actions were clearly related to broader Soviet policies.

The motivations for the new Soviet emphasis on the work of the ECE's technical committees have not been as transparent. In some cases, particularly involving plastics, synthetics and consumer goods, a desire to gain information seems to have been the dominant factor. Such information might have been considered helpful in implementing the USSR's economic plans. In addition, the Soviet technicians who have attended the sessions of the technical committees seem to have had what is probably best called a genuine scientific thirst for information. They appear to have reveled in their new contact with their Western colleagues. The technical committees have also provided a convenient opportunity for the USSR to demonstrate its technical prowess to the West.

It may also be that the Soviet Union has been forced to give greater emphasis to the activities of the Economic Commission for Europe as a consequence of its general lessening of controls in Eastern Europe. Some observers have suggested that for a time the USSR viewed ECE as an important instrument for contact with other communist states; it provided a convenient meeting place at a time when increased cooperation was desired but when revitalization of the Council for Mutual Economic Assistance would have been inappropriate. According to this theory, Soviet interest in ECE will decrease as the effectiveness of CMEA grows, as it has since 1958. Further, there has always been evidence of greater interest in ECE on the part of the smaller states of Eastern Europe—one reason for this is that they are more dependent on trade with the West—and the USSR's moves may have been partially designed to satisfy this interest. The Soviet Union may well have felt that the Economic Commission for Europe was a place where greater contact between East and West could be developed on reasonably safe terms, or at least on more desirable terms from the Soviet point of view than would be involved in bilateral arrangements between these states and the major Western powers. Moreover, the development of the European Common Market and EFTA could have quite serious economic implications for some of the smaller states of Eastern Europe, and the USSR may have felt compelled to act because of these interests.

The new Soviet policy in the Economic Commission for Europe has put the West in an increasingly embarrassing position. It has been difficult for the West repeatedly to offer objections to the Soviet proposals and always to urge their rejection. By so doing, the Western powers, especially the United States, since it has been the most adamant, have increasingly been cast in a negative role before the limited public which follows ECE's work. Moreover, as the Soviet Union has become more and more certain that its proposals have no chance of success, it has been able to recommend increasingly far-reaching action with no fear that it would be called upon to implement its suggestions. For bureaucratic reasons, the Soviet Union has sometimes, in a sense, been helped by the Secretariat of the Economic Commission for Europe. For example, the Executive Secretary's suggestions in 1960 were to some extent patterned after Soviet proposals, and while the USSR's proposals found no success, the Executive Secretary's did. The *raison d'être* of the ECE Secretariat has been to facilitate efforts to promote East-West cooperation. Since the Soviet Union has seemed to favor such efforts, while the West has questioned their efficacy, the Secretariat could hardly have been expected to have enthusiastically supported the Western position, which de-emphasized its own role.

Foreign Trade Problems of Underdeveloped Areas

A second and somewhat broader aspect of the new Soviet policy concerned the foreign trade problems of underdeveloped areas. Since 1953 the USSR has made a major effort to woo the underdeveloped countries, and, as a part of this strategy, trade between the Soviet bloc and these countries has been significantly increased. The Soviet Union used the UN in 1954 as a convenient forum from which it could announce its willingness (and ability) to engage in trade. In the Economic Commission for Asia and Far East and in the Economic and Social Council, Soviet representatives stated that the USSR would be willing to supply industrial equipment and machinery to the underdeveloped countries on the basis of long-term agreements.[39] They offered extremely attractive credit arrangements, including the possibility of repayment in local currencies. These offers had considerable appeal in view of the difficulties which the underdeveloped countries faced in obtaining needed equipment, and they were the prelude to several trade agreements.

In addition, in 1954 the USSR developed a new propaganda attack in the UN oriented toward the underdeveloped countries. The theme of this attack was that the restrictions on the export of strategic goods—particularly those against China—interfered with the growth of the underdeveloped countries' economies. Arguing from this premise, Soviet delegates introduced new resolutions condemning discrimination in international trade.[40] These were passed, but only after they were modified so as not to imply a condemnation of Western policy.

In 1954, the Soviet Union also supported the Economic and Social Council's decision to establish a Commission on International Commodity Trade, an eighteen-member (twenty-one, after 1961) body chosen in the same manner as the Council's other functional commissions. The underdeveloped countries had wanted to establish such a commission for some time, but their efforts had been blocked by the developed countries of the West. Belgium, France, Norway, the United Kingdom, and the United States all voted against the

[39] UN Document E/CN. 11/389, pp. 54-56; and, UN, ECOSOC, *Official Records* (17th Session), pp. 231-232.
[40] See UN Documents: E/1. 614 Rev. 1, A/C. 2/L. 248, and A/C. 2/L. 248 Corr. 1.

establishment of the Commission, and the United Kingdom and the United States did not participate in the Commission's work until 1959 after its terms of reference had been modified.

The Soviet Union has favored the Commission on International Commodity Trade over the other UN organ working in this field, the Interim Coordinating Committee for International Commodity Agreements (ICCICA). The latter body, established in 1947, consisted of a Chairman appointed by the Contracting Parties to GATT, a member chosen by FAO, and two members nominated by the Secretary-General. The last three were specialists in particular phases of the commodity problem. The ICCICA convened periodic conferences on specific commodities with the end purpose of negotiating agreements. The Soviet Union did not favor the creation of this Committee, and after the Commission on International Commodity Trade was established, Soviet delegates argued that it was the proper and most effective body for dealing with such questions. The Soviet exclusion from the ICCICA may have been responsible for the USSR's position. It also was in accord with the Soviet Union's general approach to organizational questions, fitting its preference for political bodies.

The USSR has used its position on the Commission on International Commodity Trade primarily to expound its interpretation of the commodity problem;[41] it has submitted no proposals for action there. Soviet delegates have consistently emphasized the gravity of the problem. The explanation which they have stressed most has varied from year to year, but certain features have been constant. They have argued that the commodity problem reflects deep-seated contradictions in the capitalist economic system and that these have been aggravated by such Western policies as the embargo on strategic exports, American agricultural policies and the development of the European Common Market and EFTA.

The USSR has generally been more sympathetic in the UN than the West to the underdeveloped countries' position concerning problems of commodity trade. It has frequently supported their proposals in the Commission on International Commodity Trade, the Economic and Social Council, and the General Assembly. How-

[41] See UN Documents: E/CN. 13/SR. 17, pp. 4-6; E/CN. 13/SR. 22, p. 4; E/CN. 13/SR. 31, pp. 4-5; E/CN. 13/SR. 36, p. 3; E/CN. 13/SR. 88, pp. 9-12; E/CN. 13/SR. 100, pp. 5-7; E/CN. 13/SR. 112, pp. 8-11; E/CN. 13/SR. 123, pp. 11-12; and, E/CN. 13/SR. 132, pp. 2-4.

INTERNATIONAL TRADE 207

ever, this verbal support has not always been accompanied by practical action. The Soviet Union is a party to the International Sugar Agreement, but it has not signed any of the other commodity agreements negotiated under UN auspices, and even though in 1959 it agreed to cooperate with the International Tin Council, this did not apply to intra-Soviet bloc trade. Further, in 1958 Soviet sales of tin seriously disrupted the international market for this commodity. Among other things this led to sharp criticism of the USSR in the General Assembly by the delegates of Indonesia and Bolivia.

Perhaps the Soviet Union's most significant actions in this field have taken place outside the United Nations; that is, the negotiation of long-term trade agreements with a number of underdeveloped countries for the purchase of their primary commodities. However, the Soviet Union publicized these moves in the UN. When such agreements were first offered, the underdeveloped countries viewed them as a significant opportunity to stabilize commodity prices, but after some experience, their enthusiasm waned somewhat.[42] Still, these agreements were of some assistance, and at the seventh session of the Commission on International Commodity Trade in 1959, the Soviet delegate attempted to argue that they were the best means of meeting the commodity problem. Similar proposals were advanced by other Soviet bloc countries at the fourteenth session of the General Assembly that fall and at the eleventh session of the Commission on International Commodity Trade in 1963.[43] Neither attempt succeeded, and the resolutions which were adopted mentioned long-term trade agreements only briefly and as one of several possible solutions.

It appears, therefore, that regardless of how much underdeveloped states may have appreciated Soviet support in the UN, they have been unwilling totally to accept the solutions proposed by the USSR and they have generally continued to accord greater importance to the views of the West in matters concerning their basic economic welfare. Nevertheless, in terms of the growing trade between the underdeveloped countries and the Soviet bloc and the increasing alignment of these two groups in UN debates, this aspect of Soviet policy must be credited as being at least moderately successful.

[42] See: Robert Loring Allen, *Middle Eastern Economic Relations with the Soviet Union, Eastern Europe, and Mainland China* (Charlottesville, Virginia: Woodrow Wilson Department of Foreign Affairs, University of Virginia, 1958).
[43] UN Documents A/C. 2/L. 429, Part B, and E/CN. 13/L. 83.

GLOBAL MACHINERY TO FACILITATE THE CONDUCT OF TRADE

The third aspect of the new Soviet policy concerned global machinery to facilitate the conduct of international trade.

Since the Havana Charter never came into force, as time passed, there was pressure to develop other machinery, and the General Agreement on Tariffs and Trade (the one concrete product of the negotiations concerning the drafting of the ITO Charter) was expanded into a semi-permanent organization.[44] This arrangement, however, was not completely satisfactory. Its seemingly temporary nature caused uncertainty in some states, and the structure was weak. Consequently, it was proposed that an Organization for Trade Cooperation (OTC) should be created to administer a revised General Agreement. In the spring of 1955 the text of the OTC Agreement was completed, and it was submitted to the Contracting Parties of GATT for ratification. Ultimately OTC, like its predecessor ITO, foundered, among other reasons because of the unwillingness of the American Senate to ratify the agreement, but for a time, the prospects of its coming into existence seemed promising. It was envisaged that states would not be able to join OTC unless they accepted the obligations of GATT and were accepted by GATT. This would have made Soviet membership difficult. Czechoslovakia is a member of GATT, but it joined before falling completely under communist control. Yugoslavia and Poland entered into a form of association with GATT in 1959, but this did not carry with it full privileges of membership. Basically, GATT has remained a "private enterprise club." Its main activities, the reduction of tariffs and quotas, have little applicability for communist states where foreign trade is completely controlled by the government.

The Soviet Union's new moves in this field have aimed at the creation of a new and universal agency for the consideration of international trade issues, or at making the United Nations the central place for such discussion rather than GATT or some similar institution. They could be interpreted as attempts to counteract the USSR's exclusion from GATT.

This aspect of Soviet policy began modestly in 1953 when the

[44] This development is described in: Raymond Vernon, "Organizing for World Trade," *International Conciliation*, no. 505 (November, 1955), pp. 163-222; and, UN Documents E/2737, "The Quest for Freer Trade," and E/2897.

INTERNATIONAL TRADE 209

USSR proposed that the Economic and Social Council should recommend that member governments should remove obstacles to the development of international trade between states with various social systems.[45] This proposal was related to earlier suggestions by members of the Soviet bloc, offered under the title of discrimination in international trade, and was clearly aimed at Western controls on the export of strategic materials. Even though it was adopted only after great modification, this proposal was the starting point for a vigorous Soviet program, and it inaugurated a program of work within the UN.

The following year, the Soviet Union submitted a similar proposal, but with the additional provision that ECOSOC should convene an international conference of experts to formulate recommendations concerning the removal of obstacles to international trade.[46] The USSR also introduced a similar resolution in the General Assembly. Although neither proposal was adopted, the Soviet initiative resulted in the adoption of ECOSOC Resolution 531 C (XVIII), which insured that the Secretariat would pay greater attention to the problem of developing East-West trade and committed the Council to discuss means of expanding international trade at its twentieth session.

The twentieth session was held in the summer of 1955. Soviet policy assumed new and unforeseen dimensions then. This occurred at the same time that the West was intensifying its efforts in connection with the Organization for Trade Cooperation. Debate was to have been based on various reports prepared by the Secretariat in response to Resolution 531 C (XVIII), which described the development of GATT and the nature of the OTC Agreement. However, a new element was introduced when the USSR submitted two draft resolutions: one concerned the removal of obstacles to trade, and the other urged member states to ratify the Havana Charter.[47] The Soviet delegate announced that the USSR was willing to support the original proposal for an International Trade Organization, and he urged that the Council should take steps to encourage member states to ratify the Charter. He stated that GATT could never

[45] UN Document E/L. 531.
[46] UN Documents: E/L. 614; E/L. 614/Rev. 1; and E/L. 614/Rev. 2.
[47] UN Documents: E/L. 677 and E/L. 678. See also: *Izvestia*, July 15, 1955, as contained in *The Current Digest of the Soviet Press*, VII, no. 28 (August 24, 1955), 25.

be a suitable agency for the conduct of trade negotiations on a global level because its membership was limited. The Soviet move was clearly designed to work against the USSR's increasing exclusion from discussions concerning problems of international trade. The Soviet Union apparently desired that a universal institution should be established where such problems could be discussed without the commitments which were involved in GATT. At the same time, through the submission of the other proposal which it offered that year, the USSR sought to use the UN as if it were such an institution. Although the Soviet proposals were not accepted, ECOSOC adopted two resolutions in this area at its twentieth session. They urged governments to take a number of steps, largely based on Western theories, designed to facilitate an expansion of trade, and also insured that the problem of organizational machinery to deal with world trade problems would be discussed again the following year. In addition, the Secretary-General was asked to produce further studies.

When the discussion of these matters was resumed at ECOSOC's twenty-second session, the Soviet Union dropped its appeal for ratification of the Havana Charter and proposed instead that an *ad hoc* committee should be established to study and make recommendations concerning the creation of an international organization for trade cooperation.[48] The Soviet delegate held that such an organization should be open equally to members and non-members of the United Nations and that it should work for the elimination of all discriminatory restrictions in trade. The result was similar to that of the previous year; although the Soviet proposal was not accepted, the Council decided to keep the problem under advisement.

Since then, similar proposals have been a regular feature of Soviet policy at nearly every session of the Economic and Social Council and the General Assembly. They have either been introduced by the USSR or by a member of the Soviet bloc. Several have sought to keep the question of creating an all-inclusive trade organization as an active agenda item within the UN.[49] One even suggested that amendments should be prepared to the Agreement for the Organization for Trade Cooperation.[50] In addition to advocating the creation of a universal trade organization, a draft proposal submitted

---

[48] UN Document E/L. 734.
[49] UN Documents: E/AC. 6/L. 178; A/C. 2/L. 332, and A/C. 2/L. 429.
[50] UN Document E/AC. 6/L. 216.

by Bulgaria, Czechoslovakia, and Poland to the General Assembly's fourteenth session in 1959 embraced and gave wider application to an idea which the USSR had advanced in the Economic Commission for Europe; that is, for the creation of all-inclusive regional organizations. Other Soviet-backed proposals have suggested the convocation of a world economic conference, either at an expert or a ministerial level.[51] Each proposal contained a draft agenda. Some of these included the creation of a new trade agency, while others appeared to treat the conference as a substitute for such an agency. All listed the "removal of barriers" to international trade as one of the main topics to be considered.

As in 1955, another series of proposals has accompanied these Soviet efforts to construct global machinery for the consideration of trade problems. In a sense, these proposals have sought to use the UN as a substitute for such machinery. They have suggested that the UN should elaborate principles which could be used as criteria for the conduct of international trade.[52] The principles which have been suggested by the USSR have been cleverly designed to appeal to the major interest groups within the UN, and especially to the underdeveloped states, but at the same time they have contained principles which could easily be used as springboards for criticisms of Western policies and institutions. In addition, they have sought to promote international scientific and technical exchanges.[53]

Until 1960, none of these Soviet-backed suggestions was accepted, and when Western proposals favoring the ratification of the OTC Agreement—when this still seemed to be a viable alternative—or endorsing present work in the field of international trade were juxtaposed, they won easily. On the other hand, it was always necessary to make some concessions to the Soviet position, and the Soviet proposals led to some studies by the Secretariat.

In 1960, at Secretary-General Hammarskjöld's suggestion, ECOSOC organized its meeting so that there could be ministerial level participation in the thirtieth session. Then that fall, at the fifteenth session of the General Assembly the USSR submitted a "Draft Declaration on International Economic Cooperation."[54] It

[51] UN Documents: A/C. 2/L. 282, A/C. 2/L. 282/Corr. 1, A/C. 2/L. 319, E/AC. 6/189, and E/AC. 6/L. 217.
[52] UN Documents A/C. 2/L. 330 and E/AC. 6/L. 215.
[53] UN Documents E/L. 837 and A/C. 2/L. 441.
[54] UN Document A/C. 2/L. 466.

had unsuccessfully advanced the same proposal earlier in the summer at ECOSOC. While the Assembly did not accept the Soviet suggestion, it did urge ECOSOC to consider it, and in 1961 ECOSOC decided to circulate the USSR's proposal to all UN member states and to solicit their views. The following year, ECOSOC decided to appoint a working group to formulate a declaration and this group was functioning in 1963. Of the twelve members, two, Poland and the USSR, were from the Soviet bloc. How successful they will be in advancing Soviet views remains to be seen.

Again nudged by the Assembly, and this time also by ECAFE, in 1962 ECOSOC decided to convene a United Nations Conference on Trade and Development in early 1964, and a preparatory committee was at work in 1963. What gains the Soviet Union will make here are problematical. What it hopes for apparently is a meeting on the lines of the International Economic Conference which was held in Moscow in 1952.[55]

It is evident that the Soviet Union and its allies have set forth an alternative concept of machinery to facilitate the conduct of world trade. One feature of this alternative concept is universal membership. A second is large open plenary meetings where suggestions such as those which the members of the Soviet bloc have advanced in the UN could be debated and broad general resolutions adopted. A final feature can be seen from another series of proposals which were advanced as part of this aspect of the new Soviet policy. The first of these proposals was introduced at the ninth session of the Economic Commission for Europe in the spring of 1954 when Czechoslovakia, with strong support from the USSR, proposed that ECE should explore the possibility of extending the technique of simultaneous bilateral negotiations to an inter-regional level.[56] Despite skepticism, the Czechoslovakian resolution was adopted in a modified form, and similar resolutions were later passed in ECAFE and ECOSOC. Although the Economic and Social Council authorized the convocation of inter-regional trade negotiations in 1955, no such negotiations have been held. Several proposals have also been

---

[55] See the intriguing article on the proposed UN conference by M. V. Nesterov, Chairman of the All-Union Chamber of Commerce, the individual who gave the principal address at the 1952 Conference, entitled "And If It Meets Again?": *Izvestia*, April 11, 1962, as contained in *The Current Digest of the Soviet Press*, XIV, no. 15 (May 9, 1962), 21.

[56] UN Document E/ECE/SR. 9/10, pp. 8-12.

submitted advocating increased technical collaboration between the regional economic commissions.[57] Their fate has been similar; they have been adopted in a modified form, but have resulted in few practical achievements. It is apparent from these proposals and from the general Soviet preference for the type of work conducted in ECE, that whatever concrete activities would be involved in the Soviet alternative would be similar to those now carried on in the regional economic commission; that is, they would consist of the facilitation of exchanges of information and the promotion of bilateral contacts. This is essentially what happened at the International Economic Conference in Moscow in 1952. The attractiveness of the Soviet alternative will in part at least depend upon how effectively the organizational machinery preferred by the West can deal with problems of international trade.

A general attitude of cooperativeness has accompanied these major changes in Soviet policy concerning the activities of the United Nations in the field of international trade. Most resolutions in this area came to be adopted by unanimous votes, and the USSR has generally preferred to abstain from voting on resolutions which it could not support, rather than to oppose them. In addition, the Soviet supply of technical and statistical data to the United Nations has increased markedly since 1955, although there are still some gaps. In 1958 the Soviet Union suddenly decided to join the Inter-Governmental Maritime Consultative Organization,[58] and it has also demonstrated an increased interest in the UN's technical activities. The USSR's participation in the Transport and Communications Commission has been more active; it has sought to stimulate this Commission's work in the field of travel, and it protested when the Commission was discontinued in 1959. The Soviet Union participated in the 1958 UN Conference on Commercial Arbitration and signed the resulting Convention on the Recognition and Enforcement of Foreign Arbitral Awards, notwithstanding its objections to signature being limited to member states of the UN or specialized agencies, the colonial and federal application clauses, and the jurisdiction

---

[57] UN Documents: E/AC. 6/L. 187, A/C. 2/L. 333, A/C. 2/L. 391, A/C. 2/L. 391/ and Rev. 1, and A/C. 2/L. 47/ and Rev. 1 and 2.

[58] See: Alvin Z. Rubinstein, "The U.S.S.R. and the I.M.C.O.: Some Preliminary Observations," *United States Naval Institute Proceedings*, LXXV, no. 10 (October, 1959), 75-79. Bulgaria and Poland joined IMCO in 1960. Yugoslavia is also a member.

given the International Court of Justice. Three years later the USSR took part in the drafting of and signed the European Convention on International Commercial Arbitration.

Despite this increased interest in the UN's technical activities, however, the question of sovereignty still is responsible for important limitations on Soviet cooperation. The USSR does not participate in any of ECE's work where licensing problems are involved, nor does it participate in the Commission's work concerning customs. And the USSR still refuses to have any contact with ICAO or with the UN's work involving the transport of dangerous goods.

CONCLUSIONS

The changes in Soviet policy in relation to the activities of the United Nations concerning international trade in part merely reflect developments in the economies of the Soviet bloc. The fundamental problem of the communist economies in the early postwar years was reconstruction, and, as matters developed, the United Nations could contribute little to this. Furthermore, Soviet leaders apparently wanted the other Eastern European states to reorient their economies internally by giving greater emphasis to industrial production, and externally by directing their foreign trade more toward one another and toward the USSR. Participation in the United Nations activities would not have aided in achieving this; it might even have interfered. By 1953, however, the Eastern economies had recovered from the war and had made substantial further progress. The desired reorientation had also occurred. The USSR and the other members of the Soviet bloc were then free to concentrate on other objectives and, if they desired, to expand their international trade on a new basis.

The decision to take advantage of this opportunity may have been prompted primarily by internal considerations. The willingness to engage in trade and to cooperate in this area of the UN's work may simply have been a product of the new Soviet leaders' desire to consolidate power through raising living standards. The composition of the expanded trade indicates that this probably was a factor. This new policy may also have been chosen as a means of reducing world tensions and thereby allowing the new leaders to concentrate more on internal problems. Further, Stalin's successors clearly desired to lessen the USSR's economic isolation.

But it is possible that the Soviet Union would have taken advantage of the new opportunity and changed its policy in the UN even if Stalin had lived, and without reference to internal considerations. Indeed, the first indication of the change in ECE came before Stalin's death. Further, the change was to some extent foreshadowed by the events of the Nineteenth Congress of the Communist Party of the Soviet Union and by Stalin's major address there.[59] If Soviet policy in the UN through 1952 can be interpreted largely as a divisive propaganda attack against the West, this attack had failed. While Soviet speeches and proposals had some effect at first, by 1952 their hollowness had been exposed. New tactics were also needed after 1952 because the situation had changed. Through the Organization for European Economic Cooperation, the European Coal and Steel Community (ECSC), and other devices, Western Europe moved, however, fitfully, toward integration. The West had also progressed in the construction of global machinery to facilitate the conduct of trade. As neither development included the Soviet bloc, it is reasonable to assume that the USSR should attempt countermoves.

While new targets have been added to the Soviet attack—the instruments of integration in Western Europe, ECSC, EEC and EURATOM, and GATT, OTC, and OECD—the Western embargo on the export of strategic goods has remained the prime target. Although there could be no doubt that the Soviet Union would have liked to eliminate this ban, it probably has not been displeased with the opportunity which the prohibition creates for exacerbating relations among Western states. There are differing interpretations in the West concerning the degree of risk involved in trade with the Soviet bloc, and, of course, each state has its own separate economic interests. Even greater differences can be found in public opinion concerning these controls. In several areas of the world public opinion is particularly susceptible to Soviet claims concerning the possibilities for and advantages of expanded trade with communist countries. The USSR has always utilized the United Nations to exploit these differences, and its new tactics have increased its capabilities to do this. Soviet tactics in the UN have probably played some role

[59] See the suggestive discussion in Herbert Marcuse, *Soviet Marxism*, pp. 64 ff. See also the insightful analyses by Marshall D. Schulman: "Some Implications of Changes in Soviet Policy Toward the West," *Slavic Review*, XX, no. 4 (December 1961), 530-540; and *Stalin's Foreign Policy Reappraised*.

in the growing opinion against the export controls and, to a limited extent, may have been responsible for the two reductions in the Coordinating Committee's list of prohibited exports. The new Soviet tactics have also enhanced the USSR's ability to play upon other divisive forces within the West, for example concerning the commodity problem.

At the same time, the changed Soviet tactics have resulted in increased trade between the Soviet bloc and some Western countries and have also allowed the UN, especially ECE, to expand its work. This has no doubt been immediately important, but its long-range significance is questionable. Although Western scholars have shown that it may be to the USSR's advantage to increase its foreign trade, particularly with underdeveloped countries,[60] there is little evidence that communist theories concerning the role of external trade—at least with noncommunist countries—have changed.[61] In public confrontations, however, Soviet scholars have disputed this and have argued that communist theory does not point toward autarky.[62] But they have been unable to indicate specific criteria which govern choices concerning foreign trade in communist states, and they have not been able to ease fears that the state monopoly of foreign trade contains countless possibilities for unseen discriminations. Furthermore, although the Soviet Union has increased its participation in the United Nations, it has not been willing to join FAO, ICAO, IMF, IBRD, or GATT, and has not significantly altered its narrow definition of national sovereignty as it bears upon the UN's more technical activities. The activities which the Soviet Union has participated in generally have been conducted on a different basis from that originally planned for the UN. They have been, as in ECE, more oriented toward bilateralism than multilateralism, and although Soviet representatives are now less forceful in asserting the superiority of the former technique, their practice is evidence of their continuing preference.

The effect of Soviet policy on the United Nations therefore appears to have been to limit the UN's activities in the early years,

---

[60] See: Stanley J. Zyzniewski, "The Soviet Bloc and the Underdeveloped Countries," *World Politics*, XI, no. 3 (April, 1959), 378-398.

[61] See: UN, ECE, *Economic Bulletin for Europe*, XI, no. 1 (June, 1959), 54-55.

[62] See: V. P. Diatchenke, "International Trade and Peaceful Co-operation," *International Social Science Quarterly*, XII, no. 2 (1960), 237-250.

and since 1953 to push the UN in the direction of bilateralism. It may be, as some have suggested, that the goal of multilateralism as envisaged by the United Nations planners was inappropriate for the conditions of the mid-twentieth century.[63] Still, the basic values of multilateralism in the sphere of international trade remain, and the West has moved increasingly in this direction. It would be a serious blow for the West if the UN took a different course.

[63] See: Leicester Webb, "The Future of International Trade," *World Politics*, V, no. 4 (July, 1953), 423-442.

8: ECONOMIC DEVELOPMENT

PERHAPS THE MOST IMPORTANT OF THE UNITED NATIONS ECONOMIC and social activities have been those which have dealt with problems of economic development. The "revolution of rising expectations" has become a prominent feature of the mid-twentieth century. The underdeveloped countries have become convinced that a change in their material status is possible and have devoted themselves to achieving this goal. It was inevitable that the United Nations should become deeply involved in this process. Article 55 of the Charter directs the UN to promote "conditions of economic and social progress and development," and the ever-increasing political strength of the underdeveloped countries in UN organs insured that attention would be focused on this mandate. Ultimately several programs specifically designed to promote economic development were inaugurated, and a concern with problems of economic growth came to pervade all aspects of the UN's economic and social activities.

The slowness with which the United Nations began concrete work in this area may be explained partially by the pressure to deal with the immense problems left by the Second World War and partially by the difficulty of beginning work in a largely unchartered field.[1] The UN's initial activities concerning economic development consisted of discussions of general aspects of the problem. These discussions occurred in the Sub-Commission on Economic Development; its parent body, the Economic and Employment Commission; the Economic Commission for Asia and the Far East; the Economic

[1] See: Robert E. Asher, "Problems of the Underdeveloped Countries," Chapter XIV in R. E. Asher and others, *The United Nations and the Promotion of the General Welfare*, pp. 581-639.

ECONOMIC DEVELOPMENT

and Social Council; and the General Assembly. Then, in the fall of 1948, the first stages of a more tangible policy were adopted. The United Nations technical assistance program was enlarged and steps were taken which led to studies of specific issues, the most significant of which concerned the problem of financing economic development. In 1949 this change was carried farther with the inauguration of the Expanded Program of Technical Assistance.

Since then, UN activities in the field of economic development have increasingly consisted of providing assistance and aid to the underdeveloped countries. Among other things, this has meant a larger role for the specialized agencies. The development of concrete programs, however, has not ended the UN's general discussions of economic development. On the contrary, such discussions have continued to be featured in the Assembly and in ECOSOC and its subsidiary bodies.

Soviet leaders—as their public pronouncements have indicated—have always been aware that underdeveloped areas have afforded opportunities for the expansion of communist influence and power, and they have sought, with varying degrees of perceptiveness and skill, to exploit these. The USSR's broad objectives have been to foment discontent in underdeveloped areas, to alienate them from the West, and to make the Soviet Union appear as their true friend and protector. Soviet leaders soon saw the United Nations as a vehicle to further this strategy. Numerous examples have already been cited of Soviet attempts to turn debates on other subjects into conflicts between developed and underdeveloped countries. The UN's economic development activities could be used for this purpose immediately, without redirection.

GENERAL DISCUSSIONS

At first the United Nations activities in the field of economic developments were vague and groping; they consisted mainly of attempts to define the UN's role and to create the appropriate institutional machinery. Attempts were also made to achieve an understanding of the processes and implications of economic development. There were several general discussions, commissions were created and studies inaugurated. Resolutions stating broad general principles were adopted. While its part in the creation of the UN's institutions which were to work in this area was largely passive, the

USSR was extremely active in the general discussions. Indeed, these were almost tailor-made for Soviet efforts.

THE SUB-COMMISSION ON ECONOMIC DEVELOPMENT

Although the Soviet position was stated frequently in general debates in the United Nations in 1946 and early 1947, it was developed most effectively in the Sub-Commission on Economic Development. This body was ideally suited to Soviet tactics. Its mandate was broad and vague and it consisted of seven "experts," nominated by Brazil, China, Czechoslovakia, India, Mexico, the United States and the USSR. The Soviet Union's "expert" was Alexander P. Morozov, a frequent delegate to ECOSOC and the General Assembly.

The Sub-Commission's work consisted primarily of preparing reports for the consideration of its parent body, the Economic and Employment Commission, and other UN organs. Mr. Morozov was extremely successful, during the drafting of the first report in the fall of 1947, in insinuating his views and in securing the deletion of items he opposed.[2] He successfully objected to the inclusion of a statement that economic development should take place within the framework of economic "interdependence" and also to a recommendation that governments of UN member states should create a coordinating agency for all of their development activities. On the other side, he was able to secure the inclusion of a statement that political dependence was a major cause of backwardness in colonial areas. Further, at his insistence, the Sub-Commission recommended that loans and credits were preferable to direct investment as the latter tended to lead to intervention in the domestic affairs of underdeveloped countries. Also as a result of his urging, the Sub-Commission stated that technical assistance should be given within the framework of the United Nations and should not be used to gain political or military privileges. His greatest triumph, though, was in the inclusion throughout the report of the concept that economic development was equivalent to industrialization. During the debate, Mr. Morozov made it clear that by industrialization he meant the development of heavy industry, and he argued that only in this way could colonies and less developed countries be liberated from economic dependence.[3]

In sum, the Soviet view—which found considerable acceptance in

[2] See: UN Document E/CN. 1/47.
[3] UN Document E/CN. 1/Sub. 3/9, p. 2.

the Sub-Commission—was that colonialism and imperialism were the principal causes of the low level of economic development in underdeveloped areas, that above all the sovereignty of these areas needed to be protected, and that the only real formula for economic development was industrialization, through the development of heavy industry. These were themes drawn from or parallel to some of the principal tenets of Soviet ideology, and they were to be heard again and again in the United Nations. The emphasis on heavy industry has been an especially prominent feature of Soviet presentations.[4] This reflected communist beliefs and the USSR's own experience. Moreover, it set the Soviet Union as the model which others should emulate. Then, too, the West has always been doubtful that industrialization, at least as conceived in communist terms, is the key to economic progress, and by stressing this concept Soviet delegates have been able to set up conflicts between the West and underdeveloped areas.

Mr. Morozov was even more successful in writing his views into the Sub-Commission's second report.[5] The only result of these reports, though, was controversy in the Economic and Employment Commission and in the Economic and Social Council. Their contentious nature was an important factor in the decision, which was taken in 1950, to discontinue the Sub-Commission.

ECAFE AND ECLA

The USSR pursued related tactics with reference to the Economic Commission for Asia and the Far East and the Economic Commission for Latin America, although it was a member only of the former. In ECAFE sessions, Soviet delegates characteristically attacked colonialism and stressed the development of heavy industry.[6] Although the Soviet views may have had considerable appeal—at one point the Indian representative "agreed that the Soviet dele-

[4] See the excellent analysis by Alvin Z. Rubinstein, "Soviet Policy Toward Under-Developed Areas in the Economic and Social Council," *International Organization*, IX, no. 2 (May 1955), 232-243.

[5] See: UN, ECOSOC, *Official Records* (9th Session), Supplement No. 11 A, "Report of the Second Session of the Sub-Commission on Economic Development."

[6] See: UN Documents E/CN. 11/SR. 25, pp. 4-5; E/CN. 11/SR. 41, pp. 6-8; E/CN. 11/AC. 5/5, pp. 1-2; and also, Alvin Z. Rubinstein, "Soviet Policy in ECAFE: A Case Study of Soviet Behavior in International Economic Organization," *International Organization*, XII, no. 4 (Autumn 1958), 459-472.

gate's analysis of the condition of the ECAFE countries was mostly correct"[7]—they were never included in the Commission's reports. Nor did ECAFE accept the Soviet proposal that it should establish a special committee to assist the development of national industries in the area. Instead, the Commission merely added "Heavy Engineering Industries" to the subjects that should be studied by its *ad hoc* Committee on Industrial Development.

During the debate on ECAFE's report at the seventh session of the Economic and Social Council in 1948, Mr. Arutiunian charged that because of the intransigence of the metropolitan countries the Commission had failed in its tasks, which he claimed were those of eliminating the colonial regime and assisting semi-dependent territories to achieve complete independence.[8] He submitted a draft resolution which contained instructions to guide ECAFE in its future work.[9] It directed the Commission: (1) to promote the development of national industries, including heavy industry, through extensive mobilization and utilization of the available national resources and through foreign assistance, although this assistance must not be accompanied by demands for political or other advantages; (2) to encourage the growth of trade between the countries of the region and also with other regions "without any discrimination whatever"; (3) to formulate recommendations for the restoration and development of irrigated lands, the organization of cheap agricultural credit for the peasants (especially "small peasants") and the means of supplying peasants with fertilizers, agricultural implements and seeds on advantageous terms; (4) "to increase the total amount of capital and credit available" from outside sources and to make it available where most needed; and finally, (5) to continue discussion of these problems and establish whatever subsidiary bodies might be necessary. The resolution's preamble stated that the reconstruction and development of the economies of the countries of Asia and the Far East should be conducted so as "to promote the elimination of colonial and semi-colonial dependence" and the "development of national independence and State sovereignty" in Asia and the Far East.

The proposal was a collection of platitudes and exhortations,

[7] UN Document E/CN. 11/SR. 42, p. 2.

[8] This analysis is based on his major address: UN, ECOSOC, *Official Records* (7th Session), pp. 186-192.

[9] UN Document E/905 and Rev. 1 and 2.

several of which had great appeal for underdeveloped countries, although few were capable of immediate realization. Some sections were related to other aspects of Soviet policy; for instance, the reference to discrimination in international trade. Subtle attacks on the West were cleverly admixed with general principles to which all gave at least lip service. It was impossible for most delegates completely to oppose the Soviet proposal. Several counter-resolutions were advanced, and a drafting committee was ultimately established to prepare a universally acceptable resolution. Their product, ECOSOC Resolution 114 C (VII), clearly reflected the Soviet draft, but the most obnoxious features from the Western point of view were eliminated. A Soviet attempt in the plenary session to reintroduce these elements was rebuffed by votes ranging from thirteen to three with two abstentions, to seven to seven with four abstentions. The Soviet bloc supported the final resolution, even though Mr. Arutiunian claimed that it was not satisfactory. Theoretically, it was to provide a basis for ECAFE's future work, and the USSR claimed credit for initiating it.

Soviet tactics with regard to the Economic Commission for Latin America were similar. As the USSR was not a member of this Commission, debates in the Council and the Assembly provided the only occasions for Soviet delegates to deal with problems of economic development in Latin America. The Soviet position on these issues was first developed in detail in 1948 at ECOSOC's seventh session. Mr. Arutiunian claimed that ECLA also had failed in its tasks.[10] He characterized the Latin-American countries as "semi-colonial economies." He felt this term was apt because: exports were limited to only one or two commodities; equipment and means of production were in short supply; and, foreign capital was in a dominant position. In his view the last feature led to the normal processes of development being subordinated to the interests of foreign capitalists and encouraged the exhaustion of Latin America's national resources. More importantly, he felt that it resulted in foreign political influence. Therefore, he argued that ECLA's main task should be to deliver the Latin-American states from their dependence on foreign capital, not to encourage further foreign penetration, as he claimed it had. He maintained that there were sufficient resources in Latin America for economic development purposes; the problem was that

[10] This analysis is based on his major address: UN, ECOSOC, *Official Records* (7th Session), pp. 559-565.

the major part of the profits earned in Latin America was not invested there, but was exported. He also argued that since the profits in semi-colonial countries were always high, foreign investment would be forthcoming without any special appeal by ECLA.

The very violence of Mr. Arutiunian's speech and the insinuation that their countries were controlled by foreign capital forced all of the Latin-American members of the Council to reply to his attack. While many of his charges were caricatures of their own criticisms, they could not allow them to be made in this form.

ECLA's report allowed Mr. Arutiunian to attack the United States in the same way that ECAFE's report allowed him to attack the major Western European countries. The concept of "semi-colonial dependence" was a counterpart to that of "colonial dependence" used in the discussion of ECAFE's report. It enabled him to identify the United States with imperialism. This attack, however, was somewhat less successful. If it had any impact, it could only have been in terms of public opinion. Mr. Arutiunian did not offer a draft resolution, but simply voted against the one which the Council adopted approving ECLA's work. Byelorussia joined in opposition, but Poland abstained. The difficulty of attacking the work of the Economic Commission for Latin America must have impressed the Soviet Union, for it never again attempted such a vitriolic onslaught.

THE CHANGING SETTING OF UN ACTIVITIES

The seventh session also marked a turning point in Soviet policy in other respects. It ended the preliminary stage of the UN's work concerning economic development; thereafter this work became more and more concrete, and the milieu within which Soviet policy had to operate was significantly altered. When the General Assembly's third session opened in the fall of 1948, the underdeveloped countries' impatience and dissatisfaction with the UN's past activities were evident; they wanted immediate and meaningful assistance. The result was the adoption of three resolutions: 198 (III) directing ECOSOC and the specialized agencies to give "further and urgent consideration to the whole problem of economic development in *all* its aspects" and requiring the Council to report proposals for new activities to the Assembly's next session; 200 (III) expanding the UN's technical assistance work; and 246 (III) authorizing the Secretary-General to make arrangements for the establishment of an international center for training in public administration. These three resolutions, to which the USSR's contribution was minimal and largely negative, laid the foundation for a concrete program of assistance to underdeveloped countries. It is true that they did not end the UN's general discussions of problems of economic development, which have occurred regularly at meetings of the regional and functional economic commissions, ECOSOC and the Assembly, but they basically altered the context within which these discussions have been carried on.

The Soviet Union has continued to use these to expound its interpretation of the problem of economic development. Soviet delegates have emphasized the themes which were developed in the UN's early discussions. They have also insisted that central planning and control are necessary if economic development programs are to be successful. Other issues, such as Western rearmament, the Western controls on the export of strategic goods and the level of commodity prices, have been integrated into this basic analysis. Representatives from the USSR have also frequently, albeit tangentially, worked the United States' racial discrimination troubles into the discussions. Although the tone of these Soviet statements has varied with the mode of general Soviet policy, and with few exceptions has become increasingly moderate since 1953, their substance has been largely unchanged. Their major purpose appears to have been to make the Soviet process of economic growth appear as the only correct one, and to create the image of the USSR as the friend and protector of the underdeveloped countries in contrast with the imperialist Western powers, which have been pictured as exploiting these states for their own benefit.

The effectiveness of these Soviet tactics is difficult to gauge. After 1948 the USSR was never able to secure the formal adoption of its position in the United Nations. Structural reorganization was one factor responsible for this. The Sub-Commission on Economic Development, the most favorable forum from the Soviet standpoint, held only two further meetings before it was disbanded in 1950. Its parent body, renamed the Economic, Employment and Development Commission, which had also been fairly receptive to Soviet proposals, was discontinued a year later. The USSR's opportunities thus were significantly diminished.

It may be, however, that the USSR will again find a favorable environment for the exposition of its views in the Committee for Industrial Development, a body composed of delegates from thirty member states which ECOSOC created in 1959 in response to a request by the General Assembly. It is noteworthy that the Soviet Union's role in the creation of the Committee was confined to supporting the initiatives of underdeveloped countries. Certainly the USSR made full use of the opportunities provided by the general debate at the Committee's first two sessions in 1961 and 1962 to expound its interpretations. On one occasion in the latter year, in arguing that developing countries should give priority to the development of heavy industry, the Soviet delegate introduced a revealing supporting argument:

> ... true economic independence could be achieved only through the establishment of a national economy with its own means of production. When a country was able to produce its own machinery, it could diversify its economy and limit the sphere of influence of private investment capital, thus ending its dependence on the advanced countries of the West.[11]

In the discussions which led to the creation of the Committee, the West had attempted to have the concept of industrial development defined carefully and broadly and felt that it had succeeded. By 1963, though, it was apparent that this was not the case.[12]

Another factor which has inhibited Soviet success has been the USSR's unwillingness to participate fully in the United Nations' developing concrete work concerning economic development. Until 1953 the Soviet Union boycotted most of these activities, and Western delegates constantly and effectively contrasted this record with Soviet claims of concern for the welfare of underdeveloped countries. The USSR's decision to participate in the Expanded Program of Technical Assistance and in several of the specialized agencies from which it had previously abstained eased this situation somewhat, but there still are a number of specialized agencies which the USSR has not joined, and its contribution to EPTA has been limited.

Perhaps the most basic obstacle which the Soviet Union has faced has been the fact that although the majority of underdeveloped countries have been greatly impressed with the USSR's achievements, they have not been willing totally to adopt its methods, nor have they been willing completely to accept its interpretations. This has been made clear time and again in United Nations debates.

[11] UN Document E/C. 5/SR. 15, p. 11.
[12] See the competing Soviet and American definitions: UN Documents E/C. 5/L. 17 and E/C.5/L. 18.

The success of the Soviet tactics as propaganda is another matter. In the United Nations, few appear to have been impressed, but the impact probably has been greater in less sophisticated circles. Even in the UN, heavy industry has received prominent emphasis and although the Soviet Union has certainly not been solely responsible, it must be given some of the credit. In 1961 the United Nations moved toward the establishment of an Industrial Development Center and began to consider whether or not a specialized agency in this field would be useful. Through its onslaught, the USSR has also probably contributed to the underdeveloped countries' dissatisfaction with their material status and has thereby intensified their demands for concrete action.

TECHNICAL ASSISTANCE

In contrast to Soviet policy concerning the UN's general discussions of economic development, which has been relatively constant, the USSR's attitude toward the UN's work in the field of technical assistance has fluctuated greatly. Soviet behavior during the first discussion of the subject at the second part of the Assembly's first session in the fall of 1946 is illustrative. The USSR initially opposed its inclusion in the agenda; then, in the Second Committee, abstained from voting on the resolution which was adopted asking ECOSOC to consider the problem of providing expert assistance to UN members; and, finally, in the plenary session, voted for the same resolution.[13] Apparently the USSR had little interest in technical assistance as such, but at the same time it appeared to be unwilling to oppose a popular measure. Similar sequences have occurred often.

Early Discussions of Technical Assistance

It was obvious from the very beginning that the underdeveloped countries within the UN were extremely interested in technical assistance. Despite this, the United Nations did little to provide such aid prior to the Assembly's third session, and the adoption of resolutions 200 (III) and 246 (III). Only one team of experts was dispatched

[13] UN, General Assembly, General Committee, *Official Records* (1st Session, 2nd Part), p. 87; UN, General Assembly, *Official Records,* Joint Second and Third Committee, *Official Records* (1st Session, 2nd Part), p. 77; and UN, General Assembly, Plenary Meetings, *Official Records* (1st Session, 2nd Part), p. 1387.

before 1949. However, there had been several discussions of technical assistance in ECOSOC and its subsidiary bodies and a number of guiding principles for the UN's work in this field had been established.

The Soviet Union's role in these discussions was minor. In the Economic and Employment Commission, Mr. Morozov insisted that the initiative must rest with the countries which desired to receive assistance, and that the UN should only act on the basis of specific requests from the states concerned.[14] There was no opposition to this position, and it was agreed that all activities should be undertaken only upon request of the government concerned and on the basis of special agreements. In later debates, Soviet delegates often restated Mr. Morozov's argument. It was consistent with the USSR's general policy of seeking to insure that the UN's competence would be limited and with its attempts to appear as the guardian of the interests of the underdeveloped countries.

The latter objective was especially apparent when the Economic and Social Council first discussed the question of technical assistance at its fourth session in the spring of 1947. Debate was based on a resolution adopted by the Assembly at its first session which asked ECOSOC to explore the question of the UN's providing expert advice to member states. Mr. Morozov proposed that one of the tasks of the Economic and Employment Commission should be to insure that technical assistance and other aid given to underdeveloped countries should not be used for the purpose of exploitation or for obtaining political, military or economic advantages.[15] This proposal, which was adopted in a modified form, was related to Soviet tactics with regard to reconstruction assistance. It was probably a caveat for the future, too. The Soviet Union could probably foresee that in the years to come the United States could and would be much more active in the field of technical assistance than the Soviet Union, and, therefore, hoped to cast aspersions on American activities in this area.

Mr. Morozov made one other significant intervention in the Council's discussion of technical assistance at its fourth session. It was to question the budgetary implications involved in the decision to establish machinery within the UN Secretariat to provide expert

[14] UN Document E/CN. 1/SR. 3, p. 13.
[15] UN Documents: E/345, p. 6; E/384, p. 4; E/AC. 6/5/Rev. 1/Add. 1; and E/AC. 19/7, p. 1.

ECONOMIC DEVELOPMENT 229

assistance to underdeveloped countries. This intervention foreshadowed a prominent aspect of Soviet policy. Thereafter, on every possible occasion during the UN's general discussion of technical assistance, Soviet delegates argued that the recipient countries should pay for the costs of the aid which they received.[16] It is hardly necessary to state that this position found little support.

The Third Session of the Assembly

As the UN's discussions became more specific, the USSR's role was reduced even more. The Soviet contribution to the discussions concerning the establishment of an international center for training in public administration, which finally led to passage of Assembly Resolution 246 (III), was completely negative. In every debate Soviet delegates argued that international action in this field would be inappropriate; it could only be treated on a national basis.[17]

Nor was the Soviet position with regard to Resolution 200 (III), the other important decision on technical assistance which was adopted at the Assembly's third session, any more in accord with majority sentiment. In this resolution the General Assembly decided to allocate funds ($288,000 was appropriated for the first year's operations) for a continuing program of expert assistance to underdeveloped countries in the form of survey missions, fellowships, local training programs, seminars and other exchanges of information. This resolution inaugurated the United Nations Program of Technical Assistance in the Field of Economic Development. It and the programs in Social Welfare, Public Administration and Human Rights were all financed from the UN's regular budget and made up the Regular United Nations Program of Technical Assistance.

According to Resolution 200 (III), the Program of Technical Assistance in the Field of Economic Development was to be administered by the Secretary-General under the supervision of the Economic and Social Council. ECOSOC was instructed to report annually to the Assembly and to formulate recommendations on technical assistance. Resolution 200 (III) grew out of a proposal sub-

[16] UN Documents: E/CN. 1/SR. 33, p. 5; E/CN. 1/SR. 59, p. 11; E/AC. 6/SR. 26, p. 26; and also E/1007.
[17] UN Document E/C. 3/SR. 5, p. 2; UN, ECOSOC, *Official Records* (6th Session), pp. 250-251; UN, General Assembly, Fifth Committee, *Official Records* (3rd Session, 1st Part), p. 728; and, UN, General Assembly, Plenary Meetings, *Official Records* (3rd Session, 1st Part), pp. 708-709.

mitted by Burma, Chile, Egypt and Peru. In terms of the schedule established by ECOSOC and the Sub-Commission on Economic Development the proposal was somewhat premature; studies of the UN's role were still in process and others were planned, but the underdeveloped countries were impatient for the inauguration of a concrete program.

The Soviet Union had very little influence on the terms of Resolution 200 (III). At one point in the debate, Mr. Arutiunian suggested that technical assistance was a delicate question for history showed that it often provided great opportunities for foreign infiltration and the spreading of foreign influence.[18] Perhaps as a result of this, or perhaps to forestall an inevitable Soviet amendment, the resolution stated that technical assistance granted by the UN should not be used as a means of economic or political interference in the internal affairs of recipient countries and should not be accompanied by political demands.

Mr. Arutiunian's major point concerning the financial aspects of the program, however, was ignored, and as a consequence the USSR abstained from voting on Resolution 200 (III). During the debate, both in the Second Committee and in the plenary session, Mr. Arutiunian stated that although his government "recognized the right" of the Secretary-General to organize, at the request of member governments, plans for expert assistance, it felt:

> . . . that the costs of the implementation of such a programme should be borne by the countries benefiting from such technical assistance. . . . It believed that the task of the United Nations was not to finance such schemes, but to provide, on an international level, impartial and highly qualified assistance. The United Nations was neither a bank nor a relief agency.[19]

This position was consistent with earlier Soviet statements on technical assistance and with the USSR's policy concerning the Advisory Social Welfare Services and the dispatch of a mission to investigate the effects of chewing the coca leaf. At this point the Soviet Union was not willing to contribute funds to programs from which it would receive no direct benefits. The Soviet position was particularly unpalatable to the underdeveloped countries, who felt strongly that

---

[18] UN General Assembly, Second Committee, *Official Records* (3rd Session, 1st Part), p. 181.

[19] UN, General Assembly, Plenary Meetings, *Official Records* (3rd Session, 1st Part), pp. 700-701.

their pressing needs had not received sufficient international attention. It erected a barrier between this group and the USSR.

The USSR's Isolation and Its Attitude Toward EPTA

Thus, by the end of the Assembly's third session, because of its general position, and particularly because of its attitude toward resolutions 200 (III) and 246 (III), the Soviet Union was rapidly becoming isolated from the mainstream of the UN's developing concrete activities in the field of technical assistance. From 1948 to 1953, there were few changes in Soviet policy, and as a consequence, the USSR's isolation increased. The USSR continued to maintain that providing training in public administration was beyond the UN's competence.[20] For a while it also continued to argue that the costs of technical assistance should be met by the recipient countries.[21] This position, however, was dropped after the summer of 1949. Although the USSR voted for resolutions on the Regular Program, there were obvious limits to its support. For instance, on one occasion the Soviet delegate opposed an ECOSOC resolution dealing with the activities carried on under Resolution 200 (III) because there was a provision which recommended that the funds should be increased.[22] On another occasion the USSR refused to vote for a resolution concerning the Regular United Nations Program because of the administrative arrangements involved.[23]

Perhaps the most important factor in the USSR's growing isolation during this period, though, was its attitude toward and abstention from the UN's newly inaugurated Expanded Program of Technical Assistance. When the Economic and Social Council began its eighth session in the spring of 1949, it had before it the three resolutions, 198 (III), 200 (III) and 246 (III), passed by the General Assembly the previous December. These insured that problems of economic development, and particularly technical assistance, would receive increased attention. The movement toward giving the United Nations more concrete tasks in this field, which these resolutions symbolized, was given added impetus by President Truman's 1949 inaugural address. In this speech he proposed a "bold new program" of aid to underdeveloped countries. His suggestion caught the mood

[20] See, for example: UN, ECOSOC, *Official Records* (9th Session), p. 455.
[21] UN Documents: E/CN. 1/SR. 79, p. 5; and E/AC. 6/SR. 78, pp. 12-13.
[22] UN Document E/AC. 6/SR. 64, pp. 13, 16.
[23] UN, ECOSOC, *Official Records* (12th Session), p. 238.

of the times, and discussions of it and its implications for the UN, rather than the three resolutions, dominated the Council's eighth session. The Expanded Program of Technical Assistance, probably the United Nations' most significant concrete program concerning economic development, resulted from these discussions.

Willard Thorp, the United States delegate, opened the discussion by suggesting that ECOSOC should elaborate plans for a much larger program of technical assistance than had been envisaged in Resolution 200 (III). He advocated that such a program should be carried out in collaboration with the specialized agencies and announced that the United States would be willing to contribute substantial funds. Most delegates responded enthusiastically, although some expressed disappointment that Mr. Thorp offered no proposals for capital investments. Soviet bloc delegates provided an exception to the general enthusiasm; they were harshly critical.[24] All but the Soviet bloc supported the resolution which Mr. Thorp submitted asking the Secretary-General to prepare a comprehensive plan for an enlarged program in the field of technical assistance.

The fact that the Soviet bloc abstained from voting indicated the dilemma of Soviet policy. Although the USSR apparently saw little merit in the proposal for the Expanded Program of Technical Assistance, especially in view of its American authorship and the obvious fact that the United States would be the largest contributor, to oppose this popular suggestion would risk alienating the underdeveloped countries. This dilemma plagued Soviet policy until 1953 when the USSR decided to contribute to the Expanded Program of Technical Assistance, and to some extent it continued to be a problem even after that.

Discussion of the American proposal was resumed at the Economic and Social Council's ninth session in July and August 1949 and the most significant negotiations occurred then. Heated discussions of trade union rights, forced labor and unemployment were also prominent features of this meeting. Mr. Arutiunian's opening speech reflected the Soviet quandary.[25] Although he did not directly attack the plans to create the UN's Expanded Program of Technical Assistance, he did so by implication. Among other things, he severely criticized the United States Point Four Program. His speech, how-

---

[24] See the major address by Semyon K. Tsarapkin, the Soviet delegate: UN, ECOSOC, *Official Records* (8th Session), pp. 432-435.

[25] UN, ECOSOC, *Official Records* (9th Session), pp. 396-404.

ever, had little apparent effect on the representatives of the underdeveloped countries.

Nor was the USSR especially successful in the detailed negotiations concerning the Expanded Program of Technical Assistance. The Soviet Union's proposal that the recipient countries should bear the costs of the assistance that they received was summarily rejected.[26] Soviet opposition to the creation of a special central account to which governments could contribute on a voluntary basis and from which the UN and the specialized agencies could draw was also ignored.[27] And Soviet opposition could not prevent the decision to convene a governmental conference to solicit and ascertain contributions to the EPTA special account. These Soviet positions indicated that the USSR would probably be unwilling (and perhaps was unable) to contribute to the Expanded Program. This diminished Soviet influence. The USSR's nonparticipation in and hostility toward several of the specialized agencies may also have been a factor determining these positions. Indeed, Soviet representatives implied several times that the specialized agencies should not be included.

Several Soviet proposals dealt with the information which recipient governments would be required to submit. For instance, Byelorussia proposed the deletion of provisions requiring recipient governments to publish or to supply publishable information on the results and experience gained from technical assistance and making it mandatory for governments when submitting requests for aid to inform the UN of all assistance which they were presently receiving in the same field of development.[28] The only proposal of this nature which succeeded was another Byelorussian amendment which limited the information required of recipient governments "strictly to questions directly related to the concrete requests for technical assistance." An amendment proposed by the USSR placing a similar limitation upon studies prepared by the Secretariat was rejected. According to the resolution which the Council finally adopted, the Secretariat was allowed to examine "the needs and conditions of the various countries requesting assistance."

[26] UN Document E/AC. 6/SR. 78, pp. 12-13, 16.

[27] The most convenient source for the Soviet proposals is UN Document E/1540, the amendment which the USSR submitted in the plenary session. This repeated several proposals which were presented first in the Economic Committee. Unless other citations are given, the following analysis is based on this document.

[28] The Byelorussian amendments are contained in UN Document E/1543.

Other Soviet amendments concerned the administration of the Expanded Program of Technical Assistance. The creation of two bodies to administer the program was envisaged: a Technical Assistance Board (TAB), composed of the executive heads of the specialized agencies participating in the Program and chaired by the Secretary-General of the United Nations or his representative (in 1952 a full time Executive Chairman was appointed); and a Technical Assistance Committee (TAC), composed of the members of ECOSOC (eventually twelve elective positions were added). Following general Soviet policy concerning organizational questions, the USSR and Poland sought to strengthen the powers of TAC over TAB.[29] Their proposals were also designed to increase Soviet bloc influence in the allocation of technical assistance. TAB would have no communist members, while TAC would. The only Soviet successes were the adoption of a Polish amendment instructing TAB to inform TAC of any request for technical assistance as soon as it was received and an amendment sponsored by the USSR requiring the specialized agencies to report to TAC on all of their technical assistance activities, not only those that were part of the Expanded Program.

The Soviet bloc scored its greatest successes in the last stage of the negotiations and with regard to the general principles which were to guide the Expanded Program of Technical Assistance. On the basis of proposals submitted by Poland and the USSR, the initial principle was amended to state that the participating organizations should:

> Regard it as a primary objective to help those countries to strengthen their national economies through the development of their national industries and agriculture, with a view to promoting their economic and political independence in the spirit of the Charter of the United Nations, and to ensure the attainment of higher levels of economic and social welfare for their entire populations.

An amendment submitted by the USSR requiring that the duties of technical assistance personnel be strictly defined in bilateral agreements between the recipient government and the organization pro-

---

[29] Poland submitted several amendments relating to this issue: UN Document E/1542. Many of these were similar to the USSR's proposals, but the Polish delegate argued that they were milder and offered them as "compromise amendments."

viding assistance was also adopted. In addition, a Soviet amendment was responsible for the deletion of a preambular paragraph stating that economic development required careful coordination in the utilization of the scarce resources of underdeveloped countries as well as "a coordinated foreign supplementation of those resources." On the other hand, several broad amendments submitted by Byelorussia, Poland and the USSR emphasizing themes which communist delegates frequently stressed concerning economic development and technical assistance were rejected.

All three members of the Soviet bloc abstained from voting on ECOSOC Resolution 222 (IX) which recommended that the General Assembly authorize the creation of the Expanded Program of Technical Assistance and, subject to this authorization, provided the institutional framework for the Program. No explanation was given for the Soviet bloc's abstention. The failure to adopt many of the Soviet amendments may have been the reason. Also, Mr. Arutiunian hinted that he either lacked instructions or was in the process of attempting to have his instructions altered.[30]

In any case, he was somewhat better equipped at the General Assembly's fourth session in the fall of 1949. Although his major speech[31] repeated most of the points which he had made in ECOSOC, and his attack on the United States Point Four program was even more violent, he submitted no amendments to the Council's proposal, and those which Poland offered were soon withdrawn.[32] Moreover, the Soviet bloc joined the unanimous vote for Assembly Resolution 304 (IV) which approved the establishment of the Expanded Program of Technical Assistance. The *New York Times* on October 12, 1949, acclaimed the Soviet vote in the Second Committee as evidence of a new policy of cooperation within the UN. In retrospect, this seems to have been rather premature.

On the basis of the authorization provided by Resolution 304 (IV), a pledging conference was held in June 1950. The Soviet bloc boycotted this conference and those held in 1951 and 1952, and these states refused to contribute to the Expanded Program of Technical Assistance during this period. Although the members of the Soviet bloc voted for resolutions concerning the program at the

[30] See: UN, ECOSOC, *Official Records* (9th Session), p. 856.
[31] UN, General Assembly, Second Committee, *Official Records* (4th Session), pp. 47-50.
[32] UN Document A/C. 2/L. 5.

Assembly's fifth session in the fall of 1950 and the Council's twelfth session in the next summer, their support was not enthusiastic. Further, at the General Assembly's fifth session, the Soviet bloc opposed the decision to create a Technical Assistance Administration (TAA) within the Secretariat to handle the administrative and operational aspects of all of the UN's technical assistance programs (on February 1, 1959, this became the Bureau of Technical Assistance Operations [BTAO] within the Department of Economic and Social Affairs), and unsuccessfully attempted to have its funds reduced.[33]

After the first session, which they missed because of the Chinese representation boycott, the USSR and the other eligible members of the Soviet bloc attended the meetings of the Technical Assistance Committee, but their role was limited. Their contribution in TAC, as in the Council and Assembly debates on the Expanded Program, consisted mainly of attacks on the United States Point Four Program and the Colombo Plan.

Starting in the fall 1951 meeting of TAC, Soviet delegates even attacked the United Nations Expanded Program.[34] They charged that it had deviated from its original purposes, and had violated the principles on which it was to have been based. In their view it was dominated by the influence of "capitalist monopolies." Outside the United Nations the USSR charged that the UN's technical assistance missions were being used as a cover for American intelligence activities.[35] After this attack began, the Soviet Union abstained from voting on all resolutions adopted in ECOSOC and the Assembly dealing with the Expanded Program. These abstentions continued through ECOSOC's fifteenth session in the spring of 1953.

Soviet criticisms did nothing to lessen the enthusiasm of underdeveloped countries for EPTA; their principal effect seems to have been to alienate the USSR from the underdeveloped states. Western delegates capitalized on the Soviet predicament. Hardly a debate

[33] UN, General Assembly, Fifth Committee, *Official Records* (5th Session), pp. 72-73.

[34] See: UN Document E/TAC/SR. 15, pp. 21-25; and UN, ECOSOC, *Official Records* (13th Session), p. 442.

[35] See: *Trud*, December 25, 1951, as contained in *The Current Digest of the Soviet Press*, III, no. 52 (February 9, 1952), 19; *Pravda*, May 21, 1951, as contained in *The Current Digest of the Soviet Press*, IV, no. 21 (July 5, 1952), 15; and, *Pravda*, as contained in *The Current Digest of the Soviet Press*, IV, no. 34 (October 4, 1952), 26.

occurred in which they did not emphasize the already evident fact that the USSR did not contribute "one red ruble" to the Expanded Program. Soviet delegates sought to counter these charges by citing the USSR's contribution to the Regular Program of Technical Assistance. However, this tactic had little success, the arithmetic of the matter was against it. During this period, the budget of the Expanded Program was approximately $20,000,000 per year, and the United Kingdom and the United States voluntarily provided about 70 per cent of the funds. On the other hand, the budget of the Regular Program never exceeded $500,000, and the USSR's contribution, which was taken from its regular UN assessment, was approximately 7 per cent. The Soviet Union's attitude toward and abstention from the UN's Expanded Program of Technical Assistance was probably the most important obstacle to the attainment of its objective of winning the sympathy of the underdeveloped states.

The Shift in Soviet Strategy

This situation was suddenly changed in July 1953 when Mr. Arutiunian announced at the Economic and Social Council's sixteenth session that the USSR would contribute four million rubles ($1,000,000 at the official exchange rate then in effect) to EPTA.[36] No prior indications had been given of the shift in Soviet policy, and the announcement itself was made during a debate on the financing of economic development. At the previous Council session the USSR had abstained from voting on a resolution on EPTA and it also did this at the sixteenth session. The Soviet press carried a factual account of Mr. Arutiunian's speech, permitting itself only the comment that the announcement of the Soviet decision "made a great impression at the meeting." [37]

Alvin Z. Rubinstein finds the change in Soviet leadership occasioned by the death of Joseph V. Stalin on March 5, 1953, to be the

[36] UN, ECOSOC, *Official Records* (16th Session), p. 142.

[37] *Pravda* and *Izvestia*, July 17, 1953, as contained in *The Current Digest of the Soviet Press*, V, no. 29 (August 29, 1953), 15. Somewhat later, *New Times* was much more voluble (See: "Aid to Underdeveloped Countries," *New Times*, no. 32 [August 5, 1953], pp. 1-3.) The account asserted: "The Soviet Union's decision has been extensively commented on in the world press which described it as an event of major significance, one which inspired the hope that U.N. technical aid to underdeveloped countries would now be put on a firm footing" (p. 1).

immediate cause for the shift in Soviet policy.[38] The abruptness of the announcement, and the fact that it was made in the wrong debate, certainly suggests that it was not a move that had been planned for a long time. However, Soviet diplomats must have been aware of the ineffectiveness of the USSR's past policies in this area much earlier, and they presumably made their views known to elements of the Soviet hierarchy. Furthermore, this shift was related to changes in other Soviet policies within the UN; for example, in the Economic Commission for Europe. Probably all of the changes which occurred in Soviet policies during this period can be traced ultimately to the USSR's improved economic situation and to the transformation in its world outlook, which was already evident in late 1952 at the Nineteenth Congress of the Communist Party. In explaining the change, Soviet authorities themselves emphasize their earlier identification of EPTA with the American Point Four Program, the shortage of material resources in the USSR during the reconstruction period, and the colonial status of many of the potential recipients of economic assistance, which raised the problem of the intermediary of the metropolitan power.

Whatever the explanation, Mr. Arutiunian's announcement had the effect of quickly lowering the barrier which had grown up between the USSR and the underdeveloped countries. Because of past Soviet policy, and because it was new, the Soviet contribution was greeted with an enthusiasm which vastly exceeded its financial significance.

Other related Soviet moves followed in swift succession. After ECOSOC's sixteenth session the USSR voted for almost all UN resolutions dealing with technical assistance. It became an active participant in three of the four most important specialized agencies cooperating in the Expanded Program of Technical Assistance: the International Labor Organization, the United Nations Educational, Scientific and Cultural Organization, and the World Health Organization. The USSR launched its own bilateral program of aid to underdeveloped countries and used the UN as a forum to publicize this.[39] In so doing it had to drop the argument, which it had ad-

[38] See: *The Soviets in International Organizations: Changing Policy Toward Underdeveloped Countries*, to be published by the Princeton University Press.

[39] For descriptions of the Soviet program see: Robert Loring Allen, *Soviet Economic Warfare* (Washington, D. C.: Public Affairs Press, 1960); Joseph S. Berliner, *Soviet Economic Aid* (New York: Harpers, 1958); V. Rimalov, *Eco-*

ECONOMIC DEVELOPMENT 239

vanced previously, that all aid should be channeled through the UN. Soviet delegates maintained that the USSR's aid did not carry with it demands for political and other advantages, implying that other bilateral programs did. For a while at least, these moves greatly facilitated the Soviet Union's efforts with the underdeveloped countries.

THE "CURRENCY UTILIZATION PROBLEM"

Even with these important changes in the USSR's policy, however, Soviet strategy still encountered difficulties; and problems in the area of technical assistance were among them. Although most delegates from the underdeveloped countries glowingly praised the Soviet decision to contribute to the Expanded Program of Technical Assistance, in practice their governments seemed more reserved. The Soviet contribution to EPTA was made in nonconvertible rubles. Therefore it had to be spent in the USSR, and could only be used for Soviet equipment, fellowships in the Soviet Union or Soviet technical advisers. Further, related administrative services (shipping charges, travel and other similar items) which could not be furnished by the USSR had to be paid from the contributions of other countries. Few underdeveloped countries desired to use the Soviet contribution on these terms. A "currency utilization problem" developed; instead of being spent, the Soviet Union's rubles accumulated in unused balances in EPTA's Special Account.[40]

Until 1961 underdeveloped countries were especially reluctant to accept or request Soviet experts, as Table 1 shows. Even in 1962, when more Soviet citizens were utilized than ever before, there were one and a half times as many Indians serving as UN experts. That same year there were 574 experts from the United Kingdom and 428 from the United States. Those Soviet citizens who have been chosen have served mainly such states as Afghanistan, Burma, India, the United Arab Republic and Yugoslavia.[41] Fellowships in the Soviet

nomic Co-operation between the U.S.S.R. and Underdeveloped Countries (Moscow: Foreign Languages Publishing House, 1962); and, L. Stepanov, "Soviet Aid—And Its 'Critics'," International Affairs (Moscow), VI, no. 6 (June 1960), 20-26.

[40] See: Robert Loring Allen, "United Nations Technical Assistance: Soviet and East European Participation," International Organization, XI, no. 4 (Autumn 1957), 615-634.

[41] Walter R. Sharp, Field Administration in the United Nations System: The Conduct of International Economic and Social Programs (London: Stevens, 1960), p. 141.

TABLE 1

NATIONALS OF THE USSR SERVING AS EXPERTS
IN UN TECHNICAL ASSISTANCE PROGRAMS

	Regular Program	EPTA	Total Soviet Citizens	Total Experts in Programs
1953	0	0	0	2,252
1954	0	0	0	2,380
1955	0	5	5	2,568
1956	1	15	16	2,895
1957	0	28	28	3,183
1958	0	40	40	3,144
1959	3	40	43	3,215
1960	2	47	49	3,225
1961	5	66	71	3,739
1962	14	118	132	3,871

Source: UN, ECOSOC, *Official Records* (18th through 36th Sessions), Supplement No. 5, "Technical Assistance Committee: Annual Report of the Technical Assistance Board for 1953-1962."

Union have been somewhat more popular, as indicated in Table 2. Even so, in 1962 when there were 536 UN Fellows studying in the USSR, there were 941 in France, 948 in the United Kingdom and 785 in the United States.

TABLE 2

FELLOWSHIPS UNDER UN TECHNICAL ASSISTANCE PROGRAMS
INVOLVING THE USSR AS THE PLACE OF STUDY

	Regular Program	EPTA	Total Fellows in USSR	Total Fellowships Awarded
1953	0	0	0	3,094
1954	0	0	0	3,374
1955	0	17	17	4,612
1956	0	104	104	4,312
1957	0	95	95	4,940
1958	20	105	125	5,090
1959	44	118	162	5,677
1960	63	246	309	6,747
1961	44	203	247	7,951
1962	136	400	536	9,936

Source: UN, ECOSOC, *Official Records* (18th through 36th Sessions), Supplement No. 5, "Technical Assistance Committee: Annual Report of the Technical Assistance Board for 1953-1962."

ECONOMIC DEVELOPMENT

The reasons for the relative lack of interest over the years on the part of underdeveloped countries in Soviet experts and, to a lesser extent, in fellowships in the USSR have never been clearly stated. There have been hints of insufficient technical qualifications, language problems (although the USSR has offered to provide interpreters without charge) and inability to adjust on the part of experts, and of failures to keep the UN informed of the progress and whereabouts of fellows.[42] The basic reasons, though, have probably been of a political nature. Some underdeveloped countries have been reluctant to take any move which might increase the possibilities for communist influence within their borders. Many have been hesitant to take actions which might jeopardize their position with the West. In addition, there have been practical obstacles. Since most underdeveloped countries have most of their trade with the West, if given a choice they would naturally prefer to receive training from the West.

In an effort to utilize the Soviet Union's contribution, and also those of other Soviet bloc states, the Technical Assistance Board developed the so-called special projects device. In the 1956 program, recipient countries were given an allocation from the general funds available in EPTA's Special Account, and, in addition, a share of the unexpended balance of "difficult" currencies, mostly rubles. This arrangement often involved what appeared to be in effect bilateral negotiations between the donor and recipient governments.[43]

Both East and West objected to the special projects device. The Soviet Union alleged that it constituted undue discrimination. The United States complained that the Soviet contribution was being "pushed," and also objected to the bilateral negotiations between the USSR and recipient governments which accompanied some of the special projects. At ECOSOC's twenty-second session, in the summer of 1956, because of the insistence of the United States, the Council adopted Resolution 623 B III (XXII) which set strict limitations upon bilateral negotiations between contributing and recipient countries and outlawed the special projects device. The resolution also urged countries to make "that part of their contribution exceeding the equivalent of $500,000 in the form of, or conver-

[42] See: Walter R. Sharp, *Field Administration in the United Nations*, pp. 141, 464 and 489. These hints can also be found in the records of TAC.
[43] Walter R. Sharp, *Field Administration in the United Nations System*, p. 219.

tible into readily usable currencies." In addition, it stated that if more than a certain amount of a contribution remained uncommitted at the time of the next Pledging Conference that currency would be defined as "not readily usable," and it brought pressure to prevent further contributions in such currencies.

The Soviet Union bitterly contested this resolution, and at the General Assembly's eleventh session that fall Czechoslovakia and Romania proposed that it be rescinded.[44] In the Assembly debate, the United States delegate, Walter Kotschnig, implied, as he had previously, that the United States would revise its attitude toward EPTA if the provisions of Resolution 623 B III (XXII) were not upheld. Perhaps as a gesture of conciliation, the Soviet delegate, Mr. Saksin, announced that the USSR would agreed to make up to 25 per cent of its contribution convertible so that the administrative costs related to its utilization could be covered. This money, however, could only be used in connection with projects financed by the Soviet contribution; no Soviet funds could be used for EPTA's general administrative costs. The American threat was apparently more effective than the Soviet concession; the draft resolution was resoundingly rejected (44-10-14).

Since then the "currency utilization problem" appears largely to have been solved, as Tables 1 and 2 imply, and within the terms of ECOSOC Resolution 623 B III (XXII). One important factor, in addition to the greater number of Soviet experts in the field and of fellows studying in the USSR, is that underdeveloped countries have become increasingly willing to accept Soviet equipment. A large share of the USSR's contribution has been used for this purpose, in marked contrast to the utilization of other countries' contributions. The accumulated balances of unexpended rubles and other Soviet bloc currencies have been significantly reduced. This has only been achieved, however, through considerable efforts on the part of TAB, the UN's Bureau of Technical Assistance Operations and the secretariats of the participating specialized agencies to "sell" Soviet equipment. Their natural bureaucratic or organizational bias toward a large and universal program has compelled them to such steps.

Despite the progress toward its solution, the "currency utilization problem" has left a residue of bitterness and suspicion. The USSR has continued to complain about the small number of its nationals

[44] UN Document A/C. 2/L. 283.

employed as experts in the Expanded Program and the relatively small number of fellows studying in the Soviet Union. Soviet delegates have sometimes spoken as if they felt that this was the result of a conspiracy against their country.[45] Outside the UN, the conspiracy thesis has been openly stated. Soviet commentators have asserted that experts from the USSR are not chosen because of the disproportionate number of posts held by citizens of the United States and other NATO countries in the Department of Economic and Social Affairs.[46] These individuals allegedly follow the policy of their governments, "which carry out political and economic expansion under the U.N. flag," and consistently choose Western rather than Soviet experts. On the other hand, some in the West have charged that the USSR has been attempting to use the Expanded Program of Technical Assistance as a cover for bilateral operations.

To date the Soviet Union has shown no evidence that it will change its policy of making the bulk of its contribution to the Expanded Program in nonconvertible rubles. On the contrary, it has often sought to emphasize the desirability of making contributions in national currency. Moreover, starting in 1961 the USSR began to assert that the Regular Program of Technical Assistance ought not to be defrayed out of the compulsory contributions of member states to the UN budget, which must be in convertible currencies: "that the United Nations Charter neither authorizes nor justifies such compulsory financing of these operations."[47] In the midst of the United Nations financial crisis in 1963, the USSR announced that thereafter it would submit that proportion of its contribution to the UN budget that would go to the Regular Program in rubles.[48] The motivation for this position, and for the USSR's general attitude on these questions, is a basic unwillingness to have its funds used to finance noncommunist experts or fellowships for study in noncommunist countries. To put it positively, the USSR makes its contributions in rubles because it wants to reap whatever political advantages might accrue from having more Soviet nationals in the field as experts, more students from underdeveloped countries studying in

[45] See, for example: UN Document E/TAC/SR. 185, pp. 10-11.
[46] See: A. Nekrasov, "Soviet Aid Within U.N. Framework," *International Affairs* (Moscow), VII, no. 9 (September 1961), 74-75.
[47] From the separate statement by A. Roschin, Soviet expert on the committee of experts on the activities and organization of the Secretariat, UN Document A/4776, p. 5.
[48] *New York Times*, May 21, 1963.

the Soviet Union, and more exports of Soviet equipment. Pride in Soviet economic and technological accomplishments is another factor. In fairness, it should be pointed out that more than half of the states which contribute to EPTA make no provision for the conversion of their contributions, and only slightly more than a quarter make contributions which are fully convertible.[49]

OTHER ASPECTS OF SOVIET PARTICIPATION IN EPTA AND THE REGULAR PROGRAM

Until 1960, the USSR showed no willingness to increase its contribution to EPTA. The annual Soviet contribution through 1960 was identical with the amount first pledged in 1953, $1,000,000. The contributions of Byelorussia and the Ukraine also remained constant during this period, being set at $50,000 and $125,000 respectively. In the fall of 1960, during the General Assembly's fifteenth session, all three states announced that they would double their contributions in 1961. Several other Soviet bloc states followed suit. The new levels established for the USSR, Byelorussia and the Ukraine ($2,000,000; $100,000; and, $250,000, respectively) have been maintained since then. Nevertheless, the United States contribution continues to be more than eight times that of the Soviet Union. The "currency utilization problem" may well have been a factor in the USSR's reluctance to increase its contribution. It was only after this issue was more or less solved that the Soviet contribution was increased. The increase in the USSR's contribution also was announced at the same time that sixteen African states joined the UN and the organization's membership jumped from eighty-two to ninety-nine.

Its unwillingness to increase its contribution was responsible for one of the few instances since 1953 when the USSR did not vote for a resolution on technical assistance. At the twelfth session of the General Assembly in the fall of 1957 the Soviet Union abstained from voting on a resolution because of a provision which urged governments to consider increasing their contributions to EPTA for the next year. A year later, at the thirteenth session, even though it voted for a similar resolution, it did so with the caveat that the size of a country's contribution was exclusively a matter of national jurisdiction.

As the years passed, the "currency utilization problem" and the

[49] UN Document E/TAC/REP/186. See also: Walter R. Sharp, *Field Administration in the United Nations System*, p. 218.

constancy of the Soviet contribution to the Expanded Program both served to dampen the enthusiasm with which the underdeveloped countries initially greeted the change in the USSR's policy. Other limits to the change also became apparent, and this had the same effect. For one thing the Soviet Union still did not belong to the Food and Agriculture Organization, the specialized agency which received the largest EPTA allocation.[50]

Soviet delegates continued to play only a minor role in the Technical Assistance Committee. They seldom intervened in debates, and when they did, it was hardly ever to advance new proposals for action. They protested TAB decisions to reduce the allocation for the Western Higher Institute of Technology in Bombay, a project largely financed by Soviet funds, and to limit the funds available for work in Europe. The points that Soviet delegates raised most frequently were those which they had emphasized earlier: that administrative costs were too high and that insufficient resources were devoted to projects dealing with industrialization. Although the first argument may have had some appeal, it probably faded with time, and the second was in reality a criticism of the underdeveloped countries, for the UN's programs were shaped on the basis of their requests. The Soviet Union has also argued that ECOSOC's regional economic commissions should have a greater role in the UN's technical assistance programs.

The USSR's attempts to use the Expanded Program of Technical Assistance as a means of promoting extraneous Soviet political objectives caused certain frictions which the underdeveloped countries disliked. In 1956 the German Democratic Republic offered 400,000 German marks ($180,000) to EPTA. The Secretary-General refused to accept this contribution. On every occasion thereafter Soviet delegates severely criticized his decision, arguing that it was incorrect to refuse any contribution on "political" grounds when funds were so badly needed. And at the fourteenth session of the General Assembly in 1959, Bulgaria and Byelorussia unsuccessfully proposed an amendment which would have allowed all states to contribute to the Expanded Program.[51] In 1956, when the General Assembly recommended that ECOSOC expand the membership of the Technical Assistance Committee by choosing six additional members, the Soviet bloc unsuccessfully sought to amend the decision so that

[50] Nevertheless, FAO has employed Soviet experts.
[51] UN Document A/C. 2/L. 416.

all states would be eligible, not just those that were members of the UN and the specialized agencies.[52] Had the amendment been adopted, it would have been possible to propose the German Democratic Republic or the People's Republic of China as candidates. The Soviet Union also argued this position in 1957 at ECOSOC's twenty-third session.[53] Although a few underdeveloped states supported the Soviet bloc on these questions, many, including some that voted with the USSR, regarded them as diversionary and as detracting from their important problems.

Soviet delegates opposed two administrative developments concerning technical assistance, which almost everyone else considered useful, the establishment of resident representatives in recipient countries and steps toward biennial programming, on the grounds that they were likely to involve violations of sovereignty.[54] Although the USSR ultimately dropped its opposition in both cases, it did so reluctantly. It has always argued that the power of resident representatives should be limited and that they should have as many nationals from the recipient countries as possible on their staffs. The underdeveloped countries do not seem to have been as concerned about their own sovereignty.

Starting in 1961, however, the Soviet Union advanced an administrative argument which might possibly have greater appeal. The USSR suggested that TAC should have final authority over the UN's Regular Program as well as over the Expanded Program.[55] Some moves in this direction had already been taken, and the suggestion had a certain logic. In addition the move was related to the Soviet attack on the Secretary-General, and in that it meant transferring power from the Secretary-General and other administrative organs to a political body, it was consistent with other aspects of Soviet policy. It also tied in with the Soviet position on financing the Regular Program.

Although the USSR has supported some of the resolutions dealing with technical assistance in public administration since 1952, it has done so reluctantly and it has also abstained in a number of cases. Further, on two occasions, once in 1953 and again in 1959, the Soviet

---

[52] UN Document A/C. 2/L. 290.
[53] UN, ECOSOC, *Official Records* (23rd Session), pp. 75, 76.
[54] See: UN, General Assembly, Second Committee, *Official Records* (8th Session), p. 31; and UN Document E/TAC/SR. 189, pp. 8-9.
[55] UN Document E/TAC/SR. 248, pp. 7-9.

ECONOMIC DEVELOPMENT

Union sought to limit the funds available for this program.[56]

The USSR refused to support a decision at the thirteenth General Assembly in 1958 to add a new type of assistance to this program, the provision, on the basis of specific requests and for a temporary period, of qualified experts to perform operational and executive duties as public servants in underdeveloped countries. This was known as the OPEX program. The Soviet attitude toward sovereignty and its unwillingness to allow the UN to expand its competence were probably responsible for its opposition.[57] The underdeveloped countries, on the other hand, were quite interested in OPEX, and requests for such assistance exceeded the available resources. Nevertheless, in 1960, when the General Assembly decided to place this program on a continuing basis, the Soviet Union abstained. It argued then, as it had previously, that it was inappropriate to place foreign nationals in positions of administrative responsibility; the correct approach would be to train indigenous people for these posts. Again, the underdeveloped countries did not seem to be as concerned about their own sovereignty as the USSR apparently was. To date, no Soviet experts have served under the OPEX Program.

The Soviet Union took an even more negative stand in 1961 when the Economic and Social Council, at its thirty-second session, voted to authorize the use of volunteer workers in the UN's operational programs. The United States introduced this proposal, which was an extension of the American Peace Corps idea. This no doubt at least partially explains the USSR's opposition.[58] Soviet delegates argued against the proposal when it was first raised in the Technical Assistance Committee and later voted against the Council resolution. Although some underdeveloped countries voiced reservations, most were favorably disposed toward the idea, and several were enthusiastic.

THE SPECIAL FUND

Perhaps the factor which hampered Soviet tactics and the attainment of the USSR's objectives with reference to the underdeveloped

[56] UN, ECOSOC, *Official Records* (16th Session), p. 295; and UN Document A/C. 2/L. 417.

[57] See the comments of the Soviet delegates in TAC on the initial operations under this program: UN Document E/TAC/SR. 192, p. 13.

[58] Soviet commentators have called the Peace Corps "a weapon in the hands of the American neocolonialists," and have asserted that it is under the command of the Central Intelligence Agency. *Izvestia*, March 1, 1963, as contained in *The Current Digest of the Soviet Press*, XV, no. 9 (March 27, 1963), 22-23.

countries the most, though, was another new initiative taken by the United States in this field. In 1957, at the twelfth session of the General Assembly, just slightly more than four years after the Soviet Union decided to contribute to the Expanded Program of Technical Assistance, the United States suggested that a special projects fund be created to supplement EPTA and provide types of technical assistance which were not possible under existing programs. In reality, this move was designed mainly as an attempt to block pressures by the underdeveloped countries for the establishment of a Special United Nations Fund for Economic Development (SUNFED) which would provide long-term, low-interest loans and grants for development projects. Although the underdeveloped countries disliked this aspect, at the same time, they welcomed the opportunity to have greater funds for technical assistance, and at the next Assembly session, the United Nations Special Fund was created.

Negotiations concerning the establishment of the Special Fund began in the Second Committee immediately after the United States made its proposal and were continued in a special Preparatory Committee, as well as at ECOSOC's twenty-sixth session. They were finally completed at the Assembly's thirteenth session. The Soviet Union played only a marginal part in these negotiations, and its tactics were largely unsuccessful. The Soviet Union's first reaction to the proposal for the creation of a special projects fund was to deride the United States for its failure to support SUNFED, and to contrast the USSR's willingness to see such an institution created. In the concrete negotiations for the Special Fund, Soviet delegates sought to press this point further by arguing that the Fund should make long-term, low-interest loans, in addition to supplying technical assistance. They also criticized the United States for suggesting that more funds should be made available for technical assistance and at the same time insisting that its percentage contribution to such programs should be reduced.

The amendments which the Soviet Union proposed would have: (1) allowed all states, rather than just the members of the UN, the specialized agencies or IAEA, to participate in the Special Fund; (2) eliminated the requirements that contributions should either be readily usable or transferable to readily usable currencies; and (3) deleted the provision whereby the President of the International Bank for Reconstruction and Development would be made a member of the Consultative Board which would advise the Managing Director of the Fund.[59] These proposals were all rejected. In addition, the Soviet Union supported an unsuccessful attempt by several underdeveloped countries to have the General Assembly rather than the Economic and Social Council elect the eighteen-member Governing Council of the Special Fund. It also argued without effect that the Managing Director was given too much power in relation to the Governing Council and that he should be a national of an underdeveloped country. That an American, Paul Hoffman, the first Administrator of the European Recovery Program was appointed Managing Director of the Special Fund after the General Assembly approved its creation shows how little influence the Soviet Union had.

In spite of the many rebuffs, the USSR voted for every resolution passed by the Assembly and ECOSOC concerning the Special Fund; it abstained only in the Preparatory Committee. And in 1958, at the Assembly's thirteenth session, after the final decision had been taken to create the Special Fund, the Soviet Union announced that it would make a contribution. Byelorussia and the Ukraine and other Soviet bloc states followed the same course. It was evident, however, that these actions represented acquiescence rather than fervent support. The United States had initiated another popular program and the USSR could do little to detract from this. Admittedly the Soviet Union was quicker to support the Special Fund than it had been to support the Expanded Program of Technical Assistance, but this appeared to be primarily the result of increased tactical skill and flexibility.[60]

This state of affairs did not change very much after the Special

[59] These amendments were proposed in ECOSOC. See: UN Document E/AC. 6/L. 229. They had been proposed previously at various points in the Preparatory Committee. See: UN Document A/AC. 93/SR. 1-20, *passim*.

[60] It is interesting to note the way in which Soviet commentators described the establishment of the Special Fund:

"The struggle waged for several years by many Asian, African and Latin American states for *the establishment of a special economic assistance fund for underdeveloped countries* also ended in definite success; the Assembly adopted a resolution outlining its basic principles. The U.N. Social and Economic Council, which met at the same time, elected the funds' leading bodies. It must be said, however, that the United States and the other imperialist Powers, who still control the voting machine, prevented the Assembly from adopting a resolution which would fully satisfy the underdeveloped countries. Even so, the results achieved are undoubtedly a major step forward, made possible by the successes of the national-liberation struggle." V. Alexandrov, "Some Results of the 15th General Assembly," *International Affairs*, p. 45.

Fund was underway. Soviet policy followed patterns which had been established in the preliminary negotiations and with respect to EPTA. The German Democratic Republic offered a contribution, which was refused, and this refusal was duly protested.

From 1959 through 1962 the USSR was the only member of the Soviet bloc on the Governing Council of the Special Fund, although Yugoslavia also held a seat during this period. In late 1962, Poland was elected to replace Yugoslavia, for a three-year term. Soviet delegates on the Council have raised a number of issues, but as of mid-1963 they had only succeeded in getting descriptions of their views included in the Council's reports to ECOSOC. The USSR's representatives have protested the concentration on "pre-investment" activities, alleging that in many cases this has merely meant doing the spadework for private investors. They have argued that when private companies continued projects begun by the Special Fund, these companies should reimburse the Fund for its services. As in the case of EPTA, Soviet delegates have argued that a higher proportion of the budget should be allocated to industrial development projects and have opposed giving aid to non-self-governing territories, arguing that this was a responsibility of the metropolitan powers. They have also argued that the portion of local costs to be met by the recipient countries should be cut. They have protested that too few Soviet nationals were involved in the Special Fund. In 1960 there was one citizen of the USSR in a senior administrative post and there were three Soviet experts in the field. As of January 1963, there were 20 Soviet experts on Special Fund assignments out of a grand total of 558. Consistent with general Soviet policy the USSR's representatives have maintained that the Managing Director's powers are too extensive and have sought to have more decisions concerning the allocation of aid brought before the Council. Soviet delegates have generally sided with the representatives of underdeveloped countries whenever they could, and have taken the line that the Special Fund should not be viewed as an end in itself, but merely as a forerunner of SUNFED. Although this last position had some appeal, it was not sufficient to detract from American leadership in this area.

Perhaps because of its lack of success in shaping the activities of the Special Fund, the Soviet Union has not increased its contribution. The USSR pledged $1,000,000 for 1959, and Byelorussia and the Ukraine pledged $50,000 and $125,000 respectively. The con-

ECONOMIC DEVELOPMENT   251

tributions of all three states were equal to their contributions to EPTA, and as in the case of EPTA only a quarter of the contribution was convertible. All three contributions were continued at the same level through 1963.

Thus it would seem that the Soviet Union has been able to do little other than to prevent its exclusion from a popular program. In terms of the events of a decade earlier, this was a gain, but it was little beyond that.

SOVIET INITIATIVES

The USSR and other communist states have made various attempts to gain the initiative in this field, but, they have not made much headway. In 1958, at ECOSOC's twenty-sixth session, the USSR proposed that the UN should convene a second scientific conference on the conservation and utilization of resources, but this suggestion was withdrawn because of lack of support.[61] That fall, at the General Assembly's thirteenth session, Poland and Ceylon proposed that the United Nations should inaugurate a training program for "middle level" technical personnel,[62] and Czechoslovakia and Romania proposed that there should be more international cooperation in technical assistance.[63] Although both suggestions were adopted in a modified form, neither has significantly affected the UN's work.

Soviet-backed proposals relating to the petroleum industry have had a greater impact, at least in terms of propaganda, if in no other way. Starting in 1958 at the thirteenth session of the General Assembly, several Soviet bloc states in combination with one another and sometimes with other states have introduced a series of proposals proposing that the UN undertake work in this field.[64] Among other things these proposals would have had the UN train personnel, facilitate exchanges of information and supply equipment to underdeveloped countries. Although none of these proposals have been adopted in their original form, they have led to some action. Moreover, one of the most extensive discussions of the problem occurred in 1959 at ECOSOC's twenty-seventh session, which was held in

[61] UN Document E/AC. 24/L. 140.
[62] UN Document A/C. 2/L. 373.
[63] UN Document A/C. 2/L. 374.
[64] UN Documents A/C. 2/L. 394 and Add. 1 and Rev. 1; E/AC. 6/L. 235; A/C. 2/L. 432.

Mexico City, an extremely fertile environment for Soviet propaganda efforts.

Nevertheless, in the area of technical assistance, it appeared that in 1963 the Soviet Union was still a long way from having wrested the leadership from the United States or even from having gained a lasting alliance with the underdeveloped countries. Although the 1953 decision to participate in the Expanded Program of Technical Assistance removed one of the biggest obstacles standing in the USSR's way, others still remained, and new ones were added. It also seemed clear, given the Soviet Union's subsequent policy, that the 1953 decision should be viewed primarily as a tactical move, rather than as one which reflected a basic change in the USSR's attitude toward this work.

FINANCING ECONOMIC DEVELOPMENT

As in the case of technical assistance, it was 1949 before the United Nations began extensive activities in the field of financing economic development. The nature of these activities, however, has been considerably different. They have consisted mostly of studies and framing proposals for action. Most of the operational work, even though it may have been first discussed within the UN, has been put into effect by the International Bank for Reconstruction and Development or agencies closely associated with it. Western countries, and especially the United States, have generally preferred IBRD to the UN for whatever concrete cooperative ventures they have been willing to undertake through multilateral agencies with large memberships. The voting structure of IBRD is such as to give the West a dominant voice, and the President has always been an American.

The International Bank's importance has been a major factor limiting the Soviet Union's participation in this aspect of the UN's activities. Its attitude toward IBRD, since the cold war began, has been one of undisguised hostility. Another limiting factor has been the fact that for some time the major Western powers—especially the United States—were the sole source of funds for financing economic development. Even with the changes in Soviet policy, the Western states have continued to be the major contributors and they have been regarded by the underdeveloped countries as the most important sources of future help. The USSR has not been willing, or perhaps able, to offer meaningful and acceptable alternatives. Its argument that the greatest share of the financial resources needed for economic development must be found within the economies of the underdeveloped countries themselves, although it reflected the USSR's own experience and may have contained elements of practical advice, has had little appeal within the UN. The Soviet Union's part in determining the course of the UN's work concerning the financing of economic development has therefore at most been marginal.

Because of its limited role and the nature of its policy, the USSR's efforts to win the sympathies of the underdeveloped countries have not been notably successful. Attacks on the International Bank and the Western powers have comprised one principal aspect of the Soviet Union's policy. Although many of the Soviet criticisms mirrored those voiced by spokesmen for the underdeveloped countries, these attacks were nonetheless directed at the most important sources of funds. It would have been difficult for the underdeveloped countries wholly to subscribe to the Soviet position, and it might even have precluded their obtaining future assistance. The other major segment of Soviet policy, supporting positions which were favored by the underdeveloped countries, although certainly more palatable to these states and generally more effective, has also had limitations. Soviet support has occasionally been welcomed with mixed feelings because of the fear that it might lead to issues becoming embroiled in the cold war. And since this support has not been accompanied with guarantees to even approximate the present level of assistance for financing economic development, it has had a hollow character.

In the spring of 1949, in response to the General Assembly's request in Resolution 198 (III) for more concrete work in the field of economic development, ECOSOC asked the Secretary-General to prepare "a report setting forth methods of financing economic development of underdeveloped countries, including methods of stimulating the international flow of capital for this purpose. . . ."[65] This was followed by other studies and then by discussions in the Council.

Because of the Chinese representation boycott, the USSR missed the most important of these discussions, which occurred at the Council's eleventh session in the summer of 1950. Guidelines were estab-

[65] ECOSOC Resolution 179 (VIII).

lished then for the United Nations functions, and the Secretary-General was authorized to appoint a group of experts to formulate definite recommendations. Although Soviet delegates participated in the subsequent talks, their role became increasingly minor. Their occasional amendments always failed, and they abstained from voting on most of the resolutions which were adopted.

Three lines of activity ultimately emerged: (1) action to stimulate the flow of private capital to underdeveloped countries; (2) efforts to establish an international finance corporation to facilitate financing productive private enterprises; and, (3) planning for the creation of a special UN fund which might make grants-in-aid and long-term, low-interest loans.

EFFORTS TO STIMULATE PRIVATE INVESTMENT

The first involved expanding programs which were already underway. As early as 1947 the Economic and Employment Commission had discussed the possibility of drafting a code for foreign investment—in fact this project owed its origins to the League—and the Fiscal Commission had planned a number of activities dealing with technical problems in this field. Other programs were added to these.

The Soviet Union has never supported the United Nations work in this field. Consistent with communist ideology, it has been fundamentally opposed to all efforts to attract foreign private capital to underdeveloped countries. Soviet delegates have argued that underdeveloped countries must rely primarily on their own resources for economic development, and that foreign funds should only be used as supplementary sources. They have charged that private foreign investment has not been directed toward the things which underdeveloped countries really needed for their development and that such investments have frequently led to economic domination.[66] Moreover, the USSR has maintained that many of the UN's activities in this area, such as the efforts to eliminate double taxation, violate national sovereignty. At first Soviet opposition to these activities was vehement. Since 1953 it has been muted somewhat, but the USSR's basic position has not been altered. The Soviet Union has either opposed or abstained from voting on all but the most innocuous of the UN's resolutions concerning this subject.

On the other hand, the USSR has supported a number of pro-

[66] See for example: E/AC. 6/SR. 282, pp. 11-13.

posals which have had the effect of discouraging private investment in underdeveloped areas. In 1952, for instance, it strongly supported General Assembly Resolution 626 (VII) which recommended that all member states should refrain from any action that might "impede the exercise of the sovereignty of any State over its natural resources."

This same question has also frequently been considered in connection with human rights. In these discussions the Soviet Union has always argued for the broadest concept of sovereignty. In 1958 it supported the establishment of the Commission on Permanent Sovereignty over Natural Resources and since then it has constantly sought to push that body toward a radical line. Although its positions have seldom been adopted, by enlarging the dimensions of the debate, it has moved the mid-point to the left and at least partially attained its goal.

In 1958, at the Assembly's thirteenth session, Byelorussia advanced an extremely far-reaching proposal in this area. It suggested that the Secretariat should prepare a study which among other things:

> . . . should ascertain the possibilities of increasing royalty and other payments by companies to countries whose natural resources are being exploited, and also the possibilities of allocating a certain percentage of the exported profits of those companies for the financing of economic development of underdeveloped countries by the United Nations.[67]

The proposal was ultimately withdrawn because of lack of support, but Mr. Arkadev argued that the mere fact that it was introduced should help underdeveloped countries by bringing "moral pressure" on the foreign "capitalist countries" and stated ominously that "sooner or later the problem would have to be settled." [68] To settle it on Soviet terms would probably mean eliminating private investment completely.

THE INTERNATIONAL FINANCE CORPORATION

The UN's second activity in this field, efforts to establish an international finance corporation, began to take definite shape in 1951. At its thirteenth session, ECOSOC, acting on a recommendation of

[67] UN Document A/C. 2/L. 392.
[68] UN, General Assembly, Second Committee, *Official Records* (13th Session), p. 274.

the group of experts which had been appointed the previous year, asked IBRD to study the possibility of creating an institution "to promote the financing of productive private enterprise either through loans without government guarantee, through equity investments or by other methods intended for the same purpose." Five years later, in July 1956, the International Finance Corporation came into being. Although an independent specialized agency, it was closely affiliated with the International Bank and it was open only to members of that institution. The actual negotiations for the creation of IFC were conducted under the Bank's auspices. The UN's role was limited to discussing these negotiations and adopting resolutions of encouragement and approval. In Council and Assembly debates, Soviet delegates frequently asserted that the IBRD had never promoted the underdeveloped countries' interests and prophesied that, because of its close connection with the Bank, the IFC would not either. But they announced that the USSR would not oppose something which was strongly desired by the underdeveloped states and for that reason abstained from voting on all but one of the United Nations' resolutions on this subject. The resolution approving the agreement between the IFC and the UN was the only one which the USSR supported. The Soviet Union's position seems to have been a conglomeration of its dislike for the International Bank, its ideological opposition to private enterprise, and its unwillingness to alienate the underdeveloped states. Such a mixture could hardly produce a positive policy.

A CAPITAL DEVELOPMENT FUND

The UN's third activity in this area had the same origins as the second. Creating a special United Nations fund to make grants-in-aid and long-term, low-interest loans was another of the recommendations which the group of experts had advanced in their report, *Measures for the Economic Development of Under-developed Countries*.[69] In 1951 the Council also asked the Secretary-General to study this proposal further and to formulate alternative means of carrying it out. This cautious beginning was given additional momentum at the General Assembly's sixth session later that fall. While ECOSOC had hesitantly decided to explore the experts' recommendation, the Assembly, where the political power of the

[69] United Nations Publication, Sales Number: 1951.11.B.2. Also issued as UN Document E/1986.

underdeveloped states was greater, enthusiastically endorsed it, and directed the Council to produce a detailed plan for establishing a special United Nations fund. In response to this request, and after examining the Secretary-General's report, ECOSOC established an *ad hoc* committee to prepare the detailed plan.

Their Report on a *Special United Nations Fund for Economic Development*[70] was considered at the Council's sixteenth session in the summer of 1953. Prior to this debate, Soviet delegates had opposed the proposal to establish a special United Nations fund. They had argued that the new institution was likely to become an instrument of American capitalism, as they alleged IBRD and IMF had,[71] and they had abstained from voting on all relevant resolutions. This pattern was continued when the detailed plan for the Special United Nations Fund for Economic Development was first considered at ECOSOC's sixteenth session, but the negativeness of Mr. Arutiunian's speech was softened by his announcement that the USSR would begin contributing to the Expanded Program of Technical Assistance. Then, within a few months, at the Assembly's eighth session that fall, Mr. Arkadev announced that because of the underdeveloped countries' interest in SUNFED, his government would support a resolution providing for further studies.

In the next four years the SUNFED proposal was studied again and again by various groups and individuals. The underdeveloped states fought desperately to keep the issue alive, despite the unwillingness of the major Western powers, especially the United States, to contemplate the immediate establishment of such an institution. During the negotiations the Soviet Union became an increasingly strong supporter of the Special United Nations Fund for Economic Development. It voted for all resolutions, and in 1954 announced that it would consider participating in SUNFED if it were established. A year later this was made a definite commitment. Although at one stage Soviet delegates maintained that there was a close connection between disarmament and the availability of resources for SUNFED, they explicitly denounced the later attempt by Western powers to make disarmament a condition of SUNFED's establishment. When the United States sought to avoid a showdown on

[70] United Nations Publication, Sales Number: 1953.II.B.1. Also issued as UN Document E/2381.

[71] UN, General Assembly, Second Committee, *Official Records* (7th Session), p. 149.

SUNFED's creation by proposing that the UN's technical assistance activities should be expanded through the establishment of the United Nations Special Fund (a deceptively similar title), Soviet delegates argued that this proposal was a maneuver designed to kill SUNFED. After the creation of the Special Fund, the USSR supported the underdeveloped states' attempts to keep the idea of establishing a United Nations Capital Development Fund an active agenda item. Their pressure continued through 1963.

Although Soviet support first for SUNFED and then for a Capital Development Fund has been appreciated by underdeveloped countries, it probably has not won as much sympathy as the USSR might have hoped. For one thing, the Soviet Union's concept of what a UN institution in this field should be like has not completely coincided with that of the underdeveloped states.[72] The USSR has insisted that contributions should be voluntary and in national currencies or in kind. It has held that the institution should only provide loans, although these might be interest free (the Soviet bilateral program consists almost exclusively of long-term credits). It has argued that the new body should have no connection with the International Bank and that all states should be eligible to participate. Underdeveloped states would prefer convertible contributions, and some, a scheme of assessments. They would like grants as well as loans. They are not unalterably opposed to IBRD, nor are they particularly insistent that membership be extended beyond the United Nations. Equally important, although the Soviet Union has announced that it would contribute, it has given no indication that it contemplates supplanting the United States as the potential major contributor. Indeed, it announced that its contribution to SUNFED would be in rubles or in equipment and machinery, and its record with respect to the Expanded Program of Technical Assistance and the Special Fund indicates that the contribution would probably be rather modest in size. The fact that some Western powers, France and the Netherlands, for example, also ultimately favored the creation of SUNFED or a similar institution, has been another factor lessening the impact of Soviet support. Finally, in 1958 and 1959 the United States proposed: the creation of the Inter-American

---

[72] The most comprehensive exposition of the Soviet position during the SUNFED debate can be found in UN Document A/AC. 83/L. 1/Add. 19. The Soviet position on the subsequent proposal can be seen in the various debates.

ECONOMIC DEVELOPMENT

Development Bank; the expansion of the capital of IMF and IBRD; and the establishment of the International Development Association. Although none of these developments took place within the UN, they made more capital available for underdeveloped countries and some of it on easier terms. To some extent and for a while they lessened the pressure for the creation of a new institution within the UN. By 1963, though, this pressure had again reached significant proportions.

To date, the Soviet Union's support has brought it closer to the underdeveloped states, but the USSR has not gained a firm alignment with these states and its role in this aspect of the UN's work has continued to be marginal. What the future will bring remains to be seen.

SOVIET BLOC INITIATIVES

Perhaps in an effort to redirect the United Nations activities concerning economic development into channels which would be more amenable to their tactics, the USSR and other communist states in 1950, 1951 and 1952 introduced several proposals for new UN programs in this field. Only one of these, that concerning land reform, led to adoption of a sustained program of work, and this was based on principles which were quite different from those advocated by the Soviet bloc. The others were either adopted in a greatly modified form, and then allowed to atrophy, or rejected immediately. In sum, the Soviet campaign had little success, and the change in the USSR's policy toward other aspects of the United Nations activities in this field may well have been related to its failure.

The Soviet bloc's efforts began with its return to the UN after the Chinese representation boycott. At the General Assembly's fifth session, Poland, with strong Soviet support, introduced two proposals; one involved land reform, the other, the distribution of national income in underdeveloped states. The Polish delegate charged that most of the national income in underdeveloped countries was "diverted from productive uses and sent abroad in the form of interest and profits."[73] He submitted a draft resolution requesting that the Secretary-General prepare a report on the level and distribution of

[73] UN, General Assembly, Second Committee, *Official Records* (5th Session), p. 55.

national income in the "economically backward countries," and directing him to pay particular attention to the part of this income which accrued to foreign countries and which was used for the liquidation of foreign debts.[74] This proposal was ultimately adopted in a modified form. However, when the question was considered again at the Economic and Social Council's thirteenth session the following spring, despite Soviet protests and another Polish proposal, it was shelved through the adoption of a resolution asking the Secretary-General and the specialized agencies to keep the problem under advisement.

The other Polish proposal which was introduced at the Assembly's fifth session, that concerning land reform, had a greater impact. The initial draft resolution which Poland submitted, after stating that anachronistic agrarian conditions were a barrier to economic development and a cause of low productivity and standards of living, requested that the Secretary-General prepare a report for ECOSOC on the agrarian structure of the "economically backward countries and territories and its effects on the conditions of the landless, small and middle peasants."[75] He was also asked to prepare recommendations with a view to improving the conditions of these groups. His recommendations were to deal with: (1) appropriate measures of land reform; (2) cheap agricultural credit facilities; (3) construction of small factories for the repair and manufacture of agricultural implements; (4) tax relief for the landless, small and medium peasants; and, (5) other measures to ease the burden of such groups. After some modification, this resolution was unanimously approved.

When the Economic, Employment and Development Commission held its next session in May 1951, the United States attempted to wrest the initiative from Poland. In a sense, the United States had originally introduced the question of land reform in the UN through Secretary of State Dean Acheson's discussion of it in his address during the general debate at the Assembly's fifth session. On the basis of American urging, the Commission recommended that when considering this problem at its thirteenth session ECOSOC should pay special attention to a number of factors such as security of land tenure, which definitely reflected free enterprise concepts. Soviet bloc delegates objected, claiming that this prejudged the Council's work, but their protests were without avail.

[74] UN Document A/C. 2/L. 37.
[75] UN Document A/C. 2/L. 36.

Nor was the Soviet bloc able to regain the initiative at the Council's thirteenth session later in 1951.

Since then the Soviet bloc's formal influence on the UN's activities concerning land reform has been limited. Explicit attempts in 1954 by Poland at the Assembly's ninth session, and in 1959 by the USSR at the Assembly's fourteenth session, to change the direction of the UN's work in this field were both rejected by overwhelming majorities.[76] In each case an amendment was proposed which would have deleted several qualifications concerning the pace of land reform.

From 1950 to 1960 then, the Soviet bloc was confronted with Western sponsored resolutions concerning land reform. It supported some and abstained on others. Its contribution, however, may well have been greater than this formal record indicates. Through its continual advocacy of radical land reform, the Soviet bloc probably encouraged the growth of pressures within the United Nations which affected the course of the organization's work in this field.

Perhaps the influx of new states will cause the UN to take a more radical course on this emotionally charged issue and the USSR will find a more receptive audience for its ideas and proposals. For a time in the fall of 1960 this appeared to be the case, but by 1962 a more moderate tone again prevailed.

Two other attempts by the Soviet bloc to redirect the United Nations work concerning economic development were much less successful. At the General Assembly's sixth session, Poland introduced a draft resolution which admixed slogans about the underdeveloped countries' need for capital goods with an attack on the Western rearmament program.[77] The proposal was adopted after great modification. A similar draft resolution which the USSR offered at ECOSOC's fourteenth session the following summer was flatly rejected.[78] The USSR has also had little success in advancing the notion that the principal purpose of the United Nations Development Decade "should be the rapid elimination of the economic consequences of colonialism." [79] In the nineteen sixties, the underdeveloped countries want more than slogans.

[76] UN Documents: A/C. 2/L. 239 and A/4321, p. 31.
[77] UN Document A/C. 2/L. 81.
[78] UN Document E/L. 388/Rev. 1.
[79] See Mr. Arkadev's speech: UN, ECOSOC, *Official Records* (34th Session), pp. 57-60.

CONCLUSIONS

Of all the changes in the USSR's policies concerning the UN's economic and social activities those in the field of economic development are the most striking, and the changes here have spilled over into other fields. Yet even in this field, there seems to have been an underlying continuity in Soviet conduct.

Soviet leaders recognized the potential importance of underdeveloped areas in world politics long before the creation of the United Nations. They had given considerable thought to these areas, though most of it went under the rubric of the "colonial problem," and had developed a body of doctrine which both explained the low level of economic development and charted a course for economic progress. When the UN began activities in the field of economic development, Soviet statesmen probably saw these as an excellent opportunity to advance communist strategy. They sought to foment discontent in the underdeveloped areas and to alienate these states and territories from the West. They also hoped to make the Soviet Union appear as the protector and guardian of these areas, and to make the Soviet Union's method of achieving rapid economic growth appear as the most effective.

The organization's early activities in this field in many ways were ideally suited to Soviet tactics. The general discussions afforded excellent opportunities for Soviet delegates to expound communist theories, and their efforts appear to have been relatively successful. Soviet doctrines were frequently written into reports, especially those of the Sub-Commission on Economic Development, and their informal impact may have been even greater.

When the United Nations turned to more concrete tasks after 1948, however, Soviet successes dwindled. The USSR's unwillingness to participate in this work belied its pretensions of concern for the underdeveloped areas. Its refusal to contribute to the Expanded Program of Technical Assistance was the most conspicuous evidence of this unwillingness, but there were others also. The Soviet Union's policy was probably partly determined by its limited financial resources during this period. Also, the United States clearly played the most important role in the developing concrete programs, and the USSR may have been reluctant to accept a secondary position. The Soviet perception of world politics may have been another factor. Soviet leaders appear to have regarded the ruling groups in underdeveloped areas as puppets of the West and did not see fully—and consequently could not exploit—the conflicts of interest that existed between these groups and the West. In any case, the results of Soviet policy were hardly those which the USSR desired, and its efforts to redirect the UN's work along lines more suited to Soviet tactics failed.

The changes in Soviet policy which began in 1953 must be interpreted in this light. They appear to be primarily tactical shifts designed to improve the USSR's position with the underdeveloped areas. There has been no evidence that Soviet objectives have changed. Nor has the Soviet interpretation of the causes of the present status of underdeveloped areas or of the most effective methods of achieving economic growth been altered. The USSR's commitment to the United Nations programs has remained limited. The Soviet Union has preferred bilateral arrangements when providing aid to underdeveloped countries even more than the United States has. Its bilateral program of long-term credits has dwarfed its contribution to the world organization's work. The USSR's decision to increase its participation in the activities of the United Nations appears to have been more a concession to popular sentiment than a change in basic attitude.

In a broad sense the changes in the USSR's policy probably stemmed from its improved economic situation and alterations in its world outlook. By 1953 the Soviet Union began to have significant resources available for external political efforts, and the proceedings of the Nineteenth Congress of the Communist Party the previous year indicated a growing appreciation of tensions in the noncommunist world. In a more immediate sense, the transformation in Soviet leadership after the death of Stalin contributed to increasing diplomatic flexibility. Moreover, the failure of Soviet policy within the United Nations was glaringly evident.

At first, the changes in Soviet policy were quite effective in terms of improving the USSR's position with the underdeveloped states. The Soviet contribution to the Expanded Program of Technical Assistance and its support for the Special United Nations Fund for Economic Development were enthusiastically welcomed by representatives of these states. But as some of the restrictive features of Soviet policy again became clear, and after the United States took new initiatives, their enthusiasm waned. Even so, the Soviet position in mid-1963 was immeasurably better than it had been a decade earlier prior to the inauguration of the USSR's new tactics.

Beyond the early reports of the Sub-Commission on Economic Development, the Soviet Union's impact on the United Nations activities in this field seems to have been extremely slight. It had a minor influence in drafting the technical assistance program and no doubt has in part been responsible for the UN's pronounced emphasis on sovereignty. The Soviet Union also deserves some of the credit for the increasing emphasis in the UN's activities on industrialization and the development of heavy industry. Beyond this the USSR's role has largely consisted of first opposing and then supporting programs which were initiated by others. But in a wider framework, the conflict between the Soviet Union and the United States, whether in its cold war or "competitive coexistence" stage, has certainly had as one of its by-products the effect of focusing increased attention on the needs of underdeveloped areas. Both sides have devoted increasing efforts to gain the allegiance of the people in these areas. Without the Soviet-American struggle it is unlikely that the United Nations would have done as much in the field of economic development as it has, and in this sense the USSR's impact has been much greater.

9: THE USSR AND THE UN'S "NON-POLITICAL" ACTIVITIES: INTERPRETATIONS AND IMPLICATIONS

HAVING EXAMINED THE RECORD OF SOVIET POLICY CONCERNING WHAT in the terminology of the League of Nations era would have been called the "non-political" activities of the United Nations, it is appropriate to return to the questions which were raised at the outset of this study. The first set of these related to the changes in Soviet policy. The second concerned the impact of the USSR's participation on the UN's institutions and functions and centered particularly on the consequences of the USSR's having an ideology, a governmental structure and political goals which were considerably different from those of the majority of the UN's member states. The third and final group dealt with the implications of Soviet policy for the theory of functionalism. Although clear and unambiguous answers to the various questions are impossible, the record contains a wealth of data which is relevant to them.

THE CHANGES IN SOVIET POLICY

The first task is to consider the changes in Soviet policy in this area, for the answers to the other questions depend to some extent on those given here. Clearly, Soviet policy concerning the economic and social activities of the United Nations has been radically transformed since September 8, 1944, when Ambassador Gromyko reluctantly agreed to the inclusion of such functions in the new world organization. The USSR's policy in 1963 showed few traces of the opposition and doubts which he voiced during the Dumbarton Oaks Conversations. On the contrary, the USSR was an active participant in almost all phases of these activities and it had even introduced a series of far-reaching proposals for new tasks.

The extent of these changes can be illustrated by comparing Mr. Molotov's opening speech at the San Francisco Conference in 1945 with the one which he made a decade later at the anniversary session commemorating the signing of the Charter.[1] In the earlier speech, he continually referred to the need to create an "international security organization" and did not mention economic and social functions. In 1955, Mr. Molotov took a much broader view. Three of the seven issues which he listed for immediate action by the United Nations were of an economic and social character:

> development of the peaceful uses of atomic energy and large-scale industrial, scientific and technical assistance to countries which are less fully developed technically;
>
> removal of any discrimination hampering the development of wide-scale economic cooperation and international trade;
>
> expansion of international cultural ties through a wide exchange of delegations and the development of tourism.

All three topics have been prominently featured in Soviet policy within the UN. They have been the areas where Soviet participation has been the most extensive, and where the USSR has even attempted to seize the initiative. The contrast between the two speeches—and the transformation in Soviet policy—is striking.

The nature of this transformation can be understood fully only when put in the context of the shifts in broader Soviet strategy which also occurred during this period. Although a detailed analysis of these shifts is beyond the scope of this study, it is necessary to consider them at least briefly. For a variety of reasons, starting in the early nineteen fifties, Soviet strategy increasingly came to rely on nonmilitary techniques and to focus on the underdeveloped areas of the world.

In part, these shifts were a reaction to developments in the international scene. The earlier Soviet course, characterized by an aggres-

---

[1] See: UNCIO, *Documents*, I, 131-136; and, UN, Secretariat, *Tenth Anniversary of the Signing of the United Nations Charter, San Francisco, 1955: Proceedings of the Commemorative Meetings* (UN Document ST/GG/6: Sales No.: 1955, I.26), pp. 103-115.

sive, hard line, had provoked a hard, yet creative, Western reaction which led to the thwarting of Soviet ambitions. Not only did the West increase its military capacity, but it also moved toward integration, a development which would have permanent effects. In addition, the West began to take creative steps in the area of its relationship with underdeveloped areas and new states, notably the inauguration of economic aid programs. These moves outside the United Nations were reflected in and accompanied by Western actions within the United Nations. From the Soviet point of view, none of these developments was helpful. The isolation of the USSR in the UN's economic and social activities, which started in 1949 and continued through 1952, was but one example of the general situation. Some writers have speculated that the Soviet Union considered withdrawing from the United Nations during this period and hoped that the Peace Movement might become a rival to the UN.[2] If so, this scheme was probably foredoomed and in any case was quickly abandoned. But if the USSR were to remain within the UN, some changes in its policies were obviously necessary so that it could break out of its isolation, and this was true generally. The shifts in Soviet strategy were also a reaction to developments in weapons technology; with the development of new delivery systems and nuclear and thermonuclear weapons the prospective costs of major wars had increased drastically. Then too, over the years, the new states and underdeveloped areas had come to play an increasingly prominent role in international affairs. Any strategy based on the realities of world politics would have to take account of this.

Developments within the Soviet orbit were also important in the shifts in Soviet strategy. The consolidation of power by communist forces in Eastern Europe was a crucial factor. Once this was accomplished, Soviet policy could have more flexibility. In addition, the USSR's growing economic capacity significantly increased its capabilities. At first the Soviet Union was preoccupied with its own recovery from the devastation wrought by the Second World War. Once this was accomplished, and patterns of economic growth were again set in process, the USSR could turn to other things; it could afford to release resources for an economic aid program and to assign technicians to foreign areas without detriment to its own economic plans. Furthermore, the USSR's gains in military technology

[2] See: Alexander Dallin, *The Soviet Union at the United Nations*, pp. 31-37; and, Marshall D. Shulman, *Stalin's Foreign Policy Reappraised*, p. 200.

appear to have given Soviet leaders increased self-confidence.[3]

Soviet ideology also changed during this period. In the years immediately after the Second World War the two-camp concept—symbolized by Joseph Stalin's election speech of February 9, 1946, and Andrei Zhdanov's address at the founding of the Cominform in September 1947—prevailed. The world was seen as divided into two hostile groups, capitalist and socialist, and the only feasible strategy for communists was held to be constant vigilance and pressure against capitalist forces. Gradually this picture came to be modified (dissenting views had actually been advanced as early as 1947, for example by Eugene Varga, though at that time they were quickly suppressed). The fact and ramifications of the process of decolonization were perceived. Indigenous leaders in underdeveloped areas were no longer indiscriminately seen as "imperialist lackeys" and the problems, frustrations and ambitions of these areas were discerned with greater clarity. Conflicts of interest within the West itself were seen in more sophisticated terms. Although communist doctrine continued to emphasize the need for vigilance and pressure against the capitalist world, it also allowed the possibility of cooperation with selected noncommunist elements. The new view was most clearly articulated in February 1956 in Nikita S. Khrushchev's report to the Twentieth Congress of the Communist Party of the Soviet Union. Whether the changes in the USSR's strategy stemmed from the revisions in communist ideology, or whether the revisions in ideology were tailored to suit decisions made on pragmatic grounds, need not concern us. For our purposes, it is sufficient to note that the two complemented one another.

Joseph Stalin's death and the subsequent changes in the Soviet leadership were certainly important in facilitating the shifts in Soviet strategy and the revisions in Soviet ideology. However, the transformation in Soviet strategy started before the death of Stalin;[4] the

---

[3] See: Herbert S. Dinerstein, *War and the Soviet Union: Nuclear Weapons and the Revolution in Soviet Military and Political Thinking* (New York: Frederick A. Praeger, 1959).

[4] This point is made most persuasively with respect to Soviet foreign policy generally in: Marshall D. Shulman, *Stalin's Foreign Policy Reappraised.* Frederick C. Barghoorn makes the same point in his book, *The Soviet Cultural Offensive* (Princeton: Princeton University Press, 1960). He states that by the time of the Nineteenth Party Congress Stalin had "come out clearly for a strategy of coexistence, relying heavily on the internal 'contradictions' in the non-Soviet world." (p. 60)

USSR's moves in the Economic Commission for Europe were an example of this in those UN activities considered here. American officials have also noted that the shift to a more moderate tone in Soviet statements in other areas of the UN began before March 1953.[5] Moreover, Stalin's last major publication, *Economic Problems of Socialism in the USSR*, which appeared in pamphlet form in October 1952 (though some of the comments had been written as early as February and had appeared in the Soviet press then), and the addresses at the Nineteenth Congress of the Communist Party of the Soviet Union, which occurred that same month, were precursors of many of the ideological revisions which were advanced in more detail and more clearly later.

The shifts in Soviet strategy coincided with certain basic changes in the United Nations, and as a consequence of both developments, the Soviet view of the UN must have changed. In 1944 the USSR probably saw the UN in terms of its interpretation of the League experience. It had joined the League of Nations as a part of its attempt to find security from the fascist powers. The failure of the League to provide this—to say nothing of its expulsion of the USSR —must have had a profound impact upon Soviet leaders. They probably regarded the Bruce Report, and its proposal to develop the League's so-called "non-political" work with the aim of preserving the organization and maintaining contact with the fascist powers, as a final diversionary attempt to deflect that body from its principal purposes. Further, the technical character and Western orientation of most of the League's economic and social activities must have discouraged any Soviet interest in them as such, except in cases of obvious necessity, such as malaria control.

To the extent that the USSR believed in international organization in 1944 and was not just acting in the interest of preserving the necessary wartime unity, it probably did so for roughly the same reasons that were responsible for its adherence to the League. It probably saw the new world organization as a possible means of protecting its security, particularly of preventing a revival of German and possibly Japanese power. The only other conceivable security function which the Soviet Union could have seen for the new organization would have involved outbreaks between minor powers. It must have recognized that the UN would provide little benefit for

[5] See Ray L. Thurston's comments: C. Grove Haines (ed.), *The Threat of Soviet Imperialism*, pp. 118-119.

the USSR in the event of a Soviet-American clash. With this perspective, economic and social functions would naturally seem unimportant. Further, in 1944 it probably appeared as if the economic and social activities of the United Nations would develop along the lines which had been established during the League years, and this precluded intrinsic interest on the part of the Soviet Union.

In reality, however, the United Nations developed in a quite different way. It soon became apparent that the UN, like the League, would not perform the security role which the USSR had probably envisaged. As the cold war developed, the Federal Republic of Germany and Japan became allied with the West, and this ruled out using the United Nations to keep these states in a subordinate position. The USSR found that the UN's principal utility was in the realm of political warfare. It was a useful forum for efforts designed both to divide the West and to undermine the position of the West through the mobilization of opinion to the Soviet side. Debates on economic and social issues could be as useful for this purpose as those involving purely political issues.

Simultaneously, other developments occurred which gave the economic and social activities of the United Nations new orientations and vastly increased importance. These activities have not followed the patterns established by the League. Partly because of Soviet participation (a matter to be considered in more detail shortly) they have not had the same technical character. The greatest change, however, has been in the tremendous amount of attention devoted to problems of economic development, a subject barely considered in the League of Nations. The "revolution of rising expectations" has had a profound impact on the character of the UN's economic and social activities.

Then too, the institutional nature of the United Nations has changed. Although this change really dates from 1960, since the West's relative strength did not decline significantly prior to that date even though the UN's membership grew, Soviet leaders probably foresaw and anticipated this development.[6] Certainly an organi-

[6] When the first session of the General Assembly opened in January 1946, the West as defined in this study included: Australia, Belgium, Canada, Denmark, France, Greece, Luxembourg, Netherlands, New Zealand, Norway, Turkey, the United Kingdom and the United States, a total of 13 states, or slightly more than 25 per cent of the total membership. In the fall of 1960, when the General Assembly's fifteenth session opened, the West constituted over 24 per cent of the total membership. Although the UN's membership had in-

zation with 111 member states and a functioning African and Asian bloc of over fifty is a more favorable arena for Soviet efforts than the original UN with 51 member states, twelve of which were from Africa and Asia.[7] Indeed, when the fundamental change in the UN's membership began in the fall of 1960, Soviet commentators devoted greater attention to the UN, noted "the new balance of forces," and gleefully asserted that "the days of United States domination of the UN are numbered."[8] Significantly, in 1960 further changes were inaugurated in Soviet policies, which had been relatively constant for a while; for example, the USSR announced that it would double its contribution to EPTA.

The changes in the United Nations and the shifts in Soviet strategy have therefore, fitted together rather well. The USSR has found that the UN's economic and social activities are much better suited to its strategy than it had foreseen in 1944. The three economic and social issues which Mr. Molotov mentioned in his 1955 address—assistance to underdeveloped countries, efforts to increase trade, and the promotion of increased contacts—have been important elements of Soviet policy outside of the UN as well as within the world organization. Of the three issues, the League would only have dealt

---

creased from 51 to 82 during this period, seven of the new members, Finland, Iceland, Ireland, Italy, Portugal, Spain and Sweden, were from the West, making a total of twenty in this group.

[7] If Mongolia is included in the Afro-Asian group, its membership totals 56. Mongolia does attend the caucuses of the group (See: Thomas Hovet, Jr., *Africa in the United Nations* [Evanston: Northwestern University Press, 1963], pp. 18 and 74). The figure 56 includes Turkey. Turkey is also included in the figure 12 for 1946, as is the Republic of China. If Turkey is not included in the group defined as the West, the constancy of the strength of that group between 1946 and 1960 is even more striking; it constituted somewhat over 23 per cent of the UN both at the beginning and at the end of this period. These figures of course are not intended to indicate that the various groups mentioned vote as units, but merely to give some indication of the relative political balance within the UN.

[8] See: *Pravda*, September 20, 1960, as contained in *The Current Digest of the Soviet Press*, XII, no. 38 (October 19, 1960), 34-38; "African and Asian Countries in the United Nations," *International Affairs* (Moscow), VII, no. 11 (November 1961), 120-122; V. Vershinin, "U. N.: Its Possibilities and Prospects," *International Affairs* (Moscow), VII, no. 11 (November 1961), 85-89; V. Vershinin, "U. N.: Its Possibilities and Prospects," *International Affairs* (Moscow), VIII, no. 8 (January 1962), 58-62; and, A. Alexeyev, "United Nations Under Western Diplomatic Fire," *International Affairs* (Moscow), VIII, no. 3 (March 1962), 34-38.

with that concerning trade, and its activities in that field would have been quite different from those of the United Nations.

Furthermore, although the changes in Soviet policy concerning the economic and social activities of the United Nations since 1944 have been significant, the transformation should not be overemphasized. There have been important elements of continuity in the USSR's position. The emphasis on sovereignty has remained. The Soviet Union has been no more willing to allow a strong international organization to develop in the economic and social field—or in any other—than it was in 1944. This has stemmed partly from the USSR's minority position. The UN's economic and social activities have continued to be basically oriented toward the West, and the Soviet Union has never been able to exercise a determining influence on these activities. Few representatives of communist states have been chosen for the top elective positions in the relevant UN organs—in 1962 Jerzy Michalowski of Poland became the first Soviet bloc diplomat to be elected President of ECOSOC—and the number of citizens of Soviet bloc states in administrative posts in this area, both at headquarters and in the field, has been unrepresentatively small. Until the late nineteen fifties and early nineteen sixties —with the exception of EPTA and certain other technical assistance programs—this situation was as much attributable to Soviet disinterest as to anything else. The Soviet bloc has won few decisive votes. A statistical analysis of roll call votes in the first thirteen sessions of the General Assembly found that the Soviet bloc had voted against the majority more frequently on economic and social issues than on any other category except collective measures.[9] The Soviet position is understandable; it is doubtful that the United States would have supported this aspect of the UN to the extent that it has if it had been in the USSR's place. With conditions as they have been, the United States has jealously guarded its sovereignty.[10] However, even allowing for the USSR's minority position, its interest in protecting its sovereignty has been distinctive, as analysts of Soviet policy in other aspects of the UN have also noted.[11] In part, the explanation

---

[9] Thomas Hovet, Jr., *Bloc Politics in the United Nations*, p. 108.

[10] See: Louis K. Hyde, Jr., *The United States and the United Nations: Promoting the Public Welfare*.

[11] See: Alexander Dallin, *The Soviet Union at the United Nations*; and, Joseph L. Nogee, *Soviet Policy Toward International Control of Atomic Energy* (Notre Dame: University of Notre Dame Press, 1961).

lies in the nature of the Soviet regime. The secretiveness of the Soviet regime in all fields is well established. It has certainly carried over to participation in this aspect of the United Nations, although perhaps to a decreasing extent. Further, believing as they do that the millennium can come in only a communist form, Soviet leaders can never have a basic commitment to a noncommunist international organization.[12] Part of the reason that the USSR has been able to adopt a more active policy has been that the economic and social work of the United Nations, because of the impact of Soviety policy, among other things, has developed so that few infringements of sovereignty are involved.[13]

Nor has the Soviet Union changed its basic attitude toward providing significant financial assistance for the UN's economic and social activities. It is true that since the middle nineteen fifties the USSR has contributed to the Expanded Program of Technical Assistance, the Special Fund, and the United Nations Children's Fund. These moves, however, appear to have been primarily concessions to popular opinion. The constant size of the Soviet contributions until 1961 and the extremely small proportion of the USSR's total aid to underdeveloped countries which has been channeled through the UN have shown the limited extent of the change. The Soviet Union's reluctance to expand its financial commitment to the UN's economic and social program has probably stemmed from the same complex of factors which were responsible for its attitude toward sovereignty.

Much of Soviet policy concerning this aspect of the United Nations has continued to consist of attacks on the policies and institutions of the capitalist West and attempts to glorify the USSR. These efforts have been more subtle and sophisticated, and therefore more likely to succeed, but they have nonetheless been propagandistic attacks. States have often used the United Nations for efforts to influence opinion, and many UN members have been willing to distort the organization's technical activities for political purposes. The American unwillingness to have the UN deal with Communist China in matters of narcotics control is an example of the latter. However, the extent to which the USSR has done these things has

[12] See: J. Frankel, "The Soviet Union and the United Nations," pp. 69-70.
[13] See: Harold Karan Jacobson, "The USSR and the UN's Economic and Social Recommendations," *Osteuropa Recht*, IV, no. 2 (December 1958), 310-314.

been distinctive. Its policies have occasionally almost shown a contempt for the intrinsic purposes of the economic and social activities of the United Nations. The USSR's limited influence in determining the direction of this work may again have been responsible for these actions, but they also appear to have reflected a disbelief, engendered by communist ideology, in the efficacy of the UN's economic and social functions.

Although the success of Soviet efforts to influence opinion is difficult to estimate, it seems to have varied over the years. Judging by the reaction within the United Nations, Soviet propaganda efforts appear to have had marked success only during two periods. The initial period consisted of the first two, or possibly three years of the UN's existence. Soviet general statements appealed to some then, and their hollowness had not yet been exposed. Many were reluctant to see the cold war develop and were prepared to make special allowances for the USSR, particularly in view of its important role in the Second World War. In 1948 this situation began to change. The West and the United States inaugurated a series of creative policies within and outside the United Nations; for example, the Marshall Plan, Point Four and the Expanded Program of Technical Assistance. The UN's procedures, especially in the Economic and Social Council were tightened. The USSR's unwillingness to participate in the developing concrete programs led to its increasing isolation. Moreover, the West developed a telling counterattack on a number of issues such as trade union rights and forced labor. By the early nineteen fifties the ineffectiveness of Soviet tactics was clearly apparent.

The second period during which the Soviet Union appeared to have had some success in influencing opinion within the United Nations was in the period from 1953 through 1958, the years immediately after the first signs of the changes in its policy. The new Soviet moves came at a time when American policy was also being changed and was peculiarly negative. An example illustrates this. On the same day in 1953 that the Soviet Union reversed its policy of abstaining from voting on resolutions concerning UNICEF, and voted for a resolution which among other things recommended that the Children's Fund should be put on a permanent basis, the Committee on Appropriations of the House of Representatives killed a provision for the United States contribution.[14] Others could be

[14] See: The New York Times, July 21, 1953, pp. 1, 9.

cited. American Congressmen reacted to the Soviet contribution to the Expanded Program of Technical Assistance with disproportionate fear. During this period the United States decided that it could not sign conventions such as those dealing with equal remuneration, freedom of association, forced labor and slavery. The controversy concerning visas for representatives of communist-controlled Non-Governmental Organizations also reached its height then. In addition, the early years of the Eisenhower Administration were marked by a general policy of financial retrenchment which affected United States policy in the United Nations. This situation began to alter in 1957, when the United States and the West generally began to take a number of initiatives within and outside the United Nations, which significantly reduced the effectiveness of Soviet tactics. Thus, the effectiveness of Soviet efforts appears to have varied directly with the positiveness and creativeness and Western and particularly United States policies.

It is yet too early to ascertain whether or not the period of Africa's entry into the United Nations, which began on a large scale in 1960, will be marked by significant gains for the USSR, as Soviet commentators so confidently predicted. They saw this period as the beginning of a permanent change in the world organization. It is true that African states and the Soviet bloc have voted together with great frequency, but this has more often been the result of Soviet support of African moves than of African support of Soviet initiatives.[15] Although the USSR's position in the UN's economic and social activities improved somewhat in the early nineteen sixties, it still usually was able to break out of its minority role only when supporting the initiatives of others. This suggests that while the USSR can affect the nature of the UN's decisions through the votes of the Soviet bloc, it can in no way control these decisions. The majority of underdeveloped states within the UN, including those from Africa, still see and prefer the West as the principal source of economic assistance and political guidance. Unless this situation changes —and the outcome will at least in part be determined by Western actions—the USSR is unlikely to score significant gains. Moreover, even if Western influence in the UN were to suffer a marked decline, this need not necessarily result in increased Soviet influence. The UN is not a two-player game.

One cannot predict with certainty that the Soviet Union will

[15] See: Thomas Hovet, Jr., *Africa in the United Nations*, pp. 171-179.

continue to be as active in the UN's economic and social activities as it has been since 1953 if the present situation prevails. There is evidence that policy toward underdeveloped areas has been a controversial subject among Soviet leaders, and Soviet writers have begun to question the simple formulation, which dominated in communist doctrine after the decline of the two-camp view, that the process of decolonization would automatically be a loss for capitalism and a gain for socialism.[16] Conceivably, the USSR could resume its isolationist stance of an earlier period, but this is unlikely. The same factors which stimulated the USSR to strive to break out of its isolation in the early nineteen fifties would probably operate to prevent a withdrawal.

Just as the changes themselves in Soviet policy concerning the economic and social activities of the United Nations should not be overemphasized, it is also important not to interpret them as indicating that the USSR has radically revised its concept of the role of the UN, or of the importance of the various aspects of the organization. The United Nations continues to play only a secondary role in over-all Soviet strategy, and its political activities continue to be regarded as the most important.[17] Countless examples such as summit conferences, the special negotiations concerning the discontinuance of nuclear weapons tests and the relatively small proportion of Soviet aid to underdeveloped countries given through the UN, illustrate the secondary role assigned to the UN in Soviet strategy. In commenting on the specialized agencies in a Soviet text published in 1960, S. B. Krylov stated that the bourgeois doctrine of international law "greatly exaggerates" their importance.

> Their importance is restricted by the special framework for their activities. . . . They not only do not guarantee peace between States, but themselves frequently reflect and experience the impact of contradictions and conflicts between States, which became particularly acute when capitalism entered its imperialist stage.

[16] On the first point see M. Z. Saburov's speech to the Twenty-first Party Congress: Leo Gruliow (ed.) *Current Soviet Policies: III: The Documentary Record of the Extraordinary 21st Congress of the Communist Party of the Soviet Union* (New York: Columbia University Press, 1960), p. 182. On the second see: Herbert S. Dinerstein, "Soviet Doctrine on Developing Countries: Some Divergent Views," The RAND Corporation, 1963, P-2725. Dinerstein points out that some Soviet writers have even begun to question the emphasis on the development of heavy industry in underdeveloped countries (pp. 17-19).

[17] See: Alexander Dallin, *The Soviet Union at the United Nations*.

It should also be borne in mind that many of these organizations are dominated by monopoly capital, which has secured control over the bourgeois state machine and directs and guides its activities.[18]

Although this will be treated in more detail later, it would be hard to imagine a more direct attack on the theory of functionalism.

It would be wrong therefore to read too much into the changes in Soviet policies toward the economic and social activities of the United Nations. Putting it in summary fashion, in 1950, 1951 and 1952 the USSR increasingly found itself isolated with respect to the UN's economic and social functions, among other reasons, because of its attitude toward these activities. By 1953 increased participation was feasible and was also in accord with broader Soviet strategy. The transformation does not appear to have resulted from fundamental changes in the USSR's attitude toward international cooperation concerning so-called "non-political" issues.

THE IMPACT OF THE USSR'S PARTICIPATION ON THE UN'S INSTITUTIONS AND ACTIVITIES

The second set of questions which were raised at the outset of this study concerned the impact of the USSR's participation on the UN's institutions and activities. Although it is impossible to measure this impact with precision, some conclusions seem warranted.

First, the limited extent to which the USSR and other Soviet bloc states have been able to determine the direction of the economic and social activities of the United Nations should be re emphasized. The positions which the Soviet Union advanced on the two items of most direct importance to it, refugees and displaced persons and relief and reconstruction assistance, were overwhelmingly rejected. Substantive proposals introduced by the USSR or the various members of its bloc dealing with other issues have almost without exception been treated in a manner quite different from that originally proposed. Soviet sponsored substantive amendments have generally been turned down. The only Soviet proposals which have met significant success have been those which have dealt with organizational and procedural questions. This is not, however, to argue that the effects of the Soviet Union's participation have been inconsequential.

In institutional terms, the USSR's participation has led to the

[18] Academy of Sciences of the USSR, *International Law*, p. 348.

"politicization" of the economic and social functions of the United Nations. Soviet structural proposals have always been designed to emphasize the political nature of these activities. For instance, when the structural framework for IRO, UNICEF and EPTA was debated, the Soviet Union sought to stress the powers of political rather than administrative bodies. The USSR's insistence that ECOSOC's functional commissions should be composed of governmental representatives instead of individuals appointed in their own right is another example of the same tendency. Although giving Non-Governmental Organizations a prominent role in ECOSOC's proceedings did not inevitably mean that political considerations would be introduced, as a practical matter, it did, because of the tactics of the WFTU. The substantive items which the USSR has introduced also have usually had political overtones. Such proposals as those concerning the effects on health of nuclear weapons tests, trade union rights, equal pay, unemployment, discrimination in international trade, technical assistance in the petroleum industry, and the profits of private foreign investment in underdeveloped countries, are cases in point. It is fair to say that the USSR has regarded the UN as an "arena for combat" concerning economic and social issues rather than as a focal point for cooperative endeavors. It has taken this view of the UN not as "a reluctant recognition of a tragic fact, but as an exhilarating ride on the wave of the future." [19] The USSR's substantive positions have been designed to contest basic Western positions concerning economic and social questions, and its procedural suggestions have been drawn to facilitate such efforts. The USSR's position on the implementation of recommendations concerning economic and social issues exemplifies this point; it was appropriate for hortatory tasks, not for detailed technical cooperative endeavors.

Although the Soviet position and the final outcome are both clear —significantly the term "non-political" is hardly ever used to describe the UN's economic and social activities—it is far from easy to establish the inter-relationship with accuracy. Clearly the Soviet position on structural and procedural issues was only accepted to the extent that, and because, other states were willing. The substantive issues, however, were another matter. Once challenges were introduced, responses almost always had to be made, and political controversy, once started in one area, had a way of spilling over into other areas and of perpetuating itself. Thus, even though sole responsibil-

[19] Alexander Dallin, *The Soviet Union at the United Nations*, p. 200.

ity for the "politicization" of the economic and social work of the United Nations should not be assigned to the USSR, that state played a substantial part in this development.

The "politicization" of the UN's economic and social activities has been decried by several statesmen and scholars who have looked back wistfully at the calmer and more technical atmosphere which surrounded the work of the League of Nations in these fields. One former League official has even suggested that the UN's economic and social functions should be reorganized so as to exclude the Soviet Union.[20] At this stage such a proposal is clearly not feasible, and perhaps it might not even be desirable. It probably would not eliminate the "politicization." The conflicts of interest in the non-communist world, particularly those between the developed and underdeveloped states could well sustain the present situation. Further, this "politicization" has had beneficial effects which should be recognized. It has focused attention in the UN on some of the basic economic and social problems of the present era, and the resulting debate, however polemical, has clarified some of the central issues involved.[21] However, the suggestion, and the thinking on which it was based, merit careful consideration in future decisions concerning what matters should be brought before the UN and the creation of new international organizations. There is clearly a more pronounced relationship between the degree of ideological consensus among the member states and the type of functions which an international organization can carry out than many American postwar planners seemed to assume in 1944.[22]

Another consequence of the USSR's participation, or lack thereof,

[20] A. Loveday, "Suggestions for the Reform of the United Nations Economic and Social Machinery."

[21] See the suggestive article by Walter M. Kotschnig, "The Economic and Social Foundations of the United Nations," *Proceedings of the American Philosophical Society*, XCV, no. 5 (October 17, 1951), 512-518.

[22] W. Friedman has consistently written insightfully on this point. See: *Legal Theory* (3rd ed., London: Stevens, 1953), pp. 390-394, 459, 462; "The Growth of State Control over the Individual and its Effect Upon the Rules of International State Responsibility," *The British Yearbook of International Law, 1938*, XIX (London: Oxford University Press, 1938), 118-150; and "Some Impacts of Social Organization on International Law," *The American Journal of International Law*, L, no. 3 (July 1956), 475-513. See also: Stephen S. Goodspeed, "Political Considerations in the United Nations Economic and Social Council," *The Yearbook of World Affairs, 1961* (London: Stevens and Sons, 1961), pp. 135-161.

on the institutions of the United Nations has been that of underscoring the decentralization which was implicit in the Charter. This tendency was most pronounced prior to 1953 when the Soviet bloc boycotted most of the specialized agencies, but it has continued to operate even after that date. In 1963, the USSR still did not belong to six of the specialized agencies, nor did it participate in the work conducted by GATT. As a consequence, most problems of international trade and finance, civil aviation, and agriculture, were handled in an almost exclusively noncommunist framework. Clearly the problem of coordination has been complicated by the differences in the membership of the specialized agencies and the United Nations. These differences have also weighed heavily in decisions concerning where various problems should be considered. While coordination is not an end in itself, and while it is utopian to expect that decisions concerning which body should have responsibility for a given item should be based on abstract criteria, it is probably also true that the over-all effectiveness of the UN system as an instrument for attacking basic economic and social problems has been less than would have been possible had it not been for these complications. On the other hand, one of the features of the present arrangement is that it has allowed varying degrees of cooperation on different issues.

So far as substantive issues are concerned, the USSR's abstention has meant that many of these activities have not had as broad a scope as many had hoped. The Soviet boycott of the specialized agencies working in the field of international trade and finance, civil aviation and agriculture has just been mentioned. In addition, the Soviet bloc has had little to do with the activities of the International Refugee Organization, the United Nations High Commissioner for Refugees, the United Nations Relief and Works Agency for Palestine Refugees, and the United Nations Korean Reconstruction Agency. By and large, the USSR has stayed aloof from the UN's program of advisory social welfares services and from the organization's activities with respect to the prevention of crime and the treatment of offenders. The Soviet Union has refused to participate in the work of the United Nations concerning traffic in dangerous goods and measures to encourage private foreign investment in underdeveloped countries.

However, it is important to recognize that even though the USSR has refused to participate in much of the economic and social activities which have been carried on with the UN framework, it has never been able to block the inauguration of such functions nor their development if majority sentiment favored the opposite course. When the majority in the United Nations has desired to ignore the Soviet position in these matters, it has done so, even on issues of great importance to the USSR, such as refugees and displaced persons. Although there have been no completely analogous cases, the majority has seldom acted when the United States has expressed its disapproval. The UN's actions with respect to SUNFED and a Capital Development Fund have illustrated this point, although they also have demonstrated that, as the largest potential contributor, as a practical matter, the United States has held a financial veto. The Soviet Union's sanction, in contrast, has generally been limited to political disapproval, and on the whole this has proved to be a relatively weak weapon. The United Nations has conducted many economic and social activities despite the Soviet Union's disapproval. Even when the Soviet Union has given its formal approval, it has been striking how little its views have been taken into account. Many debates in the United Nations on economic and social issues have sounded as if they were dialogues between the West and the underdeveloped areas of the world. The USSR's role has sometimes been almost that of a spectator, occasionally enlisted for support on this point or the other, from time to time intentionally or unintentionally insulted by one or the other side, but most frequently just ignored.

Clearly Soviet policy and the cold war have been responsible for preventing certain issues from being brought before the United Nations or for driving them out of the world organization. As a concrete example, had the USSR been more cooperative both within and outside of the UN, the organization's role in the economic reconstruction work following the Second World War might have been much more extensive. On a broader and more abstract level, Soviet policy and the ideological differences between East and West have ruled out the possibility of the UN's becoming a center for the harmonization of national policies concerning economic and social issues. ECOSOC has been far removed from being a global General Staff or High Commission for these matters. Not only has Soviet policy precluded significant cooperative endeavors with the West, it has also been directed at exacerbating conflicts within the noncommunist world. Although it is impossible to know the way in which the United Nations would have developed under different conditions, certainly the abrasive nature of Soviet policy and the ideological differences between East and West have been a profound barrier to global cooperation and planning. This is not to argue that the Soviet Union is singularly responsible for the limited nature of the UN's economic and social activities. Gunnar Myrdal has quite rightly pointed out the basic reason for the failure of the UN and the specialized agencies to develop strong programs and powers is that the governments of the Western powers "and behind them their peoples, were not prepared to let it happen." [23] It is merely to indicate that had the Western states chosen a different course, because of Soviet participation, it would have been difficult for them to utilize the UN to implement their desires, and to suggest that Soviet conduct may have contributed in some way to their reluctance to go farther. The European Coal and Steel Community, the Common Market, Euratom and the Organization for European Economic Cooperation have provided various examples to prove that the coordination of national policies can go much farther than it has in the UN, if there is agreement on fundamentals.

To the extent that the Soviet position on sovereignty has been accepted, this too has had a limiting effect. It is true that the Soviet position has been adopted only when it has won majority support, and thus the USSR has only been able to raise restrictions which, it could be said, the majority has wanted. However, by constantly stressing the issue of sovereignty the USSR has probably made other states more aware of the issue than they might have been otherwise, and by raising the issue, may have made it more difficult for them to compromise. Then, too, states which might not have wanted to compromise on matters involving sovereignty, but which perhaps could have been induced to make concessions, could always count on the Soviet Union to fight pressures on them to give in. Perhaps this has had its most significant impact on the UN's activities with respect to the economic reconstruction of Europe and economic development. In the first case especially, the UN might have made far greater inroads on national sovereignty than it did, had it not been for the USSR's participation.

Soviet policy also resulted in the creation of certain technical difficulties for some of the economic and social activities of the United Nations. Its success in eliminating colonial application and

---

[23] Gunnar Myrdal, *Beyond the Welfare State: Economic Planning and Its International Implications* (New Haven: Yale University Press, 1960), p. 284.

federal state clauses from conventions dealing with problems of social and economic welfare made it more difficult to use this technique as an instrument of control, and its insistence on the exclusion of Franco Spain weakened the international system for the control of narcotic drugs.

At the same time, Soviet policy has also had positive effects, which must not be overlooked. The USSR must be credited with initiating the consideration of some items, such as trade union rights, equal pay for equal work, and the study of the economic consequences of disarmament, which might not have been considered otherwise, or at least not at the time that they were. The Soviet Union probably also forced the United Nations to pay greater attention to the problem of unemployment than it might have in other circumstances. These were issues on which Soviet ideology differed considerably from that of the majority of UN member states, but at the same time there were important ties between Soviet ideology and that of the others. Soviet ideology after all had its origins in criticisms of practices in the West. To some extent it was the suggestion of an alternative and allegedly more effective way of achieving similar goals. Soviet policy in the UN in a sense fitted this pattern. It served as a "gadfly" to the West.

This process actually has operated in all areas of the economic and social activities of the United Nations, regardless of whether or not central ideological differences were involved. Soviet attacks, whatever the subject and their origin, have spurred the West to develop new programs both within and outside of the United Nations. Certainly the great amount of attention which the United Nations has devoted to problems of underdeveloped areas is at least partly a result of the Soviet-American struggle.

In a curious sense, then, Soviet participation may actually have served to promote the values of those Americans who during the Second World War drafted plans for the new postwar international organization. Probably the UN has done much more about the deep-seated economic and social problems which could contribute to international tension and war than the League of Nations did, and this should be attributed at least partly to the nature of Soviet participation and the competition which the USSR has engendered.

To say that the Soviet Union's participation in the economic and social activities of the United Nations has had beneficial effects, however, is not to argue that even more would be accomplished if the USSR's role were increased. Some scholars have questioned the Western position of first criticizing the Soviet Union for not participating in several of the UN's economic and social activities, and then continuing to condemn the USSR after it reversed its policy. They have argued that this has reflected a fundamental ambiguity on the part of the West, at the same time neither wanting the USSR to abstain nor to participate. The problem has been the terms on which the USSR has been willing to enter into the UN's activities. In this sense, the positive function of the Soviet Union in the UN's economic and social activities has not been to introduce its own values, but rather to make it more difficult for the West not to give effect to those which it espouses.

IMPLICATIONS FOR FUNCTIONALISM

The third set of questions which was raised at the outset of this study involved the implications of the record of Soviet policy for functionalist theory. Although the extent to which one can generalize may be subject to question, in this case at least the relationship between national policy and international organization was rather different from that envisaged in functionalist theory.

In the first place, the functionalist assumption that states could and would cooperate with respect to economic and social matters despite their political differences, seems to have been at best only partly true. Reviewing the record, one is struck by how little real cooperation the USSR has been involved in, rather than how much. Perhaps the most accurate way of putting it would be to say that the Soviet Union has fought with the West in the UN's economic and social activities. When the USSR has chosen to cooperate, its decision appears to have been based generally on political considerations rather than grounds of necessity. Perhaps the functionalist theory would hold true for small states with similar ideologies concerning economic and social matters and analogous governmental structures. In this case, however, there was little compulsion to cooperate and differences concerning economic and social issues were basic components of the political quarrel between East and West. David Mitrany's hope that economic and social collaboration would provide a way of circumventing ideology has surely proved ill-founded.[24]

Nor does the record indicate that participation in this aspect of the

[24] A *Working Peace System*, p. 23.

United Nations has had the impact on the USSR which functionalist theory postulated. There has been almost no organized public support for the United Nations within the Soviet Union.[25] An Association for the United Nations was formed in March 1956, but little is known about its membership or activities. Extremely little has been written of a scholarly nature in Russian concerning the United Nations and the paucity of periodical literature dealing with the UN has been striking.[26] The accounts which have appeared in the Soviet press have usually been highly colored and have reflected the priority assigned to the organization's political activities. It has therefore not been possible independently to influence general public opinion within the USSR through these activities. If the UN has had any impact, it must have been on the Soviet leadership in a rather direct sense.

Some writers have expressed the hope that repeated exposure to free economic and social systems through the United Nations and pressure from other states within the UN would encourage Soviet leaders to modify and liberalize their domestic rule. It is true that as Soviet policy has changed in the United Nations, Soviet domestic rule has also been liberalized; for example, the USSR's practices concerning forced labor and trade union rights have been modified somewhat.[27] However, it would be extremely difficult to trace any of the elements of this liberalization directly to the work of the United Nations. A variety of domestic factors can be cited as the basic causes for the relaxation. The most that can be said is that the UN's activities, such as the investigation of forced labor, encouraged and gave added impetus to these trends.

The record of Soviet policy also contains little encouragement for those who hoped that participation in the UN's economic and social activities would ameliorate political differences between states. Despite its participation in this aspect of the UN for over a decade and a half, the USSR's political differences with the West seem to be just about as sharp in 1963 as they were in the years immediately after the Second World War. The UN's economic and social activities have not resulted in the formation of strong links between the USSR and the rest of the world, as some hoped.

[25] See: Alexander Dallin, *The Soviet Union at the United Nations*, pp. 88-94; and, Alvin Z. Rubinstein, "The Soviet Image of the United Nations."

[26] See: Alvin Z. Rubinstein, "Selected Bibliography of Soviet Works on the United Nations, 1946-1959."

[27] See: Harold Karan Jacobson, "The USSR and ILO," pp. 421, 427.

After reviewing the record of Soviet policy with respect to the economic and social activities of the United Nations, one is tempted to state the proposition that international economic and social cooperation is determined by, rather than a determinant of, political decisions. That seems to have been the case in this instance. Certainly this is a very different relationship between national policy and international organization than that postulated by the functionalists and in the Bruce Report. Functionalist theory clearly underestimated the ability of a totalitarian state to isolate itself and the degree of ideological consensus and political agreement necessary for meaningful international cooperation concerning economic and social issues.

On the other hand, to state the relationship between national policy and international organization in this way would also put the matter too simply. Without doubt, there are other cases where the outcome would be much more like that which the functionalists envisaged. European integration is probably a case in point.[28] Even in the case under consideration the interaction is much more complicated. Because of the USSR's participation in the UN's economic and social activities certain basic features of the international arena were probably underscored for Soviet leaders, and this may well have quickened certain political decisions. The UN probably made the USSR more aware of the nature and aspirations of the noncommunist world, and especially of the underdeveloped areas.

Then too, for whatever reason, the USSR did change its policy and did begin to participate in many aspects of the economic and social work of the United Nations. Even though its new policies could hardly be described as cooperative, the USSR was forced to compete with the West.

While the functionalists saw clearly the gains which could be obtained through cooperation in international organizations concerning economic and social matters, they virtually ignored the benefits which might accrue from channeling conflict with respect to these issues into international institutions. Beneficial as well as detrimental effects have resulted from the UN's having been an arena of combat.

[28] See: Ernst B. Haas, *The Uniting of Europe: Political, Social and Economic Forces 1950-1957* (Stanford: Stanford University Press, 1958). For comparisons between the European institutions and the UN see his suggestive article, "International Integration: The European and the Universal Process," *International Organization*, XV, no. 3 (Summer 1961), 366-392.

The United Nations has probably achieved considerably more in the economic and social fields during the years since its establishment than the League of Nations did in a comparable period, and this has been at least partly attributable to the stimulus provided by Soviet participation and East-West competition. Further, the total impact of the UN cannot be measured only by what has gone on within the organization itself. Pressure for action within the United Nations has stimulated bilateral programs, especially in the field of economic development.[29] Thus, the institutionalization of conflict may well have been as important and useful as the institutionalization of cooperation would have been. Perhaps on balance there is little cause to bemoan the fact that the adjective "non-political" is seldom used in connection with the economic and social activities of the United Nations.

[29] See: John G. Hadwen and Johan Kaufmann, *How United Nations Decisions Are Made* (Leyden: A. W. Sythoff, 1960), pp. 109-110.

SELECTED BIBLIOGRAPHY

THIS STUDY IS BASED PRIMARILY ON THE DOCUMENTS, BOOKS AND ARTIcles which are listed here and on interviews and personal observations. Several other books and articles on international organization and Soviet policy contributed to the analysis, but this listing is confined to works of immediate relevance.

Many of the citations in the study are references to United Nations documents. Some of these are printed, and they are cited by their official title. Others are either mimeographed or reproduced by photo-offset, and they are cited by their document number. An elaborate system of symbols has been evolved for numbering the nonprinted documents of the United Nations. The first letter in any series is the basic symbol of the document and indicates the major organ of the United Nations responsible for its publication. Only documents of the General Assembly and the Economic and Social Council are used in this study. The basic symbol "A" indicates Assembly documents, and "E," Council documents. Other symbols have the following meanings:

Add.	Addendum
AC.	*Ad hoc* committee
C.	Committee
CN.	Commission
Conf.	Conference
Corr.	Corrigendum
L.	Limited Distribution
P.C.	Preparatory Commission or Committee
Rev.	Revision
SC.	Subcommittee
SR.	Summary record
Sub.	Subcommission

The symbols for the committees, commissions and other organs referred to most frequently are:

A/C. 2	Second Committee, or Economic and Financial Committee
A/C. 3	Third Committee, or Social, Humanitarian, and Cultural Committee
E/AC. 6	Economic Committee
E/AC. 7	Social Committee
E/AC. 24	Coordination Committee
E/C. 2	Committee on Non-Governmental Organizations
E/C. 5	Committee for Industrial Development
E/CN. 1	Economic and Employment Commission; after 1950, Economic, Employment and Development Commission
E/CN. 1/Sub. 2	Sub-Commission on Employment and Economic Stability
E/CN. 1/Sub. 3	Sub-Commission on Economic Development
E/CN. 2	Transport and Communications Commission
E/CN. 3	Statistical Commission
E/CN. 5	Social Commission
E/CN. 6	Commission on Narcotic Drugs
E/CN. 7	Fiscal Commission
E/CN. 9	Population Commission
E/CN. 11	Economic Commission for Asia and the Far East
E/CN. 13	Commission on International Commodity Trade
E/ECE	Economic Commission for Europe
E/ICEF	United Nations Children's Fund
E/REF	Special Committee on Refugees and Displaced Persons
E/SF	United Nations Special Fund
E/TAC	Technical Assistance Committee

For a more complete explanation of the symbols, see: ST/LIB/SER. B/5, "United Nations Documents Series Symbols" (Sales No.: 1956.I.4). On the general problem of United Nations documentation, see: Brenda Brimmer, Linwood R. Wall, Waldo Chamberlin and Thomas Hovet, Jr., *A Guide to the Use of United Nations Documents* (New York: Oceana, 1962).

I. DOCUMENTS

International Labor Organization
International Labor Organization. *Official Bulletin*, XXXIX, no. 4 (1956), 211-304; and XLI, no. 3 (1958), 228-241.
———. *The Trade Union Situation in the U.S.S.R.* Geneva: 1960.
———. *The Trade Union Situation in the United States.* Geneva: 1960.

League of Nations
League of Nations Document A.23.1939. *The Development of International*

Cooperation in Economic and Social Affairs: Report of the Special Committee. Geneva: 1939.

United Nations
United Nations, Economic and Social Council. *Documents*, 1946-1963.
United Nations, Economic and Social Council, *Official Records*, 1946-1963.
United Nations, Economic and Social Council. *Rules of Procedure of the Economic and Social Council.* Documents: E/33 and Rev. 1-5; E/565; E/1662; E/2424; E/2425; E/3063.
――――. Agenda Committee. *Documents*, 1947-1951; *Summary Records*, 1947-1952.
――――. Committee for Industrial Development. *Documents*, 1960-1963; *Summary Records*, 1960-1963.
――――. Commission on International Commodity Trade. *Documents*, 1955-1963; *Summary Records*, 1955-1963.
――――. Commission on Narcotic Drugs. *Documents*, 1946-1963; *Summary Records*, 1946-1963.
――――. Committee on Non-Governmental Organizations. *Documents*, 1946-1963; *Summary Records*, 1946-1963.
――――. Coordination Committee. *Documents*, 1946-1963; *Summary Records*, 1946-1963.
――――. Economic and Employment Commission (after 1950, Economic, Employment and Development Commission). *Documents*, 1946-1951; *Summary Records*, 1946-1951.
――――. Sub-Commission on Economic Development. *Documents*, 1947-1950; *Summary Records*, 1947-1950.
――――. Sub-Commission on Employment and Economic Stability. *Documents*, 1947-1949; *Summary Records*, 1947-1949.
――――. Temporary Sub-Commission on Economic Reconstruction of Devastated Areas. *Documents*, 1946; *Summary Records*, 1946.
――――. Economic Commission for Asia and the Far East. *Documents*, 1947-1963; *Summary Records*, 1947-1963.
――――. Economic Commission for Europe. *Documents*, 1947-1963; *Summary Records*, 1947-1963.
――――. Economic Committee. *Documents*, 1946-1963; *Summary Records*, 1946-1963.
――――. Fiscal Commission. *Documents*, 1946-1954; *Summary Records*, 1946-1954.
――――. Population Commission. *Documents*, 1946-1963; *Summary Records*, 1946-1963.
――――. Social Commission. *Documents*, 1946-1963; *Summary Records*, 1946-1963.
――――. Social Committee. *Documents*, 1946-1963; *Summary Records*, 1946-1963.
――――. Special Committee on Refugees and Displaced Persons. *Documents*, 1946; *Summary Records*, 1946.
――――. Special Fund, Governing Council. *Documents*, 1959-1963; *Summary Records*, 1959-1963.

SELECTED BIBLIOGRAPHY

———. Statistical Commission. *Documents*, 1946-1960; *Summary Records*, 1946-1960.

———. Technical Assistance Committee. *Documents*, 1950-1963; *Summary Records*, 1950-1963.

———. Transport and Communications Commission. *Documents*, 1946-1959; *Summary Records*, 1946-1959.

———. United Nations Children's Fund, Executive Board. *Documents*, 1947-1963; *Summary Records*, 1947-1963.

———. Miscellaneous Temporary Committees, Conferences and Subsidiary Bodies. *Documents*, 1946-1963; *Summary Records*, 1946-1963.

United Nations, General Assembly. *Documents* (all documents pertaining to economic and social issues), 1946-1963.

United Nations, General Assembly. *Official Records* (all debates pertaining to economic and social issues), 1946-1963.

United Nations, General Assembly. *Rules of Procedure of the General Assembly*. Documents: A/520 and Rev. 1-4; A/3660 and Corr. 1; A/4700.

United Nations, Preparatory Commission. *Journal of the Preparatory Commission*. London: 1945.

———. *Report by the Executive Committee to the Preparatory Commission of the United Nations*. London: 1945.

———. *Report by the Preparatory Commission to the United Nations*. London: 1945.

———. Committees 1-8, *Summary Records of Meetings*. 8 Vols. London: 1945.

United Nations, Secretariat. *Repertory of the Practice of United Nations Organs*. 5 Vols. New York: 1955, and Supplement No. 1, 2 Vols. New York: 1958.

———. *Tenth Anniversary of the Signing of the United Nations Charter, San Francisco, 1955: Proceedings of the Commerative Meetings* (UN Document ST/GG/6: Sales No. 1955.I.26).

———. Department of Public Information. *Yearbook of the United Nations*, 1946-1962.

United Nations Conference on International Organization. *Documents of the United Nations Conference on International Organization*. 22 Vols. New York: 1945-1955.

Government Documents and Publications

France, Ministère des Affaires étrangères. *Documents de la Conférence des Ministres des Affaires étrangères de la France, du Royaume-Uni, de l'U.R.S.S. tenue à Paris du 27 juin au 3 juillet 1947, et pièces rélatives aux négociations diplomatiques engagées à la suite du discours prononcé par le Général Marshall Secrétaire d'Etat des Etats-Unis, le 5 juin 1947*. Paris: Imprimerie Nationale, 1947.

Union of Soviet Socialist Republics, *The Soviet Union at San Francisco*. London: 1945.

United States of America, Department of State. Document, London Embassy, Ambassador Winant to the Secretary of State, Cable No. 327, January 22, 1942.

———. Document, Washington, Assistant Secretary Acheson to the Secretary of State, Memorandum, June 23, 1942.

———. *Foreign Relations of the United States: The Conferences at Malta and Yalta, 1945.* Department of State Publication No. 6199. Washington, D. C.: Government Printing Office, 1955.

———. *Postwar Foreign Policy Preparation, 1939-1945.* Department of State Publication 3580, General Foreign Policy Series 15. Washington, D. C.: Government Printing Office, 1949.

II. MANUSCRIPTS

Blumenthal, Irene. *The Soviet Union and the United Nations.* New York: Carnegie Endowment for International Peace, mimeographed, 1960.

Rubinstein, Alvin Z. *The Soviets in International Organizations: Changing Policy Toward Underdeveloped Countries.* To be published by Princeton University Press.

III. BOOKS

Academy of Sciences of the Union of Soviet Socialist Republics, Institute of State and Law. *International Law.* Moscow: Foreign Languages Publishing House, 1960.

Allen, Robert Loring. *Middle Eastern Economic Relations with the Soviet Union, Eastern Europe, and Mainland China.* Charlottesville: Woodrow Wilson Department of Foreign Affairs, University of Virginia, 1958.

———. *Soviet Economic Warfare.* Washington, D. C.: Public Affairs Press, 1960.

Asher, Robert E., Kotschnig, Walter M., Brown, William Adams, Jr., Green, James Frederick, Sady, Emil J., and Associates. *The United Nations and Promotion of the General Welfare.* Washington, D. C.: The Brookings Institution, 1957.

Barghoorn, Frederick C. *The Soviet Cultural Offensive: The Role of Cultural Diplomacy in Soviet Foreign Policy.* Princeton: Princeton University Press, 1960.

———. *The Soviet Image of the United States.* New York: Harcourt, Brace, 1950.

Baykov, Alexander. *Soviet Foreign Trade.* Princeton: Princeton University Press, 1946.

Beloff, Max. *The Foreign Policy of the Soviet Union, 1929-1941.* 2 Vols. London: Oxford University Press, 1947.

Brierly, J. L. *The Law of Nations: An Introduction to the International Law of Peace.* 4th ed. London: Oxford University Press, 1949.

Brzezinski, Zbigniew. *The Soviet Bloc: Unity and Conflict.* Cambridge: Harvard University Press, 1960.

Claude, Inis L., Jr. *Swords into Plowshares: The Problems and Progress of International Organization.* 2nd ed. New York: Random House, 1959.

Dallin, Alexander. *The Soviet Union at the United Nations: An Inquiry into Soviet Motives and Objectives.* New York: Frederick A. Praeger, 1962.

Davis, Kathryn Wasserman. *The Soviets at Geneva.* Geneva: Librairie Kundig, 1934.

Dennett, Raymond, and Johnson, Joseph E. (eds.). *Negotiating with the Russians*. Boston: World Peace Foundation, 1951.
Dinerstein, Herbert S. *War and the Soviet Union: Nuclear Weapons and the Revolution in Soviet Military and Political Thinking*. New York: Frederick A. Praeger, 1959.
Fernbach, Alfred P. *Soviet Coexistence Strategy*. Washington, D. C.: Public Affairs Press, 1960.
Friedmann, W. *Legal Theory*. 3rd ed. London: Stevens, 1953.
Goodman, Elliot R. *The Soviet Design for a World State*. New York: Columbia University Press, 1960.
Haines, C. Grove (ed.). *The Threat of Soviet Imperialism*. Baltimore: The Johns Hopkins Press, 1954.
Haas, Ernst B. *The Uniting of Europe: Political, Social and Economic Forces 1950-1957*. Stanford: Stanford University Press, 1958.
Hadwen, John G. and Kaufmann, Johan. *How United Nations Decisions Are Made*. Leyden: A. W. Sythoff, 1960.
Holborn, Louise W. *The International Refugee Organization: A Specialized Agency of the United Nations: Its History and Work, 1946-1952*. London: Oxford University Press, 1956.
Hyde, Louis K., Jr. *The United States and the United Nations: Promoting the Public Welfare*. New York: Manhattan, 1960.
Hovet, Thomas, Jr. *Bloc Politics in the United Nations*. Cambridge: Harvard University Press, 1960.
———. *Africa in the United Nations*. Evanston: Northwestern University Press, 1963.
Jessup, Philip C., Lande, Adolf, Lissitzyn, Oliver J., and Chamberlain, Joseph P. *International Organization*. New York: Carnegie Endowment for International Peace, 1954.
Klemme, Marvin. *The Inside Story of UNRRA*. New York: Lifetime Eds., 1949.
Lie, Trygve. *In the Cause of Peace: Seven Years with the United Nations*. New York: Macmillan, 1954.
Marcuse, Herbert. *Soviet Marxism*. New York: Columbia University Press, 1958.
Mitrany, David. *A Working Peace System*. London: Oxford University Press, 1943.
Myrdal, Gunnar. *An International Economy: Problems and Prospects*. New York: Harper, 1956.
———. *Beyond the Welfare State: Economic Planning and Its International Implications*. New Haven: Yale University Press, 1960.
Niemeyer, Gerhart, with the assistance of John S. Reshetar, Jr. *An Inquiry into Soviet Mentality*. New York: Frederick A. Praeger, 1956.
Nogee, Joseph L. *Soviet Policy Toward International Control of Atomic Energy*. Notre Dame: University of Notre Dame Press, 1961.
Penrose, E. F. *Economic Planning for the Peace*. Princeton: Princeton University Press, 1953.
Rimalov, V. *Economic Cooperation Between the U.S.S.R. and Underdeveloped Countries*. Moscow: Foreign Languages Publishing House, 1962.
Russell, Ruth B., assisted by Jeannette E. Muther. *A History of The United*

Nations Charter: The Role of the United States, 1940-1945. Washington, D. C., The Brookings Institution, 1958.
Schiffer, Walter. The Legal Community of Mankind. New York: Columbia University Press, 1954.
Schwartz, Harry. Russia's Soviet Economy. 2nd ed. New York: Prentice Hall, 1954.
Sharp, Walter R. Field Administration in the United Nations System. London: Stevens and Sons, Ltd., 1961.
———. International Technical Assistance. Chicago: Public Administration Service, 1952.
Shulman, Marshall D. Stalin's Foreign Policy Reappraised. Cambridge: Harvard University Press, 1963.
Stettinius, Edward R., Jr. (ed. by Walter Johnson). Roosevelt and the Russians: The Yalta Conference. Garden City: Doubleday, 1949.
Stoessinger, John George. The Refugee and the World Community. Minneapolis: The University of Minnesota Press, 1956.
Vernant, Jacques. The Refugee in the Post-War World. New Haven: Yale University Press, 1953.
Walters, F. P. A History of the League of Nations. 2 vols. London: Oxford University Press, 1952.
Wightman, David. Economic Cooperation in Europe: A Study of the United Nations Economic Commission for Europe. New York: Frederick A. Praeger, 1956.
Wilcox, Clair. A Charter for World Trade. New York: Macmillan, 1949.
Woodbridge, George. UNRRA: The History of the United Nations Relief and Rehabilitation Administration. 3 vols. New York: Columbia University Press, 1950.

IV. NEWSPAPERS AND PERIODICALS

The following newspapers and periodicals have been consulted extensively.
The Current Digest of the Soviet Press
International Affairs (Moscow)
International Organization
New Times
The New York Times
News (Moscow)
United Nations Bulletin (1946-1954)
United Nations Review (1954-1963)

V. ARTICLES AND PAMPHLETS

Allen, Robert Loring. "United Nations Technical Assistance: Soviet and East European Participation," International Organization, XI, no. 4 (Autumn 1957), 615-634.
Armstrong, John A. "The Soviet Attitude Toward UNESCO," International Organization, VIII, no. 2 (May 1954), 217-233.
Armstrong, Willis C. "The Soviet Approach to International Trade," Political Science Quarterly, LXIII, no. 3 (September 1948), 368-382.

Behrman, Jack N. "Political Factors in U.S. International Financial Cooperation, 1945-1950," *The American Political Science Review*, XLVII, no. 2 (June 1953), 431-460.
Benjamin, Peter. "The Work of the Economic Commission for Europe in the Field of International Commercial Arbitration," *The International and Comparative Law Quarterly*, VII, Part 1 (January 1958), 22-30.
Brügel, J. W. "Der Sowjetblock in der IAE-GENF," *Aussen Politik*, Heft 5/61 (May 1961), pp. 340-347.
Diatchenko, V. P. "International Trade and Peaceful Cooperation," *International Social Science Journal*, XII, no. 2 (1960), 237-250.
Dinerstein, Herbert S. "Soviet Doctrine on Developing Countries: Some Divergent Views," The RAND Corporation, P-2725.
Emerson, Rupert, and Claude, Inis L., Jr. "The Soviet Union and the United Nations: An Essay in Interpretation," *International Organization*, VI, no. 1 (February 1952), 1-26.
Frankel, J. "The Soviet Union and the United Nations," *The Year Book of World Affairs, 1954*. New York: Frederick A. Praeger, 1954, pp. 69-94.
Friedmann, W. "The Growth of State Control over the Individual and its Effect Upon the Rules of International State Responsibility," *The British Yearbook of International Law, 1938*. London: Oxford University Press, 1938, pp. 118-150.
———. "Limits of Functionalism in International Organization," *The Year Book of World Affairs, 1956*. New York: Frederick A. Praeger, 1956, pp. 256-269.
———. "Some Impacts of Social Organization on International Law," *The American Journal of International Law*, L. no. 3 (July 1956), 475-513.
Fuller, C. Dale. "Soviet Policy in the United Nations," *Annals of the American Academy of Political and Social Science*, CCLXIII (May 1949), 141-151.
Ginsburgs, George. "The Soviet Union and the Problem of Refugees and Displaced Persons," *The American Journal of International Law*, LI, no. 2 (April 1957), 325-361.
Goodman, Elliot R. "The Soviet Union and World Government," *Journal of Politics*, XV, no. 2 (May 1953), 231-253.
Goodspeed, Stephen S. "Political Considerations in the United Nations Economic and Social Council," *The Year Book of World Affairs, 1961*. London: Stevens and Sons, 1961, pp. 135-161.
Goodrich, Leland M. "New Trends in Narcotics Control," *International Conciliation* No. 530 (November 1960), pp. 181-242.
Haas, Ernst B. "International Integration: The European and the Universal Process," *International Organization*, XV, no. 3 (Summer 1961), 366-392.
Hoffman, Michael L. "Problems of East-West Trade," *International Conciliation*, No. 511 (January 1957), pp. 259-308.
———. "Problems of Trade Between Planned Economies," *American Economic Review*, XXXIV, Supplement (May 1951), 445-455.
Jacobson, Harold Karan. "Labor, the UN and the Cold War," *International Organization*, XI, no. 1 (Winter 1957), 55-67.
———. "The Soviet Union, the UN and World Trade," *The Western Political Quarterly*. XI, no. 3 (September 1958), 673-688.

———. "The USSR and ILO," *International Organization*, XIV, no. 3 (Summer 1960), 402-428.
———. "The USSR and the UN's Economic and Social Recommendations," *Osteuropa Recht*, Heft 2/58 (December 1958), pp. 310-314.
Jasny, Naum. "International Organization and Soviet Statistics," *Journal of the American Statistical Association*, XLV, no. 1 (March 1950), 48-64.
Johnson, Robert H. "International Politics and the Structure of International Organization: The Case of UNRRA," *World Politics*, III, no. 4 (July 1951), 520-538.
Kotschnig, Walter M. "The United Nations—Road to Economic and Social Progress," *World Affairs*, CXII, no. 2 (Summer 1949), 41-42.
———. "The Economic and Social Foundations of the United Nations," *Proceedings of the American Philosophical Society*, XCV, no. 5 (October 17, 1951), 512-518.
Loveday, A. "An Unfortunate Decision," *International Organization*, I, no. 2 (June 1947), 279-290.
———. "Suggestions for the Reform of the United Nations Economic and Social Machinery," *International Organization*, VII, no. 3 (August 1953), 325-341.
Malin, Patrick Murphy. "The Refugee: A Problem for International Organization," *International Organization*, I, no. 3 (August 1947), 443-459.
Mikesell, Raymond F. "The Role of International Monetary Agreements in a World of Planned Economies," *Journal of Political Economy*, LV, no. 4 (December 1947), 497-512.
Mikesell, Raymond F., and Behrman, Jack N. *Financing Free World Trade with the Sino-Soviet Bloc*. Princeton: International Finance Section, Department of Economics and Sociology, Princeton University, 1958.
Mitrany, David. "The Functional Approach to World Organization," *International Affairs*, XXIV, no. 3 (July 1948), 350-360.
Myrdal, Gunnar. "Psychological Impediments to Effective International Cooperation," *Journal of Social Issues, Supplement Series*, no. 6 (1952).
Pasvolsky, Leo. "Dumbarton Oaks Proposals for Economic and Social Cooperation," *International Conciliation*, no. 409, Section 2 (March 1945), pp. 203-208.
Prince, Charles. "U.S.S.R. and International Organization," *The American Journal of International Law*, XXXVI, no. 3 (July 1942), 425-445.
Read, James M. "The United Nations and Refugees—Changing Concepts," *International Conciliation*, no. 537 (March 1962), pp. 1-60.
Reston, James B. "Negotiating with the Russians," *Harper's Magazine*, CXCV, no. 1167 (August 1947), 97-106.
Rostow, Walt W. "The Economic Commission for Europe," *International Organization*, III, no. 2 (May 1949), 254-268.
Rubinstein, Alvin Z. "Selected Bibliography of Soviet Works on the United Nations," *The American Political Science Review*, LIV, no. 4 (December 1960), 985-991.
———. "The Soviet Image of the United Nations," *Proceedings of the American Philosophical Society*, CVII, no. 2 (April 1963), 132-137.

———. "Soviet Policy in ECAFE: A Case Study of Soviet Behavior in International Economic Organization," *International Organization*, XII, no. 4 (Autumn 1958), 459-472.

———. "Soviet Policy Toward Under-developed Areas in the Economic and Social Council," *International Organization*, IX, no. 2 (May 1955), 232-243.

———. "The United States, the Soviet Union and Atoms-for-Peace," *World Affairs Quarterly*, XXX, no. 1 (April 1959), 46-62.

———. "The U.S.S.R. and the I.M.C.O.: Some Preliminary Observations," United States Naval Institute *Proceedings*, LXXXV, no. 10 (October 1959), 75-79.

Rudzinski, Alexander W. "The Influence of the United Nations on Soviet Policy," *International Organization*, III, no. 2 (May 1949), 254-268.

———. "Soviet Peace Offensives," *International Conciliation*, no. 490 (April 1953), pp. 177-225.

Schaaf, Hart C. "The United Nations Economic Commission for Asia and the Far East," *International Organization*, VII, no. 4 (November 1953), 463-481.

Shulman, Marshall D. "Some Implications of Changes in Soviet Policy Toward the West, 1949-1952," *Slavic Review*, XX, no. 4 (December 1961), 630-640.

Sweetser, Arthur. "The Non-Political Achievements of the League," *Foreign Affairs*, XIX, no. 1 (October 1940), 179-192.

Vernon, Raymond. "Organizing for World Trade," *International Conciliation*, no. 505 (November 1955), pp. 163-222.

Viner, Jacob. "International Relations Between State-Controlled National Economies," *American Economic Review*, XXXIV, Supplement (March 1949), 315-329.

Webb, Leicester. "The Future of International Trade," *World Politics*, V, no. 4 (July 1953), 423-442.

Wightman, David. "Efforts for Economic Cooperation in Asia and the Far East: The Experience of ECAFE," *The World Today*, XVIII, no. 1 (January 1962), 30-42.

Zyzniewski, Stanley J. "The Soviet Bloc and the Underdeveloped Countries," *World Politics*, XI, no. 3 (April 1959), 378-398.

"At the Heart of UNICEF," *The New Yorker* (December 2, 1961), pp. 69-112.

INDEX

A

Acheson, Dean, 260
Advisory Social Welfare Services, 117-121, 230, 280
Afghanistan, 239
Africa, refugees in, 78-79
African states, 244
  entry into UN, 275
African and Asian states, 19, 55, 82, 270-271
  representation in ECOSOC, 21
Afro-Asian Organization for Economic Cooperation, 30
Agenda Committee, 26
Agricultural credit, 222
Albania, 17, 124-125, 139, 153, 193
Algeria, 79
Algerian refugees, 78, 82
American Federation of Labor (AFL), 23, 24, 26, 155, 160, 163-166
The American Way of Life, 144
Angola, 79
Arab refugees, 80-81, 82
Arab states, 80, 81
Argentina, 20
Arkadev, Georgy P., 111, 255, 257
Arms race, 111, 176, 178-179
Arutiunian, Amazasp A., 48, 105, 171, 189, 222-224, 230, 232, 235, 237-238, 257
Asian states, 119
Atomic energy, 199-200, 266
Australia, 48, 49, 93, 165n
Austria, 90, 96, 119, 193

B

Baltic refugees, 69, 82
Battle Act, 196
Belgium, 25, 65n, 67, 108, 167, 205
Berg, Pall, 166
Berlin crisis, 193
Bevin, Ernest, 90
Bidault, Georges, 90
Bilateralism, 216-217
Bolivia, 207
Brazil, 220
Bretton Woods Conference, 186, 187
Bruce Report, 6-9, 15, 55, 269, 285
Brunei, 124
Budget of the United Nations, 57, 70, 119, 122, 142, 228-229, 237, 243
  consideration of consolidation with those of specialized agencies, 39
Bulgaria, 17, 103, 123, 136, 153, 163n, 193, 213n, 219, 245
Bureau of Technical Assistance Operations (BTAO), 236, 242
Burma, 230, 239
Byelorussian Soviet Socialist Republic, 17, 90, 96, 139, 224
  contribution to EPTA, 244
  contribution to Special Fund, 250

299

contribution to UNICEF, 123
and ECE, 104
and EPTA, 233, 235, 245, 249
and ILO, 153
proposal by, 143, 233, 235, 255
and refugees, 62, 63
and UNRRA, 86
and WHO, 142

C

Canada, 65n, 89, 177
Capital Development Fund, 256-259, 281
Capitalism, USSR's views of, 131, 138, 163, 170, 173, 175, 177, 180, 181, 206, 276
Carnegie Endowment for International Peace, 29
Center for Research on Conflict Resolution, 179n
Ceylon, 251
Chile, 65n, 260
China:
 aid to children in, 124
 representation of, 20-21
 survey of, 107
China, People's Republic of, 20-21, 77, 126, 138, 141, 151, 167, 169, 246, 273
 embargo against, 205
China, Republic of, 21, 23, 65n, 99, 108, 141, 220
Chinese refugees in Hong Kong, 77-79
Chinese representation boycott, 11, 127, 174, 253, 259
Chizhov, K. Y., 163n
Claude, Inis L., Jr., 8-9
Coca leaves, investigation of effects of chewing, 140, 230
Cold War, 85, 124, 154, 163, 185, 188, 252, 253, 264, 270, 274
Colombia, 65n
Colombo Plan, 236
Colonial application clause, 129, 134, 151, 152, 159, 169, 213, 282
Colonialism, USSR's attack on, 47, 107, 147-148, 162, 165, 168, 222, 261
 USSR's view as cause of economic backwardness, 220-221
Cominform, 92, 193, 268
Commercial arbitration, 213

Committee for Industrial Development, 225-226
 origins of, 37
Commission on International Commodity Trade, 36, 205-207
Commission on Narcotic Drugs, 35, 135, 139, 141
Commission on Permanent Sovereignty over Natural Resources, 255
Commodity trade, 205-207
Communist ideology, 9-10, 11-12, 141, 150-151, 273, 274, 276, 283
 changes in, 262-263, 268-269
 concerning economic development, 221
 concerning effects of arms race, 178-179
 concerning international trade, 184-185, 216
 concerning population problems, 145-146
 concerning private foreign investment, 254
 concerning unemployment, 170
 implications for concept of experts, 33
 implications for ILO, 41
 opposition to world government, 29
Competitive coexistence, 264
Conference of Plenipotentiaries on a Supplementary Convention on the Abolition of Slavery, the Slave trade, and Institutions and Practices Similar to Slavery, 169
Conference on the Elimination or Reduction of Future Statelessness, 79
Congo, Republic of (Leopoldville), 82
Congo crisis, 51
Congress of Industrial Organizations (CIO), 23
Convention for the Suppression of the Traffic in Persons and of the Exploitation of the Prostitution of Others, 131
Convention on the Declaration of Death of Missing Persons, 80
Convention on the Recognition and Enforcement of Foreign Arbitral Awards, 213
Convention on Statelessness, 79
Convention Relating to the Status of Refugees, 79

INDEX 301

Coordinating Committee of the Consultative Committee (COCOM), 196, 202, 216
Coordination, 280
Coordination Committee, 40, 43
Council for Mutual Economic Assistance (CMEA), 85, 185, 204
Cuba, 65n, 139
Cuban invasion, USSR's protests in ECE concerning, 201
Currency utilization problem, in EPTA, 239-244
Customs treatment of samples and advertising, 190
Czechoslovakia, 17, 62, 173, 179, 211, 212, 220, 242, 251
   and Advisory Social Welfare Services, 119, 120-121
   and control of narcotic drugs, 139
   and ECE, 105
   and ERP, 92
   and FAO, 108
   and GATT, 187
   and IBRD, 186
   and ICAO, 188n
   and ILO, 153
   and IMF, 186
   and reconstruction, 96
   and refugees, 63, 65n, 75
   and UNESCO, 144, 145
   and UNICEF, 123
   and WHO, 144

D

Dallin, Alexander, 33
Danube River, 100, 104
Data, USSR's submission of, 96, 113, 137, 139, 213
Decolonization, 268, 276
Denmark, 89, 195
Disarmament, 179, 257, 283
Displaced persons, *see* refugees
Domestic jurisdiction, 79-80, 102, 133, 146, 149, 151, *see also* sovereignty
Double taxation, 190, 254
Dumbarton Oaks Conversations, 3, 12, 266
Dumbarton Oaks Proposals, 32

E

East-West trade, 169, 188, 191-204

Eastern Europe, USSR's consolidation of power in, 92, 114-115, 267
Eastern European states:
   defined, 17
   lessening of USSR's controls in, 203
   protection of interests in UNICEF, 124
   reorientation of economies of, 214
Economic assistance to devastated areas, 85-90
Economic Commission for Africa (ECA), 47
Economic Commission for Asia and the Far East (ECAFE), 46-47, 95, 99, 106-107, 160, 212, 218, 221-223
Economic Commission for Latin America (ECLA), 46, 223-224
Economic Commission for Europe (ECE), 11, 19, 45-46, 90, 91-92, 160, 171, 174, 190, 191, 195, 196, 212, 214, 216, 238, 269
   Committee on Agricultural Problems, 111-112
   Committee on the Development of Trade, 192-196
   origins of, 95-106
   technical committees of, 13, 104-105, 188, 197, 201, 203
Economic Commission for Latin America, 46, 223-224
Economic Commission for the Middle East, 46
Economic development, 11, 178, 218-264, 270, 282, 287
   financing of, 219, 252-259
Economic and Employment Commission, 94, 99, 171, 175, 187, 218, 220, 228, 254
Economic, Employment and Development Commission, 36, 225, 260
Economic and Social Consequences of Disarmament, 180
Economic and Social Council (ECOSOC), 16-22
   ministerial level participation in, 211
   politicization of, 182
   USSR's agreement to creation of, 3-4
ECOSOC Resolution 3 (II), 25-26
ECOSOC Resolution 57 (IV), 29
ECOSOC Resolution 114 C (VII), 223

ECOSOC Resolution 222 (IX), 235
ECOSOC Resolution 283 (X), 50-51
ECOSOC Resolution 290 (XI), 174
ECOSOC Resolution 531 C (XVIII), 209
ECOSOC Resolution 623 B III (XXII), 241-242
Economic Problems of Socialism in the USSR, 269
Education, 149
Egypt, 65n, 149, 230
Eisenhower Administration, 112, 275
Electric power, 97, 200
Emergency Economic Committee for Europe (EECE), 103
Equal pay for equal work, 161-163, 278, 283
Ethiopia, 180
European Atomic Energy Community (EAEC), 203, 215, 282
European Central Inland Transport Organization (ECITO), 103-104
European Coal Organization (ECO), 103-104
European Coal and Steel Community, 215, 282
European Convention on International Commercial Arbitration, 214
European Economic Community (EEC), 203, 204, 215, 282
European Free Trade Association (EFTA), 203, 204
European Recovery Program (ERP), 25, 49, 85, 91-94, 156, 170, 171, 192, 193, 249, 274
Exchanges of personnel, 145, 148, 199, 266
Expanded Program of Technical Assistance (EPTA), 13, 147, 219, 226, 231-246, 257, 258, 262, 263, 271, 273, 274
Experts, citizens of the USSR serving as, under UN programs, 118, 121, 239-241, 243, 250
Expert representation on functional commissions, USSR's attitude toward, 32-33, 35

F

Federal state clause, 130, 152, 213, 283
Fellowships: UN programs involving USSR as place of study, 121, 239-241, 243
Financial crisis of the United Nations, 243
Finland, 96, 103, 149, 193
Fiscal Commission, 36, 254
Food and Agricultural Organization (FAO), 14, 39, 43, 108-113, 186, 188, 206, 216, 245
Food shortage, 84, 85, 107-113
Forced labor, 163-167, 181, 274
France, 17, 23, 25, 63, 65, 65n, 67, 88, 108, 129-131, 195, 205, 258
Free trade, 183-184
Full employment, 154, 183
Functional commissions of ECOSOC, 31-37, 53, 54
Functionalism, 5, 15, 32, 114, 265, 277, 283, 284-287

G

General Agreement on Tariffs and Trade (GATT), 13, 14, 206, 208-210, 215, 216, 280
General Assembly:
  Fifth Committee, 165
  Second Committee, 18, 227
  Sixth Committee, 129, 131
  Third Committee, 18, 129, 131, 135
  USSR's preference for, 18
General Assembly Resolution 8 (I), 61, 62, 75
General Assembly Resolution 27 (I), 108
General Assembly Resolution 45 (I), 109
General Assembly Resolution 48 (I), 49, 89
General Assembly Resolution 57 (I), 122
General Assembly Resolution 58 (I), 118
General Assembly Resolution 198 (III), 224, 231, 253
General Assembly Resolution 200 (III), 224, 227, 229-230, 231, 232
General Assembly Resolution 246 (III), 224, 227, 229, 231
General Assembly Resolution 304 (IV), 235
General Assembly Resolution 417 (V), 122

INDEX

General Assembly Resolution 418 (V), 120
General Assembly Resolution 626 (VII), 255
General Assembly Resolution 802 (VIII), 122
Geographical representation, 20, 34, 35, 79, 126, 137
German Democratic Republic, 45, 126, 245, 246, 250
Germany, 69, 96, 125, 269
 Allied Control Authorities in, 52, 101, 106, 125
 Nazi, 56
Germany, Federal Republic of, 45, 80, 270
Goedhart, G. J. van Heuven, 77
Greece, 65n, 90, 136, 177
 aid to children in, 124
Gromyko, Andrei A., 3-4, 108, 265

H

Hammarskjöld, Dag, 21, 33, 51, 211
Havana Charter, 187-189, 208- 210; *see* ITO
Heavy industry, USSR's emphasis on development of, 220-221, 264
Hillman, Sidney, 25
Hoffman, Paul, 249
Hot Springs Conference, 186, 187
Housing, 147, 149
Howard League for Penal Reform, 29
Hull, Cordell, 3-4
Human rights, 255
Hungary, 17, 103, 132, 193
 and ECE, 105
 and FAO, 108, 113
 and ILO, 153
 and reconstruction, 90
 and UNHCR, 78
 and UNICEF, 123-125
 and WHO, 142-144
Hungarian crisis, 56
Hungarian refugees, 78

I

Ideology, its relationship to international economic and social cooperation, 14, 279, 284-285
Imperialism, USSR's views of, 221, 224

India, 20, 27, 30, 65n, 107, 109, 111, 136, 180, 220, 221, 239
Indonesia, 111, 149, 207
Industrial Development Center, 227
Industrialization, 220, 264
Inter-American Development Bank, 258-259
Inter-Governmental Committee on Refugees, 58, 60, 74, 75
Intergovernmental Committee for European Migration, 82
Inter-Governmental Maritime Consultative Organization (IMCO), 13, 188, 213
Interim-Coordinating Committee for International Commodity Agreements (ICCICA), 205
International Association of Democratic Lawyers, 28
International Atomic Energy Agency (IAEA), 13, 43, 200
International Bank for Reconstruction and Development (IBRD), 14, 41-42, 43, 186, 188, 189, 216, 248, 252, 253, 256, 257, 258, 259
International Civil Aviation Organization (ICAO), 14, 43, 188, 214
International Confederation of Free Trade Unions (ICFTU), 23, 156, 159
International Cooperative Alliance (ICA), 24, 25
International Court of Justice (ICJ), 31, 38, 130, 131, 137, 169, 213
International Criminal Police Organization, 29
International Development Association (IDA), 14, 42, 43, 259
International Economic Conference, Moscow, 1952, 195-196, 212
International Emergency Food Council (IEFC), 108, 109
International Federation of Trade Unions (IFTU), 23
International Finance Corporation (IFC), 14, 41, 43, 255-256
International Labor Organization (ILO), 13, 24, 26-27, 38, 40-42, 153-155, 156-167, 181, 238
 Conventions of, 157-159, 161, 162, 163, 166
International law, 53, 79-80, 137

International Monetary Fund, 14, 41-42, 43, 186, 188, 189, 216, 257, 259
International Narcotics Control Board (INCB), 137, 139
International Organization of Journalists, 28
International Penal and Penitentiary Commission, 132-133
International Refugee Organization (IRO), 57-75, 280
International Sugar Agreement, 207
International Telecommunications Union (ITU), 12
International Tin Council, 207
International trade, 175, 183-217, 222, 223, 266, 278, 280
International Trade Organization (ITO), 186-187, 208, 209
  Charter of, 188-189, 196, see Havana Charter
Iran, 136, 141
Ireland, 193
Italy, 90, 96, 119, 193
Izvestia, 51

J

Japan, 107, 125, 269, 270
Jews, 58, 72
Jouhaux, Leon, 25, 157

K

Kennedy, John F., 167, 170
Khrushchev, Nikita S., 21, 33, 51, 179, 268
Korea, Democratic People's Republic of, 46, 138
Korean War, 84
Kotschnig, Walter M., 242
Krylov, S. B., 31, 276

L

La Guardia, Fiorello H., 89
Land reform, 259-261
Lange, Oskar, 93, 179n, 195n, 202
Latin-American states, 17, 25, 55, 63, 119
  representation in ECOSOC, 18
League of Nations, 4-6, 31-32, 37, 40, 128, 254, 265, 269, 270, 279, 283, 287
Health Organization, 122
and narcotic drugs, 133
refugee work of, 59-60
and slavery, 168
Lebanon, 65n
Lie, Trygve, 90, 196
Lindt, Auguste, 77

Mc

McCarran-Walter Immigration and Naturalization Act, 30

M

Malaya, 124
Marshall, George C., 91-92
Marshall Plan, see ERP
Marxist theory, see communist ideology
Masaryk, Jan, 92n, 102
Measures for the Economic Development of Under-developed Countries, 256
Medical care, 148-149
Mexico, 220
Mexico City, 252
Michalowski, Jerzy, 272
Middle East, 81, 82
Middle Eastern states, 25, 63
Migrant labor, protection of, 160-161
Military technology, developments in, 267
Mikoyan, Anastas I, 81
Mitrany, David, 5, 84, 284
Molotov, Vyacheslav M., 12, 155, 266, 271
Mongolia, People's Republic of, 17n, 46, 271n
Morozov, A. P., 220-221, 228
Morse, David A., 165
Most-favored-nation principle, 200
Mudaliar, Ramaswami, 166
Multilateralism, 216-217
Myrdal, Gunnar, 90, 101, 191, 194-195, 196, 282

N

Nansen, Fridtjoff, 59
Nansen refugees, 56, 69

INDEX   305

Narcotic drugs, international control of, 133-142, 273, 283
National Association of Manufacturers, 29
National income, 259
National and International Measures for Full Employment, 174
Netherlands, 108, 258
Netherlands East Indies, 124
Neutral states, 21, 34, 96
New York Times, 235
New Zealand, 10, 23, 270n
Non-Governmental Organizations, 22-31, 175, 278
Non-Governmental Organizations, Committee on, 25-26, 28
Non-self-governing territories, 46-47, 129-130, 134-135, 146, 168, 250
North Atlantic Treaty Organization (NATO), 164, 243
Northern Borneo, 124
Norway, 65n, 89, 99, 205
Nuclear weapon tests, 126, 148-149, 278
  negotiations for the discontinuance of, 276
Nuclear weapons, 267

O

Operational, executive and administrative personnel, program for provision of (OPEX), 247
Opium, 135
Organization for Economic Cooperation and Development (OECD), 185, 203, 215
Organization for European Economic Cooperation (OEEC), 85, 185, 215, 282
Organization for Trade Cooperation (OTC), 208-209, 215

P

Pakistan, 179
Paris Meeting of Foreign Ministers, 91, 93
Pasvolsky, Leo, 7
Pate, Maurice, 121
Peace Corps, 247
Peace Movement, 267

Permanent Central Opium Board (PCOB), 134, 136, 137, 139
Peru, 65n, 230
Petroleum industry, proposals for technical assistance in, 251, 278
Poland, 17, 62, 65, 95, 131, 132, 139, 149, 160, 163n, 172, 179, 180, 195, 202, 211, 212, 224, 234, 235, 250, 251, 252, 260, 261, 272
  and Advisory Social Welfare Services, 118, 119, 120
  and ECE, 98, 105
  and ERP, 49, 92, 93
  and FAO, 108, 113
  and GATT, 187, 208
  and IMCO, 213n
  and IBRD, 186
  and ICAO, 188n
  and ILO, 153
  and IMF, 186
  and reconstruction, 90, 96
  and refugees, 63, 73, 75
  and UNESCO, 144
  and UNHCR, 78
  and UNICEF, 122, 123, 124
Political bodies; USSR's preference for over administrative organs, 68, 87, 121, 234, 278
Politicization of the UN's economic and social activities, 277-279
Population Commission, 34, 36, 146
Population problem, 145-147
Portugal, 193
Pravda, 92, 179
Preparatory Commission, 32, 57, 58, 59
Pre-investment activities, 250
Prevention of crime and treatment of offenders, 132-133
Private foreign investment, 254-255, 278, 280
Propaganda, 150, 159, 175, 181, 182, 227, 251-252, 273, 274
Procuring, 130
Prostitution, 130
Protocol for Limiting and Regulating the Cultivation of the Poppy Plant, the Production of, International and Wholesale Trade in, and Use of Opium, 135, 137
Public administration, program for training in, 224, 229, 231, 246-247

Public opinion, 53, 54, 88, 132, 150, 152, 170, 178, 181, 270, 285

Q

Quai d'Orsay, 31

R

Radulesco, Gheorghe, 202
Rajchman, Ludwik, 122
Rearmament, 225, 261
Reconstruction, 12, 84-116, 228, 277, 281, 282
Red Cross, 29
Refugees, 12, 14, 56-83, 160, 277, 281
Regional economic commissions, of ECOSOC, 27, 39, 45, 176-177, 187, 213, 245
Report on the World Social Situation, 147
Resident Representatives of TAB, 246
Revolution of rising expectations, 218, 270
Romania, 17, 103, 139, 153, 158, 159, 193, 202, 242, 251
Roosevelt, Franklin Delano, 3
Roosevelt, Mrs. Franklin Delano, 122
Rostow, Walt W., 191n
Rubinstein, Alvin Z., 237
Russian, proposal to use as working language, 45, 126

S

Saksin, G. F., 242
San Francisco Conference, 12, 22, 39, 40, 42, 48, 50, 154-155, 266
Sarawak, 124
Sayan, Enrique Garcia, 166
Scandinavian states, 103, 193
Secretariat of the United Nations, 27, 51-52, 93, 118, 133, 146, 150, 174, 177, 229, 233
  Department of Economic and Social Affairs, 52, 236, 243
  Secretary-General of the United Nations, 30-31, 32, 39, 89, 90, 157, 161, 165, 167, 168, 174, 196, 210, 211, 224, 229, 230, 245, 253, 256, 259, 260
  USSR's attack against, 21, 33, 51-52, 246

Security Council, 3, 9, 43
Senegal, 30
Singapore, 124
Single Convention on Narcotic Drugs, 135, 137-139
Slavery, 167-170
  Ad Hoc Committee of Experts on, 168
Social Commission, 27, 30, 36, 119, 131, 143, 144-145, 147, 148, 149, 160
Social defense, 128-133
Social security, 148-149
Sovereignty, 47, 51, 53, 54, 102, 114, 132, 133, 137, 141, 187, 190, 214, 216, 221, 222, 246, 247, 254-255, 264, 272, 273, 282, *see* also domestic jurisdiction
Soviet bloc, 17, 27, 35, 39, 48-49, 75, 81, 108, 109, 123, 131, 132, 139, 142, 144, 151, 161, 166, 167, 187, 190, 192, 193, 210, 211, 214, 232, 234, 263, 280
  constitution of and defined, 17n
  representation of in ECOSOC, 17-18
Soviet ideology, *see* communist ideology
Soviet Union, *see* USSR
Spain, 29, 134, 151, 152, 283
Spanish Republican refugees, 59, 70
Special Committee on Refugees and Displaced Persons, 62-69, 75
Special Fund, 247-251, 273
Special Meeting on Urgent Food Problems, 108
Special projects device, 241
Specialized agencies, 12-14, 24, 37-44, 53, 100, 101, 148, 185-186, 219, 226, 232, 233, 234, 242, 260, 276, 280, 282
Special United Nations Fund for Economic Development (SUNFED), 248, 257-258, 263, 281
Special United Nations Fund for Economic Development, 257
Stalin, Joseph V., 196, 215, 269
  effects of death of, 215, 237, 263, 268-269
Statistical Commission, 34
Statistics, USSR's submission of, 113, 137, 139, 213
Stettinius, Edward R., Jr., 3
Stoessinger, John G., 82
Strategic goods, Western controls on

INDEX 307

the export of, 111, 172, 188-190, 198, 215, 225
Strauss, F., 202
Sub-Commission on Economic Development, 218, 220-221, 225, 262, 264
Sub-Commission on Statistical Sampling, 36
Suez crisis, 199
Sweden, 67, 96
Switzerland, 45, 67, 68, 96, 193

T

Technical assistance, 219, 220, 227-247, 266
  costs of, 231
  in narcotics control, 140
Technical Assistance Administration, 236
Technical Assistance Board (TAB), 234, 241, 242, 245
Technical Assistance Committee (TAC), 234, 236, 245-247
Temporary Sub-Commission on Economic Reconstruction of Devastated Areas, 95-98
Thorp, Willard, 163n, 232
Tin, 207
Totalitarian states, and international economic and social cooperation, 285
Tourism, 266
Town and country planning, 147
Trade union rights, 155-159, 274, 278, 283
Traffic in persons and obscene publications: suppression of, 128-132
Transport and Communications Commission, 36, 213
Transportation of dangerous goods, 190, 280
Troika, 21
Truman, Harry S, 231
Truman Doctrine, 90
Trust Territories, 146, 148
Trusteeship Council, 38
Turkey, 136

U

Ukrainian Soviet Socialist Republic, 17, 65n, 90, 139

contribution to EPTA, 244
contribution to Special Fund, 250
contribution to UNICEF, 123
and ECE, 104
and EPTA, 249
and FAO, 113
and ILO, 153
  proposal by, 67, 143
and reconstruction, 97
and refugees, 62, 63, 67
request for fellowships in United States, 118
at San Francisco Conference, 154
and UNRRA, 86
and WHO, 142
Unemployment, 148, 165, 170-178, 278, 283
Underdeveloped areas and countries, 133, 147-148, 162, 247, 248, 267, 280, 286
  attitude toward free trade, 184
  desire for assistance, 227, 230, 263
  political strength in UN, 218
  power in General Assembly, 256
  USSR's alienation from, 236
  USSR's policies toward, 151-152, 205, 206, 219, 236, 245, 250, 253, 266, 276
  USSR's trade with, 216
  and UNICEF, 127-128
Union of Soviet Socialist Republics:
  agrees to include economic and social functions in UN, 3-10
  Association for the United Nations of, 285
  attitude toward League's economic and social activities, 8
  bilateral aid to underdeveloped countries, 238, 276
Census of 1959, 146
  Communist Party of, 19th Congress, 215, 238, 263, 269
  Communist Party of, 20th Congress, 268
  Corrective Labor Codex of RSFSR, 164
  drug addiction in, 136, 139, 141
  economic capacity of, 267
  isolationism, 276
  policies toward UN's economic and social activities periodicized, 12-14
  prostitution in, 132

status of trade unions in, 156
writing on UN in, 285
United Arab Republic, 239
United Kingdom of Great Britain and Northern Ireland, 17, 65, 98, 161, 164, 176, 183, 193, 194, 195, 205-206, 237
  and colonial application clause, 129, 131
  and ECE, 105, 191
  and food problem, 108
  and IRO, 66, 68
  and reconstruction, 88, 115
  supports ICA, 24
United Nations, role of, in USSR's strategy, 11, 276
United Nations Appeal for Children (UNAC), 123
United Nations Charter, 16, 20-21, 49, 140, 183-184, 234, 243, 280
  Article 55, 117, 119, 154, 183, 218
  Article 56, 48
  Article 64, 50, 94
  Article 71, 21, 23-24, 26, 28
  Article 108, 20
United Nations Children's Fund (UNICEF), 13, 43, 121-128, 152, 273, 274
United Nations Conference on Trade and Development, 212
United Nations Congresses on the Prevention of Crime and the Treatment of Offenders, 133
United Nations Development Decade, 261
United Nations Educational, Scientific and Cultural Organization (UNESCO), 13, 43, 117, 144-145, 238
United Nations High Commissioner for Refugees (UNHCR), 76-79, 280
United Nations Korean Reconstruction Agency (UNKRA), 80, 84, 280
United Nations Narcotics Laboratory, 140
United Nations Opium Conference, 135
United Nations Relief and Rehabilitation Administration (UNRRA), 58, 60, 61, 63, 65, 75, 85, 86-90, 96, 102, 117, 121, 122
United Nations Relief and Works Agency for Palestine Refugees (UNRWA), 80, 280
United States of America, 10, 17, 65, 91, 94, 95, 102, 105, 108, 118, 130, 131, 171, 176, 177, 190-194, 203-206, 220, 228, 248, 252, 262, 272, 274-275
  agricultural policies criticized, 109
  attitude toward conventions, 170, 275
  attitude toward international trade, 183-184
  Congress, 90
  contribution to EPTA, 237
  contribution to UNICEF, 122-123
  Department of State, 4, 144
  desire for interim agreement on opium, 135
  and ECE, 98, 100, 201
  Escapee Program, 82
  financial veto of, 281
  and food problem, 108, 112
  and land reform, 260
  insistence on UN's having economic and social functions, 3-8
  immigration policies attacked, 30-31
  Point Four Program, 232, 235-236, 238, 274
  position concerning forced labor convention, 167
  proposes EPTA, 231-232
  proposes Special Fund, 257-258
  racial discrimination in attacked, 225
  raises issue of forced labor, 163-164
  and reconstruction, 85, 88, 115
  and refugees, 66, 68
  Senate, 167, 170
  support of AFL, 24
  and UNRRA, 87
United Towns Organization, 30
Universal Postal Union (UPU), 12

V

Varga, Eugene, 268
Velebit, Vladimir, 202
Viet Nam, Democratic Republic of, 46, 138
Vyshinsky, Andrei, 92

W

War orphans, 73

INDEX 309

Weapons technology, 267
West, defined, 10
  position of in ECOSOC, 18-19
  position of in General Assembly, 270-271
Western European Integration, 202-204, 215
Western Higher Institute of Technology in Bombay, 245
Wetback problem, 161
White Russian refugees, 60, 70
Whitehall, 32
Wightman, David, 98
Women's International Democratic Federation, 28, 30
World economic surveys, 93-94
World Federation of Democratic Youth, 28
World Federation of Trade Unions (WFTU), 22-27, 30, 39, 53, 54, 142-143, 155-157, 160, 161-162, 172-173, 175
World Food Program, 112-113
World Health Organization, 13, 117, 142-144, 238
World government, 29, 33
World Meteorological Organization, 12
World population conferences, 146
World Refugee Year, 80

World War II, 11, 23, 56, 78, 84, 139, 183, 218, 267, 274

Y

Yalta agreements, 58, 98
Yugoslavia, 17, 62, 65n, 75, 124, 139, 149, 163n, 169, 180, 193, 239, 250
  and Advisory Social Welfare Services, 119, 120
  and ECE, 105
  and FAO, 108
  and GATT, 208
  and IBRD, 186
  and ILO, 153
  and IMCO, 213n
  and IMF, 186
  and narcotics control, 136
  and reconstruction, 90, 96
  and refugees, 59, 63, 65
  and UNESCO, 144
  and UNHCR, 78
  and UNICEF, 123
  and WHO, 142

Z

Zhdanov, Andrei, 268